W9-BZE-931

EMILE DURKHEIM

EMILE DURKHEIM

Emile Durkheim, 1858-1917

A Collection of Essays, with Translations and a Bibliography

Edited by Kurt H. Wolff

Contributors

CHARLES BLEND

PAUL BOHANNAN

LEWIS A. COSER

HUGH DALZIEL DUNCAN

JEROME D. FOLKMAN

ROSCOE C. HINKLE, JR.

PAUL HONIGSHEIM

KAZUTA KURAUCHI

JOSEPH NEYER

TALCOTT PARSONS

HENRI PEYRE

ALBERT PIERCE

MELVIN RICHTER

ALBERT SALOMON

KURT H. WOLFF

THE OHIO STATE UNIVERSITY PRESS
COLUMBUS

The publication of the volume was made possible, in part, by a grant from the Ohio State University Development Fund.

CONTENTS

v

CONTENTS

PREFACE

The essays collected in this commemorative volume fall easily into five groups. The first consists of three papers, those by Henri Peyre, Albert Salomon, and Paul Honigsheim, which present the historical, political, and intellectual setting in which Durkheim the scholar and citizen lived; some aspects of his lasting legacy, notably the work of Marcel Mauss and Maurice Halbwachs; and an inventory of the scholarship in the history, sociology, and psychology of religion that he has stimulated. The three analyses by Joseph Neyer, Melvin Richter, and Lewis A. Coser, are, when compared to the first group, more analytical than descriptive; they deal with some of Durkheim's central moral and political concerns. Albert Pierce's and Paul Bohannan's contributions connect Durkheim with more specific problems in social science: Pierce discusses Durkheim and "functionalism"; and Bohannan, the relation (a progression or a regression) between Durkheim's notion of the *conscience collective* and the current anthropological one of culture. The similarity between another pair of papers—Talcott Parsons' on the integration of social systems and Hugh Dalziel Duncan's on ritual —consists in the fact that the author of each uses Durkheim as a point of departure in the development of his own ideas. The feature common to the contributions by Roscoe C. Hinkle, Jr., and Kazuta Kurauchi is their concern with the reception accorded Durkheim's work in two countries other than his own, the United States and Japan. The collection of analyses concludes with Paul Honigsheim's personal reminiscences of some outstanding members of the Durkheim school.

This quick survey of the first part of the book may suggest— though, of course, much less vividly than a reading of the analyses themselves—the widely diversified but always concrete and specific relevance of Durkheim and his work. Durkheim's human and moral appeal, for instance, is clearly apparent in the papers—otherwise so different—of Peyre, Salomon, Neyer, and Richter, and in Honigsheim's reminiscences. And his political relevance must certainly strike the reader of both Richter's and Coser's essays, which, although Richter tends to play down, and Coser to play up, Durkheim's conservatism (with complementary traits such as liberalism and democratism receiving correspondingly different weights), are not, I believe, incompatible. In addition, Durkheim's intimate connection with major trends in contemporary sociology and anthropology are evident in the analyses by Pierce and Bohannan.

Although the essays collected here analyze many important aspects of Durkheim's intellectual enterprise, they can do no more than single out a few for major attention and, especially when taken together, give the reader some idea of, and an appetite for, the wealth and complexity of the whole. Thus more can be said than has been offered here on Durkheim's ideas on education, the sociology of organizations, nationalism, the sociology of knowledge, epistemology, such anthropological topics as incest and totemism, thinkers like Montesquieu and Rousseau, and nineteenth-century German social science. Nor is an important contemporary point of view concerning intellectual matters—that of psychoanalysis—represented; adopting it, Norman O. Brown has much to say about Durkheim that is novel.[1] But although the breadth of his interests precludes the present volume's being a full discussion of the scope of Durkheim's influence on many endeavors in many parts of the world, an influence that is probably continuing to grow—particularly in this country—it is, in all likelihood, the most devoted and diversified commemoration to date.

An important part of this commemoration is the appearance of several of his writings that have not previously been translated into English. The first of these is a hitherto unpublished letter from Durkheim to A. R. Radcliffe-Brown, the well-known and influential British anthropologist (1881-1955), which constitutes an important link between Durkheim and social anthropology. J. G. Peristiany, to whom we owe its inclusion here, has greatly increased the interest of the letter by his illuminating historical and technical analysis of its content and meaning. Three pieces that follow it—Durkheim's Prefaces to the first two volumes (1898 and 1899) of the *Année sociologique,* and the two essays "Sociology and Its Scientific Field" of 1900, and

"Sociology" of 1915—give us a set of consecutive formulations of his conception of the field. The first of these, which launched that extraordinary periodical and reports on its experiences during its initial year, is a sanguine proclamation of sociology's coming of age; it sees the science as infusing the older studies of social life, notably history, with the new vigor and the new light that come from a clearer ordering of the world.

According to a letter, dated May 23, 1958, from Durkheim's erstwhile pupil, Armand Cuvillier, the original of the second of these three statements about sociology is probably lost; the article first appeared in an Italian translation in the *Rivista italiana di sociologia,* and was not published in French until more than a half-century later when it was retranslated in Cuvillier's *Où va la sociologie française?*[2] One of the noteworthy features of this essay is Durkheim's assertion that his own conception of sociology is opposed to that of Georg Simmel, two of whose essays he had read at that time. Stating this controversy in general terms, we may say that Durkheim's critique of Simmel's "forms"[3] of sociation comes from a scholar who is fascinated by history and its changes, and who therefore condemns the comparatively ahistorical Simmel as an arid and arbitrary metaphysician. Later in the same paper, however, the two antagonists are foreshadowed in roles that are almost reversed: here it is Durkheim's insistence that society is something *sui generis* which strikes one as purely systematic, atemporal, and ahistorical—especially when compared to Simmel's later historical explanation[4] of "the great contents of historical life" by reference, in the course of history, first to God and later to the great man, an idea that preceded the still later insight that "man in all aspects of his life and action is determined by the fact that he is a social being."[5]

Durkheim's third presentation of his sociology, which he wrote for a collection of volumes on French science prepared for the Panama-Pacific Exposition held in San Francisco in 1915, is a brief account of the history of the discipline—a history which, the opening sentence proclaims, is nearly identical with the history of French sociology: "Although there is no country today where it is not cultivated, it nevertheless remains an essentially French science." And, indeed, with the exception of a brief reference to Herbert Spencer, Durkheim discusses only French thinkers, beginning with the Encyclopedists' extension of "determinism" from nature to society, continuing through Saint-Simon and Auguste Comte, and turning finally to himself and his collaborators on the *Année sociologique,* all of whom he sees as followers in the steps of Comte. He concludes his discussion by expounding the work of two thinkers who are not in the Comtean tradition, however: Gabriel Tarde, whom he admits, nevertheless, as a sociologist, and Frédéric Le Play, who, even though he stands "completely outside the movement of ideas which gave birth to sociology," does deal with "social matters."

"The Dualism of Human Nature and Its Social Conditions" presents a sociological treatment of the traditional dichotomy between soul and body. It is of relevance to our understanding of the development of Durkheim's and our own ideas about culture and society—such as those that are dealt with in the present volume, especially in the papers by Bohannan and Parsons. In its pervasive preoccupation with this "inner contradiction" of man, his position—and Durkheim quotes Pascal —between "angel and beast," it strikes notes that may well remind the reader of both Freud and Max Weber (who in H. Stuart Hughes's assessment of the four decades from 1890 to 1930, are, in this order, the two most eminent figures in the history of social thought).[6] Indeed, more specific connections of both a conceptual and affective nature could easily be established between Durkheim's paper and Freud's *Civilization and Its Discontents* (1930), on the one hand, and Weber's "Politics as a Vocation" and "Science as a Vocation" (both of 1918), on the other.

"Pragmatism and Sociology" contains translations of the first five and the thirteenth and fourteenth lectures of a course by that title that Durkheim gave at the Sorbonne in 1913-14. The French text (*Pragmatisme et sociologie* of 1955) was reconstructed by Armand Cuvillier from notes taken by two students. The essay may be interpreted as an intrafamilial controversy between pragmatism and Durkheimian sociology vis-à-vis, and under the still towering impact of, traditional rationalism, which, according to Durkheim, is in need of renovation. However, Durkheim does not give us this renovated rationalism, but offers instead a critical exposition of pragmatism as seen, above all, in William James, and also in F. C. S. Schiller and John Dewey, and an argument in favor of his sociology. There is hardly any mention of the fact that both pragmatism and his sociology came out of the same historical situation, and Durkheim does not entertain the possibility that the reason why pragmatism has not found a systematic exposition—a weakness he notes repeatedly—may be its failure to have gained insight into this fact. Two of the major features of the historical situation of both are liberalism and a technological orientation. Although Durkheim calls pragmatism "logical utilitarianism" at the very end of the selections presented here, this designation does not appear to imply any suggestion of pragmatism's affiliation with liberalism. Durkheim also fails to notice a parallel between the pragmatist distribution of necessity and freedom, as he sees it (page 116),[7] and the liberal conception of voluntary submission to freely chosen representatives, or to recognize the political importance of the diversity of minds that James accounted for ontologically by his "pluralistic universe" (page 125). Pragmatism militates "against pure speculation and theoretical thought" (page 137), and in so doing, it fuses both the liberal and the technological elements of its time, as it does in its emphasis on tolerance (fourteenth lecture), which it shares with Durkheim's sociology (page 187). The technological component clearly emerges, for instance, in Schiller's interpretation of men as "genuine makers of reality" (page 119), and in James's likening of conceptual thinking to flying (page 107). There is an affective bond between Durkheim the critic, and pragmatism, his topic; and indeed Durkheim often praises pragmatism—for instance, because it makes truth "into something that can be analyzed and explained" (thirteenth lecture). This affective bond may have prevented him from engaging in a sociological analysis of either pragmatism or his own sociology, or of the affective bond between them, and thus, indirectly, from reaffirming rationalism or from redefining it in the light of historical developments—in short, from "renovating" it. He comes closer to such re-affirmation outside this book—for instance, in the argument which he uses in developing his conception of religion in *Les formes élémentaires de la vie religieuse* (and repeats in the fourteenth lecture) that "it is impossible for us to claim that the generations which preceded us were capable of living in total error, in aberration." Yet despite this and many other instances in which he admits that human continuity exists by virtue of a common human feature that many have called reason, Durkheim persists, here and in other of his writings, in separating reason and practice, fact and obligation (page 162, and early in the fourth lecture). In such separations he exhibits rather than analyzes his historical situation, and he no more "transcends" it toward scientific mastery than do the pragmatists. Therefore, Durkheim's essay, in addition to what it intends to say, unwittingly tells us much about the fate and prospects of reason in his and our time.

The volume concludes with a bibliography, the nature of which is clarified in a prefatory note, some information on the contributors, and an index.

In addition to the contributors to this volume, I am indebted to a number of others whose part in this enterprise I gratefully acknowledge. As I stated in the Preface to the companion volume, *Georg Simmel, 1858-1918*, Everett Walters, dean of the Graduate School, Ohio State University, and chairman of the Editorial Board of the Ohio State University Press, enthusiastically received the idea of these two commemorative publications when he was first approached with it, and has been consistently helpful throughout the long period of their preparation. Most particularly Weldon A. Kefauver, editor, but also Edith C. Rinehart, co-ordinating editor, and Gerald B. Rice, editor, have worked without let-up and with truly impressive competence and thoroughness, greatly improving the manuscripts and seeing them into print. Several of my friends and former colleagues at Ohio State have also aided me very much in the editing of both the analyses and the translations: John W. Bennett (Anthropology; now at Washington University, St. Louis, Missouri), Roscoe C. Hinkle, Jr. (Sociology), Gisela J. Hinkle, Virgil G. Hinshaw, Jr. (Philosophy), and Roy Harvey Pearce and Claude M. Simpson, Jr. (English). I also wish to thank Professors Armand Cuvillier of Paris, and J. G. Peristiany of the University of Oxford, both of whom I have had occasion to mention earlier in this Preface, for various favors that have greatly facilitated my task. My acknowledgments to various publishers for granting translation rights appear in footnotes in the text.

In short, the editor is only one of many workers who have made this volume possible. Along with its readers, he is under great obligation to them.

KURT H. WOLFF

Department of Sociology
Brandeis University
Waltham 54, Massachusetts
May 7, 1960

1. *Life against Death: The Psychoanalytical Meaning of History* (New York: Random House [Modern Library Paperbacks], 1959).

2. Paris: Marcel Rivière, 1953.

3. This notion, which is fundamental to Simmel's whole outlook, has engaged many critics; cf. Kurt Gassen's bibliography of writings on Simmel in *Georg Simmel, 1858-1918: A Collection of Essays, with Translations and a Bibliography*, edited by Kurt H. Wolff (Columbus, Ohio: Ohio State University Press, 1959), pp. 357-75. A decisive breakthrough in the analysis of it may well be just beginning. See, above all, the following three essays in *Georg Simmel, 1858-1918*: "The Structure of Simmel's Social Thought," by Donald N. Levine (pp. 9-32), "Form and Content in Simmel's Philosophy of Life," by Rudolph H. Weingartner (pp. 33-60), and "Formal Sociology," by F. H. Tenbruck (pp. 61-99).

4. In Chaps. i and iii of *Soziologie* (Leipzig: Duncker und Humblot, 1908), and in *Grundfragen der Soziologie (Individuum und Gesellschaft)*, (Berlin and Leipzig: de Gruyter, 1917). For specific instances, see "The Problem of Sociology," trans. Kurt H. Wolff, in Wolff, *op. cit.*, p. 312; "Fundamental Problems of Sociology (Individual and Society)" (Part I), *The Sociology of Georg Simmel*, trans., ed., and with an Introduction by Kurt H. Wolff (Glencoe, Ill.: Free Press of Glencoe, Illinois, 1950), pp. 12-13; and "Superordination and Subordination" (Part III), *ibid.*, p. 257.

5. Wolff, *The Sociology of Georg Simmel*, p. 12. For a summary of Durkheim's "Sociology and Its Scientific Field," and a presentation of Durkheim's and Simmel's influence on German sociology, see Heinz Maus, "Simmel in German Sociology," in Wolff, *Georg Simmel, 1858-1918*, pp. 188-92.

6. *Consciousness and Society: The Reorientation of European Social Thought, 1890-1930* (New York: Alfred A. Knopf, 1958), pp. 13, 19.

7. Page numbers refer to passages in *Pragmatisme et sociologie* that are not translated in the present volume; otherwise, references are to the lectures contained herein. Some of my comments are taken from my brief review of *Pragmatisme et sociologie,* in *American Journal of Sociology,* LXII (1956), 100-101.

ANALYSES

DURKHEIM: THE MAN, HIS TIME, AND HIS INTELLECTUAL BACKGROUND

HENRI PEYRE

Baudelaire once remarked that a great man is never an aerolite. The greatest of French sociologists, whose thought dominates sociology in France to this day, knew, even when—if not chiefly when—he was taken to task, as he was by Georges Gurvitch and by Jules Monnerot, that he had had several precursors in his own country and that he was a link in a long and glorious chain. Durkheim never ceased striving for objectivity not even in the early years of the First World War, when he placed himself at the service of his country. He pursued truth, his own truth, *sine ira et studio*. Still, he could not divorce himself from his own time and place. He was profoundly concerned with the spiritual welfare of his country, eager to broaden the training of its ruling classes, anxious for moral, even more than for political, reforms. He was too independent a thinker ever to be molded by his environment; but he was too generous to disregard all that he owed to his background, to his education, to his country, and to his predecessors.

Every country is a land of contrasts. When Durkheim was born, in the France of the Second Empire, conflicting currents coexisted. In the provinces, the farmers still lived very much as they had for the previous ten centuries. There were more artisans than industrial workmen, and among the latter poverty prevailed, along with a constant fear of unemployment, disease, and accidents against which no insurance was provided. The railways, built mostly after 1848, were slowly shaking the countryside out of its lethargy: sugar, soap, candles, and matches came into use in daily life; coal was provided for fuel; gas served for lighting. Cotton goods became available at lower prices, and the level of comfort in housing, clothing, and especially in the quantity and the quality of food rose markedly around 1850-70, at least for the middle classes. In Paris, big department stores opened, and money became plentiful, both in savings banks and for speculating and lending purposes. The world of greed and corruption which had been prophesied by Balzac (who died in 1850) came to pass.

The Paris to which young Durkheim came from his native Vosges to complete his secondary education was a glamorous metropolis for the happy few and the foreign visitors. It was the city of fashionable races, vividly sketched by Constantin Guys and later by Degas, of pleasure-loving men and women portrayed by Emile Zola and Alphonse Daudet in *Nana* and *Le Nabab,* and by Manet on his canvasses. Theatregoers flocked to light comedies and to Offenbach's frothy music. International men and women of fashion followed the court of the Emperor to Compiègne, Saint-Cloud, or Biarritz. Only one year after Sadowa, which Europe had not taken seriously, kings and queens visited the second Universal Exhibition of 1867. Haussmann was modernizing Paris, which counted almost two million inhabitants. The government had become more liberal, and the small Republican opposition was popular with the intellectuals and the students in the capital.

Paris, however, had ceased to be representative of France as a whole, and every newcomer from the provinces who was temporarily exalted by the sparkling liveliness of the nerve center of France realized how out of step its swift life was with the dormant agrarian France. The aftermath of 1848 was felt for decades. In that year, for the first time, France had withstood a Parisian revolution and, in June, 1848, had applauded the repression of the bloody riots which had frightened the country. The Falloux bill of 1850 had fostered an even sharper cleavage between the Frenchmen who were trained in Catholic schools and the others. Clericalism and republicanism faced each other in bitter opposition. After the 1848 riots and the failure of premature attempts at setting up a Second Republic, a momentous event occurred which caused Durkheim's generation to ponder the country's problems: this was the humiliating defeat of 1870, and the Commune which followed. Once again, Paris had gone too far ahead of the rest of the country, and was disowned by it. Slowly, with the Third Republic, the country moved toward Republicanism and the newly coined formula of Radicalism, while Paris swung to the right and became a bastion of conservatism surrounded by a "red belt."

As a boy of twelve, Durkheim could not have reasoned about the unexpected French defeat of 1870-71 as older thinkers did: Jules Michelet, crushed by the blow dealt his country, died in grief in 1874; Gustave Flaubert, Théophile Gautier, Leconte de Lisle, who had professed impassibility and subscribed to the cult of art as divorced from local and national circumstances, were deeply shaken by the first invasion from which France had suffered since the short-lived occupation of 1815. Lucien Anatole Prévost-Paradol, one of the very few original political thinkers of France in the last hundred years, who had entered the Ecole Normale Supérieure in 1849, thirty years before Durkheim was to follow him there, shot himself in Washington, where he was the French envoy; Hippolyte Taine, Ernest Renan and a score of other thinkers, rocked to the very foundations of their thought by the victory of Prussia, undertook to reform France intellectually and morally and to re-examine the whole myth of the French Revolution with a coldly critical eye. The courage of the French troops, the foolhardy idealism of the Republicans who prolonged a hopeless fight along the Loire, vainly hoping to relieve besieged Paris, had been of no avail. The defeat was due to a lack of intelligence in the ruling classes, and to an even more disastrous lack of foresight among the statesmen. The massacres of the Commune, the burning of the center of Paris by the rioters, the ruthless repression, which culminated, May 21 to 28, 1871, in the shooting of the last Commune fanatics at the Mur des Fédérés in the Père-Lachaise cemetery, opened the eyes of many members of French university circles. It was clear that the barbarians of the interior, uncultured, sadly neglected by the elite, alienated from the middle class and the provincial and conservative farmers, freed from the constraints which religious belief had long imposed upon them, had to be brought within the fold of a France which considered itself the focus of light and civilization. A moral and civic training had to be devised, or renovated, to fill the gap caused by the growing agnosticism and the increasing social consciousness of the proletariat.

The Republic was officially consecrated in 1875, when the word, almost by chance, was inserted in the Constitutional laws then barely passed by the two French assemblies. It was strengthened by the victory of the Left over the Monarchist Right after the famous *Seize Mai* (1877), a victory which forced out the authoritarian President MacMahon and made any dissolution of the French Parliament almost impossible for decades. The confused crisis of Boulangisme, 1889-95, ended in another victory for democracy and weakened still further the latent Bonapartist complex in the French people. Meanwhile, the nation enjoyed unprecedented prosperity. Savings grew fast, comfort increased, an immense colonial empire was acquired at very small cost, and French investments spread overseas. For intellectuals like Durkheim, Henri Bergson, Jean Jaurès, the most momentous event in the country's internal history was the weakening of confessional schools and the bills of 1882-84 establishing compulsory free primary education throughout the country. The minister who initiated and carried through that reform, Jules Ferry, became, along with Victor Duruy who had organized women's secondary education under the Second Empire, one of the molders of the new France. The "instituteur" replaced the priest as the guide of the conscience of rural and industrial France.

The Third Republic proved to be the most stable of all French regimes. It weathered the tempestuous crisis of the Dreyfus case, in the last five years of the century. Durkheim, like Bergson, like Proust, whose mother was Jewish, and like many non-Jews in the university and outside, from Lucien Herr to Emile Zola and Charles Péguy, must have been profoundly moved by the venomous partisanship of that civil war. But Durkheim hardly took notice of it in his writings. His field of action lay in educating the teachers and the scholars of France. The separation of Church and State and the weakening of the clerical as well as the military groups followed the victory of the partisans of Dreyfus, among whom were a great many professors—agnostics, Protestants, and a few Jews. The search for a lay ethics went on actively among philosophers, from Marie Jean Guyau and Théodore Ruyssen to Lucien Lévy-Bruhl and Gustave Belot in the years preceding the First World War. The Church itself lost in material power but acquired independence and spiritual prestige after its separation from the State and the expulsion of religious congregations. It knew

it could gain more than it stood to lose from the competition
of lay groups like the *Universités populaires* and *L'Action pour
la vérité,* which forced it to reform itself from the inside. The
new Sorbonne, of which Durkheim eventually became one of
the outstanding leaders, was vehemently attacked. By then,
however, Durkheim's doctrine had spread through a growing
number of the happy few: in sociology, education, anthropology, linguistics, sinology, classical studies, comparative religion,
and in history, Durkheim's disciples constituted the marching
wing of France's intellectual forces in the years preceding the
First World War.

Emile Durkheim was born on April 13, 1858, in the eastern
city of Epinal, in the region of the Vosges, not very far from
Strasbourg and Nancy. Four years before him, the mathematician Henri Poincaré and Louis Hubert Lyautey, the future
marshal of France, were born in Nancy; two other Lorraine
princes—as they were to be called by the critic ,Albert
Thibaudet—Raymond Poincaré and Maurice Barrès, the former from Nancy, the latter from the small city of Charmes in
the Vosges, were respectively two and four years younger than
Durkheim. Something of the severity traditionally ascribed to
eastern France, a land of battlefields and hardy, earnest workers,
alien to the sunny indolence of the southern French, persevered
in Durkheim. To him as to Raymond Poincaré, the poet
Charles Guérin (born in Lunéville in 1873) , and the comparative scholar Fernand Baldensperger (born in 1871 in the
Vosges) , the remark made by Laurence Sterne in his *Sentimental Journey* was certainly apposite: "If the French have a
fault, they are too serious."

For a hundred years or longer, there had been more Frenchmen of the Jewish faith in Alsace and eastern France than in
the rest of the country. The French Revolution had granted
full civil rights to the Jews; and, since they represented a
relatively small number in a country which had long been
welded together solidly and in which patriotism was primarily
cultural, few Jewish Frenchmen were made to feel that they
differed in any way from other citizens. Several wealthy indus-
trialists, such as the brothers Péreire or bankers like the Roths-
childs, had played a distinguished part in reorganizing French

economy during the Second Empire. Indeed, no outbreak of anti-Semitism in modern France occurred until about 1880-90, when the Jews became a symbol of plutocracy and were therefore attacked by Socialist propaganda. Later, with the Dreyfus case and its aftermath, they were the victims of reactionary hostility and were denounced by Barrès and Charles Maurras as lacking in national feeling, and accused of fostering the eternal ferment of revolutions and social restlessness.

Following an ancient tradition revered in his family, Emile Durkheim was to become a rabbi. We know next to nothing about his parents, of whom he seldom spoke. For a while, under the influence of a Catholic woman teacher, he seemed inclined to turn to a mystical form of Catholicism. However, he soon became, and remained, an agnostic. In the *collège,* or secondary school, of his native city of some twenty thousand people, Emile Durkheim achieved a brilliant success. He passed his baccalaureate triumphantly, and won national laurels in the Concours Général. At eighteen, he went to Paris, on the advice of his teachers, to prepare for the Ecole Normale Supérieure. But his vocation was not merely that of a teacher yearning for security and a dignified career. He knew that he had in him the traits of a prophet and a missionary; that he wanted to convert disciples to a doctrine and, through teaching and thinking, enable his students to fulfill their role in the social recovery of his country, saddened by her recent defeat and the mutilation of Alsace-Lorraine. Georges Davy, one of the men who knew Durkheim best and who succeeded him in the chair of sociology at the Sorbonne, states that it became evident very early in Durkheim's career as a student that he did not share the youthful ebullience of his companions but believed that effort and even sorrow were more conducive to the spiritual progress of individuals than joy or pleasure. His family had been of modest means; his future seemed insecure; sensitive as he was, he was impatient of the constrictive discipline from which candidates to the renowned Ecole Normale Supérieure had to suffer during the two or three years of their Parisian preparation. During those years, he was a boarder at the Institution Jauffret, and attended the classes in French, Latin, Greek, philosophy, and history, preparatory to the competitive examination at the Lycée Louis-le-Grand.

The rigorous pursuit of formal studies stressing Latin verse and the principles of rhetoric more than originality scarcely suited the young man from Epinal who dreamt of a revival of French intellectual life. He was not admitted to the Ecole Normale in the 1878 competition with his class, which included, among others, Bergson and another philosopher whom politics was to seduce, Jaurès. Durkheim entered the Ecole in 1879, with the class of Pierre Janet, the future psychologist; Goblot, the logician; René Doumic; Ferdinand Brunot; and other scholars and critics destined to fame. Once enrolled (1879), he found freedom, financial security, and the stimulating comradeship of brilliant, fervent young intellectuals. He became an intimate, and occasionally a respected adviser, of Jaurès. He was a close friend of the classical scholars, Maurice Holleaux and Lucien Picard. He adored the discussion of ideas, and his sincerity and his dialectical power won him respect, but he never imprisoned himself in a library or limited himself to the study of the past. Philosophy was his vocation from the start, but a philosophy that had political and social applications. He was attuned to the people of Paris in those years when Republican enthusiasm, in the face of the reactionary threats from Bonapartists and Royalists, was rife in the capital of France. In 1880, when the Fourteenth of July was celebrated for the first time, he spent the whole day in the Paris streets, taking part in the public rejoicing.

The German chemist Wilhelm Ostwald, who was five years older than Durkheim, used to say that the surest mark of future greatness in a young man was rebellion against the teaching he received. Even in a congenial group of some fifty young and promising scholars selected annually from the whole of France, Durkheim was dissatisfied with his instruction. The director of the Ecole Normale, where Pasteur had once been vice-director, was traditionally a humanist. Ernest Bersot, a polished moralist and literary historian, was the holder of the post during the period of Durkheim's attendance. The young philosopher found him superficial and flawed by too mundane a desire to please by elegant rhetoric and surface polish. He found the well-known Latin scholar Gaston Boissier equally shallow. Philosophy was taught by Ollé-Laprune, a professor now scarcely remembered, whom Durkheim, in his eagerness to think scientifically, considered conventional and lacking in intellectual vigor. At that time, physiology and experimental psychology had no place in the training of a philosopher; Durkheim resented this the more because he had to devote most of the first year at the Ecole Normale to courses in Latin verse and Greek prose. He was happiest during his second year (1880-81), which was reserved for personal research. During the third and last year of their stay, the *normaliens* bend most of their energy to preparing for another very difficult competitive examination, the agréga-tion. Success in these competitive ordeals, in which candidates specialize as philosophers, historians, classicists, mathematicians, physicists, and so on, means that they are thereafter "aggre-gated" to the body of French teachers, with a secure position in a lycée and rights to regular promotion. The most scholarly among them may then spend several years uniting the two theses required for the French doctorate (the second one was formerly written in Latin) and occupy a chair in one of the sixteen French universities.

His friends all expected Durkheim to score a brilliant suc-cess. However, original minds are not necessarily attractive to examination committees. His rank was next to the last among the chosen few of the new *agrégés*. Durkheim was in no way daunted by this disregard of his originality. He was already planning his thesis for the doctorate and bubbling over with ideas. He realized that he would never be a conformist or an official greedy for academic honors. He was never elected to the Institut de France, and he had to wait a long time before a special professorship of sociology was created for him at the Sorbonne. In spite of all this, he always looked back with grati-tude upon his years at the Ecole Normale, and later insisted that his son André enter the same Ecole, which he did in 1911. André's promising career was cut short by his death at the front, in 1916, and the loss of his son shortened Durkheim's life.

Three teachers at the Ecole Normale had impressed Durk-heim strongly: Emile Boutroux, the philosopher, and two precise, methodical, almost scientific historians, Fustel de Coulanges (who became director of the Ecole Normale) and Jules Monod. With the perspective of years, Durkheim must later have admitted that, traditional as the training was at the

Ecole Normale, emphasizing ancient languages and rhetoric and style as it did, it had nevertheless failed to cramp the thought of such sociologists as Alfred Espinas and Jean Izoulet, who had entered that same Ecole in 1864 and 1874, or of Lévy-Bruhl, Henri Berr, Célestin Bouglé, Henri Hubert, François Simiand, Louis Gernet, Marcel Granet, and Georges Davy. Most great scientists of the past had likewise proved none the less original for having had to submit in their youth to the discipline of rhetoric, Latin verse, and traditional philosophy.

After he passed his agrégation, Durkheim was assigned to several provincial lycées as teacher of philosophy. For pupils who select the humanities as their favorite field, secondary education in France is traditionally crowned by one year almost entirely devoted to philosophy: for ten hours a week, pupils study psychology, logic, ethics, metaphysics, and elements of the history of philosophy. Those who have specialized in the sciences study only logic and ethics. In the twentieth century, thanks in great part to the prestige of Durkheim, sociology was added to ethics, but it was still, like psychology, classified under philosophy. The greatest of the French philosophers—Bergson, Brunschvicg, Hamelin—did their first teaching in provincial lycées and seldom regretted the experience. Few audiences can be more alert or more rewarding than a class of seventeen-year-old French boys—fervent, if not "silent, upon a peak in Darien" —surveying the magic world of pure speculation, questioning all that they have previously taken for granted. According to all accounts, Durkheim was an exceptional teacher. He spoke well and easily. His every word was instinct with faith and, as one of his disciples testified, "gave his hearers the impression that they had before them the prophet of a nascent religion." He was a master of dialectics. Without oversimplifying philosophical questions, he threw new light on the age-old controversies about freedom and determinism, the infinite, teleology, and epistemology. He endeavored to appear austere and cold, but the students who went to his home to engage in philosophical discussion with him soon discovered that he was a man of warm heart and unusual sensitiveness.

The lycées in which Durkheim taught between 1882 and 1887 —Sens, Saint-Quentin, and Troyes—were all near Paris, where he frequently went to pursue his research. In 1885-86, he took a year's leave of absence to explore the state of philosophical research in Germany. He seems to have been especially impressed by Wilhelm Wundt's *Ethik,* less so by Albert Schäffle. It is not probable that he met Georg Simmel, whose ideas he discussed in an article in Italian reprinted as an appendix to Armand Cuvillier's volume of 1953, *Où va la sociologie française?*[1] His important doctor's thesis, *De la division du travail social,* was completed and published by 1893. Two years later, his essential methodological chart, *Les règles de la méthode sociologique,* established Durkheim as the founder of a school. A professorship of social science had been created for him at the University of Bordeaux in 1887. In 1902, he was at last called to the University of Paris, where he was made a full professor in 1906. Sociology as such appeared to many to be a dangerous innovation, and for a number of years Durkheim occupied a chair of ethics and of philosophy of education. Far from fretting under official timidity, however, he rejoiced in not having to sever the new discipline from philosophy and ethics. His turn of mind predisposed him to the observation of individual cases. "Only the universal is rational. The particular and the concrete baffle understanding," he had declared in his thesis; and he had added in his methodological volume: "Science does not describe the individual, but the general." Education interested him vitally, as the most efficacious means of which a society can avail itself to mold the persons it wants. No finer work on the history of French education has been written than his two-volume *L'Evolution pédagogique en France,* the posthumous publication (1938) of his course given at the Sorbonne in 1904-5.

With the closing years of the nineteenth century, Durkheim's thought was fully formed, and it ceased, thereafter, to derive much from outside influences. The last twenty years of his life (1897 to 1917) were devoted to the expansion of his own ideas. The result was the great work on *Les formes élémentaires de la vie religieuse* (1912), which followed his remarkable series of lectures on education. Although he never pursued anthropological or sociological inquiries among primitive peoples themselves, never ventured into Central Africa, Australia, or New Guinea, and lived at a time when ethnological research had not yet formulated its method and learned patient empiricism, Durkheim divined a great deal that actual observers of primitive tribes in Australia and elsewhere were later to prove accurate. In this respect, Bronislaw Malinowski, who admired much in Durkheim, and the American school of anthropologists (Ruth Benedict, Clyde Kluckhohn, Margaret Mead) owed a good deal to him, even, or chiefly, when they contradicted several of his conclusions. For the admirable essays of Marcel Mauss (on magic, the gift, the techniques of the body, swaddling clothes, and the weaning of babies) led them to pursue their research boldly into cultural and social anthropology. Mauss, also from Epinal, was not only Durkheim's nephew but his disciple. Durkheim's influence over his students was never imperiously exercised: his role was, rather, that of a liberator, as Nietzsche wanted the educator's role to be; and he might even have subscribed to the ironical remark of a contemporary thinker, Ernest Renan, with whom he had more affinities that he would acknowledge, that the disciples he would cherish most would be those who rebelled against him.

The literary atmosphere in the year 1888 appears, in retrospect, to have been permeated with naturalism in fiction and on the stage (De Maupassant, Zola, and the Théâtre Libre), and with the nascent and eccentric manifestations of symbolism in poetry. Durkheim appears to have taken little interest in those contemporary movements, which seem much more important to us than they did to those who lived through them. Few contemporaries perceived the profundity which lay behind the poetical search of Stéphane Mallarmé for an Orphic explanation of the world, or the imaginative force which drove Zola to underline the coarseness of common life but also to transfigure it into visionary hallucinations. The professors of literature at the Sorbonne in those days were as remote from the turmoil of contemporary literature as Durkheim may have been; they preferred to study the literature of the past with an almost scientific determination to be objective rather than to order the chaos of living literature around them.

In philosophy, Bergsonism was attracting the young but meeting with tenacious resistance from the Sorbonne professors. In 1900, Bergson had been appointed to the Collège de France.

His *L'Evolution créatrice* (1907) represented the apex of his fame; Edouard Le Roy in philosophy, Albert Thibaudet in literary criticism, and the poet and essayist Charles Péguy were to campaign for him against the traditional philosophers who stood for intellectualism as against intuition, and against the neo-Scholastics who, with Jacques Maritain, fought for a return to St. Thomas Aquinas. Durkheim and Bergson had little in common but appear to have retained mutual esteem for each other's thought. Both, being of Jewish origin, must have suffered from the unleashing of passionate vituperation which accompanied the protracted Dreyfus trial. Durkheim's own wife had been a Mademoiselle Dreyfus, but of a different family from that of the sorely tried staff officer. More and more, as he grew older, Durkheim ceased to appear to be the iconoclast he had been taken for in his youth. He did not ally himself with the Socialists who emerged victorious from the successive Dreyfus trials and soon turned their "mystique," as Péguy, once one of them, called it, into politics. Several of his disciples judged him overconservative and almost timid. He certainly could not be charged with demoralizing France. His chief concern was to explain morality and the origins of religious beliefs, not to destroy them. He eschewed mysticism as he eschewed materialism. "The true function of society is to create the ideal." These words of Durkheim might have been signed by Renan or Bergson.

The new Sorbonne, as it was termed, was vehemently indicted by young Frenchmen of the Right, as being overscientific and Germanized, as having forsaken the traditional Christian and patriotic French ideals. The Royalists and the conservatives, often allied with elements of the army and of the Church whom their defeat in the Dreyfus battle had embittered, founded a daily, *L'Action Française,* and several weeklies and monthlies. They discovered a rich panoply of anti-Republican weapons in the reasoning of Charles Maurras, and reveled in Pierre Lasserre's onslaught against the Sorbonne and its so-called official philosophy, and in an even more vicious attack by Henri Massis, a friend and admirer of Maurras, who signed himself "Agathon." Those strictures of partisans who refused to move with the age had little effect on Durkheim. He had never entertained an excessive esteem for the classical age of France, for which those neo-classical reactionaries were nostalgic. He had regretted the scorn for science which first Montaigne, then the Jesuits, had instilled in their students, and the preference given by the seventeenth century to polished style over erudition and science.

Durkheim could not burden his life with idle polemics. He was devoted to his family, to his teaching, to the writing which he did and inspired others to do for the *Année sociologique.* That publication was not an ordinary learned journal but a series of long and often very important monographs which carried the rich teaching of Durkheim to sociologists of all countries. Thanks to the close and affectionate relationship which linked most of those young researchers and Durkheim, sociology became a catalyst which literally transformed a number of disciplines: law, with Georges Davy, Georges Scelle, Marcel Mauss, and Maurice Hauriou; economics and political thought, with Hubert Bourgin and François Simiand; geography, with Lucien Febre, Gourou, Roger Dion; archaeology, with Henri Hubert, who revived the study of the Celts, and Marcel Granet, who revitalized sinology; linguistics, with Antoine Meillet, De Saussure, and Benveniste; anthropology and ethnology, with Marcel Griaule and, after Durkheim's death, Claude Lévi-Strauss and Roger Caillois; the history of art, with Louis Hourticq; sociology proper, with Marcel Mauss, again, and Maurice Halbwachs. The latter wrote the Preface for and edited Durkheim's course on *L'Evolution pédagogique en France* (1938) and interpreted and extended Durkheim's views on the elementary forms of religious life and on totemism in Australia in a slim volume entitled *Les origines du sentiment religieux* (1925). Earlier still, in 1918, he analyzed Durkheim's doctrine in a sixty-page essay in the *Revue philosophique.* He became, along with Mauss, the most brilliant continuer of Durkheim's work. Because of his Jewish origin, he was deprived of his professorship at the Collège de France and put to death in the Buchenwald in 1945. The collaborators on the *Année sociologique* seldom made sufficient use of the empirical method; they proffered very bold theoretical views based on an inadequate foundation of concrete data; they preferred philosophizing in Paris to undertaking patient inquiries in remote lands. But, unlike sociologists in other countries, they never isolated themselves from philosophy and ethics. English and American anthropologists and sociologists, such as Bronislaw Malinowski, A. R. Radcliffe-Brown, Robert Redfield, and Talcott Parsons, have generously acknowledged the debt which their own discipline, practiced in a very different spirit, owed to Durkheim's impulse.

Throughout his life, which was lived under the sorrowful shadow of the Franco-Prussian War of 1870-71, and under the ominous threat of another and broader cataclysm, which came in 1914, Durkheim had been anxious to bring his knowledge and his reflection to bear upon the problems of his own time and country. He had been attracted to sociology because it worked with the living and not with the dead; he had preferred it to other branches of philosophy because it was at one and the same time theoretical and practical. In the Preface to his first volume, *De la division du travail social*, he had declared:

> We would not judge our research to be worth one hour's trouble if it were to have only a speculative interest. If we carefully separate theoretical problems from practical ones, it is not in order to neglect the latter, but, on the contrary, to become better able to solve them.

At the very beginning of his last important volume, on the elementary forms of the religious life, Durkheim was just as precise and affirmative:

> Sociology proposes to itself other problems than history and ethnography. It does not seek to know the defunct forms of civilization in order to reconstitute them. Like any positive science, it has primarily as its object the explanation of a reality which is close to us, and which thus can affect our ideas and our behavior. That reality is man, and more especially the man of today.

Jules Michelet, in his famous Preface of 1869 to his *Histoire de France;* Renan in his *L'Avenir de la science* written in 1848 but not published until 1890—and then, probably, read avidly by Durkheim; Nietzsche in his *Use and Abuse of History* (*Thoughts out of Season*), had likewise insisted that history only betrayed its secret to those who were vitally interested in the present, and that the motto of any speculative research or of any study of the past was not a woeful *memento mori* but a *memento vivere.*

When the First World War extinguished the lights in Europe, Durkheim considered it his duty to place his great scientific authority at the service of his country. A manifesto issued by well-known German intellectuals had been noisily publicized in Germany; it acclaimed the war and even approved the invasion of Belgium; the German Social Democrats had scarcely uttered a protest against the mass slaughter that was taking place; even Thomas Mann was to extol Pan-Germanism in a rapturous nationalistic volume, *Betrachtungen eines Unpolitischen* (1918). Durkheim wrote the chapter on sociology (Bergson had done the one on French philosophy) for a volume sponsored by the French Ministry of Education and published on the occasion of the world's fair at San Francisco, *La science française* (1915). He drew up several pamphlets among them *Qui a voulu la guerre?* and *L'Allemagne au-dessus de tout,* and arranged for the publication of a collection of papers, *Lettres à tous les Français.* With distress, he saw promising young teachers and scholars of his country decimated during the war. Over half the class which had entered the Ecole Normale in 1913 were killed before the war was over. Eighteen of the class of 1911, among them Durkheim's only son, died in the Serbian retreat of 1916. Durkheim and his wife bore their grief stoically, but his family and his friends saw Durkheim's health decline as the discipline he imposed upon himself to master his distress became too much for a weakened body. On November 15, 1917, his heart gave way.

The French phrase *le passé vivant* is an apt one to denote the role played by the living past in the molding of an intellectual, novel as his methods may appear to timid contemporaries. Durkheim was trained in an educational system which stressed a thorough acquaintance with the past rather than curiosity about the new sciences. His early specialization in philosophy led him, at the age when he was most receptive, to ponder over the philosophers of antiquity and of the last three centuries in France. Like all of us, he discovered lineaments of his own developing thought among his predecessors, and he realized that, cutting across time, there are such things as families of minds or spirits, and that he himself belonged to such a group. More grateful than other pioneers, "the Descartes of sociology," as Durkheim has been called, paid generous tribute to those before him who had turned their attentions to social problems.

His second thesis, in 1892, was, according to the tradition, a Latin dissertation: Durkheim wrote it on Montesquieu, whose first name was Secondat de la Brède. It was entitled *Quid Secundatus politicae scientiae instituendae contulerit*, and it was dedicated to the great historian of Roman religion, Fustel de Coulanges. Its importance justified a translation into French, by F. Alengry, in the *Revue d'histoire politique et constitutionnelle* (July-September, 1937). In 1953, a new and improved version was published in book form, with an important introduction by Georges Davy. It was followed by a later study by Durkheim on Rousseau's *Contrat social*: the volume is entitled *Montesquieu et Rousseau précurseurs de la sociologie.*

Durkheim did not praise Montesquieu unreservedly. He started from the fundamental principle proclaimed in the *De l'espirit des lois* that institutions, customs, men, must be studied from a relative, not an absolute, point of view; for they vary, not arbitrarily, but according to the nature of the individual, and even more with the nature and the conditions of society. A historical view of political and social phenomena was thus introduced. It became possible to compare, to classify, to explain. Behind the multiplicity of particular cases, some unity was described which allowed a grouping of allied phenomena. Demography, geography, climatology, the adaptation of several forms of government (democracy, despotism, and monarchy) to different eras of history and to diverse lands thus entered into social science. Montesquieu's explanations were often erroneous: laws were too sharply separated from customs and mores; deductive reasoning too often replaced prudent induction. Principles, as Montesquieu admitted in the proud preface to his great work, were posited, and individual cases bowed

18

meekly to them. Teleology entered insidiously into some of Montesquieu's reasonings. Still, Montesquieu was the first to define the object of social science and to recognize social phenomena as a fitting subject for observation. The progress achieved since the *De l'espirit des lois,* especially in the empirical study of specific cases and the rigorous definition of laws, often was to go against the father of social science, but it originated in that great work.

The years when Durkheim studied literature and history in Paris were not altogether favorable to a full appreciation of the French eighteenth century. The defeat of 1870 and the Commune had made many a French intellectual turn against the myth of the French Revolution as the dawn of the new era and the redressment of all the evils of past ages. De Tocqueville, Renan, and Taine evinced hostility to the thought of the century which had prepared that Revolution. They longed for a return to the wise hierarchy and the polished wisdom of the classical age. In literary criticism, Ferdinand Brunetière and Emile Faguet were to immolate Voltaire, Diderot, and the archvillain, the plebeian Rousseau, on the altar of their predecessors who had lived under Louis XIV. Before a fair reappraisal of the empirical and reforming spirit of the Age of Enlightment could be reached, a vast amount of first-hand research into the polemical and political literature of the eighteenth century was necessary (it was undertaken, after 1900, by Gustave Lanson, Durkheim's colleague, friend, and disciple). The Encyclopedists were dismissed by French academic orthodoxy, in the years 1870-1900, as superficial popularizers of science and light-handed peddlers of abstractions, bent on overthrowing the legacy of the past and on rebuilding *in vacuo.*

A few scattered allusions in Durkheim's writings, especially on the subject of education, indicate that he was not deceived by the partial and uninformed view of the Encyclopedists. He did not subscribe to Taine's indictment of their thinking as theoretical and purely destructive. He could, however, in the course of a busy life, grant only scant attention to the historical re-evaluation of eighteenth-century thought. He was content to encourage scholars to pursue such a study, when, early in the twentieth century, the confused writings of the "Philosophes" were read with new insights and with an open mind. His reward did not come until 1923, when René Hubert, a social scientist who owed much to him and to Lucien Lévy-Bruhl, published a solid and penetrating thesis on *Les sciences sociales dans l'Encyclopédie*. Hubert showed that in the mass of articles of unequal merit and of even more unequal originality of which the great encyclopedic dictionary is made, it is possible to discern a coherent sociological theory. The thinkers of the eighteenth century realized that the higher manifestations of human thought could take place only in a group, under the influence of the collective; they introduced a positive spirit into the social sciences.

Their gravest flaw was their shallow conception of religion. Bernard de Fontenelle, in his very curious *Essay on the Origin of Fables* (written in 1695, published in 1724, and dealing with what we would today call myths); a very perceptive magistrate and independent thinker, Des Brosses, in a piece entitled *Dissertation on the Fetish Gods* (1760); occasionally even Voltaire in his *Dictionnaire philosophique* had had some premonitions of the modern anthropological explanation of the origins of mythology and religion. But the Encyclopedists were too engrossed in their struggle against the Church to be impartial in their attitude toward the religious phenomenon. They enjoyed branding priests as imposters playing upon the people's credulity. They accomplished a useful critical task. But only after the German Hegelians, and later Renan, had recognized that religion was far more solidly rooted in the mind of man and in the structure of society, was it possible for Durkheim to stress the social origin of religious phenomena, which originate in the interaction of many minds and owe their "sacred" quality to their social character. "A social fact is to be recognized," in Durkheim's favorite formula, "by the power of external coercion which it exercises over the individual." In that sense, religion is pre-eminently social.

Much of French sociological thinking, long inextricably bound up with the favorite pursuit of French thinkers since Montesquieu, the search for a philosophy of history, revolved around the concept, or the dynamic idée-force, of progress. That concept impregnated the famous preliminary discourse by D'Alembert to the *Encyclopédie* and, in the last decade of the eighteenth century while the Revolution was raging at its most destructive, Condorcet's *Esquisse d'un tableau historique des progrès de l'espirit humain* (1794). Durkheim lived in an age in which many of the illusions of the years 1750-1848 had been shattered, among them the blind faith in progress as inevitable, continuous, and indefinite. He perceived the rashness of Condorcet and of his successor, Auguste Comte, in viewing mankind as one great Being necessarily and infallibly marching toward the progress of a positive era. Anthropology and ethnology had, by 1880, begun to stress diversity at the expense of such a mythical unity of mankind. But in Condorcet, Durkheim admired a great educator and the synthesizing boldness of a powerful mind. All his life, Durkheim taught pedagogy as well as sociology. As an educator, he was cool to the achievement of the humanists, even Montaigne and Erasmus, because he believed that they scorned science and erudition. He was equally critical of the teaching of the Jesuits, who were too intent, in his opinion, on erasing national and local features in order to mold a uniform, general, malleable man. After Comenius (1592-1670), the educators who won his praise because they recognized the value of the exterior world as a storehouse of practical and technical lessons were Rousseau and Condorcet. In education, as those eighteenth-century pioneers conceived it, society may find its most potent tool to mold the kind of men that it needs and wants. Through it, the adults can transform the young and permeate them with the religious and moral practices, the national traditions, and the group consciousness which are the essential heritage of social beings. The impact of education upon the individual was not conceived by Durkheim as that of a blind and automatic mechanism. A true successor to Montesquieu, who had nobly defined liberty in the eleventh book of his *De l'espirit des lois,* and to Rousseau, Durkheim insisted that if society makes man, society also endows him with the possibility of freedom. "Liberty is the daughter of authority properly understood . . . . To be free is not to do what one pleases; it is to be master of oneself, to know how to act with reason and to accomplish one's duty."[2]

Durkheim's admiration for Rousseau should hardly surprise us. At a time when the author of the *Contrat social* was under suspicion as a pure theorist who had reasoned in the abstract and disregarded all facts, Durkheim read the controversial texts of Rousseau with great attention. He clearly recognized that Rousseau had never envisaged the state of nature he advocated as one which had historically existed, but used it as a convenient abstraction to distinguish the traits man may owe to his social life from those which are inherent. The former, however, are only the logical and "natural" development of innate characteristics. Man's intellectual and moral growth is a consequence of social life. In his early years of teaching, Durkheim gave a course on the *Contrat social* at the University of Bordeaux which was printed in 1918 in the *Revue de métaphysique et de morale* and reprinted in the volume mentioned earlier, *Montesquieu et Rousseau précurseurs de la sociologie* (1953). It ranks among the sanest elucidations of that controversial work ever attempted. Again in April, 1906, in Volume VI of the *Bulletin de la société française de philosophie,* in an essay on "La détermination du fait moral," Durkheim incidentally remarked: "Rousseau demonstrated it a long time ago: if all that comes to him from society is withdrawn from man, he is reduced to sensation and to a creature hardly distinguishable from the animal." Durkheim admired not only Rousseau's ingenious dialectics but his perception of those individual characteristics which are the specific result of social forces and cannot be attributed to natural endowment. To Rousseau, the social is a new realm, superadded to the purely psychic one. In the same article, Durkheim said: "Such a conception is far superior to that of recent theorists like Spencer, who believe they have founded society upon a solid natural basis when they have shown that man feels a vague sympathy for man and that he has a great interest in exchanging services with his fellow men" (pages 136-37). Unafraid of the paradox he was stating, Durkheim added that, for Rousseau, the social state is the most perfect, since it turns a stupid animal into an intelligent human being; but, unhappily, it has been misused by mankind.

Speculation in the early nineteenth century in France was predominantly shaped by the Revolution, which had broken

French history into two halves that were never to be fully reconciled. Traditionalists saw in the Revolution a punishment inflicted by God and attempted to justify its massacres and its wars as part of a broad divine scheme. Others read in it a lesson intended to improve and benefit mankind. Still others glorified France's revolutionary mission, interrupted while still unfulfilled, and destined to be steadfastly pursued through further political and social reform. A few—among them Henri de Saint-Simon—understood that another era was dawning, a mechanical and industrial civilization emerging, in which a new division of labor would take place and immense technological, hence social, possibilities would open up for mankind. No more un-French thinker than Saint-Simon existed among the French, unless it was Pierre Joseph Proudhon, another revolutionary social thinker. Social scientists in our century, Bouglé among others, have been drawn to him. Durkheim paid unstinted tribute to Saint-Simon in *La science française:* "With him a new conception [of the laws of social life] appeared . . . . He was the first to offer the formula for it, to declare that human societies are realities, original to be sure and different from those which are to be found elsewhere in nature, but subject to the same determinism."

Saint-Simon had proposed the term "social physiology" for the new study. He suggested that a new and more scientific history might establish the basic law of that study, the law of progress. His disciple Auguste Comte, far more systematic, and logical to the point of madness, deduced the most far-reaching consequences from his views. Like Sainte-Beuve, Renan, Taine, and French thinkers in general, Durkheim proved critical of the founder of Positivism. They were irked by his dogmatism and by the pomposity with which he expressed his ideas, but they owed him a greater debt than they realized. The best of Comtism passed into their own thought, but with many a corrective nuance and none of the extravagance on which both the system and the reason of its prophet foundered.

It is fair to say that Durkheim had a positivistic perspective and occasionally seemed to belong to the same family of eager, encyclopedic thinkers as Comte. Comte coined the word *sociology.* He defined the method of the young science and divided its realm into provinces, notably social statics and dynamics, but he was carried away by his fallacious law of the three stages, and he wrongly assumed that mankind is one whole which inevitably develops according to the same pattern. Thus for too many years he barred the way to empirical observation of the heterogeneous. Nevertheless, after offering many correctives to the system of the godfather of sociology, Durkheim concluded: "In spite of those reservations, a vivid feeling of social reality is ever present in Comte's works. No better initiation to sociology exists."

Durkheim was not attracted for any length of time to Herbert Spencer, whose ideas were widely discussed in French philosophical circles while Bergson and Durkheim were at the Ecole Normale, or to Espinas, whose views paralleled to some extent those of the English evolutionist. A young science must validate its claim by the discussion of its aims, principles, and methods. It must philosophize, before it can free itself from the fascination of philosophy. It must, first of all, define the autonomy of its object (in the case of sociology, of the social fact) and not allow it to be merged either with the psychological (thus making sociology a branch of psychology) or the biological. Durkheim waged a tenacious battle against the analogy which tended to compare human societies with animal societies and the division of social work with the organs of the body. Social facts are things, he would tirelessly assert; that is to say, data; they are, to use the French past participle, objectively *donnés*. One cannot reduce societies to agglomerations of animals as Alfred Espinas had attempted to do in his book *Les sociétés animales* (1876).

Espinas, however, was no mere organicist; like Durkheim, for whose work he paved the way, he had aimed at reconstituting the moral being of France after the defeat of 1871. If he had argued at length that society was an organism, he had also shown that the organism is a society. "A society is a living consciousness, or an organism of ideas," he wrote. He and Théodule Ribot, the leading French psychologist of the time, translated Herbert Spencer's *Principles of Psychology,* which enjoyed wide success in France. Early in his career (1880-85), Durkheim absorbed much of Spencer's organicism, and a little of Schäffle's. Biological metaphors and a frequent recourse to the struggle for life as an explanation of the division of labor bear witness to the influence Spencer exerted over his future adversary. Later, Durkheim became far more idealistic, and also more traditionalistic, in his thinking. He rejected Gabriel de Tarde's famous thesis on imitation as the key to societies and his stress on biological contagion, which in effect negated sociology as such. In formulas which smack of neo-Kantianism and sometimes of the basic ideas of Renan, he proclaimed that "society is not a system of organs and functions . . . . It is a focus of moral life . . . . Its true function is to create the ideal."

Three more names were important in constituting the intellectual milieu in which Durkheim developed: Renouvier, Taine, and Renan. One of Durkheim's most ardent admirers, the sociologist René Maublanc, who entered the Ecole Normale in 1911, wrote in 1930 that when he first met his master, he was advised by him to devote himself to the study of a great thinker, to break down that thinker's system and discover its secrets. "That is what I did," he added, "and my educator was Renouvier." It seems likely that Durkheim was indebted to Renouvier primarily for a method and a turn of mind which tended to separate philosophy from literature and to link it with science, and that Renouvier's example was chiefly a dialectical one: as a sociologist, Durkheim could not have found much in his system.

Charles Renouvier, born in 1815, at Montpellier, the birthplace of Auguste Comte, was, like Comte, a mathematician by training. He went through the Ecole Polytechnique, was an ardent Saint-Simonist for a while, then became a republican in 1848. A man of independent means, he was not bound by academic ties, and devoted his time to the publication of a long series of massive works. In 1867, he was brought to the attention of the philosophical public by a distinguished philosopher of the day, Félix Ravaisson, who praised his ideas. Ravaisson had been entrusted with the official *Rapport sur la philosophie en France au XIXᵉ siècle.* His *La science de la morale* appeared in 1869, and he founded and directed the companion periodicals *La critique philosophique* and *La critique religieuse,* which exercised a considerable influence until his death in 1903. In his last years, Renouvier attempted to rally the French to a broadened Protestantism, but with scant success. He has often been called a neo-Kantian; he himself christened his system "neo-criticism." From Kant, he had borrowed his view of the categories of our understanding and his strong faith in duty and moral obligation. However, Renouvier can hardly be said to have thought within a sociological framework. His system of ethics was deductive and took little consideration of social aspects. His philosophy revolved around the assertion and the demonstration of freedom and the dignity of personal autonomy. It is likely that Durkheim was chiefly in debt to the philosopher whom he hailed for a while as his master for the principle that the whole is radically different from the sum of its parts. From Renouvier, he also learned to remain independent from the official doctrines of the French universities and to favor seriousness and scientific rigor over literary brilliance.

Hippolyte Taine, who was thirty years older than Durkheim, was still regarded as one of the most remarkable alumni of the Ecole Normale when the future sociologist entered that institution. After the Franco-Prussian War and the Commune, Taine had bent all his energies to the reinterpretation of French history and the reform of higher education in France. He strove hard to orient French teaching away from rhetoric and arbitrary impressionism toward greater precision and strict determinism. He devoted especial attention to political and social factors in history, and was instrumental in creating the Ecole des Sciences Politiques in Paris. His social ideas occupy an important place in his philosophy of history, and have been repeatedly discussed by subsequent scholars.[3] It does not seem, however, that Taine's later works greatly impressed Durkheim: their antirevolutionary, even antirepublican, bias, as well as their dangerous tendency to generalize from a few data, cannot have held much appeal for him.

Taine's earlier writings on psychology and literature were eagerly read by students and professors, in the years 1875-85. *Les philosophes classiques du XIXᵉ siècle en France* (1857), a brilliant satirical volume on the academic philosophers such as Victor Cousin, who for decades had professed a timid eclecticism and clipped the wings of philosophical speculation, had been hailed by all independent thinkers in France as a liberating influence. The theory of criticism expounded in the epoch-making Preface of the *Histoire de la littérature anglaise* in 1863, and earlier, in the Preface to the first series of *Essais de critique et d'histoire,* had been the first manifesto of scientific criticism in Europe. As Harry Levin put it in *Literature as an Institution,* Taine rid us "of the uncritical notion that books dropped like meteorites from the sky." He stressed the close bonds between art and the society in which that art grew. He attempted to dispel the mystery which always surrounds genius. In a famous peroration to his chapter on Byron, in the fourth volume of his *Histoire de la littérature anglaise,* he had opened up new vistas for the science of man. "It is the soul itself which science will now explain." Taine made a bold attempt to explain genius in terms of race, milieu, and "moment" (which he apparently uses to designate both the period of history and the acquired momentum). Durkheim was to disagree sharply with Taine's assertion regarding racial determinism. He aligned himself with Michelet, who denied the doctrine, and with Renan who expounded his theory in the famous essays "Qu'est-ce qu'une nation?" and "Judaisme: Race ou religion?" In his *Les règles de la méthode sociologique,* Durkheim later declared, "We know of no social phenomenon which can be placed under the undeniable dependency of race." In the very same ethnic group, indeed, the most diverse social institutions may be encountered. Heredity explains very little, far less than social milieu. Like many thinkers and writers of the last twenty years of the nineteenth century, however, Durkheim owed a debt of gratitude to Taine and Renan for providing him with a basis for criticism and progress in the development of his own theories. Like them, in his formative years Durkheim was intoxicated with scientific and moral fervor. With Taine, who concealed a burning intellectual passion under a cold and objective exterior, Durkheim might have confessed, "I am dogmatic and the opposite of a skeptic. I believe that nothing is impossible to human intelligence," or, "To think, to order and to write one's thoughts is a delight; it is the tête-à-tête of love."

When Durkheim studied at the Ecole Normale, anxious for a faith to replace the beliefs of his ancestors to which he could no longer subscribe, he expressed his views of Renan with passionate conviction. Renan, who sang the over-elaborate strains of his "Prière sur l'Acropole" in 1876 and, in 1883 indulged in reminiscences of his Breton childhood in *Souvenirs d'enfance et de jeunesse,* enjoyed an immense popularity with the public at that time. A philosopher in his youth (he was born in 1823 and at the age of twenty-three he abandoned preparation for an ecclesiastical career), he had gradually shifted his interest to philology and history. His writings, contrasting with the heavy and inelegant prose of Comte and Renouvier, and with the self-conscious works of Taine, inspired professional philosophers with distrust. His overconcern with all the nuances of meaning and his unctuous manner of eschewing blunt assertions and dogmatism displeased the young, who expected their elders to fire them with a faith. No less judicious a reader than young William James, reviewing Renan's *Dialogues et fragments philosophiques* in 1876, charged them with "insincerity and foppishness . . . unmanliness of tone and histrionic self-conceit." We know from the testimony of his young friends that Durkheim, also, was a severe critic of Renan. The two men belonged, to be sure, to different spiritual families. Montaigne, Fénelon, Chateaubriand, Bergson, and Gide are Renan's brothers, while Durkheim is closer to a Pascal without Christ, to Rousseau, or to Péguy.

In spite of his frank distaste for Renan's writings, Durkheim was influenced by them more than any historian of ideas has yet shown. Those who were most impressed by Renan's thought were not, perhaps, those who appeared to imitate him, like Anatole France, but those who, fulfilling his own wish, contradicted him and appealed to his earlier and dogmatic self against his later nonchalant dilettantism. Dominique Parodi, a historian of French philosophy and a moral thinker contemporary with Durkheim, put it thus: "The prestigious literary talent of Renan concealed the philosophical importance of his thought. Between Comte and Bergson, there is Renan."[4]

Renan's early thought, apparent in the essays he wrote from 1848 to 1859 and in the chaotic but often bold and profound volume, *L'Avenir de la science* which was written in 1848 but not published until 1890, developed around an unbounded enthusiasm for science. But science, in his view, was not necessarily mathematical knowledge; it was not susceptible merely of analytical treatment; it did not aim at reducing the complex to the simple. "The fallacious principle that simplicity is anterior to complexity is to be denounced," he asserted in his youthful treatise *De l'origine du langage*. Universal determinism is not to be proclaimed as the law of all phenomena, including psychological and social. "Laws are only true in a certain average state, and they cease to be verified in extreme cases." The science of the human mind cannot be bent to the rigid methods of physical science. Criticism is the crucible in which all must be tested, but "criticism and enthusiasm are not mutually exclusive." Durkheim, likewise, was to oppose the explanation of the complex by the simple. Social facts, which are complex, must be explained through society. The category of the social is rooted in the individual consciousness but ranges far beyond it.

Durkheim's rejection of the theory that ethnic origin is a primary factor in social evolution paralleled Renan's stubborn denial of the doctrine of racist determinism which had tempted the historian Augustin Thierry and the philosophical amateur, Joseph Arthur Gobineau. Like Renan, Durkheim was a fervent patriot, concerned with revitalizing national feeling, with arousing that collective awareness of the past and that surge toward the future which constitutes a nation. The most apt definition of a nation ever offered in French was the one which Renan gave in a public lecture which was delivered at the Sorbonne on March 11, 1882, "Qu'est-ce qu'une nation?" The young sociologist Durkheim, who was preparing his agrégation, may well have heard it. Behind his affectation of skepticism, Renan never ceased dreaming of "organizing mankind scientifically," and even hinted in his youthful eagerness that when reason had organized mankind, it would organize God (God being defined elsewhere as the category of the ideal). He wished to base ethics on science, severing it from religion. This was Durkheim's ambition, too: to derive an ethic from the science of society, to evolve rules of conduct, characterized by obliga-

29

tion and desirability, founded on science. Like Renan (for example, in his five *Essays in Ethics and Criticism* of 1859), Durkheim proclaimed that society is a compound of ideas, beliefs, and feelings, foremost among them the moral ideal which is the *raison d'être* of a society.

Durkheim's later evolution, which brought him to a closer and more sympathetic study of religious phenomena, again seemed to take him back to many familiar assertions of Renan. Like the Breton whose faith had collapsed while he studied Hebrew in the seminary, Durkheim negated the supernatural. Neither of the two men ever wavered on that point. But behind rites, dogmas, and the externals of religion, they both perceived a social substratum. Symbolically interpreted, every religion is true. Historically viewed, every one was at some time valid. Durkheim's last great work, *Les formes élémentaires de la vie religieuse,* frequently has Renanian echoes. "Deep down, no religion is false . . . . Each in its own way is true, for each answers given conditions of human life." As he grew older, Durkheim became more concerned with the breakdown of religion, which he attributed to modern letters, and with the need for more social discipline; suicides seemed to be on the increase and a new social cult was needed to replace weakening religious faith. Renan had preceded him in the same evolution. After the defeat of 1870-71, he had drawn the outlines of a comprehensive moral reform of France which was to rest on education. In a famous reply to a journalist questioning him on the symbolist poets (then considered by many to be anarchists destructive of all traditions), he had compared them to babies sucking their thumbs. Soon, however, he had leniently smiled at his own age and enjoyed his role of official and benign lay saint of French literary life. He had spoken slightingly of history, "that poor, small conjectural science," and stepped in with fanciful reconstructions of the "might-have-been" when documents were missing. Durkheim was always more rigid. He indulged no arbitrary speculation, but he was too much of a philosopher to be content with a lean empiricism. The formula of his disciple François Simiand might already have been his: "No facts without ideas, no ideas without facts." Durkheim himself, in his *De la division du travail social,* had revealed at the outset of his career how deeply French he was (if preferring the universal generalization to the particular detail is characteristically French) when he wrote: "Only the universal is rational. The particular and the concrete baffle understanding."

Such, roughly sketched, is the intellectual environment in which Durkheim grew. Most of his masters, from Montesquieu and Rousseau through Comte and Taine, to teachers like Boutroux, were philosophers. He oriented French sociology, for better or worse, toward philosophy. He was convinced that the contribution of France lay precisely in such a philosophical orientation. France, in his eyes, had uprooted her old social organization more thoroughly than any other country; traditionalism had been dealt decisive blows there, and no complacency with respect to the legacy of the past could be condoned. Hence French reflection could freely be directed to social problems. Moreover, France was, and remained, the land of Descartes; she insisted upon translating the most elusive and the most complex of realities into clear, definite notions. Durkheim may well be said to have been French of the French. A hundred years after his birth, forty-one years after his death, his place among sociologists, ethical thinkers, educators, and philosophers remains pre-eminent.

1. See the English translation in this volume, pp. 354 ff.

2. See Emile Durkheim, *L'Evolution pédagogique en France* (Paris: Félix Alcan, 1938) and the Preface by Maurice Halbwachs; and Durkheim, *Education and Sociology,* trans. and with an Introduction by Sherwood D. Fox (Glencoe, Ill.: Free Press of Glencoe, Illinois, 1956, pp. 89-90, for the quotation above.)

3. Notably by Paul Lacombe, *Taine historien et sociologue* (Paris: Giard et Brière, 1909), and René Gibaudan, *Les idées sociales de Taine* (Paris: Editions Argo, 1928).

4. "Renan et la philosophie contemporaine," *Revue de métaphysique et de morale,* XXVI (1919), 41. A little later, another philosopher, René Berthelot, writing in the same journal (XXX [1923], 365-88), defined Renan's achievement as the incorporation of German romantic idealism into a broadened scientific rationalism.

INDIVIDUALISM AND SOCIALISM
IN DURKHEIM

JOSEPH NEYER

Emile Durkheim's first efforts in sociology were directed toward identifying his own position in relation to the socialism of some of his fellow students at the Ecole Normale Supérieure. Marcel Mauss informs us that *De la division du travail social* was first conceived as a work to be entitled "Relations between Individualism and Socialism."[1] This projected work was never written, but from some of Durkheim's less-known writings, we can derive his conception of individualism and its relation to socialism; and by so doing we may be able to convey something of his image of modernity. At the same time, we may be able to contribute toward the demise of an interpretation of Durkheim—now happily on the wane—which has made him out to be a reactionary, a disciplinarian in education, and one who upheld the rights of the group mind and limited the free expression of individual reason.

The fact is that Durkheim vigorously defended the same values of freedom which John Stuart Mill espoused in his *Essay on Liberty*. However, he did not share the conception of man and society in terms of which Mill and other liberals formulated these values. His polemic against that conception has too readily been taken as an attack upon those values. In Durkheim's view, it does not follow from the fact that one must go to society, which is a "reality *sui generis*," in order to understand the development of individual reason, that this reason ought not to be freely expressed—expressed especially against those forces which seek to return to a type of society in which the reason of the individual has very little place. Nor does it follow from the fact that all communication of the cultural heritage from one generation to another necessarily involves an element of discipline[2]—or even of "constraint"— that our system of education must cease to create "autonomous" personalities, whose ideal of social relationship shall be that of "free co-operation."[3]

The fact that Durkheim drew upon a great variety of sources of insight, many of which were traditionally regarded as incompatible, aroused the suspicions of Durkheim's colleagues among the parties of "progress" in the Third Republic. Although he took his stand upon the methods of empirical science, Durkheim early developed the conviction that the accounts of human and social nature given by the metaphysicians and the idealists were in certain respects more adequate than those of the students of society in the tradition of empiricism. These insights of the idealists, which were expressed in metaphor, were, he believed, waiting to be translated into the literal and empirical terms that would be acceptable to science. Durkheim perceived that the persuasiveness of the transcendentalists (the "idealists" and "metaphysicians") of the nineteenth century lay in the fact that the sociological point of view of the tradition which they opposed (the "empirical" tradition which derived from Hobbes) could not do justice to the nature of moral and religious phenomena.[4] This perception did not imply, however, that he found the methods of empirical science inadequate. It meant rather that he must make an effort (it lasted three decades) to develop scientific sense out of the sociological awarenesses of the antiscientific tradition.[5]

Some of the philosophers upon whom Durkheim drew were not only antagonistic to the notion that empirical science could deal adequately with man and society, but were also social "reactionaries." Their rejection of the sociological individualism associated with the empirical tradition was used to derogate, more or less, the values of *ethical* individualism, the "rights of man," and the aspirations of 1789. Durkheim shared with them the proposition that society is much more than can be contained in the utilitarian conception of free individuals exchanging their goods for the purpose of better satisfying their interests. Did he also share with them their political authoritarianism?[6]

Durkheim's allies in the struggle for a secular education in the Third Republic, those who took their stand with the values of 1789, faced the problem of understanding his relations with the anti-empirical and reactionary philosophies. Perhaps the most difficult problem for some of them, however, was the manner in which Durkheim brought his studies of primitive society to bear upon contemporary issues. It was easy for them to understand and to accept Lucien Lévy-Bruhl's studies of "primitive mentality," for his approach involved a radical discontinuity between the "collective faith" of "prelogical" primitive society and the "individual reason" of contemporary man. The assumption of such discontinuity corresponded to the climate of the Enlightenment, in which these men were comfortable and on the basis of which they looked forward to the elimination of "superstition" from the affairs of men.[7] For Durkheim, however, the study of primitive modes of thought was always directed toward shedding light upon the contemporary mind; he emphasized the aspect of continuity. He had come to perceive that contemporary "reason" is "collective," and that if we are to comprehend its nature, we must understand the "primitive" strata that have gone into its making.[8]

The apparently "reactionary" consequences of this conception appeared very early in his work. For instance, in *De la division du travail social,* a theory of punishment is offered, in which the utilitarian conception of punishment as primarily a deterrent to the potential criminal, is seriously challenged, together with other "enlightened" views of punishment which, by implication, are also called into question. Durkheim offers the suggestion that punishment has the function of enabling "upright consciences" to reaffirm and strengthen their own attachment to the values that have been challenged and weakened by the crime. The aspect of vengeance in punishment is not completely "irrational," for it is only with passion that a society can defend itself against a challenge to its basic norms.[9] In reply to those who would refer to their own contemporary ideas of the functions of penal practices, Durkheim says: "The nature of a practice does not necessarily change simply because the conscious intentions of those who apply it are modified."[10]

A further instance of this refusal to take the contemporary individual consciousness at its face value appeared on the occasion of Durkheim's discussion of the nature of moral phenomena before the *Société française de philosophie* in 1906. One of the philosophy professors present challenged his notion of the essential relation between morality and religion, and Durkheim replied, "The most elementary caution obliges us to consider as altogether suspect the image which each of us constructs of his own moral conscience."[11] The caution with which the sociologist must regard the data of introspection follows not only from the ordinary requirement of good scientific method, according to which private data must be made publicly verifiable; nor only from the fact that any individual conscience reflects the collective conscience but inadequately; but also from the fact that primitive strata lie concealed (and congealed) in the contemporary mind.[12] The unfolding of the institutional life of the past is required for an adequate understanding of the meaning of the present.[13]

For Durkheim the attempt to perceive the present as continuous with the past did not mean, however, that the values of modernity were to be denied. Thus, in his view, one cannot overstress the significance of the gradual emergence of the ideal of a society of autonomous persons in a democratic community. However, the relationship between this ideal and those who aspire to it is the same as that which has always existed between mankind and its faiths and idealisms.

Perhaps the meaning of this proposition can be conveyed by calling attention to the role which Durkheim played in the Dreyfus affair, for he was able to focus upon this national crisis all his theoretical concerns—even those arising from his increasing interest in primitive religion. The issue that Durkheim debated was not the guilt or innocence of Dreyfus, however; rather he undertook to answer the question raised by the press, the question which concerned the right of men to protest what they considered an act of injustice: Were there not times when for the sake of a strong army and national security it would be well for Frenchmen to quit bickering over their rights? And was not their inability to understand this need due to their rampant individualism, *cette grande maladie du temps présent?*[14]

Durkheim accepted this challenge, and he defended the rights of the individual in an article entitled "L'Individualisme et les intellectuels."[15] He begins by dissociating himself from the individualism of Spencer and the economists, which "reduces society to . . . a mechanism of production and exchange." He defends instead the individualism that is expressed in Kant, Rousseau, and the Declaration of the Rights of Man. Such individualism, he says, is no mere dignification of "private interest."

> The human person, the definition of which is the keystone in accordance with which good must be distinguished from evil, is considered sacred, in the ritual sense of the word, so to speak. It has something of that transcendental majesty which the churches of all times lend to their gods; it is conceived as invested with that mysterious property which creates a void around holy things . . . . Such an ethic is not simply a hygienic regimen or a prudent economy of existence; it is a religion of which man is, at one and the same time, the worshipper and the god.[16]

Such individualism is not merely a philosophical construction. It has "entered into the facts" of the social organization of France. Like other religions, it does not "cater to men's instincts"; it offers men an ideal. As evidence of the fact that such individualism calls for self-abnegation, Durkheim points out that neither Kant nor Rousseau overlooks "the rights of the collectivity," and that the individualism of the French Revolution achieved the goal of "national concentration."

Neither Kant nor Rousseau ever demonstrates satisfactorily how their individualism is compatible with the extent to which they subordinate the individual to law and to the collective will, for they attempt to deduce their morality "from the notion of the isolated individual." They oversimplify their first principles and then try to derive from them more than logic permits. They do not understand that it is possible to aspire to the values of individualism "even while holding that the individual is a product of society more than he is its cause." "Individualism itself is a social product, like all the moralities and all the religions. The individual derives from society even the moral beliefs which deify him."[17] From the point of view of the social scientists, however, these philosophers have the function of expressing in as rationally systematic a form as possible certain existing "moral facts."[18]

The religion of individualism, Durkheim continues, has "the autonomy of reason as its first dogma and free discussion as its first rite."[19] The defenders of the army in the Dreyfus case argued that the recognition of the right (and rite!) of free discussion would destroy the kind of basic agreement that is essential to the security of the state. Durkheim scorns such fears. The right to criticize freely is not the right to incompetence. There is no incompatibility between respect for authority and rationalism "provided that the authority is founded rationally."[20] In regard to the case under consideration, however, Durkheim has this to say: "Now, in order to know whether it is permissible for a tribunal to condemn an accused without having heard his defense, one does not require any special illumination."[21] To decide this question the common moral judgment of men is quite competent.[22]

Durkheim says further that he is in agreement with those who are anxious concerning the disunity of France and who hold that only a religion can provide the harmony so vital to national existence; the only real question concerns the kind of religion that can unite France. It can only be "the religion of humanity, the rational expression of which is the ethics of individualism."[23]

> We know today that a religion does not necessarily imply symbols and rites, . . . temples and priests; this whole apparatus is only the superficial part. Essentially religion is nothing but a group of collective beliefs and practices that have a special authority.[24]

That this religion can only be the cult of the individual, follows, Durkheim says, from the whole development of modern Western society. He develops as part of his argument the conception of social development that is offered in *De la division du travail social:* Because of the diversification of outlook that is associated with the differentiation of functions in society, respect for the individual is the only value that is held in common by all men, although different nations will develop somewhat different conceptions of the individual who is to be the object of the cult. In order to arrest the development of individualism, it would be necessary to check the growing division of labor, lead society back to the old type of conformity, and put an end to the tendency of societies to grow larger and more centralized—but this is a task beyond our capacities.

To offer Christianity as the religion of modern society and as a protection from the supposed dangers of individualism is to ignore the fact that the "originality of Christianity consisted precisely in a remarkable development of the individualistic spirit." It was Christianity which first found the essential condition of piety in the faith and personal conviction of the individual. If individualism is dangerous to the integration of society, then so is Christianity.

The appeal for justice in the case of Dreyfus, Durkheim argues, rests not upon sympathy for an unfortunate individual, but upon the need to uphold the basis of the moral structure of France. Every violation of the rights of the individual is a blow at its foundations. "A religion which tolerates sacrilege abdicates its power over the consciences," says Durkheim, a statement that recalls the theory of punishment expounded in *De la division du travail social*. The alternative to individualism is not authority in any genuine form, but anarchy. It is from France that many other peoples have learned the forms of expression of individualism. Therefore, for France, in particular, to violate the demands of individualism is to commit "moral suicide."

In concluding this article, Durkheim recalls that in the days of his youth during the beginnings of the Third Republic, France was engaged in destroying the old barriers to freedom and was caught up in an enthusiasm for the values of individualism. It is historically understandable, he suggests, that the negative side of freedom should first engage the energies of men. But when political freedom is achieved, it must be employed as a means to positive achievements if it is not to become lifeless.

> Therefore, let us utilize our liberties in order to see what is to be done, and to do it; in order to ameliorate the functioning of the social machine, still so harsh in its effects upon individuals; in order to place within their reach all the possible means for developing their capabilities without handicaps; in order to work finally to create a reality of the famous precept: To each according to his achievements.[25]

Durkheim's position regarding the Dreyfus case has been delineated rather closely for a number of reasons, despite the fact that its formulations are somewhat careless and that the article containing them was written hastily and was published in a non-professional journal. In the first place, it seems clear that if this political pamphlet had been readily available to Americans at the time when they first began to read Durkheim's work, it might have prevented their hasty conclusions concerning his "reactionism." In the second place, the article presents the doctrine of the sacredness of the individual in concentrated form, and spares us the task of bringing together all the references to it that are scattered throughout Durkheim's works.[26]

It is interesting to note the difference between Durkheim's defense of civil liberties and that of nineteenth-century utilitarianism. The general argument of the latter was that unless men were allowed to think their thoughts and to speak their minds freely, society would lose the benefit that results from the competition of ideas in the market, where the best in each field (the most "true" in the field of ideas) is bound to triumph. The argument further asserted that society as a whole benefits when all its members and groups are allowed to speak out concerning their own interests, since every man is, in the long run, the best judge of what his own interests are.

This utilitarian argument contains empirical propositions that are at least open to debate. Antidemocratic philosophies, for example, have pointed to the wastefulness of parliamentary and other democratic procedures (in the same way, John Stuart Mill argued *for* democracy by pointing to the wastefulness of bureaucratic centralization and its failure to tap the ideas and initiative of its human resources). However, Durkheim is not obliged to take up the issue on this pragmatic level; he regarded it as an argument that was destined to be forever inconclusive. Even the question whether the pursuit and dissemination of truth is always socially useful does not need to be argued in these utilitarian terms. Durkheim's position was that the values of individualism, upon which Western society must take its stand, place upon us the moral requirement of speaking the truth in social relations. This is what he means by "rationalism," which he says is "one of the aspects of individualism: it is the intellectual aspect . . . . Intellectual bondage is only one of the types of servitude which individualism combats."[27]

For Durkheim, "individualism" is the most inclusive term. It includes democracy,[28] rationalism, and all related values, such as liberty, freedom, and the development of individual responsibility.

In more than one context, Durkheim informs us that individualism, which has become the basic value complex of modern society, has had a development that dates back far beyond the present period. It is possible to be misled by the fact that in his remarkable study of suicide Durkheim discovers relations between the development of Protestantism, free thought, and individualism, and the type of suicide he terms *égoiste*. However, in the same study, he gives us the following reason for not seeing a revival of Catholicism as a remedy for the high rate of suicide: "The history of the human mind is the history of free thought itself. It is therefore puerile to wish to check a current which everything proves irresistible."[29] Durkheim's reply to the philosophy of Auguste Comte, which tends to regard many of the aspects of individualism as social traits representing the transition from medieval authority to a new type of authoritarian social organization, is well put in his criticism of Saint-Amand Bazard (who, with Comte, was a disciple of Saint-Simon):

> Everywhere one sees different systems of beliefs being elaborated successively, systems that arrive at a maximum of coherence and authority and then succumb progressively under criticism. What escaped the attention of Bazard was that the more one advances in history, the more one sees the characteristics of the critical period prolonging themselves up to the very heart of the organic period.[30]

We have noted that in Durkheim's intervention in the Dreyfus affair, he maintained that there is no incompatibility between the right of free criticism and the respect for authority, "provided only that the authority be founded rationally." Not only does this statement appear to raise many problems, but it carries a very strange sound to those of Durkheim's readers who are acquainted with his frequently repeated assertions to the effect that individuals in a healthy society are spontaneously aware of their moral obligations. His criticism of the utilitarian moral theory consisted, in part, in pointing out that the science of sociology is only beginning to develop insight into the utility of established institutions.[31] The same point is involved in his criticism of Spencer's "natural reactions" theory of education, which held that education should merely provide the child with opportunities for learning the consequences of his own acts.

> Morality is not so simple a thing as Spencer imagines . . . .
> The acts which it disapproves owe their character to . . . re-percussions which cannot be perceived with the naked eye, but which science alone, thanks to its special procedures and specialized information, comes gradually to discover.[32]

In *L'Education morale*, Durkheim discusses the development of autonomy in a moral education that begins with the inculcation of the "spirit of discipline." This discussion throws some light on the general problem of reconciling the demands of rationalism with the authoritarian aspects of social life. It is evident that Durkheim was troubled by this problem for a long time. At the age of twenty-seven, he writes: "A society without unexamined judgments would resemble an organism without reflexes; it would be a monster incapable of living."[33] In his early reviews and articles, he repeatedly raises the question, What shall we teach our people concerning their relation to society so that they will have a rational account of the nature of their duties and loyalties? In dealing with this question, there is, at first, a despairing note,[34] but very soon Durkheim comes to believe that sociology can provide not only a theory of social institutions, but also an account of the individual's place in society which can serve the same function in moral education as that which was served by the old "mythologies."[35]

Without attempting to discuss the many difficulties implicit in this last goal,[36] let us consider briefly the suggestions which Durkheim offers for reconciling authority and autonomy in *L'Education morale*. The two basic elements of morality which must be inculcated in the developing personality, we are told, are the "spirit of discipline" (respect for authority) and "devotion to social groups." These have always been recognized by moral philosophers in the abstract notions of duty and the good. Among modern Western peoples, however, a third, and novel, element enters into morality: the requirement that the moral will be autonomous. Philosophers (Kant, for example) have attempted various "dialectical" solutions of the antinomy between duty and autonomy, but the fact that the requirements of autonomy have increased with time indicates that the solution is historical. In utterances that take on a Spinozistic tone, Durkheim suggests that freedom comes with the advance of understanding in both the physical and the social order.[37]

If we combine this discussion with what Durkheim has said in "L'Individualisme et les intellectuels" concerning the rational recognition of authority in an individualistic society, something like the following conclusion emerges: The rationalization of authority must be conceived as a continuing process in which a reality, much of which lies beyond our awareness, is penetrated by intelligence. And we must be careful not to deny the importance or the reality of that which is as yet closed to the light of reason. The right of free discussion and criticism requires that any existing authority or accepted moral principle be open to examination upon the occasion of any deepening of insight into the social reality.

This conception of autonomy, as an ideal to be realized progressively in social history, is also applicable on the level of the moral education of the individual. The first respect for authority, says Durkheim, is achieved through the susceptibility of the child to suggestion. "Thanks to his suggestibility, we can . . . give him a first impression of the moral forces which surround him and upon which he depends."[38] The schoolmaster adopts an imperative tone,[39] but he must impress the children as representing social forces beyond himself. This early discipline must be such as to result in liberation, and Durkheim offers many suggestions concerning methods for preparing the way through discipline for the gradual emergence of autonomy; for instance, we must not allow the child to remain too long under any one master. Parenthetically, we should note Durkheim's view that without social discipline there can be no individual freedom since "self-mastery" is learned at the "school of duty."[40]

The healthy adult individual recognizes many moral obligations the rationale of which he does not pretend to know. There is always a limit beyond which the attempt to understand action results in impotence. But in an individualistic society, any individual has the right to apply his developing awareness by making proposals for social change.[41] There is no incompatibility between such "free discussion" and the recognition of authority.

> It is necessary that moral rules be invested with the authority without which they would be ineffective, but this authority must not be withdrawn from discussion after a certain moment in history, it must not be made into idols to which man does not, so to speak, raise his eyes.[42]

In thus holding that there is "no incompatibility," Durkheim expresses the tension between the more ancient demands of morality and the newer claims of rationalism.

However, rationalism is only "one aspect of individualism." In a sense, Durkheim's account of egoistic suicide is a dramatic presentation of the tension between individualism and the older dimensions of social and moral life. In order to develop the significance of this point, it will be useful to recall briefly the scheme by which he explains variations in the suicide rate in *Le suicide*.

Both anomic suicide and egoistic suicide are consequences of a weakening of the integration of social groups,[43] but the two phenomena are distinguished in that each is a consequence of one of two ways in which society acts upon its members. Society is both "transcendent" and "immanent": on the one hand, its norms regulate and limit the expression of men's desires; and, on the other hand, it is a source of strength and inspiration, and determines the content of men's desires—offering ends beyond individuals to which they want to devote their energies.[44]

In developing the meaning of anomie, Durkheim offers correlations between the increase in divorce and the rise in suicide rates—a rise due principally to the suicides of married men. From this Durkheim concludes that the movement toward easier divorce has a serious effect upon the institution of marriage in that marriage can no longer serve so effectively as it once did in stabilizing the impulses and energies of men.[45] The other important statistical datum that he offers in connection with anomie is the rise in the suicide rate that accompanies periods in which standards of living and normal expectations of reward change at an abnormal pace. The suicide rate will rise not only in a depression but also when prosperity is suddenly increased. The important fact is that the balance in the scheme of men's expectations has been shaken by such disturbed situations—a balance which in normal times has the effect that men's ambitions are, in general, realizable.[46] The effects of anomie are found in the frustration which follows the breakdown in the authority of those moral norms which regulate the satisfaction of desire. "By itself, abstracted from all external power [that is, moral authority] which might regulate it, our sensibility is an endless abyss which nothing can fill."[47]

Egoistic suicide, on the other hand, is the consequence of a dearth of objects beyond the self which can enlist its energy and devotion.[48] In support of this notion, Durkheim offers the following data: There are more suicides among Protestants than among Catholics; there is a decrease in the number of suicides when there is an increase in the size of families; and there is a decline in the suicide rate in times of national emergency when "the individual thinks less of himself and more of the common issue."[49] The egoist searches in vain for the "meaning of it all"; he finds life empty because he has devoted arduous labors to the development of capacities which have become detached from their social roles.[50]

Durkheim looked upon the values of individualism as an aggravating factor in egoistic suicide:

> In those societies and milieus in which the dignity of the person is the supreme goal of conduct, and in which man is a god for man, the individual is easily led to take as God the man which is himself, and to set himself up as an object of his own cult. When morality is oriented primarily toward giving him a very high idea of himself, certain combinations of circumstances suffice to render him incapable of perceiving anything which is beyond himself.[51]

The cult of personality encourages the development of individual capacities as ends in themselves. Furthermore, as Talcott Parsons has emphasized,[52] it places certain requirements on the individual—he must be "independent and responsible"—requirements that are sometimes found to be incompatible with the maintenance of normal group relations (marriage, family, and so on), and thus it deprives the individual of the fortifying effects of normal situations of "emotional dependence."[53]

A parallel to this relationship between the ethics of individualism and egoism is found in the relationship between the ethics of progress and anomie. If men are taught that it is a duty to contribute to the advancement of society and to the improvement of their own lot, it becomes difficult for them to accept any definition and limitation of their own social role and status. "Consequently, the number of the discontented and the restless cannot fail to increase."[54]

For Durkheim, the practical conclusion drawn from these disturbing insights is not a "reactionary" stand in opposition to both individualism and the associated ethics of progress. Rather, he advocates the acceptance of a certain increase of egoism and anomie as inevitably linked to the conditions of modern life.[55] He tells us, for instance, that if modern society is to retain its required flexibility—its readiness to "break the yoke of tradition" and to revise its beliefs when necessary— then an "exaggerated individualism" is to be expected in a certain number of its members.[56] It is in such a mood that Durkheim confronts the dilemmas of modernity.

Durkheim regarded the development toward a "socialist" organization of society as an inevitable response to the ethics of individualism and progress, as well as a consequence of what he termed the "emergence of the individual." As a preliminary to a consideration of this topic, it will be useful to add a few notes concerning the manner of his treatment of individualism.

It will have been observed that in his article on the Dreyfus case, Durkheim appeared to waver on the question whether individualism is a morality or a religion. This article was written at the same time as his first explicit effort to define religion, "De la définition des phénomènes religieux,"[57] in which he suggests that religious phenomena are "obligatory beliefs as well as the [ritual] practices relative to the objects given in these beliefs." Morality and law, therefore, are distinguished from religion by the fact that they have no mythology or cosmogony. In the same way, the ideas and beliefs connected with democracy and progress, though they are sacred, are not, strictly speaking, religious beliefs since they have no cult. These ideas involve *general* modes of action, but they are neither minutely regulated nor intimately related to belief; at the "religious stage" of society, action and representation cannot be disassociated. In writing on the Dreyfus affair, however, Durkheim does speak of individualism as a religion.

Later in his development, Durkheim identifies the sacred as the element which distinguishes religion from morality.[58] At the same time, in his discussions of the secularization of moral education, he reminds us that in detaching morality from theology we must be careful not to destroy the element of the sacred in morality.[59] To make matters more confusing, there are occasions when Durkheim, in stressing the difference between the past and the present and in defending a moral education that is independent of religion,[60] seems, contrary to his own explicit injunctions, to be making the religious synonymous with the theological. These apparent inconsistencies in Durkheim's terminology derive from his efforts to express, through comparative studies of institutions, his insights concerning the contemporary psyche as a transformation of—not a radical departure from—the past.[61]

In addition to the difficulties which arise in the treatment of individualism from the problem of defining religion, there is a certain ambiguity in the manner in which Durkheim relates the conception of the cult of the individual to his other views. For instance, in his article on the evolution of punishment, a distinction is made between *criminalité religieuse* and *criminalité humaine,* and, consequently, between two categories of crimes.

> [Crimes in] the former [category] are directed against collective things . . . of which the principal ones are public authority and its representatives, customs and traditions, and religion; [those in] the latter are injuries against individuals (murder, theft, acts of violence, and frauds of all sorts).[62]

Durkheim's view is that the punishment for the two sorts of crimes must differ because the collective sentiments which they offend are of a radically different nature. In primitive society, the sentiments are collective in two senses: they are not only the sentiments of a "collective subject," but also have collective things for their objects. In "advanced" societies, the individual is the object; the individualistic ideal is "not deprived of all transcendence," but this transcendence is, he says, "much less accentuated" than is the case with more primitive ideals.

In *De la division du travail social,* we are informed that the collective sentiments involved in the cult of the individual occupy a unique place in the collective conscience. For although they derive their force from society, they attach us not to society but to ourselves. As a consequence, the cult of the individual "does not constitute a genuine social bond."[63] However, the view which Durkheim expresses in the Dreyfus article is more in accord with the totality of his thinking on this subject; in that article Durkheim is quite certain that individualism constitutes "a genuine social bond"—in fact, a most important one.[64]

A good deal of *De la division du travail social* is devoted to exhibiting how the individual personality emerges from the homogeneity of primitive society. The individual becomes more autonomous[65] even as he grows more dependent upon social relations for his existence. This process is explained in terms of the growing division of labor, which involves a progressive differentiation of the elements of society. Durkheim seems to be saying that the collective or common conscience gradually disappears, as "solidarity" ceases to be "mechanical" and becomes "organic"—that is, as the interdependence of individuals that is a consequence of the division of functions in society, rather than shared mentality, comes to constitute the bonds of social unity. It may have been a concern for the architectonic of this thesis that led the young Durkheim[66] to assert that the cult of the individual "does not constitute a genuine social bond."

The fact is that in all the works which follow *De la division du travail social,* the idea of the collective conscience remains fundamental to the interpretation of contemporary society. Significantly, it is no longer referred to as a *common* conscience, for the system of collective representations is a system involving differentiation. Different groups of individuals participate in it in different sectors although all are united by their adhesion to certain common values. In the Preface to the second edition of *De la division du travail social,* Durkheim already recognizes that his simple explanation of organic solidarity will not suffice.[67] His idea concerning the future of occupational groups, which is contained in the Preface, is enough to make the point. For the occupational groups will perform not only economic functions, but will also fill the "moral gap" between the individual and political society by "inculcating in the heart of the workers a lively sentiment of their common solidarity."[68]

The thesis concerning the progressive diminution of the *common* conscience remains valid. As a consequence, the general distinction between mechanical and organic solidarity in so far as it refers to the *quality* of the sentiments upon which social integration depends remains basic for an understanding of modernity. The important point, we may suggest, is that in a differentiated society, man must learn to respect authorities that are not absolute. The sentiments which support his own norms are not truly "religious" because religion does not tolerate sacrilege, and the individual is constantly confronted by individuals whose values are not his own and whose behavior violates his own norms. In these terms, we may understand Durkheim's paper on the evolution of punishment. The quality of punishment has changed because, in general, the quality of the sentiments offended has changed. "Although social discipline, of which morality properly speaking is only the highest expression, extends little by little its field of action, it loses more and more its authoritarian rigor."[69] The emergence of the individual can then be conceived in terms put by that faithful and clear-minded Durkheimian, Célestin Bouglé:

> The number of groups to which a single individual can belong is ever increasing. This explains the kind of intellectual and emotional subtlety which we found characteristic of the civilized state of mind as opposed to the state of mind of the primitive.[70]

The individual personality begins to emerge, in Durkheim's view, with the breakdown of the "segmental organization" of society, that is, with the breakdown of that type of organization based on a repetition of similar units, whether the primary unit be considered to be the horde, clan, village, family, or whatever.[71] As society becomes organic, the number of social relations into which individuals enter is vastly multiplied. In his university course on the family, Durkheim was concerned with demonstrating, in line with this development, that the gradual "contraction" of the system of relations that may be said to constitute the family results in the formation of the conjugal family, which consists only of a married couple and their immediate progeny.[72] Through study mainly of the changes in law, Durkheim attempts to show that this development may be looked upon as a breakdown of primitive communism, in which all possessions are held in common.[73] As the institution of the family contracts, the individuals develop independent spheres of action, and the political authority acquires a greater control over the internal affairs of the family.

In this context the rights of inheritance are seen to be vestiges of "familial communism" that has prolonged itself "into the regime of personal property."[74] The right of testament is one of the first encroachments upon the rights of kin; it occurs as the "zone" of family relationships becomes narrower.[75]

> There is no doubt that this regression is destined to continue. By this I mean not only that the right to make one's will is becoming absolute, but that a day will come when it will no longer be permitted a man, even by way of testament, to leave his fortune to his descendants, just as he has not been allowed (since the Revolution) to leave to them his social functions or his high offices. For the testamentary transmissions are only the final and most reduced form of hereditary transmissions.[76]

Elsewhere, Durkheim is less dogmatic concerning the proposition that all forms of inheritance are bound to disappear.[77] Certainly, in the present order, the future of one's progeny constitutes a primary end of action; indeed, a concern for their prospects is an important preventative against egoistic suicide.[78] However, Durkheim's main conception is clear. Far from being a requirement of individualism, the right to inherit property is one of the last remaining features of a society in which the individual has not yet emerged. In the same context, Durkheim indicates that the elimination of inequalities at birth becomes necessary to "the moral conditions of our time."

Durkheim's formulation of the relation between the primitive and the modern has certain advantages over most partisan attempts (especially those made around the turn of the century) to draw conclusions for or against private property from the study of primitive society. He opposes those who use supposed evidence of primitive communism as grounds for asserting that "human nature" is capable of abandoning the individualistic emphasis made by contemporary society; for Durkheim envisages the "socialism" of the future as being, from the point of view of social structure, at the farthest possible remove from primitive communism: he sees it, in fact, as the very extreme of individualism. However, he also differs from the anthropologists who point to the regulations governing property in some primitive societies as support for the view that "private property" is "eternal";[79] for from Durkheim's point of view, these regulations are of such a nature that, when they are seen in the context of comparative legal history, they serve to exhibit rather that the distinction between primitive communism and individual property is not so sharp as it might appear to be at first. Such comparative study shows that in all societies—even in our regime of private property—the manner in which material goods are allocated is regulated in accordance with social norms (both legal and moral); the differences are seen to be matters of degree and emphasis.[80] In Durkheim's terms, therefore, both primitive communism and what is today called private property are linked to a type of social structure whose disappearance is correlated with the emergence of the individual.

Although Durkheim anticipated the disappearance of inheritance, he did not believe that it meant the end of all property rights. Inheritance is only one mode of acquiring property. "Individualism would be no more than a name if we did not have some physical sphere of action within which we could exercise a kind of sovereignty."[81] What is required by the values of individualism is the elimination of such inequalities as stand in the way of men's arriving at "just contracts." This is a persistent theme with Durkheim. "The task of the most advanced societies is, we may say, a work of justice."[82] From the beginning Durkheim was aware that the unhealthy state of the moral conscience of Western man would continue until the anarchy of economic life had been moderated by some measure of control. It should not be surprising, therefore, to find that Durkheim was, as Mauss informs us, sympathetic with some of the socialists of his day.[83]

Durkheim defined socialism as follows: "We call socialist every doctrine which calls for the joining of all economic functions—or of certain of them which are at present diffuse—to the governing and conscious centers of society."[84] In stating this definition Durkheim does not raise the question concerning the nature of the governing centers of society. It is possible that direct contact with economic life will change the character of the state, and what is called for is contact, not subordination. Furthermore, the question of how far economic life is to be related to the central organ of the state, and how far to the intermediary occupational groups, is not settled. The important element, however, is the attachment of economic functions to organized centers of authority.[85]

As thus defined, socialism is distinguished from "communism," which is an ancient and recurrent ideology in the history of human thought. Communism is motivated by an awareness of the antisocial effects of wealth. It advocates consumption in common, but it is not concerned with the regulation of production, which it seeks to remove as far as possible from the center of social life.[86] It is a dream, which comes to man from time to time, a dream of a society in which all trace of antisocial impulse has been erased from human existence. Socialism, on the other hand, is a distinctly modern phenomenon. Its aspirations develop out of the awareness that the activities of large-scale industry have grown to such proportions that they must become associated with the governing centers of society if human existence is to be made tolerable. Therefore, Durkheim considers Saint-Simon the first important "socialist" thinker, for he was the first to have perceived the significance of the emergence of large-scale industry.[87]

From Durkheim's conception that the emergence of the individual brings about changes in the character of inheritance, from his idea that individualism demands the elimination of inequalities at birth, and from his appreciation of Saint-Simon's treatment of industrialism, it is clear that Durkheim believed in the future of socialism. In the context of a rather aloof analysis of the socialist movement as a social phenomenon, he says, "Far from being a turning back, socialism, *as we have defined it,* appears, on the contrary, to be implied in the very nature of the higher societies."[88] What, then, is the explanation of his rather impatient condescension toward socialist theory?[89]

Absorbed as he was in the minute details of the comparative study of institutions, Durkheim was unable to tolerate the claim of the socialists that their doctrine was "scientific." He maintained that broad generalizations of the sort indulged in by the Marxists must await the test of new knowledge to be gained from the advance of studies of the family, property, political organization, morality, law, and economics. It is not difficult to sympathize with Durkheim's criticism and with his view that the socialists have failed to distinguish properly between science and its "application" in social action.[90]

There are occasions, however, when Durkheim's critical remarks might be judged excessively zealous.[91] For example, he suggests in more than one context, that there are two approaches that may be taken to the study of socialism. The one which he adopts is that of regarding socialism as a social phenomenon, the genesis and historical causes of which are the object of inquiry. The alternative approach is to treat it as a system of propositions "outside of space and time" and "outside of historical becoming"; in this case, the inquiry concerns the truth or falsity of the system. In regard to the latter approach, Durkheim says that "sociology has only one word to say: it must . . . refuse to recognize it [socialism] as a scientific enterprise."[92]

Now it would seem that sociology should have more than "one word" to offer here. The notion that one is required to give a simple positive or negative reply to the question of whether or not socialist doctrine is "scientific" is not in accordance with Durkheim's general conception of the nature of science and its development. In his appreciation of writers like Montesquieu and Condorcet, for example, Durkheim is careful to separate their "scientific" contributions from the other ingredients of their thought.[93] In making this sharp distinction between the two approaches to socialism—the one, historical; the other, "outside of space and time"—Durkheim is far from his later insight that scientific reason is itself a "social fact."

Durkheim's more significant criticism of socialist thought, however, attacks the general ideas in terms of which socialist writers interpreted the functioning of social institutions. At this deeper level, he was challenging ideas which were shared by socialism and by laissez-faire liberalism. It will be convenient, in considering this point, to follow Durkheim's analysis of Saint-Simon.

Both Saint-Simon and the classical economists emphasize the principle of industrialism, namely, that "economic relations constitute the warp and woof par excellence of the collective life."[94] They differ, of course, in that for the economists, economic activities are private affairs which arise from the initiative of individuals; whereas for Saint-Simon, "society can become industrial only if industry socializes itself." In both views, the aim of social institutions becomes the achievement of the most effective organization of production.

Another principle which Saint-Simon and the economists share, according to Durkheim, is that of anarchism. In the views of both all social "constraint" (including that exercised by government) is destined to disappear.[95] The reason for this, says Saint-Simon, is that the supreme council of industry derives its authority sheerly from its competence, and one can no more think of violating its directives than one can conceive of disobeying the physician or the engineer. "Order will be maintained by the simple play of spontaneities without . . . any coercive discipline."[96] The social system has an authoritarian aspect; but the only true authority is science, which ministers to society as a system of economic interests, and no constraint is required to persuade men to follow their own interests. The economists, however, believe that this harmony of interests already exists. Unlike Saint-Simon, they do not anticipate a social reorganization which would attach the economic functions to central governing agencies; for them the only function of governmental authority is the maintenance of liberty.

In favor of the economists, Durkheim finds that their view is an "ideological" expression of modern individualism, the significance of which escapes Saint-Simon.[97] However, in spite of certain important reservations, he goes along with Saint-Simon's "collectivism" in that, as we have seen, he regards social development as moving in the direction of a centralized regulation of many features of social life which have hitherto been under the control of the social segments. He also accepts Saint-Simon's "industrialism." That society must be organized, for the most part, on an "industrial base," that the primary social institutions of the future must become affiliated with the productive organization of society,[98] is a proposition that is persistent in Durkheim's thought, and is, in fact, involved in his definition of socialism.

However, Durkheim's conception of the nature of such institutions differs from that of Saint-Simon and of socialist theory in general. For Durkheim, the organization of society on an industrial base does not imply that the sole function of social institutions is the ordering of "economic interests." In another context, in which Durkheim discusses the relations among the various social sciences, he suggests that at different stages of social development different types of institutions play a preponderant role.[99] Nevertheless, identical social functions are carried out in all social organizations, although often in a disguised form. Therefore, we can say that "economic" institutions may perform moral functions, and "religious" institutions may serve economic ends. The fact that industrial organization predominates does not entail society's becoming concerned solely with the production of goods.[100]

Thus the error of both Saint-Simon and the economists lies in their notion that "individuals and peoples must no longer pursue anything except economic interests," a notion that results in their view that all social constraint is destined to disappear. For they regard the social problem as being mainly that of harmoniously ordering the interests of men; and they share the optimistic belief that this can be accomplished without appealing to anything beyond those interests—even though the method of Saint-Simon is based upon collectivism and that of the economists on laissez-faire individualism. The sole task of

54

Saint-Simon's collective administration is to "render as fruitful as possible the production of wealth so that each may receive as much as possible. . . ."[101]

In his account of the passing of the military and the theological structures, Saint-Simon demonstrates the disintegration of those forces which formerly kept in check all the tendencies toward greater production and industrialization. Then, in what Durkheim calls a *non sequitur,* he says that in the new society there can be no limitations upon economic development, for society secures the adherence of its members by distributing its products in such a manner that everyone, "from the top to bottom of the scale," receives a sufficient reward—as much reward, in fact, as is possible. Durkheim's criticism of this conception touches at the root of the problem of socialist social organization. From the fact that the old checks upon industrial activity are no longer effective, it does not follow that a new type of regulation will not come into being. The conception that a sufficiently productive economic organization can, by the fact of enormous production alone, satisfy men's needs, is based upon a naïve notion of human nature and its relation to social organization.

> In any social organization whatsoever, no matter how skillfully it may be administered, the economic functions can co-operate harmoniously and maintain themselves in a state of equilibrium only if they are submitted to moral forces which go beyond them, which contain and govern them.[102]

It is in this context that Durkheim expounds his view of the unlimited expansibility of human needs, which we have considered in the discussion of anomic suicide. Durkheim believed that any realistic socialist view must cope with the fact that the rewards received by the different classes of society are unequal. The question is not merely one of providing "motive" for social services: the sheer fact of social differentiation must create different orders of needs.[103] In order that men may be content with their lot, they must recognize the authority of moral norms which contribute to the definitions of what is their due.[104]

The problem of social reorganization is, therefore, in large part, that of seeking to determine the nature of the "moral checks which can regulate the economic life." Saint-Simon's error lay in his failure to perceive that industrial organization would have to perform other than industrial functions. The function of a social institution, according to Durkheim, even when it is "industrial," is not only to satisfy the interests of men, but also to develop and sustain a complex of norms and values. These norms and values regulate and limit the "pursuit of interests," but, more than this, they also determine, in considerable measure, the content of these interests.[105] With this conception of their role, Durkheim looked to the development of "occupational groups." He was impatient with *ad hoc* "positivistic religions," which some theorists added to their systems in a desperate attempt to make up for their inadequacy in solving the problem of social order.[106] The theorist can aid only by anticipating the dim outlines of future structures: he can only suggest how the "collective and moral forces" may be launched upon their work.

Durkheim expected these moral forces to develop a socialist organization of society, and, as we have seen, he envisaged the termination of what we know as private property; but it is clear that he did not believe that these ends would be achieved by the stroke of a pen or the shot of a gun.[107] The present order allows for the emergence of this organization through the regrouping of men and the development of new institutional realities. Society will yield to the rights of the dispossessed when it is compelled to recognize that they have actually achieved social and moral power. Consequently, men must be guided in organizing themselves in such a way as to enable them to discover their own moral selves. In these terms, the development of trade unionism, to use an American term, can be conceived not only as an instrument for securing higher wages and better working conditions, but also as one of the means of filling the "moral gap" created by the final breakdown of segmental society.[108]

In the immediate future, Durkheim expected existing "syndicates" of both employers and employees to organize along occupational lines and to establish "contact" with existing legal and political authority. That the syndicates of employers and employees remain separate is "legitimate and necessary."[109] Some institutional contact between the two must be devised, however, in order that their relations may be something more than a state of war interrupted by truces in the form of contracts. That some "common authority" that makes "contact" with political authority must be established does not mean that company unions or state-controlled syndicates must be formed. It is clear from Durkheim's whole conception of the occupational group that no "organization from above" would have satisfied his meaning.[110]

It is also evident from Durkheim's account that he expected the relations between employers and employees to be maintained in a moving equilibrium. It was not his belief that all conflict could be eliminated from these relations. "It is neither necessary nor possible that social life be without struggles. The role of solidarity is not to suppress competition but to moderate it."[111] Durkheim suggests that employers and employees should be represented on various legislative, administrative, and judiciary organs "in proportions corresponding to the respective importance attributed by opinion to these two factors in production."[112] And Durkheim does not expect such "opinion" to remain always the same.

It is in these same terms that Durkheim envisages the development of solutions to the problems of distributive justice. It will be recalled that, in the discussion of anomic suicide, Durkheim suggests that there is, in "the moral consciousness of societies," a certain range of rewards which are considered appropriate to the various social services. "In vain the economists protest." The "sentiments" which determine this range of rewards change with variations in collective production and with moral ideas, but unless they can maintain some minimum of stability, individuals will suffer. Even though inheritance is abolished, individuals will still start life with different talents and propensities, and those who insist that remuneration be equal will have to secure the acceptance of this standard by the more talented. Whatever the prevailing standard, it must be accepted as just. The very fact that there are diverse modes of life raises questions concerning the appropriateness of alternative schemes for the allocation of social energies.[113] In short, Saint-Simon's theory to the contrary notwithstanding, the problem of justice is not merely technological.

It is Durkheim's conviction that men will find solutions to

the problems of justice when they learn to organize themselves in the kind of groupings that are appropriate to modern industrial life. Under such circumstances, they will make contracts in which "equivalent values" are exchanged—that is, "just contracts." The demands of the values of individualism contribute to the development of conditions under which such contracts are the rule.[114]

It has been the aim of this paper to convey, through an analysis of the relation between individualism and socialism in Durkheim's thought, the general image of the situation of modern man that dominated his work. It would not have furthered this aim to have paused to point out errors in the details of his work; nor have we taken the time to consider the extent to which his anticipations concerning the future have or have not been fulfilled. Perhaps his conception of a secular and individualistic society is unrealizable, because in formulating it he overlooked certain important factors. The main point, however, is that his manner of conceiving modern man, in relation to his past, was novel, and it has entered as an important ingredient into our own self-awareness.

It is clear that Durkheim was no reactionary. Was he a pessimist? If a man has the strength and the faith in life to look at things directly, he may expect to be regarded as a "pessimist." Durkheim destroyed certain illusions of traditional liberalism. He perceived the uniqueness of the quality of unhappiness that is associated with freedom. And he understood the futility of the utilitarian view that the principal problem of "emancipated" man is the effective production of goods for the satisfaction of his needs. Very early in his career, he said: "In order for a society to be in good health, it is neither sufficient nor always necessary that it use up a lot of coal or consume a lot of meat. . . ."[115]

The full explication of Durkheim's supposed pessimism—the complete account of how Durkheim's thought calls for a reformulation of the traditional philosophy of liberalism—would demand that we attempt to lay bare the basic ideas in his theory of the human psyche.[116] That level of analysis has been avoided in this paper. However, the discussions of individualism and socialism may have suggested that Durkheim rejected the notion of the psyche as a "bundle of desires" to which the "additional faculty" of reason functions as the "servant." This notion had dominated empiricism and liberalism since Hobbes, and under its aegis utilitarian liberals and Marxists had devised programs which would secure a greater sum of pleasures for all men. However, their inadequate conception of the human psyche led them to advocate measures that seriously endangered its health; and this health, Durkheim insisted, is a necessary condition of the capacity for pleasure. It is in this light that many of Durkheim's "illiberal" and "pessimistic" recommendations for social policy are to be understood—for instance, his criticism of certain aspects of progressive education, and his polemic against the introduction of divorce by mutual consent.

Let us make a final note on Durkheim's pessimism. In an article published in 1895, he criticizes the teaching of philosophy in the lycée. He urges the recognition of the need for an education which will develop an understanding of the "spirit of science" and will cultivate the student's awareness of his relations to society. He assures the reader, however, that he has no intention of eliminating philosophy from the curriculum. The reason he gives for retaining it is a simple one. "There is no subject more alive; and life, in itself, is always something to be respected."[117]

1. In Mauss's Preface to Durkheim's posthumously published *Le socialisme* (Paris: Félix Alcan, 1928). Between 1884 and 1886, Mauss tells us, Durkheim came to realize that his problem involved the advancement of the new science of sociology. Thus he was drawn away from the study of socialism to devote his efforts to the establishment of sociology as a science. In 1895, he returned to the study of socialism with the intention of writing a history of socialist theory and a sociological analysis of the "socialist ideology," but this work was interrupted by the founding of *L'Année sociologique.* The part of this endeavor that was published posthumously in *Le socialisme* contains the definition of socialism, an analysis of its historical beginnings, and a masterly presentation of the work of Saint-Simon.

2. Durkheim, *L'Education morale* (Paris: Félix Alcan, 1925), Leçon II.

3. In this connection, see Talcott Parsons, *The Structure of Social*

Action (Glencoe, Ill.: Free Press of Glencoe, Illinois, 1949), p. 384, for an excellent note on the relations between "discipline," "constraint," and Jean Piaget's "co-operation."

4. "Does not the favorite and most telling argument of the metaphysical moralists consist essentially in demonstrating that the empirical doctrines cannot give an account of the elementary principles upon which every society is based?" "La science positive de la morale en Allemagne," *Revue philosophique,* XXIV (1887), 33. (All translations are my own unless the reference is to a specific translation.)

5. Through the years Durkheim became bolder in his efforts in this direction, a fact that certain critics have interpreted as indicating a development toward philosophical idealism. However, his purposes, which were clearly consistent with his method, were already set forth in his early writings. See, for instance, "La philosophie dans les universités allemandes," *Revue internationale de l'enseignement,* XIII (1887). The same idea is found in the writings from the middle of his career; see, for example, Durkheim and Paul Fauconnet, "Sociologie et sciences sociales," *Revue philosophique,* LV (1903), 497. Although the assertion is not always that sociology will utilize insights of the philosophers, but often that sociology will throw light upon philosophical problems, the point is the same since sociology helps to solve the problems of the philosophers only in so far as it succeeds in restating those problems in empirical terms. The awareness of a "problem" is already insight.

6. What were the defenders of 1789 to think of a sociologist who claimed that he took his stand upon "science and progress," but who associated in friendship with Hamelin, the defender of Hegel, and who was able to utilize Hamelin's analyses of Kant, Charles Renouvier, and Hegel in his own sociological work? See the Preface which Durkheim wrote for Octave Hameline, *Le système de Descartes* (Paris: Félix Alcan, 1911); and Georges Davy, "Emile Durkheim," *Revue de métaphysique et de morale,* XXVI (1919), 185-86, in which Davy says that Durkheim had a definite antipathy for Joseph Ernest Renan, the apostle of "science and progress."

7. Joseph Neyer, "Lévy-Bruhl's Concept of 'L'Art moral rationnel,'" *Social Research,* XV (1948), 213-14.

8. See especially his article, written in collaboration with Marcel Mauss, "De quelques formes primitives de classification: Contribution à l'étude de représentations collectives," *Année sociologique,* VI (1903), 1-72. The word "primitive" has tended to become discredited in recent years, owing partly to its association with an outmoded conception of social development. Perhaps the reader will permit its use in the exposition of the intellectual history of half a century ago.

9. This theory is formulated again in "La pénalité scolaire," in *L'Education morale,* with interesting implications for the problems of school discipline. A similar theory is suggested in Freud's *Totem and*

Taboo: "An individual, who has violated a taboo, becomes himself taboo because he has the dangerous property of tempting others to follow his example . . . . He is therefore really contagious." *The Basic Writings of Sigmund Freud,* trans. and ed. A. A. Brill (Modern Library ed.; New York: Random House, 1938), p. 822.

10. *De la division du travail social* ([1893] 5th ed.; Paris: Félix Alcan, 1926), p. 53.

11. "La détermination du fait moral," *Bulletin de la Société française de philosophie,* VI (1906), 182.

12. The use which Durkheim makes of knowledge of the primitive mind in understanding the contemporary, and his general conception of the relation of the primitive to the contemporary, has much in common with Freud's procedures and notions. The two men were born within two years of each other, and they studied the same ethnological material, but, as far as I know, neither was influenced by the work of the other.

A good deal of attention has been paid to Durkheim's article "Représentations individuelles et représentations collectives," *Revue de métaphysique et de morale,* VI (1898), for the light which it throws upon the problem of the so-called group mind. Actually, from the point of view of that problem, the article is immature. Of far greater significance is the fact that here Durkheim points the way to a development of the notion of the psychical, and argues for an acceptance of "unconscious representations." In an extremely competent manner, Durkheim sums up the contemporary evidence for the "unconscious mind" (pp. 277, 289-91), concluding his defense in the following manner: "Moreover, if everything that is psychical were conscious and if everything that is unconscious were physiological, psychology ought to return to the old introspective method." This is to say that both the method of introspection and the emphasis upon the nervous system are twin products of the same Cartesian dualism that must be superseded by a new conception of the psyche.

13. This emphasis on the continuity between past and present will be unacceptable only to those who make too much of the distinction between "mechanical" and "organic" solidarity, a distinction which Durkheim introduces in *De la division du travail social* as characterizing the difference between societies of the past and modern society. See n. 67 in this paper.

14. Ferdinand Brunetière, "Après le procès," *Revue des deux mondes,* CXLVI (1898). It was to this article that Durkheim directed his reply.

15. *Revue bleue,* Series 4 (1898), 7-13.

16. *Ibid.,* p. 8.

17. "L'Individualisme et les intellectuels," p. 12, n. 1.

18. In the Introduction to the first edition of *De la division du travail*

social, Durkheim defines a "moral fact" as a "rule of conduct to which a diffuse repressive sanction is attached" (as opposed to the "organized" sanction attached to legal rules). The word "sanction" is interpreted in a broad sense. The sanction is not the "essence" of the moral fact, but its presence is the "external" sign of the existence of feelings of obligation. *De la division du travail social,* pp. 21-38.

19. "L'Individualisme et les intellectuels," p. 10. I have translated *libre examen* as "free discussion."

20. This suggestion certainly raises questions, and it will be discussed later.

21. "L'Individualisme et les intellectuels," p. 10.

22. Durkheim notes that the artists, writers, and scientists who rose to the defense of Dreyfus acted not in their function as intellectuals but as ordinary men interested in justice. He adds that it is natural, however, for these intellectuals to be especially concerned since their professions are linked to the rights at stake. Brunetière had criticized the intellectual specialists for presuming to judge in matters beyond their special competence.

23. "L'Individualisme et les intellectuels," p. 11. This is one of the very few contexts in which Durkheim employs the phrase "the religion of humanity." The *h* in "humanity" is not capitalized, and it is clear that his thought is not following the path of Auguste Comte. There is little awareness in Comte of what Durkheim means by the value placed upon the human person in modern society. The vestiges of Comte's "Religion of Humanity" to be found in Durkheim are in the idea of "attachment" to society. In general, the influence of Comte upon Durkheim has been exaggerated. Durkheim himself is responsible for this. In his effort to establish sociology upon French soil, he stresses the fact that it had its beginnings in France in his accounts of the history of social science. In an interesting exchange of letters between him and Simon Deploige, Durkheim objects to Deploige's view that his (Durkheim's) sociology is chiefly of foreign (German) origin; see Deploige, *Le conflit de la morale et de la sociologie* (Paris: Félix Alcan, 1912), pp. 139 ff. Deploige had a point, but his chauvinism caused him to misuse it. In *Le socialisme,* pp. 148 ff., Durkheim says that the credit for most of Comte's basic ideas belongs to Saint-Simon.

24. "L'Individualisme et les intellectuels," p. 11.

25. *Ibid.,* p. 13.

26. Several examples are: *De la division du travail social,* pp. 140-41, 146-47; *Le suicide* (Paris: Félix Alcan, 1930), pp. 378-84; *The Elementary Forms of the Religious Life,* trans. Joseph Ward Swain (London: George Allen and Unwin; New York: The Macmillan Co., 1915), p. 203; and "Deux lois de l'évolution pénale," *Année sociologique,* IV (1901), 89.

27. *L'Education morale,* p. 13.

28. Durkheim's most developed discussion of political democracy is to be found in the only recently published *Professional Ethics and Civic Morals,* trans. Cornelia Brookfield (Glencoe, Ill.: Free Press of Glencoe, Illinois, 1958), which was first published in French in Turkey in 1950. These lectures, which the editors tell us were delivered between 1898 and 1912, cover many of the topics in the present paper, which was prepared largely in ignorance of them. It is satisfying to be able to report, however, that they support the emphases made here. Durkheim tells us that democracy does not depend upon "the number of those governing" but rather upon "the way in which the government organ communicates with the rest of the nation" *(ibid.,* p. 85). "Democracy indeed, as we have defined it, is the political system that conforms best to our present-day notion of the individual" *(ibid.,* p. 91). See *ibid.,* p. 54, where Durkheim opposes the statism of Hegel. "Our own country, which has hitherto been deaf to this (Hegelian) argument, now seems ready to welcome it. Since the old individual aims I have just set forth no longer [seem to] suffice, there are those who throw themselves in despair on the opposite faith, and renouncing the cult of the individual which was enough for our fathers, they try to revive the cult of the City State in a new guise."

29. *Le suicide,* p. 430. Cf. *De la division du travail social,* p. 146. "Individualism and free thought do not date from our day, nor from 1789 . . . They are phenomena which begin in no particular place, but develop without stopping throughout the sweep of history. This development is, of course, not in a straight line."

30. *Le socialisme,* p. 313.

31. Introduction to the first edition of *De la division du travail social,* pp. 12-15.

32. *L'Education morale,* p. 197. "In a certain large sense, one can say that a bad act always has bad repercussions. However, these repercussions are not of such a nature that they can be perceived by the child. . . . For example, the child must respect his father. Why? It is because the respect for paternal authority, within the limits in which it is legitimate, of course, is indispensable to the maintenance of the domestic spirit; and because, on the other hand, a serious weakening of the domestic spirit would have disastrous consequences for the collective vitality . . . . But how can the child apprehend these remote consequences of his act?" *Ibid.*

33. "Les études de science sociale," *Revue philosophique,* XXII (1886), 69.

34. In Durkheim's very first published writing, a review of Albert Schäffle, *Bau und Leben des socialen Körpers,* in *Revue philosophique,* XIX (1885), 99. One can trace this theme through all of Durkheim's

writings—the hoary problem of the rationalization of authority in a secular society, a problem which in modern times begins with Hobbes.

35. Durkheim speaks of the building of a "scientific culture" in "L'Enseignement philosophique et l'agrégation de philosophie," *Revue philosophique,* XXXIX (1895), 142.

Paul Lapie, one of the original collaborators on the *Année sociologique,* became director of *l'éducation primaire* in France and reorganized the system of normal schools so that prospective teachers received a general training in sociology. See Célestin Bouglé, *The French Conception of "Culture Générale" and Its Influences upon Instruction* (New York: Bureau of Publications, Teachers College, Columbia University, 1938), p. 29.

Consider the criticism of Jean Izoulet, a sociologist and a Catholic: "The obligation to teach the sociology of M. Durkheim in the two hundred normal schools of France is the most serious national peril which our country has known for a long time," as quoted by Célestin Bouglé, *Bilan de la sociologie française contemporaine* (Paris: Félix Alcan, 1935), p. 168.

Although Durkheim is opposed to many aspects of the progressive education associated with the name of John Dewey, the roles of these two men in the intellectual life of their countries are parallel in many ways. They were born within a year of each other.

36. Relevant here would be Durkheim's notion that sociology—in particular "la science de la morale," one of the social sciences which constitute sociology—could fulfill the function formerly performed by moral philosophy. It is when he is concerned with this aim—in "La détermination du fait moral" and *L'Education morale,* for example—that he may perhaps be justly charged with "personifying" society.

37. "To wish that it [morality] were other than what is implied in the natural constitution of the [social] reality which it expresses, would be to talk nonsense on the pretext of exercising autonomy." *L'Education morale,* p. 133.

38. *Ibid.,* p. 160.

39. Durkheim was not a member of the "spare the rod and spoil the child" school of thought. We are still reacting against an era of severe discipline, and we tend to see only the two extremes.

40. "Self-mastery is the first condition of all true power, of all liberty worthy of the name . . . . Moral discipline serves not only the moral life properly speaking . . . . It also plays a considerable role in the formation of character and of personality in general. Indeed, what is most essential in character . . . is the capacity for inhibition . . . . For a real person is a being who is capable of placing on everything he does a mark which is his own, which is constant, and by which . . . he is distinguished from any other . . . . It is precisely this self-mastery in

which moral discipline trains us . . . . It is therefore generally in the school of duty that the will is formed." *Ibid,* pp. 50-53.

41. Presumably, the account of the methodology of such criticism of social institutions is to be found in Durkheim's many discussions of *l'art morale* and *l'art sociologique.* For example, see the Introduction to the first edition of *De la division du travail social,* pp. 33-38; *"La détermination du fait moral,"* pp. 116 ff.; and "Rules for Distinguishing between the Normal and the Pathological" (Chap. iii), *The Rules of Sociological Method,* trans. Sarah A. Solovay and John H. Mueller (Chicago: University of Chicago Press, 1938). Durkheim's own applications of this "art" are to be found in the social-policy recommendations of almost all of his writings. At times, Durkheim's "democratic" bias leads him to talk as though he expects all citizens to share the sociological point of view and to act upon it. This situation leads to a duality within action and within awareness—the duality of participant actor and sociologist—which raises problems in the logic of action and awareness similar to those raised by the psychoanalytic point of view. Thus, when Durkheim demonstrates that a certain amount of crime is useful, he adds that "it does not follow that we must not abhor it" (*The Rules of Sociological Method,* p. 72, n. 13), a statement that leads Tarde to ask, "But since when is it permitted to hate a benefactor?" Gabriel Tarde, "Criminalité et santé sociale," *Revue philosophique,* XXXIX (1895), 150. However, the thinking involved in social action will never be limited to what can be validated by science. "Science is fragmentary and incomplete; it advances but slowly and is never finished; but life cannot wait. The theories which are destined to make men live and act are therefore obliged to bypass science and complete it prematurely." *The Elementary Forms of the Religious Life,* p. 431. This would appear to indicate a relaxation of the rigid position maintained in the earlier *The Rules of Sociological Method.*

42. *L'Education morale,* p. 60. Although no individual has the whole story concerning the meaning of all the moral rules which men feel obligated to accept, Durkheim believed that a general theory of the moral reality could be given which would take the place of the "mythological" accounts that have in the past served to "validate" moral action. This general theory, which had, he believed, "scientific value," would constitute an essential part of moral education. Thus it would furnish the answer to the question with which Durkheim began his sociological enterprise: What shall we teach our people? Fortunately, it is not within the compass of the present paper to evaluate Durkheim's efforts to provide such a general moral theory. See n. 36 in this paper.

43. "Society allows too great a number of its members to escape the effects of its action too completely." *Le suicide,* p. 428. The context here is the discussion of egoistic suicide.

44. This dual aspect of the relation between the individual and society recurs in all of Durkheim's thought, and is worthy of more attention

than has been devoted to it. In "La détermination du fait moral" and elsewhere, we are told that it corresponds to the distinction between the awareness of the duty and the aspiration toward the good in discussions of moral philosophy. In *The Rules of Sociological Method,* there is the distinction between "constraint" and "spontaneity." In *L'Education morale,* this distinction appears in the two elements of morality, the "spirit of discipline" and the "devotion to social groups." On the level of religion, we have "awe" and "love of God" (desire for communion). Is there an important kinship here with the Freudian duality of fear and love of the father? The father limits the expression of impulse, but he also shows the way to "legitimate" pleasure as well as the way to sublimation.

45. See Durkheim's polemical discussion of the question of the introduction of divorce by mutual consent, "Le divorce par consentement mutuel," *Revue bleue,* V (1906), Series 5, 549-54.

46. "At each moment of history, there is in the moral consciousness of societies an obscure sentiment of what the different social services are worth, of the remuneration that is due each of them . . . . In vain the economists protest." *Le suicide,* p. 276.

47. *Ibid.,* p. 273.

48. The translation of these notions into the terms of contemporary psychiatry and the criticism of these notions in these terms is a job waiting to be done. Durkheim was not so clear as could be desired concerning the relation between sociological analysis and analysis on the psychological level. This is due to the fact that at the time of writing *Le suicide* he had not yet transcended the point of view that there are two psychologies, individual and social. See Daniel Essertier, *Psychologie et sociologie, essai de bibliographie critique* (Paris: Félix Alcan, 1927), pp. 18-24.

It will not advance the purpose of the present paper to complete the account of Durkheim's explanatory scheme in *Le suicide.* "Altruistic suicide" occurs more frequently in the less advanced societies. In contemporary Western societies, it is found in the army more often than in the civilian population. It results from conditions that are the direct opposite of those of egoism, for in this type of suicide the individual's devotion to ends which transcend his own existence is so great that he places very little value upon his own personal existence. There is also a fourth type, *suicide fataliste,* which bears the same relation to anomie that altruism bears to egoism. Durkheim mentions this fourth type in a footnote without developing its significance *(Le suicide,* p. 311, n. 1). *Suicide fataliste* involves a regulation and limitation of men's desires beyond the individual's endurance. We may sum up the general schema in the following way: altruism=too much self-transcendence; egoism=not enough self-transcendence; fatalism=too much regulation; anomie=not enough regulation. In Durkheim's moral terms, altruism and egoism are concerned with the good, while fatalism and anomie are concerned with duty. Self-transcendence corresponds to the action of society as immanent; regulation corresponds to the action of society as transcendent.

Le suicide has a tremendous richness of content. It is to be hoped that the necessarily schematic and slender presentation of its ideas in these pages does not lead the uninitiated reader to conclude otherwise.

49. *Le suicide,* p. 222.

50. *Ibid.,* p. 227.

51. *Ibid.,* p. 416.

52. Parsons, *op. cit.,* pp. 330-34.

53. Is there, in certain of their manifestations, a fine line between autonomy and "narcissism"?

54. *Le suicide,* p. 417.

55. Durkheim anticipated that therapeutic consequences would follow the reorganization of modern social organization in accordance with its "professional" groupings; but he believed that a certain permanent increase of egoism and anomie was inevitable. In this whole discussion, the word "egoism" is used in the technical sense required by Durkheim's account.

56. *Le suicide,* p. 417. In more than one context, Durkheim has recourse to this general idea that a healthy society will have minorities of "abnormal" individuals who will "exaggerate" certain socially necessary traits. For instance, in any society in which individuals submit to moral standards in the pursuit of their private interests, one must expect to find a small minority of members who are ascetics.

57. *L'Année sociologique,* II (1899).

58. "La détermination du fait moral," pp. 184-85. In *The Elementary Forms of the Religious Life,* Durkheim appears to integrate some of his definitions in the following formulation: "A religion is a unified system of beliefs and practices relative to sacred things, that is, things set apart and forbidden—beliefs and practices which unite into one moral community called a church all those who adhere to them" (p. 47). The latter part of the definition serves to distinguish religion from magic.

59. *L'Education morale,* pp. 8-12. In "La determination du fait moral," Durkheim distinguishes *religiosité morale* from *religiosité théologique.* Durkheim says that the former is more open to "criticism."

60. For example, *L'Education morale,* p. 7.

61. In the Preface to *L'Année sociologique,* II (1899), (see pp. 341-353, in this volume), Durkheim notes that the sociology of religion has come to dominate the interests of his group. "There has been some astonishment over the primacy which we have thus accorded to this sort of phenomena; but they [religions] are the seed from which all others—or, at least, almost

all others—have been derived. It is from myths and legends that science and poetry have emerged; it is from religious ornamentation and the ceremonies of cults that the plastic arts have come; law and morality have been born of ritual practices. One cannot understand our representation of the world, our philosophical conceptions concerning the soul, immortality, and life, if one does not know the religious beliefs which have been their first form. Kinship began by being essentially a religious bond; punishment, contract, the gift, and homage are transformations of expiatory, contractual, communal, honorary sacrifice, and so on. At the most, one may wonder whether economic organization constitutes an exception and derives from another source; although we do not think so, we agree that the question ought to be reserved" (p. iv). "Precisely because religion is a primitive fact, it must give way more and more to the new social forms which it has engendered" (p. v, n. 1). The new forms must be seen in light of their "religious origins" in order to be understood; but, Durkheim concludes, they must not be confused with these origins. Cf. Alexander A. Goldenweiser, as quoted in Robert M. MacIver, *Society: Its Structure and Changes* (New York: Long and Smith, 1931), p. 429: "The fact remains that the supernaturalistic as well as the social tendencies of totemic days live on in modern society. But in our civilization these same tendencies, in the absence of a crystallization point, remain in solution, whereas in primitive communities the same tendencies . . . function as a highly distinctive vehicle of culture."

62. "Deux lois de l'évolution pénale," *Année sociologique,* IV (1901), 89.

63. *De la division du travail social,* p. 147.

64. Durkheim may have been influenced in this by his desire to provide a neat theoretical schema based upon sociology as a substitute for traditional ethical theory. In the schema which he developed, one of the basic elements in morality is the attachment to *group* ends. From this point of view, he hesitated to consider individualism "a genuine social bond." See nn. 36 and 42 in this paper.

65. Owing to limits on space for this paper, I must resist the impulse to pursue the treatment of autonomy in Durkheim's various writings. For those readers—who are, I hope, few in number—who would raise the question of how a determinist like Durkheim can speak of freedom and autonomy, the reply must be limited to a suggestion. Durkheim had support in a respectable philosophical tradition for the view that the acceptance of determinism does not stand in the way of distinguishing between the free man and the man in bondage. He could always look to Spinoza and John Stuart Mill. Besides, Durkheim did not believe that the decision to apply the methods of science to man and society required that he rule out metaphysical indeterminism. Somewhat in the role of the devil quoting scripture, he says: "There are philosophers who have rediscovered in organisms, and even in inanimate things, a sort of free will and contingency. But neither the physicist nor the biologist has changed his method because of

this: they have calmly continued their way without concerning themselves with these subtle discussions." "Cours de science sociale: Leçon d'ouverture," *Revue internationale de l'enseignement*, XV (1888) , 27-28.

66. Although *De la division du travail social* was published in 1893 when it was submitted for the doctorate, Mauss informs us that it was first outlined in 1884 and first written in 1886. See Mauss's Preface to *Le socialisme*, pp. v, vi.

67. "In the body of this work, we tried to show that the division of labor . . . does not necessarily produce dispersion and disintegration, and that the [diverse] functions, when they are sufficiently in contact with one another, tend of themselves to become stabilized and regulated. But that explanation is incomplete. For if it is true that the social functions seek spontaneously to adapt themselves to one another, . . . this mode of adaptation becomes a rule of conduct only if a group consecrates it with its authority. A rule is not only a habitual manner of acting; it is above all an *obligatory manner of acting.*" *De la division du travail social,* p. v. The inadequate account of the formation of organic solidarity in the text of the book suggests the influence of the German economist Gustav Schmoller, whose work Durkheim reviews in one of his early articles on German social science. In that review, we learn that social relations crystallize themselves around economic relations and acquire the "obligatory force" that comes from the "authority of usage" and from the conviction that public utility demands the stability of the relations established. "La science positive de la morale en Allemagne," *Revue philosophique*, XXIV (1887) , 39-41.

68. *De la division du travail social,* pp. xi-xii.

69. "Deux lois de l'évolution pénale," p. 93. This helps to explain the following observation by Durkheim: "To the extent that *criminalité humaine* gains ground, it reacts in turn upon *criminalité religieuse* and, so to speak, assimilates it."

70. *Leçons de sociologie sur l'évolution des valeurs* (Paris: Armand Colin, 1922) , p. 72. Cf. Karl Mannheim's statement, "Life in terms of an inner balance which must be ever won is the essentially novel element which modern man, at the level of individualization, must elaborate for himself if he is to live on the basis of the rationality of the Enlightenment." *Ideology and Utopia,* trans. Louis Wirth and Edward A. Shils (New York: Harcourt, Brace & Co., 1936) , p. 31.

Is it the sin of modern man that, in times of stress and crisis, he desires to return to the state of "absolute" and unquestioned unity of feeling with which social and individual life begins?

71. Durkheim gave up the dogmatic view of primitive organization that is suggested in *De la division du travail social.* (See *The Rules of Sociological Method,* p. lvii.) However, the notion of segmental society, as opposed to organic, remains. He comes to look upon the relations among the individuals in segmental societies as kinship relations—under-

standing, of course, that these do not necessarily involve actual blood ties.

72. Emile Durkheim, "La famille conjugale: Conclusion du cours sur la famille," *Revue philosophique,* XC (1921), 1-14. The course on the family, from which this posthumously published article was taken, was conducted around 1892.

73. The point at issue does not concern the hypothesis of primitive group marriage. It may be the case, as Malinowski argues, that the "wider" kinship bonds always arise in the individual's history as an extension of the "primary, . . . personal bonds based upon procreation, socially interpreted." ("Kinship," *Encyclopaedia of the Social Sciences.*) I am aware of the fact that from the point of view of present-day anthropology, some of the issues discussed in these pages may be outmoded—the very questions they raise are based upon assumptions that are no longer acceptable. However, my purpose here is to explain Durkheim's conception of socialism; and this purpose would not be served by diverting our attention to such questions.

74. "La famille conjugale," p. 9.

75. Malinowski provides us with an interesting example of the actual process of the encroachment made upon hereditary right by voluntary transmission. The Trobrianders are matrilineal in theory, and "it is the duty of every man to hand over to his maternal nephew or younger brother the hereditary possessions of the family, such as family myth, family magic and family songs . . . ." Actually, most men will try to turn these over to their own sons, who are members of another family. The conflict presents itself as between family duty and paternal affection. Bronislaw Malinowski, *Sex and Repression in Savage Society* (London: Kegan Paul, 1927), pp. 120-21.

76. "La famille conjugale," p. 7. Mauss tells us that at this point the manuscript contained some notes concerning the progressive encroachment made upon the rights of kin to such possessions as literary property.

77. "We sometimes have to keep such survivals where they are needed. The past persists beneath the present, even when they are at variance. Every social structure is full of these paradoxes . . . . It often occurs that a continuity of some sort has been kept up whereby the older forms are preserved to nourish the newer." *Professional Ethics and Civic Morals,* pp. 174-75. "The old institutions never disappear completely; they only pass into the background and fade away by degrees. This one has played too great a role in history for it to be conceivable that nothing of it should survive. It would only survive, however, in a weakened form. We might, for instance, imagine that every head of a family would have the right to leave to his children specified portions of the heritage." *Ibid.,* p. 217.

78. Durkheim does not expect the "family" to disappear; he insists

that as the family contracts, the marriage bond becomes stronger. Monogamous marriage and the conjugal family are the institutions of the future, but they have lost many of the functions of "kinship" groupings in the past.

79. Cf. Bronislaw Malinowski, *Argonauts of the Western Pacific* (London: Kegan Paul, 1922), p. 167.

80. Thus the Roman patriarchal pattern, which forms the basis of our emphasis on individualism, was the gradual result of a concentration of the communal authority in one person. However, the patriarch did not follow his own individual whims in the disposal of his property: his obligations were sharply defined. "La famille conjugale," p. 3.

81. *Professional Ethics and Civic Morals,* p. 172. The chapters on the religious origins of property in this work remind us of Durkheim's rich contributions in *L'Année sociologique.*

In seeking a definition of socialism, Durkheim rejects the conception which sees it as the abolition of property. According to him, Marx denies the individual the right to own the means of production, but he does not refuse him all right to have property; individuals "retain an absolute right over the products of their labor." *Le socialisme,* p. 15.

82. *De la division du travail social,* p. 381.

83. Mauss informs us, in the Preface to *Le socialisme,* p. ix, that in 1883 at Bordeaux (where Durkheim was teaching), the socialist leader Jean Jaurès gave a lecture in which he "glorified" the work of Durkheim. This lecture had been organized through the collaboration of *le Parti ouvrier* and a Marxist study circle composed of some of Durkheim's students. Mauss goes on to say: "It was Durkheim who, in 1885-1886, had turned him [Jaurès] away from the political formalism and barren philosophy of the radicals" (p. viii). Jaurès accepted Durkheim's definition and analysis of socialism (p. ix). Georges Sorel and later representatives of French "revolutionary syndicalism" explicitly utilized Durkheim's conception of the role of occupational groups (pp. vi-vii).

84. *Le socialisme,* p. 25.

85. "Socialism is a tendency to effect a change in the economic functions, either abruptly or slowly, from the diffuse state in which they now exist to an organized state." Emile Durkheim, "Note sur la définition du socialisme," *Revue philosophique,* XXXVI (1893), 510. The distinction between "organized" and "diffuse" authority recurs throughout Durkheim's writings. In *De la division du travail social,* the distinction between the organized and diffuse sanctions defines the difference between law and morality.

86. *Le socialisme,* pp. 44-49. Durkheim offers the example of Plato's *Republic.*

87. *Le socialisme,* p. 96. This distinction between communism and socialism has little relation to the ordinary use of the two terms. It has some

kinship with the Marxist distinction between "utopian" and "scientific" socialism, although Engels places Saint-Simon among the utopians. Furthermore, communism as defined here has little or no connection with the "primitive communism" referred to in the previous discussion of property and inheritance. "Primitive communism" refers to a social organization that Durkheim assumes existed at one time. In the present context, "communism" designates a recurrent ideology.

88. "Note sur la définition du socialisme," p. 512. In *De la division du travail social,* Durkheim argues against the Spencerian laissez-faire view that with the emergence of the individual the functions of the state diminish. The data gathered by Spencer demonstrate only that political power becomes less "absolute"; but this is not to deny that the functions of the state increase in number and complexity. "Nothing is less complex than the despotic government of a barbarian chief." *De la division du travail social,* p. 199. It is this that Durkheim has in mind when he says that socialism is not a "turning back." Cf. "Deux lois de l'évolution pénale," p. 69, where he says, "Nothing is more simple than the government of certain petty barbarian kings; nothing is more absolute." The laissez-faire interpretation of history confuses the degree of absolute power with the number and complexity of the functions of the state. Clarity on that point would help to eradicate the notion that Durkheim is a political "authoritarian."

89. For a comparison of Durkheim and Marx from a Marxist viewpoint, see Armand Cuvillier, "Durkheim et Marx," *Cahiers internationaux de sociologie,* IV (1949), 75-97.

90. *Le socialisme,* pp. 4-5. In Durkheim's review of Gaston Richard, *Le socialisme et la science sociale* in *Revue philosophique,* XLIV (1897), 204, he says, "The propositions which it [socialism] asserts have too large an extension." Cf. "Les principes de 1789 et la sociologie," *Revue internationale de l'enseignement,* XIX (1890), 451, where Durkheim refers to socialism as a "faith," and not a scientific doctrine.

91. In the Preface to *Le socialisme,* Mauss informs us that Durkheim's promotion to one of the professorial chairs in Paris was delayed by rumors of his "collectivism" (p. vii). Durkheim was also subjected to pressures from the other side of the political fence.

92. Durkheim's review of Richard, *Le socialisme et la science sociale,* p. 204.

93. See Durkheim's dissertation, submitted in 1892, "Montesquieu: Sa part dans la fondation des sciences politiques et de la science des sociétés," trans. from the Latin by F. Alengry, *Revue d'histoire politique et constitutionelle,* I (1937), 405-63. Durkheim seems to recognize this point when he says that socialism "has awakened reflection, stimulated scientific activity, called forth research, and formulated problems, so well

that, on more than one point, its history is associated with the history of sociology itself." *Le socialisme*, p. 4.

94. *Le socialisme*, p. 201. For Saint-Simon, as for Spencer, social development is conceived as moving away from a "military" organization toward an "industrial" one. For Saint-Simon this development involves the substitution of "scientific" for "religious" ideas.

95. The meaning of the term "constraint" in Durkheim's writings is a rich topic. It must suffice here to say simply that it includes both political and moral sanctions, the sanction being an "external sign" of felt obligation. Thus constraint includes the lure exercised by moral ideals. That constraint has these various phases does not indicate that there is "confusion" in Durkheim's definition, but rather that his insights grasp the continuum of constraint in its many aspects.

96. *Le socialisme*, p. 224.

97. For Saint-Simon, "liberty" is a slogan of the "metaphysicians," who are useful in destroying the order of the "theologians," but who must eventually give way to the "scientists." For Saint-Simon, "the theory of the rights of man . . . is only an application of high metaphysics to high jurisprudence." *Le socialisme*, p. 178. Saint-Simon anticipates the disappearance of legal forms in the industrial society, but Durkheim sees only their transformation.

98. *Le socialisme*, pp. 212-15. Cf. *De la division du travail social*, p. iv; *Professional Ethics and Civic Morals*, pp. 102-6.

99. "This is the same as the manner in which in the zoological series the pre-eminent function changes in accordance with the species; here the word 'pre-eminent' has a meaning that is rather vague and somewhat figurative." (Durkheim and Fauconnet, "Sociologie et sciences sociales," p. 476.) Durkheim means that in some animals the whole structure appears to be adapted to the processes of digestion; in others, to the business of locomotion, and so on. Yet all the essential life processes may be discerned in all the forms.

100. We may suggest that a modern industrial strike, the avowed goal of which may be the achievement of a higher wage, fulfills many noneconomic needs of the workers. The picket line is a ritual, the repercussions of which may enrich the lives of the participants in many ways. Cf. n. 61 in this paper.

101. *Le socialisme*, p. 282.

102. *Ibid,* p. 287.

103. The notion of a leveling in remuneration belongs to communism, which does not face the facts of modern industrialization.

104. We have already noted that Durkheim was much concerned with the fact that a progressive social ideal involves a certain amount of

anomie. In *L'Education morale,* he suggests that especially in a secular democracy, where the ancient barriers are broken down and where all careers are open to everyone, it is important to inculcate a sense of duty and to demonstrate that this sense is "founded in the nature of things." Without discouraging legitimate ambitions or concealing actual injustices, it must be taught that happiness is associated with objectives that are at hand and realizable.

105. The statement appears to be largely tautological if we accept Talcott Parsons' definition of "institutions, or institutional patterns" as being *"normative* patterns which define what are felt to be, in the given society, proper, legitimate, or expected modes of action or of social relationship . . . . They are patterns supported by common moral sentiments." ("The Motivation of Economic Activities," *Essays in Sociological Theory* [Glencoe, Ill.: Free Press of Glencoe, Illinois, 1949]) , p. 203. Durkheim's proposition includes the view that such patterns develop and acquire "authority" in the course of group activities of certain types.

106. This explains the ambiguous role of pantheism in the system of Saint-Simon. Durkheim says, "It is not the sentiment of cosmic unity . . . that suffices to dominate egoisms and make men actively co-operative." *Le socialisme,* p. 295.

107. In his Preface to *Le socialisme,* Mauss says that Durkheim "considered political revolutions and parliamentary evolutions superficial, costly, and more theatrical than serious" (p. viii) .

108. Cf. John Dewey's statements in this regard. "The problem . . . involves development of local agencies of communication and cooperation, creating stable loyal attachments, to militate against the centrifugal forces of present culture . . . . To a very considerable extent, groups having a functional basis will probably have to replace those based on physical contiguity." *Freedom and Culture* (New York: G. P. Putnam's Sons, 1939) , pp. 160-61).

109. *De la division du travail social,* p. viii.

110. Durkheim says that when the Roman industrial unions finally became a part of the state, they were placed in a position of "miserable dependence." They became part of the state "not so they could occupy the status to which their services might have rightfully entitled them, but simply so that they might be more efficiently watched over by the governmental power." *Ibid.,* p. xxiii. Durkheim anticipated certain contemporary movements toward political authoritarianism when he said, "A society composed of an infinite mob of unorganized individuals, which a hypertrophied state attempts to encompass and to restrain, constitutes a veritable sociological monstrosity." *Ibid.,* p. xxxii.

111. *Ibid.,* p. 357.

112. *Ibid.,* p. xxviii, n. 2. In this context, the reference is probably to

organs of the syndicates within the larger political organization. But Durkheim anticipates an eventual transformation of the mode of representation in the national assemblies. See *Professional Ethics and Civic Morals*, pp. 102-6, in which Durkheim sees the corporative bodies as the "true electoral units" of the future.

113. "From the fact that wealth will no longer be transmitted in accordance with the principles that exist today, it does not follow that the state of [economic] anarchy will have disappeared; for the question is not simply whether wealth is . . . in certain hands rather than in others, but concerns instead the determination of the activity by which this wealth shall be utilized." *De la division du travail social*, p. xxxv.

114. See Chap. xvii, "The Right of Contract," *Professional Ethics and Civil Morals*. It would be a fruitful enterprise to bring together and analyze Durkheim's various suggestions concerning economic value. The attempt to reconcile his earlier view, which contains elements of both laissez-faire and Marxist theory, with his later view, in which the novel components of his own position emerge, would be a task of considerable difficulty.

In his early work, he appears to accept much of the laissez-faire framework and directs his criticism only at the questionable assumption of the mobility of labor *(De la division du travail social*, p. 194). He also suggests that as contract law develops, it tends to deny the validity of contracts made under "unequal conditions"—conditions under which it is impossible to obtain justice (the exchange of equivalent values). His later view, however, seems to indicate that the very meaning of "equivalent values" and the very determination of what shall be considered appropriate bargaining conditions are derived from the general scheme of non-economic values which integrate the society in question. Therefore, the values of individualism would appear to be crucial in the development of contract law; and the version of the "labor theory of value" that Durkheim appears to accept (in *De la division du travail social*, p. 376) would seem to be the consequence of one type of emphasis given to the "cult of the individual."

See the reaction of the economists to Durkheim's part in the discussion, "De la position de l'économie politique dans l'ensemble des sciences sociales," *Journal des economistes*, XVIII (1908), 108-21. Here Durkheim says that the value of things depends on their "objective properties" as well as on "collective opinion."

In *The Elementary Forms of the Religious Life*, he says, "Only one form of social activity has not yet been expressly attached to religion: that is economic activity . . . . Economic value is a sort of power or efficacy, and we know the religious origins of the idea of power. Also, richness can confer mana: therefore it has it. Hence it is seen that the ideas of economic value and of religious value are not without connection. But the question of the nature of these connections has not yet been studied" p. 419, n. 1). Cf. the Preface of *Année sociologique,* II (1899), iv [in this volume, see p.   ].

In one of Durkheim's last papers, which is devoted to the problem of value judgment, economic value takes its place as one form of the "ideal" whose investigation constitutes the chief business of sociology, along with other "systems of values"—religious, moral, legal, and aesthetic. "Jugements de valeur et jugements de réalité," *Revue de métaphysique et de morale,* XIX (1911), 452.

115. "Suicide et natalité," *Revue philosophique,* XXVI (1888), 447.

116. Or what Talcott Parsons calls the "schema for the analysis of action."

117. "L'Enseignement philosophique et l'agrégation de philosophie," *Revue philosophique,* XXXIX (1895), 123.

CONSCIENCE COLLECTIVE AND CULTURE

Traiter des faits d'un certain ordre comme des choses, n'est donc pas les classer dans telle ou telle catégorie du réel; c'est observer vis-à-vis d'eux une certaine attitude mentale.

> EMILE DURKHEIM,—Preface to the second edition
> of *Les règles de la méthode sociologique*

Durkheim has had a tremendous influence on social anthropology—that branch of the subject which defines man as a social animal interacting in an idiom of culture—but his influence on cultural anthropology—which defines man as a tool-making animal and regards his social organization as still another tool[1] —has been negative, non-existent, or denied. A few cultural anthropologists have roundly rejected Durkheim;[2] others have rephrased him to their own ends;[3] most have simply ignored him. Social anthropology, however, received Durkheim through A. R. Radcliffe-Brown and is more permeated with Durkheimian theory than even its practitioners are sometimes aware.

It is the thesis of this essay that Durkheim covered the same ground with his notion of *conscience collective* and *représentations collectives* that such cultural anthropologists as Edward Sapir, Bronislaw Malinowski, A. L. Kroeber, and Robert Redfield (to name a few) did with their various developments of the idea of culture and its related concepts. However, the two conceptual schemes cannot be directly translated one into the other. To see both, one must search for a general framework which allows the identification and assessment of the different categories used in each conceptual scheme.

In carrying out this task I shall first review the relevant Durkheimian concepts, as I understand them, then explain various concepts of culture both in their own terms and in terms of the Durkheimian concepts, and follow with some suggestions and conclusions.

Durkheim, like all original thinkers, had to stretch the lan-

77

guage he used for the exposition of his ideas to its limits, and perhaps beyond. Communication of new ideas obviously affects language, the instrument of communication. Once the ideas have become familiar, one can begin to notice the obvious and systematic, even if unintentional, ambiguity at work in the expository writing in which the ideas were first expressed. Such is the case with Durkheim, for perhaps no social scientist ever used ambiguity with better effect.

Durkheim's ambiguity has been pointed out by many writers in the past, and new facets of it are continually coming to light. As early as 1915, Gehlke showed that Durkheim used *société* in two senses.[4] In 1926, Lacombe presented a penetrating analysis of Durkheimian ambiguity: among other things, he found that Durkheim had used the word *contrainte* in three ways, and he accused him of shifting from one of these meanings to another.[5] Alpert, in 1939, found five senses in which Durkheim used *individuel,* and showed conclusively that the development of Durkheim's thought depended on the ambiguity which he allowed the word.[6]

Durkheim himself noted in his career[7] that his use of the term *conscience collective* was not without ambiguity. He never analyzed this ambiguity, but it is plain that he meant at least three things by *conscience,* and it was this very triunity that allowed him to think with the concept. The first ambiguity is inherent in the French language. English requires two words —"conscience" and "consciousness"—to translate *conscience.* That these two form a single concept in French means, for all French sociologists, that internalized sanctions are amalgamated, at least to some extent, with awareness of the social milieu. This factor is not unique with Durkheim, and it is not the point I wish to stress. Rather, attention must be paid to a more subtle ambiguity, one that cannot be untangled by reference to dictionaries. *Conscience* was used by Durkheim to mean the instrument of awareness, a meaning which is more or less equivalent to the English "consciousness." But the third and more important meaning of *conscience* is "that of which someone is (or many persons are) aware," and the only suitable English word for this notion is the anthropologist's term "culture." Thus the French term *conscience* means three things: internalized sanctions, awareness, and perceived culture. It is with the latter two that we shall deal.

This ambiguous assimilation of the knowing instrument and the known thing—of consciousness and culture—into a single concept was vital to Durkheim's thought. Its separation in modern anthropology, important though it has been, has also been the source of much misunderstanding and much theorizing. Encompassing what are for English-speaking thinkers, at least those in social science, two substantives, the knower and the known, Durkheim focused his attention on the verbal connective between them: the "knowing," or, as he called it, the process of representation. Even when he argued that representations may not be conscious, even when he called the collective conscience greater than and independent of individual consciences, he was not separating the thinker from the thought (or, as we shall see, the subconscious from the linguistic category).

American and English interpretations of Durkheim—and even, perhaps, some French interpretations—have separated the two substantive elements which Durkheim intended to leave conjoined. In the separation, the processual (or verb-like) concept has disappeared. Gehlke,[8] in one of the earliest analyses of Durkheim's sociology, severed the tie between the knower and the known, ignored the latter and gave us a concept of the group mind which haunted social psychology for decades. Undoubtedly, this notion had origins outside of both Durkheim and Gehlke's typical Anglo-American reading of him; yet Durkheim is often cited by social psychologists for holding a "group-mind" view. They cite his terms *l'esprit commun, l'âme sociale,* or *conscience collective* and read his statements that collectivity makes of the whole more than the sum of its parts as if that "more" were substantive.

On the other hand, Kroeber[9] and many of his followers have tried to understand Durkheim in terms of "culture," and in so doing they have indeed made Durkheim intelligible in their own terms, but they have also cut off some of the most characteristic aspects of his thought: all those which deal with how culture is perceived by the consciousness.

To read Durkheim's concepts of *représentation* and *con-*

science as interaction of a subject and an object is to misunderstand them. Their vital characteristic is a blending of subject and object into a single unit. In Durkheim's theory something which we view as an interaction between two processes is analyzed as a single process.

Basically, Durkheim was interested in the many aspects of a single problem: to set epistemology on a scientific basis. All of his researches go to illuminate this problem, and all of his writings—including those on education—touch upon it, even when they have practical aims. For that reason, he never gave up his interest in psychology, in the mechanics of the working of the mind. For that same reason he carried forward the notion of the collective quality of most representations, and he meticulously differentiated between individual representations and collective representations because it seemed to him that since each had a different source, each was a different way of knowing or becoming aware. Today, students and even scholars have difficulty in reading Durkheim because his psychology is dated and seems to obscure his social thought. Yet, once one realizes what problem Durkheim is trying to solve, one sees that any particular school of psychology is beside the point.

In the English-speaking world, sociologists and anthropologists have never found the epistemological problem central to their disciplines. Today, sociologists tend to consider the problem of the categories of perception or that of the folk system of perceiving social action solely within the interests of *Wissenssoziologie.* Anthropologists, because of obvious problems of translation, confuse such interests with a "linguistic approach."

Durkheim was, in short, interested in dealing with some of the persistent problems of philosophy from the standpoint of the social sciences. Such an approach has seldom appealed to the imaginations of English-speaking social scientists. Men like Kroeber and Sapir recognize and build upon their philosophical positions, but do not see their work as fundamentally a contribution to philosophy. However, Durkheim never ceased to work toward philosophical ends, and his greatest contribution was to create a viable epistemological structure that can lead social scientists not only to philosophical comparison, but to their own problems of cross-cultural perception and translation.

80

Perception, if I may paraphrase what I understand to be Durkheim's ultimate position, can be of two sorts: the relationship between the consciousness and the thing perceived, and the relationship between the subconscious and the categories which are impressed upon it. The latter is a restatement of Durkheim in the light of more recent psychological ideas; the former is his own statement.

For communication, perception is broken up into "representations." Representations are images (communicable) in a mind or else categories (linguistic, and in that sense communicable) into which a mind classifies data. The images and the categories are learned as one is socialized and as one learns to speak. The representations refer either to material objects or to categories of material objects, on the one hand, and to expectations of behavior, on the other. The representations are, as it were, a reflection of culture: culture as one perceives it in communicable images and categories.

Thus representations are, in one sense, culture: they are learned; they are manifest in act and artifact (I would include language as a special type of act and artifact); they are subject to almost any of the other defining characteristics of culture—for example, it endures beyond the individual and is something external impressed upon him in his socialization. However, representations are not just culture—"neat" culture. The mode of perception is still of the essence. A representation, then, is something external perceived or impressed. If the representation is characteristic of many persons—that is, if they can communicate about it and act with a reasonable degree of mutual expectation on the basis of that communication—then that representation is collective or "social," in Durkheim's usage of the words.

A collective representation is either a concept or a category of thought held in sufficiently similar form by many persons to allow effective communication. However, it is more than that. Its being collective gives it, Durkheim says—and nobody in anthropology today would disagree with him—an additional dimension. It makes it independent of any particular mind or set of minds—anybody can learn it, given the social opportunity. Kroeber made this same point about culture when he described it as "superorganic."

Thus the collective representations, in being greater than the sum of the individual representations, "outgrow" the psychological explanation, which, however, does not for that reason cease to be relevant. We have now left the realm of exact science and entered the realm of metaphor, and it must not be forgotten that Durkheim used the notion of *conscience collective* in a metaphorical manner, just as Kroeber used "superorganic." Metaphorically, the representation, when it is collective, is superordinate to the individual minds. This metaphor is always present because one cannot speak of the existence of the representation without speaking of its association with mind.

Thus the metaphor reads: The representation is held in the mind (whatever we choose to mean by that statement) of individuals, but it is greater than the minds of any given individuals because it occurred as a result of social action instead of mere ratiocination, and because it may be both prior and posterior in time to any individual minds. For the anthropologist's purpose, the psychophysiology of the matter is beside the point. Since, as I have interpreted Durkheim, the collective representation is both a thing perceived (consciously learned or subconsciously impressed) and a perceiving (conscious or subconscious) agent, one can say that it is "perceiving." Seen in this way, the mass of collective representations—of "perceivings"— becomes the *conscience collective*. *Conscience collective* is the cultural idiom of social action. If one omits either the perceivers or the notions perceived, one lets Durkheim's analysis fall into triviality. The *conscience collective* is, thus, the totality of the *représentations collectives* put together in a certain way that Kroeber would call "style."

Now it is the business of sociology, according to Durkheim, to investigate and elucidate the *conscience collective* in this sense. Because the *conscience* is the body of perceiving agents and perceived notions, the representations, it reflects the qualitative aspects of the social organization. It must because it is an aspect (both a result and a cause) of social action and ultimately of social organization. The social organization is the matrix of the conscience and the experience which shapes its representations. The *conscience collective* is a reading or a folk system of the morphology, the characteristic events, and the cultural idiom of social groups.

When anthropologists have in the past investigated the same general field that we have just discussed, they have done so with different problems in mind and different tools to work with. Not only did modern anthropological theory derive from German rather than from French social science, but ethnology, during its critical years, was closely associated with archaeology in America, and this association has left its mark.

The lines of the separation of culture from what we might call "the perceived social life" is fully evident in Sir Edward B. Tylor, the first great cultural anthropologist, although Tylor himself did not separate them. Tylor developed a notion of culture and gave in his famous definition a list of things and notions which were "acquired" by man in the process of social life. Spiro has pointed out that the separation of culture and personality as concepts in anthropology stemmed from this point, and claimed that it was a "false dichotomy."[10] But we can go even further. Tylor was, like Durkheim, interested in perception. He, as well as Sir James Frazer and many others after him, wrote about "culture" as perception. The entire theory of animism is a theory of perception. Tylor's mistake was that he considered perception wholly a conscious, intellectual process. The French sociologists never made that particular mistake.

However, theories of survival advanced by Tylor, Lewis H. Morgan, and others did prepare the way for the excision of the concept of culture from the social life. The break was actually made by American anthropology at the turn of the century. Although more insight than obscurity resulted, we must, nevertheless, note the obscurity.

In America at least, most ethnologists were also archaeologists—what we today call "all-round anthropologists" when we mourn their passing. Archaeologists use the word "culture" for the artifacts that they dig up. They use the term "a culture" for an identifiable group of artifacts or culture traits which always appear together. "A culture," then, has both a temporal and a spatial dimension. The latter could be mapped; the former could be conveyed by a succession of maps. In this context, culture refers to material objects and to concatenations of material objects which are recognizable and distinguishable as characteristics of a certain time and place.

The same general anthropologists applied identical criteria of culture to living societies and to archaeological collections. To the anthropologists, the things that Indians made were of primary concern. However, behavior items and ideas also seemed significant. With their ready-made culture concept, they considered non-material ideas and attitudes as culture items. They mapped them and traced their movements in time. What they did not realize is that they were thinking in metaphorical terms. Only metaphorically is a habit a "culture item" in the archaeologists' sense. But when they reread Tylor and the early Germans, they read with new eyes: culture was an object. Tylor's intellectualist error, which they could correctly refute, led them to refutation of the culture as perceived social life. The idea of survivals confirmed their refutation.

The main difficulty with this mode of working and this way of looking at the human process is that the separation of culture from the perception of it (as archaeologists must do—good ones make a virtue of it) created a problem for later generations of anthropologists who inherited the culture concept. Many of them failed to see that the problem had been artificially created in the history of their own discipline. If culture is conceptually severed from its perception in ideas and behavior, then sooner or later the anthropologist working with living people must postulate a relationship between people and culture.

In short, the atomistic, materialistic view of culture which the archaeologist must assume passed over into ethnology. Its acceptance in ethnology created a major problem—the problem of perception: "the locus of culture," as Herskovits and Sapir and many others have called it. Herskovits found the locus of culture in human beings;[11] Sapir found it in social relationships as well.[12] Both took the "perceiving" unit and cut it into two interconnected substantives, whereas Durkheim studied the single unity, perception or representation, which had its poles in the psyche or mind and in the "external" phenomenal (including the social) world.

The problem of locus of culture and of its agent became crucial with the culturologists when they began to examine situations of culture change. Defined as material or pseudo-material traits, culture must either have an agent to work the change or

84

it must be said to evolve *sui generis,* without intervention. In any but a metaphorical sense, the latter statement is nonsense. It is obvious that even though there is, metaphorically, a *sui generis* element in the growth of culture, that growth must still be mediated by agents of some sort. When Durkheim spoke of representations *sui generis,* he was, obviously, including the agent. When the agent is included, such a statement says only that people seek rationality and consistency—whatever mode of rationality their culture may decree. Hence the statement as Durkheim made it merely tells us that perception conditions and creates new perception.

Because the atomistic, materialistic notion of culture is not very serviceable in studies of culture change, most theorizing about culture in recent years has been either tacitly or overtly aimed at solving the problem of agent. Of the many attempts, only three can be reviewed here, and they are to be read as examples, not as a survey of the field. Two of these bodies of theory are reductionist: one reduces the perceiving agent to culture; the other reduces culture to mere learning. Both, it seems to me, miss the point. The third is a struggle toward Durkheimian simplicity in culture terms. To illustrate these three points I have chosen the work of Bronislaw Malinowski, Ralph Linton, and Robert Redfield. It should be understood that I am not trying to typify the work of any anthropologist; I am only seeking examples to make clear three logical positions that can be held in this matter.

Malinowski avoided the problem of the agent by a conceptual framework which he erected around the "institution." An institution to Malinowski was a chunk of culture, but it was a bigger one than a culture trait, and the means of identifying it were much more complex. An institution is

a group of people united for the pursuit of a single complex activity; always in possession of a material endowment and a technical outfit; organized on a definite legal or customary charter, linguistically formulated in myth, legend, rule and maxim; and trained or prepared for carrying out its task.[13]

Malinowski's definition of an institution is almost identical with his definition of culture. His avowed fundamental starting place is "a group of people united." He then gives them a purpose—pursuit of some activity; a technique for achieving that purpose, and finally a system of ideas which makes it desirable of attainment; he also provides a means of intellectualizing, or externalizing, as it were, what is being done.

By thus defining culture teleologically[14] and by breaking it down according to purpose and to the institutions which serve one or more of these purposes, Malinowski included the human being in his culture. By including the people in the institution, and then making the institution the unit of culture, Malinowski bootlegged the agent into culture by definition. Culture, therefore, contains its own motive power. Defined in this way, the culture can indeed change *sui generis,* but on another level the problem still remains.

Linton made precisely the opposite move. He noted that no culture change can take place without changes in the habits of the people who accept the new situation.[15] Therefore, he reasoned, culture change consists in learning on the part of individuals. Culture, then, is reduced to learned habits. After explaining how new culture is acquired, Linton must explain the spread of the new culture; he resorts to the stratificational norms of the society in question.

The difficulty with Linton is not that he interrelates and interdefines society, culture, and personality. It is rather that he does *not;* instead, he interdefines a society, a culture, and given personalities. He does not talk about viewpoints or analyses to be interrelated, but about classes of things to be juxtaposed. He avoids the problem of agent, but only by reducing culture to a psychological state and begging the question of social action on the basis of diffusion and the facts of social stratification.

Malinowski's institutional analysis is extremely valuable so long as one does not confuse it with the analysis of culture. There is something cultural about any institution, but to regard institutions as the units of culture seems of doubtful utility. In the same way, learning new culture is a vital process in all culture change and indeed in all cultural processes. But to make it the fulcrum between culture and personality is to slight the more important problem of comparative perception.

Linton's great contribution was, of course, that he faced the dilemma and, following Sapir, elaborated the field of study called "culture and personality." Both were investigating, with very different tools, Durkheim's chief problem and doing it, largely to their loss, without benefit of Durkheim. That is, they studied the field of perception as a relationship between two substantives—culture and personality. Durkheim covered the same area by studying the representations which are the basis or idiom of both culture and personality. The two views are not contradictory; they are gained from different perspectives.

The differences can be appreciated by reading Kluckhohn's recent summary of culture and behavior[16] within the same week that one rereads the major works of Durkheim. Perception becomes, in Kluckhohn's summary, one of many relationships between culture and behavior; others include "internal biological behavior," "sexual behavior," "motor habits," "cognition," "affect," and "phantasy and unconscious processes." Durkheim would have treated most of the same material in terms of representations and *conscience.* He would thus have seen both culture and behavior in a philosophical view of perception, not perception viewed as one of several points of juncture of anthropological and psychological interest.

Redfield all but solved the agent problem with his idealist definition of culture. However, he did not hold to this definition in his later work, and practically no one has accepted the philosophical and methodological implications of it. In 1941, Redfield defined culture as "an organization of conventional understandings manifest in act and artifact."[17] This definition gets rid of the dominating idea that culture is a totality of traits or of institutions without denying that, on one level, such an idea is useful. What to earlier writers may have been a "culture trait" or an institution is to Redfield a mere manifestation of culture. The systemization is in the common understandings that are to be manifested, and only secondarily—if at all—in the manifestations themselves.

"Conventional understandings" is the best English equivalent of *représentations collectives* to be found in anthropological writing. The similarity and utility of the two views can be seen in a brief comparison of their backgrounds.

Durkheim's view was that the mass of associated individuals forms the "substratum" of society, and that on this base social life can emerge. Social life consists in relationships among individuals and groups of individuals, and is realized by them in representations. A representation is collective if it is held by all or many of the members of the social body. Redfield, on the other hand, tells us that a social relationship is present when the behavior of two or more individuals undergoes reciprocal modification. The social relations which define societies exist in terms of, or are expressed in the medium of, those conventional understandings that Redfield calls culture. Whereas Durkheim postulates a *conscience collective* as the organization of collective representations as they are manifested in social relationships, Redfield postulates a culture as an organization of conventional understandings manifested in act and artifact. The difference between social and cultural anthropology could not be more starkly exposed.

Redfield and Durkheim do, however, work on similar problems. We can equate, if only roughly, the mechanical-organic continuum of the early Durkheim with Redfield's folk-urban continuum. For Durkheim, at the time of *De la division du travail social,* a social system which expressed mechanical solidarity was one comprised of a homogeneous mass of units which derived their unity from their homogeneity. The polar opposite was organic solidarity, in which the units were differentiated but correlated by interdependence. Redfield, in studying four communities in Yucatan, found that the smaller, more isolated community was characterized by a tightly organized culture which varied little from one person to another, whereas the larger, less isolated community had a less tightly organized culture which was subdivided among people of various ranks and orders. He called his poles folk and urban culture. To paraphrase Redfield's conclusions in Durkheim's terms, we can say that the collective conscience of Tusik, the isolated Maya village, is more precise and covers a far wider range of life than is true in Merida, the urban center of Yucatan. In Merida, more and more representations have become the prerogative of specialist groups while the collective conscience becomes less specific.

Durkheim expressed a similar, but not empirical, situation in these terms: in a small society everyone lives under approximately the same conditions, and the "collective environment" is essentially concrete, made up of people like oneself and institutions like those in which one participates. But as society becomes "more voluminous" it changes its nature. The very fact that it is spread over a larger surface means that the common conscience must "rise above all local diversities," and be held in the minds of more people, many of whom are not in firsthand contact; and hence it becomes more abstract. As conditions of life change from one part of a group to another, even if only very slightly, conditions in the environment are no longer so homogeneous, and the sentiments which arise are no longer identical.

In order to proceed with the description, I find I need both sets of terms: Durkheim's and Redfield's. As the size of the social system increases, the *conscience collective* becomes more abstract and the culture becomes richer and more diverse. This process is seen by the investigator in terms of Redfield's variables: individualization, secularization, and the rest.

At this stage, both terminologies, both sets of concepts, make a better analytical tool than either alone. The representation and the *conscience* are, in a sense, a connecting link between the culture and the psyche, but they are independent of specific theories or views of either culture or psyche. They are verblike notions, and hence the substantives are changeable.

In a recent article of Kluckhohn's, already cited, still another attribute of culture has been pointed out: a basic ambiguity similar in kind but not in content to that found in Durkheim's use of *conscience*. "Culture," Kluckhohn said, is used to denote the analytical construct which is derived by the anthropologist from the behavior and statements of the people he studies. It is also used to denote "these patterns or norms as internalized in the individuals making up the group."[18] That is, "culture" is an analytical concept, while at the same time referring to a means of social action in so far as it is, "the patterns or norms as internalized in the individual." In the latter sense, it is the medium of social action; in the former, a method of scientific explanation. Kluckhohn noted that this ambiguity is not gen-

erally disruptive and found it necessary to keep the two meanings separate in only a few places in his long essay. However,
for understanding Durkheim's problem, the ambiguity is fatal.

When we talk about the process of representation, we must
compare it with just one sense of culture: the organization of
tools for social action. When dealing with social analysis, Durkheim used a very different set of concepts. He bade us "regard
social facts as things." It seems to me that what he meant by a
social fact was (in addition to other things, such as suicide
rates) a *représentation* or a *conscience*.[19] The art of regarding
them as things is to duplicate consciously on the analytical level
the process of representation as it takes place on the action
level. That is to say, on the action level one regards a culture
trait as a thing and calls it by name. By doing so, one is creating
(or re-creating) its representation—its socially relevant aspect.
Similarly, on the analytical level, one must treat the representation itself as a "thing," for the representation is that which
has analytical relevance. Social analysis thus deals not with
culture traits (the stuff of action) but with representations of
them.

Hence on the level of social action, there is a knower (the
individual), a known (the culture trait), and a connection
between them—words, categories, deeds, or some other sort of
"representation." On the analytical level, the same structural
elements are repeated: there is a knower (the anthropologist),
a known (the representation), and a connection between them
by hypotheses, theories, or what you will: what we might call
(though Durkheim did not) sociological representations.

Thus it is possible today to interpret Durkheim's statement
that social facts should be regarded as things to mean that the
unit of sociological study is the collective representation. To
study anything else, as I read Durkheim, is to study the culture
item of a foreign culture in terms of our own subconscious or
unconscious categories or representations, without focusing on
the relationship between knower and known.

Having now found that the culture approach and the
conscience approach can be profitably combined for describing
culture in so far as it is an aspect of social action, it remains
for us to investigate the possibility of their advantageous com-

bination in analysis. In order to do so, I have found a promising starting point in the work of Kurt Lewin.

Lewin noted that habits cannot be looked upon simply as static conditions, but must rather be viewed as forces in equilibrium. Food habits, like culture patterns, are constellations of forces which remain more or less the same or in constant equilibrium over a longer or shorter period of time. Habits, Lewin tells us, "will have to be conceived as a result of forces in the organism *and* in its life space, in the group *and* its social setting."[20]

The life space is a social situation seen from the point of view of a given individual. In Durkheimian terms the life space is a concatenation of individual representations. Lewin took several life spaces focused on the same empirical situation and examined the ways in which they represented the situation differently. He thus was working with overlaps and failures of overlap in several sets of individual representations—several individual consciences, if you will. He found that if the differences in representation were great enough the various individuals had to "sit down and talk things over" or otherwise work out some common ground in their life spaces—that is, reach some kind of collective representation of the situation.

Lewin referred to this process of forming representations as putting the individual and his life space into a group setting or "social field." "Social field," as an analytical concept, is "social" in only a very limited sense. Lewin saw social fields as collectivities of psychological fields which coincided sufficiently for action. Such a view is necessary but, by itself, inadequate for the anthropologist.

By examining Lewin's idea of psychological field, one can discover clues for establishing a more satisfactory notion of what a social field may be. One must examine the analysts' transference from the organism with its life space to the social group in its setting—what might be better amended to read "the social relationship in its field."

It is impossible to define social relationship as precisely as one can define an organism. Even though we are all agreed that human personalities or minds or psyches are analytical constructs, we are also surely agreed that the psyche or mind or personality "attaches" to an organism, and organisms can be counted. But social relationships are not easily counted by means of our presently developed concepts. One cannot count them at first sight; if they can be counted at all, it is only after one has a comprehensive knowledge of the culture and social systems of a people. An organism has a life space in another way than a social group or a social relationship has a setting. The problem, "Is this a human organism?" seldom plagues the psychologist. The cognate problem, "Is this a social relationship and if so in what sense?" is one of the recurrent plagues of the sociologist. The human organism is itself the criterion for the forces which impinge on its life space. The social relationship, lacking materiality and "natural" unity, must be more rigorously defined before it can stand as criterion of its own social setting.

The difficulty is obvious. A psychological field or "life space" consists of the characteristic representations of the organism which it describes. But a sociological field or "social setting" does not and cannot attach to a single perceptive agent. It must, obviously, attach to two or more—the players of the roles which make the social relationship of the players possible. A relationship cannot have a "life space" or a "social setting." It cannot perform the act we have called "representing." For a social relationship to exist, a certain common representation must exist for the individuals who play it out.

Thus if an individual exists in a life space of individual representations, a social relationship must exist in a "social field" of collective representations. Again, Durkheim's difficulty arises: a collective representation is "superior to" the individual minds which must hold it, yet it must be held in several individual minds.

To the foremost problem, "What are we comparing to the organism?" we have answered, "the social relationship." Several other answers can be, and have been, given; perhaps the most common is the concept of social role. The second problem is "What is the social setting we are comparing to the life space of the organism?" and our answer is "the collective representations in which the social relationship exists." Traditional answers have said that the "social setting" of a role comprises other roles; the analogue is that social relationships link roles that are played by human organisms. But, without denying this, we can also look at the obverse situation: social systems are made up of social relationships, not merely of roles. Roles played by people, instead of being linked by social relationships, can themselves be seen as linkages between and among social relationships. We have changed our focal length; instead of a husband with a life space and a wife with a life space, linked by the overlap in life space, we have a husband-wife relationship in a social field.

To sum up, the most important difference between life space and social field is that a husband-wife relationship cannot have a view of its social field as a wife can have a view of her life space or a husband of his. We are back to Durkheim's problem: the representation "supersedes" any individual at the same time that it must be associated with the mind or psyche of individuals. Thus the representations about the husband-wife relationship *must* be collective to some extent. The husband-wife relationship must be perceived by the husband and wife and many others in terms of collective representations about what it should be. A social relationship exists in a field of collective representations.

Although only individuals, being apprehending organisms, can perceive collective representations, the representations are, nevertheless, social phenomena. The husband-wife relationship or either of its defining roles exists, then, within a field of collective representation in much the same way as the individual exists within his life space as the latter was elucidated by Lewin.

In Lewin's illustration we saw conflict between individuals which was resolved when they "talked things over." Conflict, in social terms, is not conflict between two individuals but between two relationships: between, say, the husband-wife relationship and the mother-daughter relationship. If the collective representations which provide the field of the husband-wife relationship have, in a particular situation, come into conflict with those that provide the field of the mother-daughter relationship or the employer-employee relationship, that conflict is likely to lead to changes in the structure of the collective

93

representations, and ultimately in the relationships. On the other hand, in situations such as the impact of the West on primitive societies, new relationships are forged quickly and forcibly. They must be given a social field—a collectivity of representations has to be worked out. The resultant changes in representations have a far-reaching effect on the social fields of all the other relationships in which the holders of the new representations act, and hence on the collective conscience.

Seen from this point of view, social change is analogous to, but much more complex than, the sitting down and talking things over (or indeed the muddling along) which leads to the adjustment of the life spaces of individuals: the changes in collective representations and of relationships must adjust toward some sort of rationality.

Talcott Parsons and others have discussed this matter in terms of role conflicts;[21] anthropologists have often discussed it in terms of culture conflict. Both viewpoints are more microscopic than the one suggested here without being in any way contradictory to it.

If the position that has been adopted here is called "Neo-Durkheimian," we can sum it up by calling it the science of representations, which are perceptions of the acts and artifacts as manifestations of culture (as an analytical construct), and of the social relationships, which exist in the field of collectively held representations. "Culture" can be studied independently of its representations. So can social relationships and social systems. So long as these studies do not deny or contradict their data—the actors who hold collective representations or the things about which they are held—no falsification need take place in this sort of analytical partitioning.

However, "representation" itself is a field which demands more careful study than has been given it since Durkheim's pioneer efforts. We can put it this way: "Individual representation" refers to the configuration of a knower connected by a representation to a culture trait. "Collective representation" refers to the configuration of two or more socially interacting knowers connected by a representation to the same culture trait when that representation is sufficiently similar to allow mutual understanding for social action among the knowers.

94

Both these situations are in the field of action, and only in a very special sense in the field of social analysis (that is, you can quibble and say every actor must analyze the situation before he acts).

In the science of representations, an analyst is added. He must consider the collective representation as his "culture trait," as his "thing," as Durkheim said. He perceives it in terms of a sociological representation. In such a view, then, an organized concatenation of sociological representations, in terms of which sociologists and social anthropologists can communicate, is sociological theory.

1. Cf. Claude Lévi-Strauss, in *An Appraisal of Anthropology Today*, ed. Sol Tax, Loren C. Eiseley, Irving Rouse, and Carl F. Voegelin (Chicago: University of Chicago Press, 1953), p. 224.

2. Ruth Benedict, *The Concept of the Guardian Spirit in North America* ("Memoirs of the American Anthropological Association," No. 29 [1931]).

3. A. L. Kroeber, "The Concept of Culture in Science" (1949), *The Nature of Culture* (Chicago: University of Chicago Press, 1952), p. 118.

4. Charles Elmer Gehlke, *Emile Durkheim's Contributions to Sociological Theory* (New York: Columbia University Press, 1915), p. 16.

5. Roger Lacombe, *La méthode sociologique de Durkheim* (Paris: Félix Alcan, 1926), pp. 41-42.

6. Harry Alpert, *Emile Durkheim and His Sociology* (New York: Columbia University Press, 1939), p. 135.

7. *De la division du travail social* (2nd ed.; Paris: Félix Alcan, 1902), p. 46.

8. Gehlke, *op cit., passim.*

9. Kroeber, *op. cit., passim.*

10. Melford E. Spiro, "Culture and Personality: The Natural History of a False Dichotomy," *Psychiatry*, XIV (1951), 19.

11. M. J. Herskovits, "Cultural and Psychological Reality," in *Social Psychology at the Cross-Roads,* ed. John H. Rohrer and Muzafer Sherif (New York: Harper & Bros., 1951), p. 156.

12. Edward Sapir, "Cultural Anthropology and Psychiatry" (1932), in *Selected Writings of Edward Sapir,* ed. David G. Mandelbaum (Berkeley, Calif.: University of California Press, 1949), p. 515.

13. *The Dynamics of Culture Change* (New Haven: Yale University Press, 1945), pp. 49-50.

14. Cf. R. F. A. Hornlé, "Philosophers and Anthropologists," *Bantu Studies*, XIV (1940), 395-405.

15. Ralph Linton, *Acculturation in Seven American Indian Tribes* (New York: D. Appleton-Century Co., 1940), pp. 468 ff.

16. Clyde Kluckhohn, "Culture and Behavior," in *A Handbook of Social Psychology*, ed. Gardner Lindzey (Cambridge, Mass.: Addison-Wesley Publishing Co., Inc., 1954), II, 924.

17. Robert Redfield, *The Folk Culture of Yucatan* (Chicago: University of Chicago Press, 1941).

18. Kluckhohn, *op. cit., passim.*

19. In *The Structure of Social Action* (New York: McGraw-Hill Book Co., 1937), pp. 365 ff., Talcot Parsons investigated this point of view and claimed that Durkheim rejected it because it did not answer his needs for demographic and statistical studies. It seems to me that Durkheim later enlarged the category of social *choses,* but not that he ceased to consider representations as *choses.*

20. *Field Theory in Social Science*, ed. Dorwin Cartwright (London: Tavistock Publications, Ltd., 1952).

21. Talcott Parsons and Edward A. Shils (eds.), *Toward a General Theory of Action* (Cambridge, Mass.: Harvard University Press, 1951), *passim.*

THE DEVELOPMENT OF DURKHEIM'S
CONCEPT OF RITUAL AND THE
PROBLEM OF SOCIAL DISRELATIONSHIPS

HUGH DALZIEL DUNCAN

There are many unresolved problems in functional interpretations based on ritual. The whole concept of ritual is derived from a religious context. The work in sociology and economics of Fustel de Coulanges,[1] W. Robertson Smith,[2] Emile Durkheim,[3] Bronislaw Malinowski,[4] and A. R. Radcliffe-Brown,[5] as well as that of Max Weber, Ernst Troeltsch, R. H. Tawney, and Joachim Wach, indicates how much social theory owes to the study of religious institutions. Jacob Burckhardt reminds us in his discussion of the reciprocal determination of society by religion, the state, and culture, that many rulers follow Francis Bacon's words, "Religion [is] the chief band of humane society."[6] However, criticism of ritual concepts derived from religious experience must not commit the error of substituting the "reality" of the social bond for the "illusion" of the religious bond by asserting that what is said of religion is really what should be said to society, and following such an assertion with a description of societal bonds by means of analogies drawn from ritual moments in religious experience.

The development of Durkheim's conception of ritual by Malinowski and Radcliffe-Brown (among others) indicates the vitality of his thought. Those interested in creating a theory or method based on symbolic function owe much to Durkheim for his emphasis on the social reality of symbols and the reciprocal relationships between forms of expression and society. In attempting to develop hypotheses which can be applied to the data of sociation as it occurs in and through communication, we find that Durkheim has already cleared paths which we should do well to explore. We are fortunate in having a collection of Radcliffe-Brown's papers which deal with problems attendant on the use of Durkheim's concepts.[7]

Since this paper is not an analytic description, or even a critique, of Durkheim's theory as such, but is rather concerned with the relevance of his theory of ritual to our present concerns in social theory, I shall use Radcliffe-Brown's papers as a point of departure for the discussion that follows. Although Radcliffe-Brown differed from him in many ways, Durkheim was his master in theory. Consequently, what he has to say about the problems involved in using Durkheim's conception of ritual is of profound interest to those concerned with how to make use of the concept in their own work.

Radcliffe-Brown argues that Durkheim's belief that the totem owes its sacred or ritual character solely to its position as the emblem of the group is at once too limited and too general. "Durkheim's theory is that the primary object of the ritual attitude is the social order itself, and that anything becomes an object of that attitude when it stands in a certain relation to the social order." Radcliffe-Brown assents to this readily enough, but he adds that we need a more precise definition of the more important types of relation to the social order that cause the object which stands in such a relation to become an object of ritual attitude. Radcliffe-Brown states his own position on ritual as follows:

A social group such as a clan can only possess solidarity and permanence if it is the object of sentiments of attachment in the minds of its members. For such sentiments to be maintained in existence they must be given occasional collective expression. By a law that can be, I think, readily verified, all regular collective expressions of social sentiments tend to take on ritual form. And in ritual, again by a necessary law, some more or less concrete object is required which can act as the representative of the group. So that it is a normal procedure that the sentiment of attachment to a group shall be expressed in some formalized collective behavior having reference to an object that represents the group itself.[8]

The ritual relation between man and nature in primitive society is a general one between the society as a whole and its sacra. Thus, "any object or event which has important effects upon the well-being (material or spiritual) of a society, or anything which stands for or represents any such object or event, tends to become an object of the ritual attitude." This

98

ritual attitude among primitive men is governed not by a recognition of what we call natural laws but by a cosmology which is moral and social. In Australia the natives have, in innumerable ways, built up between themselves and the phenomena of nature a system of relations which are similar to the relations between one human being and another that they have built up in their social structure. The function of this personification of natural phenomena is to permit them to think of nature as if it were a society of persons; in this way, nature is made into a social or moral order. We may then describe Australian totemism as a "mechanism by which a system of social solidarities is established between man and nature."

What Radcliffe-Brown proposes is a refinement of Durkheim's theory:

> The suggestion I put forward, therefore, is that totemism is a part of a larger whole, and that one important way in which we can characterize this whole is that it provides a representation of the universe as a moral or social order. Durkheim, if he did not actually formulate this view, at any rate came near to it. But his conception seems to have been that the process by which this takes place is by projection of society into external nature. On the contrary, I hold that the process is one by which, in the fashioning of culture, external nature, so called, comes to be incorporated in the social order as an essential part of it.[9]

What is meant by the conception of the world as a moral order?

> In every human society there inevitably exist two different and in a certain sense conflicting conceptions of nature. One of them, the naturalistic, is implicit everywhere in technology, and in our twentieth century European culture, with its great development of control over natural phenomena, has become explicit and preponderant in our thought. The other, which might be called the mythological or spiritualistic conception, is implicit in myth and in religion, and often becomes explicit in philosophy.[10]

In his essay, "Taboo,"[11] Radcliffe-Brown subsumes the concept of taboo under ritual and searches for more functional definitions of ritual. The basic question, he maintains, is,

99

"What is the relation of ritual and ritual values to the essential constitution of human society?"[12] He begins by rejecting the use of the term "sacred value" since it refers exclusively to holy things. In its place, he offers "ritual value," arguing that anything, even if it is unclean or unholy, can become an object of ritual—if only of ritual avoidance. Ritual value, therefore, has both a positive and a negative aspect: anything "that has value in positive ritual is also the object of some sort of ritual avoidance or at the least of ritual respect." One does not arrive at an understanding of rituals through consideration of "their purpose or reason but of their meaning . . . [and] whatever has a meaning is a symbol and the meaning is whatever is expressed by the symbol."[13]

How are we to study ritual meanings?

Since each rite has a myth associated with it we have similarly to investigate the meaning of . . . myths. As a result we find that the meaning of any single rite becomes clear in the light of a cosmology, a body of ideas and beliefs about nature and human society, which, so far as its most general features are concerned, is current in all Australian tribes.[14]

The social function of ritual is not simply to provide a more abundant supply of food for the tribe but to maintain the "order of the universe of which man and nature are interdependent parts."[15] Social structure is, therefore, connected in a very special way with cosmological ideas as expressed in myth, and the maintenance of the continuity of the social order is assured by keeping such ideas alive by expressing them regularly in myth and rite.

Briefly the theory is that the rites are the orderly expression of feelings appropriate to a social situation. They thus serve to regulate and refine human emotions. We may say that partaking in the performance of rites serves to cultivate in the individual sentiments on whose existence the social order itself depends.[16]

These sentiments are both negative and positive, and we cannot understand one without the other. Rituals of avoidance, although negative in form, are positive in effect, for they allow

100

us to share our fears as well as our hope and confidence in such a way that the social bond is not weakened but strengthened.[17] Sentiments expressed in the "general ritual idiom" of society are known to us through symbols. Human societies depend upon the "efficacy" of symbols of many different kinds. Thus only as we understand "a general theory of symbols and their social efficacy" can we understand society. The primary task of ritual is to attribute "ritual value" to objects and occasions which are either themselves objects of important common interests that link together the persons of a community, or are symbolically representative of such objects.

Radcliffe-Brown, Malinowski, and others who lean heavily on Durkheim's concepts of ritual seem to be saying something like this: Society functions through symbols, and thus our understanding of society is determined by our understanding of symbols. But in order to understand symbols and learn how they function, we must turn to systems of symbolic expression such as religion. For unless we think of function within a structure, and ultimately within a societal structure, we cannot reduce our notions of symbolic experience to social theory that will lead to hypotheses which are useful in ordering the data of sociation. The problem bequeathed to us, then, is no longer one of "discovering" that symbols do determine some aspect of sociation. There is no need to repeat endlessly that human relations exist in symbols, or that social interaction is really symbolic interaction after all. Only a pseudo science which confuses technique with knowledge can be blind to the fact that the observable facts of sociation are symbolic. Explanations which take us "beyond" symbols are not hypothetical or even theoretical—they are fictional. And when we return from the "beyond" (be it social process in a new variant of equilibrium, the Marxian apocalypse of a classless society toward which we are "tending," "scientific" method based on mathematical notation derived from study of non-human events, or of instinct), we must still describe the reality "beyond" symbols in symbols.

If the problem of ritual interpretation is a problem of symbolic interpretation, our problem may be stated as follows: If we say that society exists in and through symbols, what is specifically social about the structure in which symbols are used? And how do we create a model of sociation in which the structure is the form of the function described by the structure? Our model of reciprocally determined structure and function must be derived from some conception of symbolic action. Structure is *what,* function is *how,* but the what and the how must be about the same kind of act. We cannot ground social content in "nature," in drives, instincts, or self-regulating mechanisms such as homeostasis, equilibrium, and so on, and then talk about symbolic forms in their relation to these. For if society is self-regulating and mechanical, why do we need symbols?[18]

Simmel selected sociability as his theme of sociation; Weber, authority (as the legitimation of the power which determines action); and Durkheim, religion. Simmel's sociability functions in social space, in degrees of being with, for, and against each other. Weber's authority functions in the forms of the legitimation of power through charisma, tradition, law, and custom. Durkheim's social bond functions through collective representations. But neither Simmel, Weber, nor Durkheim relates function to dramatic communication. Parsons, Kluckhohn, Shils, and Merton gravely admonish us to consider the problems of communication, but then proceed to create mechanical models of sociation in which communication must be reduced to signals, not symbols.[19] Malinowski keeps talking about the "context of situation" of the symbol but says little about *symbolic* context in relation to meaning.[20] Sapir[21] and Whorf[22] warn us that how things are named will determine sociation, but they shed little light on the society which is being determined by language.[23]

Whatever our theory of the social bond, and whether we discover our "cause" for society in nature (Darwin, Pavlov, and Freud), in sociopolitical structure (Marx, Frazer, and Weber), in God (St. Thomas Aquinas), or in the resources of language in rhetoric and drama (Aristotle, and, in our time, Kenneth Burke), the observable facts of these "causes" are symbolic expressions. And while symbols are used in religion, art, politics, and other social institutions, the kind of language in which these symbols are expressed will determine how they will function. Thus when we refer to ritual as a source from which we can derive an understanding of sociation, we must think of ritual as a symbolic act which, like all symbolic acts, depends for its power of identification on the dramatic resources of language as such.

Role-playing is an enactment, an address to others who in turn address us. While it is true that we enact roles as players in games and sports; as members of families; as rhetoricians in disputation, discussion, and argument; or as partisans in politics, we do so through language in which, like the characters in drama, we express agreement, disagreement, and doubt. These three basic modes of adjustment are possible only because we act together in the name of some social bond which transcends, but does not obliterate, differences. Differences, in so far as they are social, are hierarchical. The structure of social order is always a hierarchy in which superiors, inferiors, and equals communicate to achieve common ends. But these ends do not arise in sociation before they are communicated: they arise in communication, and sociation occurs through symbolic action.[24]

The concept of ritual can become fruitful if we turn to ritual drama, as did Aristotle and Freud, both of whom dealt with Sophocles' *Oedipus Rex* (in honor of which Freud named his central concept, the "Oedipus complex"). The first thing we note about drama is that it is a struggle, and a struggle over authority, or what is proper to social order. Oedipus is a king, a proud man who once saved Thebes and solved the riddle of the Sphinx; but he is also a man who has unknowingly committed incest and parricide. Sophocles warns us of the dangers faced by the rulers of men who may come to think themselves equal or superior to the cosmic powers; such men forget that the good life, as Aristotle reminds us in his *Ethics,* consists not in one or a few intense and heroic acts, but in the lifelong practice of moderation, that is, in submission to judgments created in discussion by men seeking truth.

In great dramas, like *Hamlet, Faust,* and *Don Giovanni,* and in novels like *Don Quixote* and *War and Peace,* we find the problem of authority enacted on a symbolic level.[25] Legitimations of authority are shown not only as "structures of power" but as enactments in communication by superiors, inferiors, and equals seeking to make sense out of a principle of authority. Charisma (Hamlet's self-willed "I"), tradition (his father's ghost), law (the justice of the realm), custom (the manners of the court), develop in communication between characters and among various aspects of the ego which must resolve conflict in order to be able to act.

Most important of all for our plan to use ritual drama to construct a theory of sociation that is useful for creating hypotheses to deal with the observable facts of social life, ritual drama deals with failure and doubt as well as with success and belief. In the Dionysia, the great dramatic festival at Athens, a satyr play was performed after every three tragedies. When the three tragedies formed a trilogy, the satyr play was connected with them in subject matter. They were not given for comic relief but as part of the religious rite, like the medieval miracle plays which depicted the shrewish humors of Noah's wife, the thieving shepherd who kneels in reverence before the Christ child in the stable at Bethlehem, or the burlesque Devil, complete with horns and tail.[26]

Tragedy is but one face of ritual drama and of all art, as the paired classical dramatic masks remind us. This double face of art, the tragic and the comic, is unique among human institutions. Unlike the Christlike saviors of men who absolve us through suffering and death, the buffoons and fools of great comic art offer us images of our own vices which sometimes shame us into wisdom. For the comic image allows us to confront our problems without fear. No longer are they locked within ourselves where, like a dream, they were beyond communicating to others. Ingratitude from inferiors, rejection by superiors, unfriendliness from equals, and, most terrible of all, complete indifference from those we deeply need are common disrelationships in every hierarchical system. They are expressed in many ways—we wish for the deaths of loved ones, we invent fantasies in which once cherished superiors are degraded, and we imagine hells full of torture and anguish to which we damn our enemies (and ourselves). Yet only as we placate superiors, inferiors, and equals significant to us, do we escape hierarchical guilt. If we fail, guilt soon becomes pathological, as when we feel deep contempt for those we despise yet must obey.

The comic scapegoat lies within ourselves. In scourging him, we scourge our own follies. In this way, we hope to purge the community of evil, as Athens is purged in Aristophanes' *The Frogs*. The play is set in the terrible year of 405 B.C. The city has only a few more months of freedom before it is vanquished by Lysander and his Spartans. Guilt lies heavily upon the city, but none of this guilt is projected onto hapless scapegoats who must suffer and die. Like Job of the Israelites, the Athenians challenge the power and justice of their gods. But this challenge, a pride and presumption which the God of Israel punishes in Job and which the Greek gods punish in tragic dramatic rites, becomes in the ritual comedy of Aristophanes a challenge to the Athenians themselves to search their own hearts and minds to discover cause for the fearful calamities that are imminent. For the gods whom they indict are only representations of the fierce longings of men: Heracles is a glutton; Dionysius a wanton, a drunkard, and a coward. Like the famous men of Athens, the gods are often clever but not always wise. Frequently, they are plain fools saved from danger by sturdy servants such as Xanthias. The curse of Athens is madness, unreason—not sin. The final chorus in *The Frogs,* like the chorus of all Greek comedy, speaks for community ideals. It asks the deities to "grant . . . wise and healthy thoughts to [Athens]." Such thoughts are born only in the discourse of free men who must learn to distrust even the revelations of their gods. Laughter, sacred laughter, is the guardian of reason.

Sentiments and attitudes necessary to community survival are created through comedy as well as tragedy. Indeed, it may well be argued that comedy surpasses tragedy as a means of social control in daily life. Few relationships are without tension of some sort. At best, as William Graham Sumner said, we act together in antagonistic co-operation. Hate lurks in the deepest moments of love. As inferiors, we find cherished superiors cold and distant; as superiors we find inferiors surly and disloyal; as equals we find each other "putting on airs." Thus we find that superiors make fun of venal, cowardly servants,[27] that inferiors lampoon the arrogance and pride of

105

their superiors,[28] and that equals tease the pretentions of friends.[29] In laughter we plead with each other to recognize group demands. We say to superior, inferior, and equal alike: "Oh, come now, we have to live together, so get down off your high horse and be one of us once more. None of us is perfect. We need each other. So, for better or worse, we must get along."

Comedy brings disrelationships to light and allows us to submit them to public communication. Tragedy enshrouds disrelationships; comedy uncovers them. Both seek to affirm the norms and principles of the group by invoking transcendent principles of group life. But comedy, unlike tragedy, keeps its victim within the group. We say to the comic victim, "If you will but mend your ridiculous ways, you can be one of us again." We say to the tragic victim, "You have sinned against the group, and as a result of your sin we all suffer. You must be driven from us, pursued, tortured, and killed as a sacrifice to our gods; for only in such atonement can we purge ourselves of sin." So long as the comic victim wants to remain in the group, he must submit to group laughter. Unlike the tragic victim, he is not a heretic who must be hunted and killed. He errs, but even in error he can appeal to the audience to laugh at those who are laughing at him. Comedy is a social form, an enactment of critical intelligence, for in comedy we assume that truth can bear the light.

Comedy, unlike tragedy, helps us to live in doubt. This is particularly characteristic of irony, which permits us to smile at what we cannot, or will not, change. Irony allows us to express social embarrassments which do not, like rejection, make acting together difficult or impossible. So long as we can express our confusion or perplexity, we can act. Thus in communicating with minority groups, we use ironic playfulness as a means of reducing tension. We act as if our group norms made sense, but we are careful to let each other know that they really do not. There is always an air of complicity in irony as if we were to say, "You and I know how absurd it is that things are this way, but that is the way our society wants it, so let us endure what we cannot change."[30] In some sexual Utopia, men and women may find their sexual differences a source of perpetual joy. But here on earth there is much suffering, and at best haunting doubt, over the perfectibility of sexual relationships. When we speak ironically of sex, we admit that we cannot change it, that we are animals after all, but we are human, too, and must laugh at what we cannot change.

While it is true, as Freud has pointed out, that jokes serve as a resistance against authority and an escape from its pressure, it is also true that they are used to discipline those who threaten group solidarity. The laughter of Americans at successive generations of immigrants (German, Irish, Scotch, Scandinavian, Italian, and Yiddish), like Molière's laughter over parvenus, serves to keep them in their place, or to sensitize them to the proper forms of social-climbing. The German was admonished to give up his "dumb" rural ways, the Irishman to curtail his "blarney," the Scot to abandon his thrift, the Jew to stop seeing everything in terms of money. The burst of glory in humor arises out of the sudden confidence that even though we are being laughed at, or that doubt or question over authority is being brought to light, the group as such is not threatened. In laughing with the group, we laugh at ourselves. We understand very well that group judgment has been passed on us; and if we choose to remain in the group, we must accept this judgment and mend our ways. Yet in laughter there is no fear, and if the American of native birth can poke fun at the immigrant, the immigrant too (like the Norwegian Thorstein Veblen) can bring our follies into public view where we must be prepared to defend ourselves against those whom we have exposed to scorn and ridicule.

Ridicule can become a savage weapon. The laughter arising out of deep scorn and mockery is never genial. We ridicule others so that we may congratulate ourselves for not sharing their defects. A person who is the object of ridicule is always inferior. Therefore, malign ridicule is never reflexive. Aristocrats of the sword reacted sharply and swiftly when ridiculed, for, as La Rochefoucauld said, "Ridicule dishonors more than dishonor." In irony we create and sustain to a high degree a conscious elaboration of the possibilities of social solidarity, but in ridicule we reduce the burden of sustaining it by arousing hate. Ridicule is the first step toward the total estrangement of the scapegoat; in making the Jew a German scapegoat, Hitler began by making him ridiculous. The victim is consecrated for sacrifice; otherwise, his guilt remains our guilt, and we must expiate it ourselves. Once we subject another to ridicule, he cannot attack us, for who will knowingly follow a fool? The victim of ridicule remains within the group; because he *is* ridiculous, he cannot become an enemy whose defeat will demand great sacrifice and complete submission to the will of the leaders.[31]

Obscene comedy is another way of reducing disrelations so that we can act together. In the great art of Rabelais and Swift, as in the filthy curses of soldiers, hated authorities are covered with symbolic filth, reviled, and then buried or washed away. Falstaff is hidden beneath stinking sheets in a laundry basket. Panurge's Lady of Paris is drenched with dog urine. The majesty of Elizabeth's court is rudely shattered by Sir Walter Raleigh's roaring flatus (in Mark Twain's *1601*). In Swift's Court of Brobdingnag, the land of the giants, the stink and corruption of every small blemish on the bodies of the great ladies nauseates Gulliver. The soldier knows he cannot do without his officers, his whores, and his profiteers. Without leaders he cannot win battles, without sluts there will be no sex with women, without traders there will be no contraband liquor, food, or tobacco. So he turns to obscenity (as the gentleman turns to irony) to endure what he hates but cannot change. With his curses and grim laughter, the soldier reduces the mystery of rank, as medieval priests did with their depictions of bishops and Biblical heroes in farcical treatments of the mysteries of the Old Testament and Christ's Passion, or as schoolboys do with their drawings of teachers falling into toilets. Old soldiers laugh grimly at their inversion of civilian manners. They have seen a world unmasked, a world become brutish, savage, and filthy. So, like the Devil, they make a kingdom of their misery; but, unlike Shaw's sentimental Devil, they refuse to turn their eyes from it. In obscene laughter, they *present* their misery to each other and to their group.

As we laugh together, we cannot hate, for in our common plight we feel a deep sense of brotherhood. The golden social moment in comedy is the reaffirmation of a common bond which is born of our recognition that there is difference and there is similarity. When we laugh at the haughty gentleman who slips into the swimming pool as he backs away from the lady to whom he bows, we feel superior because his formal dress becomes ridiculous in a swimming pool, and the elaborate status pantomime of bowing to a lady has ended incongruously. However, if in helping the drenched plutocrat out of the pool we too tumble in, our laughter mounts until in a moment of complete disregard for the expense of our plutocratic trappings, we all jump in the pool, we are "in the drink" together, and we flounder about in a mad but glorious moment of solidarity, as we reaffirm once again our common human bonds.

Comedy, then, is a kind of running commentary, an enactment of critical intelligence as a social value, a counter to the dark majesty of tragedy, which so easily leads to priestly mystification. In comic play we do not escape our burdens; we face them in reason after the pain of social inequality and all the disfunctions to which the social body is heir are made so absurd that we can face them. Like the gods of Olympus, we laugh at these mortals here below. In these benign moments we even enjoy our differences and disagreements. We can do so because faith in our capacity to overcome disrelationships runs high. We laugh as we laugh at hypocrisy when we discover that it, after all, pays homage to virtue. The strain of rigid conventions, of majestic ideals, of deep loyalties, is lessened, for in laughter they are open to examination. When they are expressed freely, there is hope for correction; and even when hope dwindles, we have company in our misery. As we huddle together beneath skies which threaten doom, we are no longer locked within ourselves or forced to submit to gods whose power lies only in our submission. As we laugh, our spirits lighten, and we take heart for another try. For when all is said and done, what do we have but each other?

If we view ritual as drama, the structure of our dramatic model must contain five elements. We must say something about the setting of the act, the nature of the act, the kind of persons who perform the act, the means used, and the end or purpose of the action. The social function of dramatic action is to uphold some principle of social order.[32] Since we use a dramatic model, we assume that all relationships involve struggle over such principles. We think of this struggle as a presentation to an audience that is differentiated into (1) a general public; (2) a public which is assumed to be the guardian of public welfare and is responsible for judging acts in relation to community goals; (3) other actors—superior, inferior, and equal—whose responses define our motives (as we, in turn, define theirs); (4) other aspects of the self (as when we soliloquize); and (5) some great transcendent principle of social order. Or, to expand Meadian terminology, we internalize a "they," a "me," a "you," an "I," and a "we" by objectifying them in symbols whose meaning is created in the give-and-take of dramatic discourse.[33]

In ritual drama, we address the general public which constitutes the whole audience, the community guardians who make up the chorus, the other actors who as heroes and villains struggle for the same goal, a self that plays many roles whose internal disagreement and conflict are so difficult to resolve within ourselves that we "allow" our struggle to be "overheard," and some great transcendent goal or principle of social order which all invoke to resolve their struggle. In the great ritual drama of American politics we see all of these. The politician addresses his speech first to his "fellow Americans" and then to the honored guests on the platform, "leaders of the great city of Chicago." As he speaks, he enters into dialogue with friends and enemies (heroes and villains) who seek to uphold or destroy the "American Way of Life." He turns aside to recall his own difficulties as "On that day when I said to myself. . . . " In closing, he invokes the Constitution, freedom, God, and democracy. Then the audience files out under the benediction of a musical expression of the great transcendent symbols of community: God and Country.

All social order and the legitimation of belief in authority rests on belief in the transcendent power of (1) persons, (2) methods, (3) traditions and manners, (4) acts of creation, or (5) ends—on any one, several, or all of these. In the first type of belief, we resolve conflict under the leadership of a prophet whose personal charisma shows us the way. In the second, we follow magical incantation, rites and techniques whose efficacy depends on strict adherence to a specific way of invoking laws, fate, destiny, or the gods. In the third, we appeal to traditions (the way it has always been done) or manners (the way everybody is doing it). In the fourth, we invoke a creative act of origin as when we accept Edenic myths as a social charter. In the fifth, we invoke ends or goals such as a "classless society," the day of "God's judgment," or "freedom under law."

All dramatic depictions define order through disorder, and provide ways for dealing with disorganization through appeals to these five types of transcendent powers. Authorities expect disobedience, and those who disobey must be provided with a means of atonement and expiation to relieve them of guilt. Equals anticipate disagreements with their peers and must have a means for adjudicating their differences. Expiation is "outer" when we load the comic or tragic scapegoat with our sins and then either kill him symbolically through ridicule (as Charlie Chaplin does with the "social swells" in his early comedies), or actually kill him, as Hitler did in his massacre of the Jews. Expiation is "inner" when we purify the self through mortification of the flesh ("If thine eye offend thee, pluck it out").[34]

Radcliffe-Brown and Malinowski hold that "ritual idiom" in cosmological myths and myths of origin must be understood if we are to understand a society. Yet despite their constant reference to ritual idiom and to the fact that the context of the situation in which it occurs offers a clue to understanding its meaning, they give no explicit method for analyzing the symbolism of rites. We cannot simply reduce ritual drama to a kind of myth, any more than we can reduce it to philosophy and imply that the enactment of the moment of origin in community ceremonial is but a roundabout way of saying what philosophy can say directly. When Polynesians dance, they enact their society in ritual drama. They do not have social bonds and then dance about them: they create and sustain them as they dance. But their dance, like any drama which becomes the enactment of group solidarity in ritual drama, is a narrative, and subject, therefore, to the laws of narrative development. If we accept this view, there is no need to consult myths

111

created in strange tongues spoken by people far distant in time and space. We can begin closer to home with "dramatistic" interpretations of symbolic expressions. No matter where we assign our causes of motivation—in nature, sociopolitical events, personal-familial experience, supernatural realms, or even language itself—such causes are described and communicated through symbols whose meaning is heavily infused with ideas and images of social order. This method of analyzing symbols, which Kenneth Burke calls socio-anagogic[35] breaks through the circularity of ritual theory. By using it, we are able to show *how* sociopolitical order, or what has been called hierarchy in this paper, is enacted on a symbolic level.

Burke admonishes us to respect "terministic factuality" which is contrasted with the analysis of symbols in terms of "analogy." When a totem sign "bear" appears in two contexts, we do not begin by asking what esoteric "symbolic" meaning a bear might have in religious, cosmological, social, or psychoanalytic allegory or myth. We simply begin by noting that "bear" (in whatever symbolic guise) bridges various contexts. And even if we know that "bear" has some well-established meaning in the "ritual idiom" because of its "significance" as a community symbol in cosmological myth, the fact would still remain that the term is used in a specific way in a specific ritual drama. This is very different from explaining the term by meanings established before we have looked at the ritual drama we intend to investigate. We may even agree with Malinowski that "all the meaning of all words is derived from bodily experience,"[36] but this merely shifts the problem to the realm of bodily experience. We must make clear what we mean by bodily experience. And even if we describe in minute detail, and define clearly what we mean by "bodily" in some theory such as homeostasis, how do we establish the connection between the body and the symbols used in ritual drama?

If we believe that society exists in and through communication, and if we take the next obvious step and conclude that as we analyze communication we analyze society, we must state clearly which form of communication we accept as characteristic of all communication. For purposes of social analysis there is little use in dealing with language "in general," for what we need to know is how language functions in role enactment in particular. We do not use language in the same way when we chat informally, make a business deal, and worship God. But in so far as these acts depend on language, they depend on language as developed in the specific social forms of expression in the ritual dramas of community life as we see them on the stage, in ceremonies, pageants, parades, and all other celebrations of our social bonds which depend on dramatic form for their presentation.

A drama has a beginning, a crisis, a struggle to resolve the crisis, and a resolution of the crisis. That is, a drama develops or unfolds, and the stages in such development determine what symbols mean. As Oedipus comes staggering from Jocasta's body, his blinded eyes dripping blood, whatever principle of social order he then invokes *is* the principle of the drama. As the dancer swoons in ecstasy before the village fire, whatever principle of order is invoked in tribal chant *is* the social bond of the tribe. The actor does not choose these stages in the development of the drama. They have a form, one precedes and follows the other, and the actor must adhere to this form. The forms of magic, games, and play function like rules which in and of themselves have power. When children agree on how an ice cream cone is to be eaten as it is passed among them, they are jealous guardians of good form. Magic is believed to be effective only if its formulas have been uttered perfectly and its routines have been complied with to the last detail. The masochist or sadist mounts a drama of lust in which the prostitute must follow to the letter every detail of the play created by the man who seeks sexual release with her.

Dramatic development is poetic as well as rhetorical. Symbolic expressions may be synonymous, although this may not be indicated by the meanings given for them in dictionaries. In moments of terror, love, wonder, mystery, power, silence, and guilt, oppositions become appositions. Soliloquy, the expression of the deepest moment of a character's inwardness, like the moment of conflict, forges new meanings from old terms. All terms for order and for the passage from one position to another tell us much about the social structure underlying the superiority, inferiority, and equality of roles in the drama.

Movement within the hierarchy, either upward or downward, is indicated in various ways. There is the ladder of language itself, in which a Platonist mounts from particulars to higher and higher orders of generalization. There is some kind of social ladder with more or less clearly defined classes and ranks. There is a ladder in nature, for some beings or conditions are lower or higher than others. There is a spiritual ladder, which ends in celestialization, as when the voice of the people becomes the voice of God, and the simple worker casting his vote becomes sanctified in the radiance of "God's will."

Social, linguistic, and supernatural ladders are always interwoven. There are terms that are assigned to the celestial order; there are symbols that are used only in referring to the worldly order. There are terms used to bridge sacred and secular realms. There are terms explicitly social but implicitly celestial; and there are symbols speciously celestial but actually social; in general, these matters become obvious when any character presents himself before the community, for then sociolinguistic pageantry, the cults of parade, exhibition, and appeal, are manifest. There are many moments in dramatic ritual when communities and institutions within the community act out their social hierarchy. Even the simplest processional must be ordered. Some must come before others. Some will speak, others will be silent. Some will ride, others walk. In all forms of symbolic expression, the social order is expressed in dramatic presentations of hierarchy which must be communicated frequently and intensively to remain in force as a social bond.

1. *La cité antique* (1864).

2. *The Religion of the Semites* (1889).

3. *Les formes élémentaires de la vie religieuse: Le système totémique en Australie* (Paris: Félix Alcan, 1912).

4. *Magic, Science and Religion* (1922).

5. *The Andaman Islanders* (1922).

6. Unlike Durkheim, Burckhardt tries to relate art and politics, as well as religion, to social consensus. The neglect of Burckhardt by anthropologists—and, indeed, by all social scientists—limits the range of social data. And even if we agree with Bacon, de Tocqueville, and, more recently, Toynbee, that religion is the most substantial bond of community, we

should ask, as does Burckhardt, "What kind of community will come out of what kind of religion?"

7. A. R. Radcliffe-Brown, *Structure and Function in Primitive Society*, with a Foreword by E. E. Evans-Pritchard and Fred Eggan (London: Cohen and West, 1952).

8. *Ibid.*, p. 124.

9. *Ibid.*, p. 131.

10. *Ibid.*, p. 130.

11. *Ibid.*, Chap. vii, pp. 133-52.

12. *Ibid.*, p. 142.

13. *Ibid.*, p. 143. The words "symbol" and "meaning" are "coincident." This distinguishes such meaning from meanings derived from "false assimilation of . . . [ritual actions] to technical acts," when "an adequate statement of the purpose of any particular act or series of acts constitutes by itself a sufficient explanation."

14. *Ibid.*, p. 144.

15. *Ibid.*, p. 145.

16. *Ibid.*, p. 146.

17. *Ibid.*, p. 149. Radcliffe-Brown points out that while magic and religion give men confidence, comfort, and a sense of security, it could equally well be argued that they give men fears and anxieties from which "they would otherwise be free—the fear of black magic, or of spirits, fear of God, of the Devil, of Hell."

18. If symbols are only "signals" which "trigger incipient social responses," what is the function of the individual?

19. Cf. Talcott Parsons, *The Social System* (Glencoe, Ill.: Free Press of Glencoe, Illinois, 1951), esp. p. 327; Talcott Parsons and Edward A. Shils (eds.), *Toward a General Theory of Action* (Cambridge, Mass.: Harvard University Press, 1952), esp. p. 160; Robert K. Merton, *Social Theory and Social Structure* (revised and enlarged ed.; Glencoe, Ill.: Free Press of Glencoe, Illinois, 1957), esp. p. 351; and Clyde Kluckhohn, "Values and Value-Orientations in the Theory of Action: An Exploration in Definition and Classification," in Parsons and Shils, *op. cit.*, esp. pp. 396, 398.

20. Cf. Bronislaw Malinowski, "The Problem of Meaning in Primitive Language," in C. K. Ogden and I. A. Richards, *The Meaning of Meaning* (New York: Harcourt, Brace & Co., 1945), esp. p. 325.

21. Cf. Edward Sapir, *Language: An Introduction to the Study of Speech* (New York: Harcourt, Brace & Co., 1921), esp. pp. 24-43.

22. Cf. Benjamin Lee Whorf, *Language, Thought, and Reality*, ed. John B. Carroll (New York: John Wiley & Sons, Inc., 1956), esp. p. 244.

23. That is, if grammatical "patterns" are interpretations of experience, how we achieve these patterns will determine the kind of experience we have. This requires a theory of social action as well as a theory of symbols.

24. Any social act contains much more than the communication of hierarchy, and the exercise of authority involves more than symbolic action. A bullet lodging in one's skull is more than symbolic, but the social meaning of this can be observed only in the symbolic action of those involved in the act.

25. This is not all that is contained in these works of art, but it is a specific social content, and from it we can learn how to think of authority in general.

26. Close examination of any of the ritual used by Jane Harrison and others as a basis for their theory of social cohesion shows their neglect of the comic elements in ritual drama. Anthropological studies which tell us nothing about primitive humor violate common sense. The psychoanalysts have not made this mistake. Whether we agree or not with their theory of laughter, we find them recognizing its importance. Until the appearance, in 1940 and 1949, of Radcliffe-Brown's two articles on joking relationships, there was very little sustained consideration given to the function of humor in primitive society. This neglect betrays at once the inadequacies of theories of social structure and function which are derived from religion. Gods, or at least Christian gods, seldom laugh; but human beings (even Christians) laugh over the burdens of hierarchy in art if not in religion.

27. As in *Don Giovanni*.

28. As in Charlie Chaplin's *City Lights*.

29. As in *Così fan tutte*.

30. Much of the fun of *Huckleberry Finn* stems from this device. Shaw's *Pygmalion*, Anatole France's *Penguin Island*, and John Gay's *The Beggar's Opera* are but a few of the dramas exemplifying that "what can't be cured, must be endured."

31. We war strenuously against villains, not fools.

32. Drama has other functions, of course. I have based my dramatic model on the work of Kenneth Burke, whose *Grammar of Motives* (1945) and *Rhetoric of Motives* (1950) offer new foundations for a social science founded on the analysis of symbolic action.

33. George Herbert Mead used a conversational image. The dramatic image increases our range of observation of the date of symbolic action.

34. The "inner" drama is also played out before an audience—an imaginary one, but one that is nonetheless powerful.

35. Although Burke developed his method for the analysis of literary symbolism, his insistence that sociopolitical order infuses literary meaning,

116

and that literary meaning also affects sociopolitical order—and his concrete analyses of this reciprocity—reduces vague generalizations about "ritual idiom" and "context of situation" to hypotheses which can be tested. He gives an explicit statement of his approach in "Fact, Inference, and Proof in the Analysis of Literary Symbolism" (Chap. xix) , in *Symbols and Values: Thirteenth Symposium of the Conference on Science, Philosophy and Religion,* ed. Lyman Bryson, Louis Finkelstein, R. M. MacIver, and Richard McKeon (New York and London: Conference on Science, Philosophy and Religion in Their Relation to the Democratic Way of Life, Inc. [Distributed by Harper & Bros.], 1954) .

36. In his discussion of the function of language in Part IV of *Coral Gardens and Their Magic* (1935) , Malinowski is not very consistent. The meaning of words lies beyond their use as words, in the body, in work, in social organization, and so on. If this is so, how do we know the meaning of the body, work, and social organization? It must be communicated to us in some way. And even if we accept meanings beyond words, how do we show how we discover such meanings?

DURKHEIM'S CONTRIBUTION TO THE THEORY OF INTEGRATION OF SOCIAL SYSTEMS

TALCOTT PARSONS

It is appropriate at this time, just a little over one hundred years after the birth of Emile Durkheim, to take stock of his contributions to what was perhaps the central area of his theoretical interest. The development of theoretical thinking that has taken place in the intervening years enables us to achieve greater clarity in the identification and evaluation of these contributions.

It can be said, I think, that it was the problem of the integration of the social system, of what holds societies together, which was the most persistent preoccupation of Durkheim's career. In the situation of the time, one could not have chosen a more strategic focus for contributing to sociological theory. Moreover, the work Durkheim did in this field can be said to have been nothing short of epoch-making; he did not stand entirely alone, but his work was far more sharply focused and deeply penetrating than that of any other author of his time. Because of this profundity, the full implications of his work have not yet been entirely assimilated by the relevant professional groups. Furthermore, in addition to the intrinsic complexity of the subject, the rather special frame of reference of French Positivism in which he couched his analysis has made it difficult to interpret him.

The present essay will not attempt to be a scholarly review either of Durkheim's own printed work or of the secondary literature. It will rather attempt—in the light of a good many years of preoccupation with the problems for which Durkheim gave what were for his time classical formulations—to assess some of the main lines of his special contribution and to indicate the ways in which it has been both necessary and possible to try to go beyond the stage at which he left them.

There are two essential reference points in Durkheim's initial orientation: one is positive and the other negative. The positive is the Comtean conception of "consensus" as the focus of unity in societies. This was the primary origin of the famous concept of the *conscience collective*; this rather than any German conception of *Geist* is clearly what Durkheim had in mind. It was a sound starting point, but it was much too simple and undifferentiated to serve his purposes; primarily, perhaps, because it could not account for the fundamental phenomenon of unity in diversity, the phenomenon of the integration of a highly differentiated system.

The negative reference point is the utilitarian conception of the interplay of discrete individual interest, as first put forward by Herbert Spencer who conceived of an industrial society as a network of "contractual relations."[1] The importance of relations of contract, that is, relations in which terms are settled by some type of *ad hoc* agreement, was an immediate consequence of the division of labor which had been emphasized in the long tradition of utilitarian economics deriving from Locke and from Adam Smith's famous chapter. Durkheim made this tradition the focal point of his criticism, tackling it in one of its main citadels; and, in so doing, he raised the problem of the differentiated system which Comte had not really dealt with.

In this critique, Durkheim shows, with characteristic thoroughness and penetration, that Spencer's assumptions—which were those common to the whole liberal branch of the utilitarian tradition—failed to account for even the most elementary component of order in a system of social relations that was allegedly based on the pursuit of individual self-interest. To put it a little differently, no one had been able to answer Hobbes's fundamental question *from within the tradition,*[2] since Hobbes's own solution was palpably unacceptable. As is well known, Durkheim's emphasis is on the *institution* of contract, which at one point he characterizes as consisting in the "noncontractual elements" of contract. These are not items agreed upon by contracting parties in the particular situation, but are norms established in the society, norms which underlie and are independent of any particular contract. They are partly embodied in formal law, though not necessarily only in what in a strict technical sense is called the law of contract by jurists, and partly in more informal "understandings" and practice. The content of these norms may be summed up as follows:

They consist, first of all, in definitions of what content is permitted and what content is prohibited in contractual agreement—in Western society of recent times, for instance, contracts that infringe on the personal liberty of either party or of any third party in his private capacity are prohibited; second, in definitions of the means of securing the assent of the other party that are legitimate and of those that are illegitimate—in general, coercion and fraud are considered illegitimate, however difficult it may be to draw exact borderlines; third, in definitions of the scope and limits of responsibility which may be reasonably (or legally) imputed to one or another party to a contractual relation, either originally on the basis of his "capacity" to enter binding agreements—as agent for a collectivity, for example—or subsequently on the basis of the consequences to himself and others of the agreements made; and, fourth, in definitions of the degree to which the interest of the society is involved in any particular private agreement, the degree to which private contracts bear on the interests of third parties or on those of the collectivity as a whole.[3]

Durkheim postulated the existence of what he called organic solidarity as a functional necessity underlying the institutionalization of contract. This may be characterized as the integration of units, units which, in the last analysis, are individual persons in roles, who are performing qualitatively differentiated functions in the social system. The implication of such differentiation is that the needs of the unit cannot be met solely by his own activities. By virtue of the specialization of his function, the unit becomes dependent on the activities of others who must meet the needs which are not covered by this specialized function. There is, therefore, a special type of interdependence that is generated by this functional differentiation. The prototype is the kind of division of labor described by the economists. Clearly, Durkheim's conception is broader than this. For example, he describes the differentiation of function between the sexes, in social as well as biological terms, as a case of the division of labor in his sense.

What, then, is indicated by "organic solidarity"? The most important problem in interpreting the meaning of the concept is to determine its relation to the conception of the *conscience collective.* Durkheim's primary interest is in the fact that units agree on norms because they are backed by values held in common, although the interests of the differentiated units must necessarily diverge. Durkheim's original definition of the *conscience collective* is as follows: "L'ensemble des croyances et des sentiments communs à la moyenne des membres d'une même société forme un système déterminé qui a sa vie propre; on peut l'appeler la conscience collective ou commune."[4] The keynote of this definition is, clearly, beliefs and sentiments that are held in common. This formula is essential, for it indicates that the problem of solidarity is located in the area of what may very broadly be called the motivational aspects of commitment to the society, and to conformity with the expectations institutionalized within it. Taken alone, however, it is too general to serve as more than a point of departure for an analysis of the problems of solidarity and hence of societal integration. Furthermore, Durkheim himself was seriously embarrassed by the problem of how to connect the *conscience collective* with the differentiation resulting from the division of labor.

It seems to me that Durkheim's formula needs to be further elaborated by two sets of distinctions. He himself made essential contributions to one of these, the distinction between mechanical and organic solidarity; but one of the main sources of difficulty in understanding his work is his relative neglect of the second set of distinctions, and his tendency to confuse it with the first. This second set concerns the levels of generality achieved by the cultural patterns—values, differentiated norms, collectivities, and roles—that have been institutionalized in a society. It also concerns the controls that articulate these levels and that determine the direction in which the controls operate. A discussion of the levels of generality of these four cultural patterns will provide a setting for a consideration of mechanical and organic solidarity and of the relations between them.

I think it is correct to say that in the course of his career Durkheim gradually crystallized and clarified a conviction which can be stated in terms more modern than he himself used: The structure of a society, or of any human social

121

system, consists in (is not simply influenced by) patterns of normative culture[5] which are institutionalized in the social system and internalized (though not in identical ways) in the personalities of its individual members. The cultural patterns just outlined are the four different types of components of this structure. Elsewhere, they are referred to as "levels of generality of normative culture." Though all are institutionalized, each has a different relation to the structure and processes of the society. Societal values constitute the component which reaches the highest level of generality; for they are conceptions of the desirable society that are held in common by its members. Societal values are thus distinguished from other types of values—such as personal ones—in that the category of object evaluated is the social system and not personalities, organisms, physical systems, or cultural systems ("theories," for example).

The value system of the society is, then, the set of normative judgments held by the members of the society which define, with specific reference to their own society, what to them is a good society. In so far as this set of values is in fact held in common and is institutionalized, it is descriptive of the society as an empirical entity. This institutionalization is a matter of degree, however; for members of a going society will, to some extent, differ in their values even at the requisite level, and they will, to a certain degree, fail to act in accordance with the values they hold. But with all these qualifications, it is still correct to say that values held in common constitute the primary reference point for the analysis of a social system as an empirical system.[6]

The paramount value system is relevant to the description of the society as a whole, but it does not distinguish normative judgments which refer to differentiated parts or subsystems within the society. Therefore, when a difference of values is imputed to the two sexes, to regional groups, to class groups, and so on, one has gone from describing societal values to describing those that characterize another social system, one which should be treated analytically as a subsystem of the society of reference. When this step has been taken, it becomes essential to make another distinction, the distinction between value and differentiated norm.

At the subsystem level, members of the society who do and who do not participate in the subsystem of reference have evaluative judgments which they apply to the qualities and performances of those members who do, as distinguished from those who do not, participate in it. These judgments are "specifications," that is, applications of the general principles of the common societal value system at a more concrete level. The expectations of behavior of those who are members of the subsystem are not the same as those of non-members. Thus, in the case of sex role, the values applying to the behavior of the two sexes are shared by both, but the norms which regulate that behavior apply differentially to the two sexes. In so far as a pattern of behavior is sex-specific, members of one sex group will conform with it, the other not. This is to say that values are shared, presumptively, by all members of the most extensive relevant system, whereas norms are a function of the differentiation of socially significant behavior which is institutionalized in different parts of that system.

It follows from this that values as such do not involve a reference to a situation, or a reference to the differentiation of the units of the system in which they are institutionalized. Norms, on the other hand, make this differentiation explicit. In one respect, they are derived from the evaluative judgments that have been institutionalized in the value system; but independently of this component, they also include, as is clear in the case of legal systems, three other specifications. The first specifies the categories of units to which the norm applies; this is the problem of jurisdiction. The second specifies what the consequences will be to the unit that conforms and to the unit that does not conform to the requirements of the norm (variations in degree are, of course, possible); this is the problem of sanctions or enforcement. Finally, the third specifies that the meaning of the norm shall be interpreted in the light of the character and the situations of the units to which it applies; this constitutes the problem of interpretation, which is roughly equivalent to the appellate function in law. It should be noted that in this case the reference to the situation is confined to the one in which the unit acts vis-à-vis other units. It is thus intrasystemic. When the reference is to situations external to the system, the levels of collectivity and role structure, to be outlined later, must be brought into the picture.

Values, then, are the "normative patterns" that are descriptive of a positively evaluated social system. Norms are generalized patterns of expectation which define differentiated patterns of expectation for the differentiated kinds of units within a system. In a particular system, norms always stand at a lower level of cultural generality than do values. Put a little differently, norms can be legitimized by values, but not vice versa.

A collectivity stands at a still lower level in the hierarchy of the normative control of behavior. Subject both to the more general values of the system and to the norms regulating the behavior of the relevant differentiated types of units within the system, the normative culture of a collectivity defines and regulates a concrete system of co-ordinated activity which can at any given time be characterized by the commitments of specifically designated persons, and which can be understood as a specific system of collective goals in a specific situation. The functional reference of norms at the level of the collectivity is, then, no longer general, but is made specific in the particular goals, situations, and resources of the collectivity, including its "share" in the goals and resources of society. This specification of function, though it is of varying degree, emphasizes the fact that it is the goal of the collectivity which defines its level of concreteness, since the goal of a unit in a system is, in so far as the system is well integrated, the basis on which its primary function in the system is specified.

The normative character of a collective goal is precisely given by this specification of function in a system, but it is subject to given situational exigencies that are external to the system. This specification is not necessary for the definition of a norm, but it is essential for further specification at the level of the organization of the collectivity.

Collectivities constitute the essential operative units of social systems, to such an extent that where relations of co-operation and "solidarity" for a given functional unit goal do not exist within collectivities, and the function is performed by a single independent individual—by the independent artisan or professional practitioner, for example—it is legitimate to speak of this as the limiting case of the collectivity: it is a collectivity consisting of one member.

All social systems arise out of the interaction of human individuals as units. Hence the most important exigencies of the situation in which collectivities as units perform social functions are the conditions for effective performance by the constituent human individuals (including their command of physical facilities). But since the typical individual participates in more than one collectivity, the relevant structural unit is not the "total" individual or personality, but the individual in a role. In its normative aspect, then, a role may be thought of as the system of normative expectations for the performance of a participating individual in his capacity as a member of a collectivity. The role is the primary point of direct articulation between the personality of the individual and the structure of the social system.

Values, norms, and collective goals—all in some sense control, "govern," and "regulate" the behavior of individuals in roles. But only at the level of the role is the normative content of expectations specifically oriented to the exigencies presented by the personalities or "motives" of individuals (and categories of them differentiated by sex, age, level of education, place of residence, and the like) and by the organic and physical environment.

In their functioning, social systems are, of course, subject to still other exigencies. But such exigencies are not normative in the sense used in this discussion; they do not involve the orientation of persons to and through conceptions of what is desirable. Thus the sheer facts of the physical environment are simply there; they are not altered by any institutionalization of human culture, although they may, of course, be controlled through such human cultural media as technology. This control, however, involves values, norms, collectivities, and role-expectations; and, as part of the social structure, it should be analyzed in these terms.

Values, norms, collectivities, and roles are categories that are descriptive of the structural aspect of a social system only.

In addition to such categories, it is necessary to analyze the system in functional terms in order to analyze processes of differentiation and the operation of these processes within a structure. Furthermore, process utilizes resources, carrying them through a series of stages of genesis, and either "consuming" them or incorporating and combining them into types of output or product, such as cultural change. The structure of institutionalized norms is the main point of articulation between these societal structures and the functional exigencies of the system. These exigencies, in turn, determine the mechanisms and categories of input and output relative to integration. Let us try to relate these considerations to the categories of mechanical and organic solidarity.

Durkheim's conception of mechanical solidarity is rooted in what I have called the system of common societal values. This is evident from the strong emphasis which he places on the relation of mechanical solidarity to the *conscience collective*. As a system of "beliefs and sentiments" that are held in common, Durkheim's *conscience collective* is more broadly defined than the system of societal values which I have given above. But it is certain that such a system is included in Durkheim's definition, and it can be argued that a system of values is the structural core of the system of beliefs and sentiments to which he refers. It should be clear, however, that Durkheim did not attempt to systematically distinguish and classify the components of the *conscience collective*, and this would seem to be essential if a satisfactory analysis of its relation to the problem of solidarity is to be made.

Such an analysis must do at least two things. In the first place, the value component must be distinguished from the others, that is, from cognitive (existential) beliefs, patterns of motivational commitment (these are close to Durkheim's "sentiments"), and patterns of legitimation of collective action (these will figure in the discussion presently). The second task involves the determination of the variations in the levels of generality and degrees of specificity of the components—of values, in particular—which eventuates in a scale corresponding to the differentiation of a society into numerous subsystems. Because of his failure to perform these two tasks, Durkheim was not able to be very exact about the relation of the *conscience collective* to mechanical solidarity, and was forced to resort to contrasting this relation with that of the *conscience collective* to organic solidarity—and this relation gave him considerable difficulty.

Mechanical solidarity is rooted in the common value component of the *conscience collective* and is an "expression" of it. Its relation to the other components is problematical. There is, however, another major aspect of mechanical solidarity, namely, its relation to the structure of the society as a collectivity. Every society is organized in terms of a paramount structure of the total system as a collectivity. In the highly differentiated modern society, this structure takes the form of governmental organization. In addition, there is, of course, an immensely complex network of lower-level collectivities, some of which are subdivisions of the governmental structure, while others are independent of it in various ways and degrees. The problem of mechanical solidarity arises wherever a collectivity is organized, but it is essential to understand what system is under consideration.

The focus of Durkheim's analysis of mechanical solidarity, in so far as it concerns the structure of the social system, lies, I suggest, in the relation between the paramount values of the society and its organization as a collectivity at the requisite level; that is, the governmental organization of the society where the system of reference is, as it is for Durkheim, the society as a whole. Mechanical solidarity is the integration of the common values of the society with the commitments of units within it to contribute to the attainment of collective goals—either negatively by refraining from action which would be felt to be disruptive of this function, or positively by taking responsibility for it.

This duality of reference is brought out with particular clarity in Durkheim's discussion of criminal law as an index or expression of mechanical solidarity. On the one hand, he makes reference to common "sentiments"; on the other, to obligations to the organized collectivity as such.[7] Also, since in all advanced societies government is the paramount agent for the application of coercion, Durkheim strongly emphasizes the role of the element of sanction in the repressive type of law. Two of the four primary functional references of a legal system noted above, legitimation and enforcement through sanctions, figure importantly in what Durkheim calls repressive law.

The above considerations account for the location of the phenomenon of mechanical solidarity with reference to the structure of the social system. This solidarity or integration of the system is brought about by the interplay of the system of common values, which legitimizes organization in the interest of collective goals, with the commitments of units of the system (which are, in the last analysis, individual persons in roles) to loyalty and responsibility. This loyalty and responsibility are not only to the values themselves, but to the collectivity whose functioning is guided by those values and which institutionalizes them. This location in the social structure does not, however, tell us anything about the mechanisms by which the integration is generated.

Before approaching the question of the mechanisms which produce integration, it will be well to raise the corresponding question of structural location with respect to "organic solidarity." My suggestion is that, by contrast with the question of mechanical solidarity, this one does not concern the value system directly, but rather the system of institutionalized norms in relation to the structure of roles in the society. This is not putting it in Durkheim's own terms, for he did not use the concept of role which has become so important to sociological theory in the last generation. The importance of the reference to norms in his analysis is, however, entirely clear.

Furthermore, Durkheim's discussion is fully in accord with the distinction made previously between values and differentiated norms as structural components of the social system, since he so strongly emphasized the relation of organic solidarity to the differentiation of functions among units in the system, and specifically to the differentiation of expectations of behavior.[8]

Though he enumerated a number of other fields, it is also clear that there is, for Durkheim, a special relation between organic solidarity, contract, and the economic aspects of the organization of societies. This relation can, I think, provide the principal clue to the way in which roles are involved. Collectivities, it has been suggested previously, constitute the primary operative agencies for the performance of social function. The resources necessary for that performance consist, in turn, besides solidarity itself and the related patterns of "organization," in cultural resources, physical facilities, and human services. "Solidarity" cannot be treated as a component for Durkheim's purposes because it is his dependent variable; he is concerned with the conditions on which it depends. He does not treat cultural resources—knowledge, for example. He is careful, nevertheless, to take account of the role of physical facilities in discusing the institutionalization of property rights. His main concern, however, is with human services and the ways in which they can be integrated for the performance of social function.

The central problem involved here may be looked at, in the first instance, in a developmental setting. It is a general characteristic of "primitive" societies that the allocation of resources among their structurally significant units is overwhelmingly ascribed. This is most obvious in the economic sphere itself. The factors of production are controlled by units which do not have specialized economic primacy of function, and they are typically not transferable from one unit to another. Indeed, even products are seldom exchanged, and when they are, the transfer is likely to take place as a ceremonial exchange of gifts rather than in barter, as we understand it—to say nothing of market exchange. This is particularly true of labor, the central factor of economic production.

The division of labor brings freedom from ascriptive ties regarding the utilization of consumable goods and services and the factors of production themselves. The structural location of organic solidarity thus concerns the dual problem of how the processes by which the potentially conflicting interests that have been generated can be reconciled without disruptive conflict (this leads, of course, into the Hobbesian problem), and of how the societal interest in efficient production can be protected and promoted.

Every society must, as a prerequisite of its functioning, presume some integration of the interest of units with those of the society—elsewhere I have called this the "institutional integration of motivation."[9] But this by itself is not enough. One path to further development is to use the organs of the collective attainment of goals as the agencies for defining and enforcing integration or solidarity of this type. This involves a near fusion of mechanical and organic bases of solidarity of the sort that is most conspicuous in socialistic economies. An independent basis of integration can develop, however, from the institutionalization of systems of norms and mechanisms that without centralized direction permit the allocation of fluid resources to proceed in a positively integrated manner.

This set of norms and mechanisms is organized in terms of two complementary reference points. One of these is the sociological reference to economic analysis and interests, the process by which generalized disposability of resources builds up. This concerns above all the institutionalization of contract, of property, and of the disposability of labor service through employment in occupational roles. Property and labor then become generalized resources. They can be allocated and controlled through processes which establish functionally specific claims, rather than through prior (and, therefore, in all likelihood, functionally irrelevant) bases of ascriptive claim, such as membership in a common kinship unit. This, of course, involves some sort of process of exchange among functionally differentiated units in the system.

It is an essential aspect of Durkheim's argument that this generalizability and fluid disposability of resources requires more than a freeing from irrelevant, usually ascriptive constraints. It also requires a positive institutionalization of correlative obligations and rights which are defined in terms of a normative structure. From the point of view of the definition of resources, this type of normative regulation becomes the more imperative the further removed the ultimate utilization of the resource is from what may be thought of as a "natural," to-be-taken-for-granted set of rights to this utilization. From the point of view of the resource, then, a dual process is necessary: First, the resource must be "generalized"—this involves freeing it from ascriptive controls; and, second, the positive obligation to enter into the generalized allocative system must be established. Thus in a primarily ascriptive society, the equivalent of what are occupational roles in our own were filled on the basis of kinship obligations, as in the case of a son who follows his father as the proprietor and cultivator of the land held by the continuing kinship unit. In our own society, to train for an occupation in which one can compete in the labor market, and to be willing to take one's chances on finding satisfactory employment constitute a positively institutionalized obligation of the normal adult male, and of a considerable number of the members of the other sex. Therefore, there is, in a sense, a "speculative" production of labor power which precedes any specification of its channels of use. This is, of course, even more true of the control of physical facilities.

At the same time, there must also be a series of mechanisms which can determine the patterns in which such a generalized resource is utilized. As the division of labor becomes more highly developed, the proportion of such resources which are utilized in collectivities that have specific functions becomes greater. These collectivities command monetary resources which can in turn be used to contract for labor services and to provide necessary physical facilities. The institutionalization of contract is the normative system which offers access to such resources— whatever the function of the organization itself may be. The institution of property, then, regulates monetary resources and physical facilities; the institution of occupation controls human services.

It is important to note here the complex relation which exists between the economic and non-economic aspects of the constellation of factors that I am outlining. Economic production as such is only one of the primary societal functions served by the processes of production and mobilization of fluid resources through the institutionalization of contract, markets, money, property, and occupational roles. Indeed, any major function may be promoted in that way—education, health care, scientific research, and governmental administration. There are only certain special limiting cases, like the family and certain aspects of the political process, which cannot be "bureaucratized" in this sense.

At the same time, it is correct to say that the mechanisms involved here—regardless of the ultimate function that they subserve in any particular case—are primarily economic; namely, contract, markets, money, and the like. We must exercise great care, therefore, when using such a term as "economic" in this kind of analysis.

The generalized disposability of resources, then, is one major aspect of the functional complex which is institutionalized through organic solidarity. The other aspect concerns the standards and mechanisms by which their allocation among alternative claimant units of the social structure is worked out. Here it is clear that, within the institutional framework of contract, property, and occupation, the primary direct mechanisms concern the structuring of markets and the institutionalization of money.

This brings us back to the subtle ways in which conventional economic and non-economic elements are involved. The market may be regarded as the structural framework for the allocation of disposable resources in so far as the mechanism of this allocation is primarily freely contractual at the level of the operative organization or collectivity. Two other types of mechanism must be distinguished from this one, however. The first is administrative allotment, which is a "free" disposal of resources by those who supposedly enjoy nearly full control of them. Theoretically, this would be the case if the economy were fully socialized, for a central planning body would simply make decisions and assign budgetary quotas—indeed it might also directly distribute labor and physical facilities. The second mechanism involves negotiation between the higher agencies which hold the resources and their prospective users in such a way that political power plays a prominent part in determining the outcome whether or not governmental structures are prominently involved. An example of this would be the distribution through legislative action of public works benefits on the basis of regional and local interests, a procedure which often involves a good deal of "log-rolling."

Empirically, there is shading-off between these types. Typologically, however, in the market the bargaining powers of the contracting partners are approximately equal; neither the holders nor the utilizers of resources are simply "told" where they are to go or what they are to get; and the degree of power held by the higher level of the goal-directed organization of the relevant collectivity structure is not the decisive mechanism in the process of allocation. The market is an institutionalized mechanism which neutralizes both these potential mechanisms of allocation in a number of areas, preventing them from being the primary determinants of more detailed allocations. This means essentially that there is a hierarchy of allocative mechanisms, whose relations to each other are ordered by institutionalized norms. Among these norms are those which define the areas within which, and the occasions on which, the more "drastic" controls may and may not be allowed to supersede the "freer" mechanism of the market. Thus the taxing power of government determines a compulsory allocation of monetary resources; and certain allocations are subject to legislative control in that limitations are placed on the freedom of individual units to contract for them at will.

However, it is clearly in accord with Durkheim's views of organic solidarity to point out that within the market sphere freedom is balanced and controlled by complex sets of institutionalized norms, so that the freedoms themselves and the rights and obligations associated with them are defined in terms of such institutionalized norms. There are, in this area, two main categories of such institutionalized structures. One concerns the institutionalization of the monetary mechanism itself, the definition of the sphere of its legitimate use, and, of course, the limits of this sphere. The other concerns the institutionalization of conditions under which market transactions involving different subcategories of resources may be entered into. Let us take up the latter class of norms first.

In general terms, norms of the highest order in a modern society clearly have the status of formal legal rules and principles. They are subject to the legislative power, and the task of interpreting and administering them is the responsibility of the courts of law. For organic solidarity, as noted above, the complex of contract, property, and occupation is central; whereas leadership, authority, and what I have elsewhere called "regulation" are central to mechanical solidarity.

Freedom of contract, then, includes the freedom to define the conditions and limitations of the various terms which—as I have previously set forth—are involved in a contractual system with respect to the content of agreements, the means of securing assent, the scope of responsibility, and the societal interest. At both the legal and informal levels, then, these conditions and limitations vary in accordance with the societal functions performed by the contracting units, the various aspects of the situations in which they operate, and other similar considerations. Thus a private relationship between a physician and a patient, established to serve the interest of the patient's health, is sanctioned. However, the offering of certain types of health service is restricted, partly by law and partly by informal institutionalization, and may be performed only by licensed and "adequately trained" physicians; and the acceptance of such services is, if it is legitimate, restricted, in a more informal sense, to persons who are really "sick." There is abundant evidence that there is wide area in which illness is not so much an objective "condition" as a socially defined role.

Therefore, the problem of the content of contractual relations involves differentiating between role-categories which are regarded as the legitimate bearers of various social functions and those which are not. A "consumer" or "client" may contract for a very wide range of goods and services, but he is not completely free to choose the agencies with which he will contract, since institutional norms define the functions which certain agencies may perform.

In addition, the ways in which the terms of the contract are settled are institutionalized in various ways, and this influences the structure of the market. Economists have been particularly concerned with one type, the "commercial" market, where prices are arrived at on the basis of "competition," and where it is an institutionalized expectation that the right of the purveying agency to continue in operation is a function of its ability to meet expenses and to show a profit. Furthermore, it is the customer's expectation that the price he pays will cover the full cost of what he purchases. However, the structure of the market in which a large number of governmental, professional, and other services are purveyed, is quite different. Although a service may be entirely free in the monetary sense, the conditions of eligibility may be sharply defined, as in the case of those regulating admission to public hospitals. Or, as is often the case in private medical practice, there may be a sliding scale of costs, so that one participant in the contract, the patient—contrary to what is expected of the customer in the commercial market —fulfills only part of his obligation in that the fee he pays covers only a portion of the costs of performing the service contracted for.

Furthermore, there is the problem of the scope of the responsibility involved in such a relation. The Spencerian version of the idea of contract tended to assume that the question of the participants' abilities to "deliver" presented no complicated problem. The typical economic exchange in which the buyer has sufficient money and the seller sufficient goods is taken as the prototype. But this is by no means always the situation. As an illustration, let us again take a certain type of professional relationship. A sick person cannot be held responsible for ending his deplored condition simply by making a voluntary effort: his helplessness is a primary criterion by which his need of, and right to, professional service is determined. But he is responsible for recognizing his helplessness and for actively co-operating with therapeutic agencies in bringing about his recovery. These agencies, in turn, though their role may be defined in terms of technical competence, must recognize a wide variation in the capacities of individuals so that if there is a failure in certain cases, the physician is not held responsible, provided he has done his best. Another good example is found in education where because of the youth of the ignorant person, ignorance is not considered culpable. Nor is a child expected to educate himself without the help of schools. He is, however, expected to work hard in acquiring his education within the framework of the school. And some children are harder to educate than others, and failures are not treated as being always or wholly the teacher's fault. There are elaborately institutionalized norms covering fields such as these.

The protection of the interest of society in contractual relations is more diffusely institutionalized; it is, in a sense, an aspect of all the norms in this area. At the legal level, however, there are a number of provisions which enable the courts and other governmental agencies that represent the public interest

135

to intervene in order to prevent or modify such arrangements. Because of its very nature, the institutionalization of a contractual system involves the imposition of a whole system of limitations on the powers of government. But the residual opportunities for private interests to exploit their freedom against the rest of the society require the maintenance of a delicately balanced equilibrium of integration.

The monetary mechanism is essential because, in the first place, the division of labor cannot develop very far if all exchanges are restricted to the level of barter. In a fully developed system, money has four primary functions. It serves, first, as a measure of the economic value of resources and products. It is in this connection that we speak of the gross national product as a monetary sum. Second, it serves as a standard for the rational allocation of resources, for comparing cost and outcome. Only in the "business" sector, where productive function in the economic sense has primacy, is the monetary standard the primary one applied. But in other functional areas, too, such as education or health, monetary cost is a very essential evaluative mechanism in that it is, from the point of view of the unit, the basis for evaluating one major component in the conditions necessary to accomplish whatever goal is involved, and is, from the point of view of the system at large, a measure of the sacrificed uses to which the resources in question might have been put.

It is thus essential to discriminate profitability as a measure of the worth-whileness of a function from the use of monetary cost as one component of the conditions which must be weighed in arriving at a judgment of worth-whileness. The capacity somehow to cover monetary cost, the ability to raise the money somehow, is, of course, a necessary limiting condition of those functions which require resources that are acquired through the market.

In serving as a measure and standard, money does not circulate; nothing changes hands. In performing its other two functions, however, money is a medium of exchange. In the first of these, money is an essential facility wherever the attainment of goals is dependent on resources accessible through market channels. Not only is it necessary to have it, but, it must be noted, in a highly developed market system, there is an extraordinarily wide range of choices open to the unit that possesses sufficient funds. The other mediating function of money is to serve as a reward. Here the reference is in the nature of the case comparative and relative; what counts is the amount of monetary income received by one unit or resource as compared with that received by another. It is this function of money which is the primary focus of the regulation of the process of allocation of resources, in so far as this is the result of market transactions. The basic principle is the economic one: A resource will flow to that one of the situations in which it is utilized which offers the highest relative reward, the reward being, in this case, monetary.

Here again it is essential, however, to insist on the same basic distinction which was made in connection with the standards of allocation. Money is not the sole component of the complex of rewards. It has primacy over other components only when the function of economic production has primacy over other functions, that is, in the "business" sector of the organizational and occupational system. It is essentially for this reason that the monetary remuneration for human services in that sector is higher than other sectors such as government, education, and so on. But even where other components of reward—political power, integrative acceptance or solidarity, or cultural prestige —have primacy within a given subsystem, it is essential that the monetary remuneration correspond to the quality of the services performed, as determined on the basis of the dominant criteria for that subsystem. In the academic profession, for example, contrary to the situation in the business occupations, the amount of one's income is not a valid measure of one's relative prestige in the general occupational system. Within the profession, however, and especially within the same faculty, there is strong pressure to establish a correspondence between professional competence and the salaries paid. Failure to do so is a prime source of integrative strain.

I have taken the space to discuss the relation among the allocation of fluid resources, the institutionalization of contract, property, and occupation, and the market and money in some detail because such an analysis is more comprehensive than any Durkheim was in a position to give, and thus provides a larger setting in which to evaluate the true importance of his basic insights about organic solidarity. His crucial insight is that there must be, in this area, a whole complex of institutionalized norms as a condition of the stability of a functionally differentiated system. In *De la division du travail social*, Durkheim did not go very far in analyzing the motivations underlying adherence to such norms. But he was entirely clear on one central point, namely, that this adherence on the part of the acting unit in the system could not be motivated primarily by considerations of expedient utility. This is the basic reason why the concept of the *conscience collective* as consisting in "beliefs and sentiments held in common" is of such central importance. In his later work, he took three major steps bearing on this question of motivation. Before attempting to outline these, however, it is well to discuss briefly the relation of the *conscience collective* to organic solidarity and the relation of organic and mechanical solidarity to each other.

Concerning the first of these two problems, Durkheim seems to have been genuinely confused, for he failed to clarify the structural distinction between values and norms, which I have presented earlier, and did not see that this distinction applies and is relevant equally to organic and mechanical solidarity. Instead, he got bogged down in the identification of mechanical solidarity with a lack of differentiation of structure, and hence with the similarity of roles which are personal expressions of the community of beliefs and sentiments. Consequently, he had no clear criteria for defining the relation of functionally differentiated norms to the *conscience collective*. Durkheim's treatment of the conception of the "dynamic density" of a social system and its relation to competition, represents, as Schnore has pointed out,[10] a valid attempt to solve the problem of the processes of structural differentiation, but he did not succeed in linking it to his master concept of the *conscience collective*.

It is now possible to state this fundamental relation more adequately: As noted above, the crucial component of the *conscience collective* is common societal values. Commitment to such values, carefully interpreted with reference to the object concerned—that is, the society as such—and to the level of generality or specification, is one major component of the general phenomenon of institutionalization. Institutionalization is, in turn, the primary basis, at the level of the integration of the social system, of Durkheim's "solidarity." But with respect to any fundamental function of the social system, values must be specified in terms of their relevance to that particular function. Furthermore, values must be brought to bear on the legitimation of the differentiated institutionalized norms which are necessary to regulate behavior in the area of that function—to regulate it, on the one hand, in relation to the concrete exigencies under which it operates, and, on the other, in relation to the interest of the society as a system. Legitimation itself, however, is not enough; in addition, there must be the functions of defining jurisdiction, of defining and administering sanctions, and of interpreting the norms themselves.

This basic complex of relationships and functions can be quite clearly worked out for the division of labor as an economic phenomenon and for the institutions clustering around it. This complex was Durkheim's primary reference; and, except for the fact that his formulation of its relation to the *conscience collective* is ambiguous, he made an excellent start on analyzing it. But he did not see that the properties of the contractual complex are directly paralleled by those of the complex involving mechanical solidarity. I have suggested that this parallel primarily concerns the relations between common values and the institutionalization of political function in the society. Here also, the values must be specified at a concrete level in order to legitimize not only society in the broadest sense, but also the type of organization which is institutionalized in it for the attainment of collective goals. This organization is, however, a differentiated functional area which in certain fundamental respects is parallel to, or cognate with, that of the mobilization of fluid resources. Furthermore, it involves differentiated structures within itself at the norm, collectivity, and role levels. Hence the relation of values to norms is essentially the same in this area as in the economic. The norms must be legitimated, but, in addition, jurisdictions must be defined, sanctions specified, and norms interpreted. The *conscience collective* does not perform these functions directly or automatically. The differentiated normative complex which centers on the institutionalization of leadership and authority parallels the complex which centers on contract, property, and occupational role in the economic area. Power is a measure and medium that in those respects which are relevant is parallel to money.[11]

Durkheim's treatment involves a further complication, namely, the problem of evolutionary sequence. He made two crucially important points in this connection. The first is that the development of the patterns of organic solidarity that are connected with an extensive division of labor presupposes the existence of a system of societal integration characterized by mechanical solidarity. The second is that the economic division of labor and an elaborated and differentiated governmental organization develop concomitantly. It is not a case of one's developing at the expense of the other.

Sound as these two insights were, Durkheim's association of mechanical solidarity with a lack of structural differentiation inclined him toward identifying this association with primitiveness in an evolutionary sense, and prevented him from making the essential connection between common values and the legitimation of the political order and organization in a more differentiated, modern type of society. The relation of modern political institutions to solidarity—very much like that of economic institutions to solidarity—was simply left hanging in the air.

I should like to suggest, therefore, a refinement of Durkheim's classification. If organic solidarity and mechanical solidarity are correlative terms, one should refer to the type of solidarity which focuses on the legitimation of political institutions, and the other to that type which focuses on economic institutions. Broadly speaking, we may say that, although the situation varies substantially with the type of social structure, both exist simultaneously in parts of the same social system, parts that can be distinguished on the basis of structure and through analysis; and there should be no general tendency for one to replace the other. The solidarity which exists prior to the development of any of the higher levels of social differentiation is not the same thing as this "political" type. The latter is closer to the principal referent of Durkheim's mechanical solidarity, but I should prefer another term—"diffuse solidarity," for example. It is the common matrix out of which *both* the others have emerged by a process of differentiation.

Durkheim seems to have faced a very common difficulty in dealing with the processes of differentiation. When a component of a system retains the same name at a later, more highly differentiated phase in the development of the system that it had at an earlier, less differentiated one, the component carrying the original name will have less importance in the later phase. This follows inevitably from the fact that in the earlier phase it may have designated one of, say, four cognate components, and in the later phase one of eight. This diminishing of importance is often attributed to "a loss of functions" or "a decline in strength" on the part of the component named. Good examples in contemporary Western society are "family" and "religion."[12] These names have been used throughout the successive phases of our development, but the components they have designated have not remained cognate. The modern urban family whose function of economic production has been transferred to occupational organizations is not cognate with the peasant household which is a principal unit of production, in addition to being, like the modern one, a unit for the rearing of children and the regulation of personality. In its capacity as a unit of production, the peasant family is, in fact, a "family firm," but the term "firm" is usually not applied to it.

One qualification of this argument, touching upon the hierarchical ordering of functions in social systems, should be made. This is that political organization, within an institutionalized framework of order, must indeed precede, in the developmental sequence, the emergence of a highly differentiated market type of economy. Hence there is some empirical justification, even within the framework I have sketched, for Durkheim's saying that mechanical solidarity precedes organic solidarity.

As previously noted, in *De la division du travail social* Durkheim had much to say about the role of institutionalized norms but little about the character of the motivation underlying commitment to values and to conformity with norms. However, his clear insight that the operation of the "rational pursuit of self-interest" as interpreted in utilitarian and economic theory does not offer an explanation of this commitment, provided a setting for approaching the problem. In his earlier phases, Durkheim tended to be content with the formula of "exteriority and constraint" in an interpretation which treated norms as though they were simply among the "facts of life" in the situation of the individual, a formula which did not help to solve the fundamental difficulty presented by utilitarianism. In *Le suicide,* however, and in his work on the sociology of education, he took two important steps beyond this position which I shall sketch briefly.

The first is his discovery and partial development of the idea of the internalization of values and norms. The second is the discrimination he makes, with special reference to the problem of the nature of modern "individualism," between two ranges of variation. One of these concerns types of institutionalized value-norm complexes, and is exemplified by the distinction between egoism and altruism. The other concerns the types of relations that the individual can have to whatever norms and values are institutionalized. Here the discrimination between "egoism" and "anomie" is crucial; it is parallel to that between "altruism" and "fatalism." I shall briefly take up each in turn.

Concerning the internalization of values and norms, we may say that, within certain limits, actual behavior in the economic and political fields can be relatively well interpreted in terms of the processes by which the individual adapts himself rationally to the existence of the norms and the sanctions attached to them, so that they simply become a part of the "facts of life." Durkheim saw clearly that the existence and functional indispensability of the institutionalization of these norms is independent of the interests of the units, but he did not have a theory to explain, in terms of motivation, the process by which institutions are established and maintained. His "sociologistic positivism"[13] prevented his formulating such a theory.

Durkheim was led to make his study of suicide by a paradox: According to utilitarian theory, a rising standard of living should bring about a general increase in "happiness"; however, concomitant with the certain rise in the standard of living in Western countries, there was a marked rise in the suicide rate. Why was it that as people became happier, more of them killed themselves?

It is not necessary to review here Durkheim's famous marshalling of facts and his analysis of them. What concerns us is that the decisive break-through in solving the paradox came about with his working out of the concept of anomie. To be sure, anomie was only one of the four components in his analysis of the reasons underlying variations in the suicide rate, but it is the decisive theoretical one in the present context.

The older view, which the early Durkheim shared, saw the goals of the action of the individual as located within his own personality, and saw social norms, which were "exterior" to him, as located in society, which was a "reality *sui generis.*" Because they were located in two different systems, the goals of the individual and the norms of society were dissociated from each other. Durkheim's concept of anomie was a formulation of his great insight that this dissociation was untenable, that the goals of the individual could not be treated as being independent of the norms and values of the society, but were, in fact, "given meaning," that is, legitimized, by these values. They must, therefore, belong to the same system. If personal goals were part of the personality, then values and norms, the *conscience collective,* must also be part of the personality. At the same time, Durkheim could not abandon the doctrine of the independence of institutional norms from the "individual." This was the very core of his conception of solidarity, and to abandon it would have meant reverting to the utilitarian position. Hence the only solution was the conception of the interpenetration of personality and social system, the conception that it must be true, in some sense, that values and norms were parts of the "individual consciousness," and were, at the same time, analytically independent of "the individual." In the earlier stages, Durkheim attempted to solve this problem by the conception that there were two "consciousnesses" within the same personality, but gradually he tended to abandon this view.

It is noteworthy that Durkheim, working in sociology, discovered essentially the same basic phenomenon of internalization and interpenetration as did Freud in his study of the personality, and that the same discovery was made independently by Charles Horton Cooley and George Herbert Mead. This convergence is, in my opinion, one of the great landmarks in the development of modern social science.

To restate Durkheim's main point concerning the operation of anomie: An individual does not commit suicide primarily because he lacks the "means" to accomplish his goals, but because his goals cannot be meaningfully integrated with the expectations which have been institutionalized in values and norms. The factors responsible for this malintegration may be social, cultural, or psychological in any combination, but the crucial point of strain concerns the meaningfulness of situations and of alternatives of action. This problem of meaning could not arise if norms and values were merely parts of the external situation and not of the actual "beliefs and sentiments" of the individual.

Durkheim left many problems connected with the clarification and interpretation of anomie unresolved, but his concept clearly pointed the way to a theory of the problem of social control which was not susceptible to his own criticism of utilitarianism, and could, when linked to modern psychological insight into the personality, lead to a theory of the motivation underlying conformity and deviation, and hence to a theory of the mechanisms by which solidarity is established and maintained.

On psychological grounds, it can be said that since internalized values and norms, as well as some of the components of goals, are involved in the motivation to conformity, certain crucial components of that motivation, and of the mechanisms by which it is established, maintained, and restored, are not fully or directly attributable to "reason." In other words, it is not enough merely to make clear to the actor what the situation is and what the consequences of alternative courses of action are likely to be; for the mechanisms and components of motivation, and the components of the mechanisms of social control that mirror the various aspects of this motivation, are non-rational. This puts the mechanisms of social control in a class that is different from that of the market, the ordinary exercise of political leadership and power, of legislation and of the administration—in its higher judicial aspects—of the legal system.

Those aspects of illness which can be associated with "psychic" factors, and the corresponding features of the therapeutic process which treats them, can serve as a prototype of this kind of mechanism, and can be systematically related to the processes of interaction that are involved in the socialization of the child.[14] It is, however, equally clear that there is need for an elaboration of theory in this field which is parallel to that which I have previously outlined for the problem area of organic solidarity in so far as it concerns economic institutions and markets. Clearly, not all social control that is oriented to motivation concerns illness and therapy. For example, it seems very likely that the practice of law has cognate functions over a considerable area in our own society. Lawyers, however, are not therapists. The subsystem of the society which presents problems of social control to which lawyers are relevant is not an individual personality, as is the one to which physicians are relevant, but a system that involves two or more parties in their relations to the normative system which regulates all of them. Hence there is more than one attorney, and there are courts. Here the analogue of anomie is a situation in which norms, and possibly the values that lie behind them, are not sufficiently well defined to place clients in a meaningful situation for action so that the pressure of this situation tends to motivate them to act "irrationally." This need not, however, imply that they have psychopathological personalities. Again it is the relational system, not the individual, which needs straightening out. It seems to me that Durkheim's own treatment of religious ritual provides another example, on which I shall remark briefly later.

It should also be noted that in following up this line of reasoning in the years following the publication of *Le suicide,* Durkheim made, in his work on education, the first major contribution to the sociological analysis of the socialization of the child.[15] It was in this connection that he was able to clarify more fully his theory of the nature of the internalization of values and norms by redefining constraint as the exercise of moral authority through the *conscience* of the individual. In this way, it became clear that the moral component of the *conscience collective* is social: first, in that it is made up of values that are common to, and shared by, the members of the society; second, in that through the process of socialization the new members of the society undergo a process by which these values are internalized; and, third, in that there are special mechanisms which re-enforce the commitment to the values thus made in ways that involve the non-rational layers of the personality structure, so that deviation is counteracted by curative mechanisms. With this definition, Durkheim provided a new understanding of the operation of the social system—one which was scarcely within the purview of the Durkheim of *De la division du travail social*.

The other main contribution of *Le suicide* to the present discussion is the conception of what may be called "institutionalized individualism," at the center of which is Durkheim's concept of *égoïsme* as distinguished from anomie. This is an extension of the basic insight of *De la division du travail social*, but here Durkheim applies it in an altogether novel context and links it with the problems of social control just discussed.

Utilitarianism and with it the methodological individualism (verging on reductionism) of our intellectual tradition have tended to interpret the emphasis placed on the sphere of freedom and the expected independent achievement of the unit of a system as meaning that the unit is free from the controls of the system. It has thus reduced the importance of the integration of the system, whether positively or negatively valued. Spencerian individualism was the negation of social control in the present sense of this concept.

There is, of course, an obvious sense in which this is true, for immediate control by direct authority is incompatible with individual freedom. But there is another and deeper sense in which it is not true. An institutionalized order in which individuals are expected to assume great responsibility and strive for high achievement, and in which they are rewarded through socially organized sanctions of such behavior, cannot be accounted for by postulating the lessening of all aspects of institutionalized control. Instead, such an order, with its common values, its institutionalized norms, its sanctions and media, its mechanisms of social control, represents a particular mode of institutional structuring. It emphatically does not represent anomie, which is the weakening of control in the sense of the weakening of solidarity.

The classic empirical formulation of this point in *Le suicide* is in connection with the Protestant-Catholic differential. The Catholic is, in matters of religion, subjected to the direct control of the authorities of his church: he must accept official dogma on penalty of excommunication; he must accept the sacramental authority of the priest in the matter of his own salvation, and so on. The Protestant church as a collectivity does not exercise this kind of authority. A Protestant is free of these types of control. But he is not free to choose whether or not to accept such controls, for he may not, if he wishes to remain a good Protestant, relinquish his freedom to accept religious responsibility imposed on him in his direct relation to God. The obligation to accept such responsibility is legitimized by the common values of the Protestant group and is translated into norms governing behavior.

Largely for ideological reasons, this basic insight is still far from being fully assimilated into the thinking of social scientists. But there are few of Durkheim's contributions which do more in relating the theoretical approach to the analysis of social systems, to the empirical interpretation of the major features of the modern type of society.

This problem brings us around to another very important link between the two dominant themes in Durkheim's original treatment of the problems of social integration; namely, the relation between organic and mechanical solidarity. Clearly, there is a relation between the egoistic factor in suicide and organic solidarity, and between the altruistic factor and mechanical solidarity. This becomes manifest in the association between areas of the social structure in which the collectivity is tightly integrated (such as the army) and there is a high incidence of altruistic suicide, and those in which market relations predominate (the professions and business, for example) and there is a high frequency of egoistic suicide. A parallel correlation may be seen between types of societies.

However, correlations such as these raise the question of the kinds of mechanisms which are associated with the different problems of integration. Very early Durkheim emphasized the importance of the definitions of certain acts as criminal and of prescriptions for punishing them as mechanisms that re-enforce mechanical solidarity. In *De la division du travail social,* he used this re-enforcement primarily as a foil to highlight the contrast with the functioning of civil law in relation to organic solidarity. In this connection, his primary reference was clearly to the solidarity of the collectivity as the main structural focus of the problem of integration.

It is noteworthy that, in his last period, Durkheim came around to a field which is, in terms of the above analysis, very closely related to the problems of mechanical solidarity, but this time the relation is seen from the point of view of values rather than from that of their political implementation. I am referring to his analysis of religion in its relation to society in *Les formes élémentaires de la vie religieuse.* There are many notable features in this work, but the one of special interest here is the treatment of religious ritual as a mechanism for the re-enforcement of social solidarity.

The most important link between this work and *De la division du travail social,* written twenty years earlier, is Durkheim's continuing concern with the *conscience collective.* However, in the earlier work this concept was used merely as a reference point for the analysis of the economic level of social differentiation, and the attendant problems of integration. In the later one, by contrast, the question of the primary role of the *conscience collective* in the social system as a whole comes to the center of the stage. As Durkheim treats it, ritual of the communal sort is the direct expression of the commitment of members of the collectivity—that is, the highest-level relevant social system—to the values which they hold in common. But it is, at the same time, more than just an expression of them, for it is a way in which through "dramatization" these commitments may be renewed and any tendencies to weaken them may be forestalled.

It is quite clear that religious ritual as it is conceived in this work is not directly concerned with the formulation and implementation of norms, but rather with the "inward," the internalized aspects of the systems of values and norms, with their direct involvement in the structure of personalities. Moreover, it concerns their relation to motivation in the context of the non-rational components referred to above. Therefore, in this last major phase of his work, Durkheim was clearly building on the results he had attained in his studies of suicide and education. But here for the first time he regarded the maintenance of the institutionalized value system in the society as a focus of social process, rather than as a point of reference from which to analyze other structures and processes.

There is, at the same time, an interesting return to his original reference points, for he explicitly takes up the problem of the role of the *conscience collective*—that is, of collective values —at the level of the value system, rather than at that of the structure of the concrete collectivity and of the obligations to it. Therefore, he ends up placing his original problem of organic solidarity within a more general framework of order, one in which there is a political organization which can enforce a uniform criminal law, but in which there is also a system of values which can legitimize norms that are independent of the particular political order and its "organs."

This was a major step in the differentiation of the theoretical components of the hydra-headed problem of social integration. It is perhaps significant, however, that Durkheim dealt with the problem of religious ritual in empirical detail only in the context of the primitive religions. I interpret this to mean that the old problem of the relation between the genetic and the analytical aspects of the problem of discrimination of components still plagued him. In a way, he simply drove the problem of mechanical solidarity back to a more generalized level, seeking the "origins" of repressive law in the religious commitments that are ritualized in the great tribal ceremonies. In so doing, he contributed enormously to our understanding of processes of social control at this level, an understanding that definitely included their motivational reference. But by virtue of his unfortunate confusion, he obscured rather than illuminated the problem of the relations of solidarity to the structural differentiation of modern society, the analysis of which was his original point of reference.

There is almost complete agreement that Durkheim was one of a very small company of sociological theorists who, during a critical phase in the development of the discipline, penetrated to deeper levels of analysis than had been reached by any of their predecessors and who formulated the main problems on which we have been working ever since. The subject of this paper is, I think, the focal center of Durkheim's contribution to theory. He was the theorist par excellence of the problem area of social integration. He was more concerned with the primary core of the social system itself than with the relations of that system to those that border it—culture, personality, and the organism in the physical environment. In addition, he was not, in a sense, greatly concerned with problems of social structure. Though he always retained an interest in making comparative studies, he did not attempt to probe the crucial problems of comparative morphological classification so deeply as did his contemporary Max Weber.

Durkheim's central problem, the solution of which he pursued with rare persistence, was to determine the major axes around which the integrative functions and processes of a society are organized. His analysis was marred by many crudities, and there are many aspects of it which have become obsolete; but his criticism of the utilitarian tradition and his conceptions of the *conscience collective,* and of mechanical and organic solidarity—though raising many problems of interpretation—served both him and the discipline well.

The important thing about these conceptions is that they cut across the lines of the conventional structural analysis of social systems, which broke them down into political, economic, religious, and other similar categories. Only with a conceptualization such as Durkheim's was it possible to approach the problems of social integration on a level that is general enough to permit the establishment of a new theoretical orientation. The fact that he succeeded in developing this conceptualization is the basis of Durkheim's stature as a theorist.

Durkheim discovered determinate theoretical relations among a whole range of empirical subject matters which are usually parceled out among different disciplines and specialties within disciplines. In *De la division du travail social,* he established relations between law and the traditional empirical subject matter of economics, subsuming both of them under a larger theoretical perspective. He also included fruitful discussions of political matters, in which he observed that government has developed concomitantly with the economy of private enterprise. In his later work, he carried his analysis of connections into the field of psychological theory; he was driven to this by the logic of the problems he wished to solve, although he had said originally that psychological considerations are irrelevant to sociological problems. His investigations into psychological theory enabled him not only to enrich his own analysis but also to establish the basis of a remarkable convergence with Freud, thereby providing a means by which the conceptions of rationality of the economic tradition of thought and the role of the non-rational components of motivation in the psychoanalytic tradition could be linked. Finally, in his later work he analyzed the relevance of religion to the secular aspects of social organization.

This remarkable ability to see relations among fields usually treated as unconnected was possible only because Durkheim constantly kept in mind the fact that he was dealing with the problem of integration of a single system, not a congeries of discrete subsystems. He was a theorist par excellence of the functioning of systems.

In the above discussion, I have stressed many of the complications and difficulties underlying Durkheim's analyses. He was undoubtedly highly selective and was, therefore, in a sense, "biased"—take, for example, his confusing of the evolutionary and the analytical problems in relation to the status of mechanical solidarity. The structural problems can be greatly clarified by building on the tradition of Weber, and the relations to personality can be greatly clarified by mobilizing psychological knowledge which either did not exist in Durkheim's time or was contained in works in which (like the earlier ones of Freud) he showed no interest.

Such critical analysis results in considerable revision of Durkheim's positions. It does not result in refutation of them, however. It involves only extension and refinement, for Durkheim established the basic foundations for developing a fruitful theory of social integration.

1. I have always considered the focal point of Durkheim's early work in this respect to lie in "Organic and Contractual Solidarity" (Book I, Chap. vii), *The Division of Labor in Society,* trans. George Simpson (Glencoe, Ill.: Free Press of Glencoe, Illinois, 1947). It starts as a critique of Spencer but actually goes clear back to Hobbes.

2. One reason for this is that the hypothetical turning-over of absolute authority to an unrestricted sovereign was empirically incompatible with the existence of the liberal governmental regimes which were a commonplace in the Western World of Durkheim's time. On this phase of the history of thought the best source is still, without question, Elie Halévy, *The Growth of Philosophic Radicalism,* trans. Mary Morris ([1901-4] New York: Macmillan Co., 1928).

3. Durkheim does not, of course, in his more general discussion, confine himself to contract at the legal or other levels. He relates organic solidarity also to domestic, commercial, procedural, administrative, and constitutional law. Cf. *The Division of Labor in Society,* p. 122.

4. *De la division du travail social* (Paris: Félix Alcan, 1893), p. 46.

5. The term "normative culture" will be used a number of times below. Here "normative" refers to any "level" of culture, the evaluative judgments of which govern or define standards and allocations at the level below. This usage is to be distinguished from those which refer to differentiated norms designating, in a particular system, one level in the hierarchy of normative culture.

6. Such a system of societal values may, of course, change over a period of time, but it is the most stable component of the social structure.

7. "The acts that it [repressive law] prohibits and qualifies as crimes are of two sorts. Either they directly manifest very violent dissemblance between the agent who accomplishes them and the collective type, or else they offend the organ of the common conscience."—*The Division of Labor in Society,* p. 106. The context makes clear that by the "organ" Durkheim means the government.

8. There is, of course, a sense in which the criminal law also lays down norms. Essentially, these norms concern the minimum standards of behavior which are considered acceptable on the part of members of the society—regardless of their differentiated functions—who are not disqualified by mental incapacity, and so on. In a highly differentiated society, however, the largest body of norms increasingly concerns the relations between differentiated functions in the fields Durkheim enumerated; namely, contract, family life, commerce, administration, and the constitutional structure of the collectivity.

9. Talcott Parsons, *The Social System* (Glencoe, Ill.: Free Press of Glencoe, Illinois, 1951), pp. 36-45.

10. Cf. Leo F. Schnore, "Social Morphology and Human Ecology," *American Journal of Sociology,* LXIII (1958), 620-34.

11. Unfortunately, space does not permit developing this line of analysis further. Several statements, which, though brief and incomplete, are somewhat more extensive than the one found here, will be found in Talcott Parsons, "Authority, Legitimation and Political Process," in *Authority*, ed. Carl J. Friedrich (Cambridge, Mass.: Harvard University Press, 1958), and Talcott Parsons, " 'Voting' and the Equilibrium of the American Political System," in *American Voting Behavior*, ed. Eugene Burdick and Arthur J. Brodbeck (Glencoe, Ill.: Free Press of Glencoe, Illinois, 1958). Max Weber's treatment of authority constitutes an essential complement to Durkheim's of mechanical solidarity.

12. I have dealt with these two cases in, respectively, *Family, Socialization and Interaction Process* (Glencoe, Ill.: Free Press of Glencoe, Illinois, 1956), Chap. i, and "Some Reflections on Religious Organization in the United States," *Daedalus*, LXXXVII (1958). This, and the paper from *Authority* cited in n. 11 above, are included in the collection of my essays published under the title *Structure and Process in Modern Societies* (Glencoe, Ill.: Free Press of Glencoe, Illinois, 1960).

13. Talcott Parsons, *The Structure of Social Action* (New York: McGraw-Hill Book Co., 1937), Chaps. viii-ix.

14. Parsons, *The Social System*, Chap. vii.

15. Most notably in *L'Education morale* (Paris: Félix Alcan, 1923), and in the volume of essays, *Education and Sociology*, trans. Sherwood Fox ([1922] Glencoe, Ill.: Free Press of Glencoe, Illinois, 1956).

DURKHEIM AND FUNCTIONALISM[1]

ALBERT PIERCE

It is commonly assumed that Emile Durkheim has exerted considerable influence on contemporary functionalist schools in sociology and anthropology. In order to understand the true nature of this influence, however, it is necessary to determine in what sense, if any, Durkheim himself can be classified as a functionalist.[2] This does not mean that a definition of functionalism that is sufficiently broad to include Durkheim's work has never been formulated, for as Buckley sagaciously observes:

> If the label [functionalism] means only that social systems are seen as integrated to some extent and can be analyzed into certain elements that may be related to other elements and to the operation of the system as a whole—then as someone has suggested, we are all functionalists.[3]

I shall attempt herein to discover the degree to which we are justified in calling Durkheim a "functionalist" in any modern meaning of the term. An obvious first step in this undertaking is to analyze the various ways in which Durkheim used the word "function" (la fonction), being careful to avoid certain errors. First, one must not confuse Durkheim's incidental use of the word as it occurs in everyday language with his usage of it as a key technical term. Second, in analyzing a concept one should be aware of possible discrepancies among its *explicit meaning,* as given in its formal definition; its *implicit meaning,* as indicated by the way it is used in a context; and its *implicit use,* which is revealed by the organization of the research and analysis. Third, we must not assume that contemporary usage of the term is in accord with Durkheim's. There is, for instance, as we shall subsequently see, a widespread modern tendency to equate "functions" with "needs," whereas there is cogent evidence that Durkheim sharply distinguished between them. Finally, there is the question whether function, however it is defined, represents only a limited aspect of Durkheim's thought or one of its major focal points.

154

In Simpson's English translation of *De la division du travail social*, we find two statements which would seem to establish rather conclusively that for Durkheim "function" and "social need" are virtually synonymous: "[We shall look first for] the function of the division of labor, that is to say, what social need it satisfies," and, "To ask what the function of the division of labor is, is to seek for the need which it supplies."[4] In the French original, the passages read: "Nous chercherons d'abord quelle est la fonction de la division du travail, c'est-à-dire à quel besoin social elle correspond," and, "Se demander quelle est la fonction de la division du travail, c'est donc chercher à quel besoin elle correspond."[5] A meticulously precise analyst like Durkheim would not have used *correspondre* as a synonym for *servir* or *satisfaire*. His usage clearly implies a distinction between "need" and "function."

Although for Durkheim "needs" are highly impersonal, they are something that can be satisfied, fulfilled, or served. Yet he very explicitly states:

> One assumes that in a healthy organism, each detail, so to speak, has a useful role to play; that each internal state corresponds exactly to some external condition and consequently performs its part in assuring vital equilibrium and diminishing the likelihood of death. However, it is legitimate to suppose to the contrary that certain anatomical or functional arrangements serve no direct purpose but exist simply because they exist—because they cannot not exist, the general conditions of life being as they are.[6]

It is clear from this passage that Durkheim made an analytical distinction between "function" and the utility which the term "need" implies; and although he specifically states that one important activity of the sociologist is to demonstrate the social need to which the function is related, this distinction must not be obscured.

So far as I have been able to discover, Durkheim never speaks of the function of the whole of society. He uses the word only when discussing some part or aspect of a society, such as the division of labor or religion. Conversely, he always uses the term "need" to designate a characteristic of the totality because there is no specific component of the society to which the need can be ascribed. The exception to this is his use of the term to refer to individual needs, but in this case his reference only serves to deny their sociological importance.

Perhaps these terms can be clarified by noting certain additional distinctions which Durkheim makes. If we have a social phenomenon that is to be explained, we may distinguish the following: (1) its cause; (2) the effect of that cause, that is, the phenomenon itself; (3) its function; (4) the social need that it serves; and (5) the mental anticipation (*l'anticipation mentale*) of individual members of the society. This last category refers to the conscious expectations or aspirations of individual members of the society, which may be represented by an end or a goal. Mental anticipations relative to the phenomenon in question may or may not exist. Even if they are present, however, they have no causal efficacy, and are, in any case, too indeterminate and indeterminable to be very useful for sociological analysis. They are the result, rather than the cause, of the social need. As evidence of the distinctions we have claimed, we may cite the following passages:

> . . . Social phenomena do not result from a mental anticipation of the function they are required to perform, for that function is, at least in a number of cases, to maintain the pre-existent cause of the phenomena. One will easily find the function if the cause is already known.[7]

> Therefore, when one undertakes to explain a social phenomenon, it is necessary to seek separately the efficient cause which produces it and the function that it fulfills.

> We use the word "function" in preference to "end" or "goal" because, in general, social phenomena do not exist in anticipation of the useful results they produce. What one must determine is whether there is a correspondence between the fact in question and the general needs of the social organism, and in what that correspondence consists, without concerning oneself with whether or not it has been intentional. All these questions of intention are, moreover, too subjective to lend themselves to scientific treatment.[8]

> Intention is too intimate a thing to be comprehended by outside observation [*du dehors*] save in a grossly approximate manner. It

is even hidden from self-observation. How many times we misunderstand the true reasons for our actions! We repeatedly impute to generous impulses or lofty motives actions inspired by petty sentiments and blind habit.

Moreover, in general, an act cannot be defined by the end envisaged by the agent since the same system of actions can, without changing its nature, be adapted to too many different ends.[9]

. . . The causes which determine the social current, act at the same time on the individuals and dispose them to yield to the collective action.[10]

. . . In a word, just as society to a large extent molds the individual, it shapes him, correspondingly, in its own image. It cannot fail to have the material it needs because it is, so to speak, prepared by its own hands.[11]

The use of the verb "needs" in the last passage should be noted for subsequent reference. One should further note that Durkheim was well aware of "voluntaristic" or "means-end" analysis and acutely sensitive to its shortcomings.[12]

Since functionalism as used today has reference, as we shall see, to either "functions" or "needs" or both, and since Durkheim retained these as analytically distinct categories, the question arises as to what he meant by each of these terms. By the "function" of a social phenomenon, Durkheim appears to mean any significant but unobvious effect it has on the general condition or development of the society. In some instances, the function of a phenomenon is the contribution it makes to maintaining the causes that have given rise to it.

In fact, the bond of solidarity which unites the cause with the effect has a reciprocal quality which has not sufficiently been recognized. No doubt the effect cannot exist without its cause, but the cause in return needs its effect. It is from the cause that the effect draws its energy, an energy which returns to the cause. Consequently, if the effect disappears, there are repercussions on the cause. For example, the social reaction that demands punishment is brought about by the intensity of the collective sentiments that have been offended by the crime. However, the crime has the useful function of maintaining these sentiments at the same degree of intensity; for they would soon lose their force if the offenses

157

that they opposed were not punished. Similarly, as the social milieu grows more complex and variable, any disturbing of existing beliefs causes them to become somewhat more indeterminate and flexible, and the faculties of reflection are developed. These faculties are indispensable to societies and to individuals in that they enable them to adjust themselves to a more mobile and complex environment. As men are obliged to labor more intensively, the products of that labor become more numerous and of better quality, for more abundant and better products are necessary to compensate for the expense that the greater work entails. Therefore, social phenomena do not result from a mental anticipation of the function they are required to perform, for that function is, at least in a number of cases, to maintain the pre-existent cause of the phenomena. One will easily find the function if the cause is already known.[13]

Other examples are not difficult to find.

> We are thus led to consider the division of labor from a new point of view. . . . [from which] the economic services that it can render are seen to be of little consequence when compared with the moral effect that it produces, its true function being to create among two or more individuals a sentiment of solidarity.[14]

Many more illustrations could be adduced, but the point would seem to be established. One additional qualification, however, should be noted: Although Durkheim was apparently willing to regard some non-effective elements in the make-up of society as having "functions," he did not regard as "functional" anything that was so destructive of an organism as to threaten its very existence.[15]

Having considered the meaning of "function" in Durkheim's work, we may now turn to his definition of "needs." According to the anthropologist Radcliffe-Brown, for Durkheim "needs" are the conditions necessary to the existence of human societies.[16] I cannot agree with this interpretation, which appears to be rather widely accepted; for although it reflects accurately the complete impersonality of Durkheim's "social needs," it misses entirely the essentially dynamic nature of his conception of society. His concept of a society's needs might more aptly be described as being the immanent consequences of its development. For whatever resemblance Durkheim may bear to modern functionalists, he differs radically from them in his preoccupation with social change. The interpretation of Durkheim's analysis of societies in terms of survival is seductively simple. It is important to recognize, however, that he never really concerned himself with the question of why societies survive. When he took cognizance of the fact that the "needs" of a society must in their aggregate be compatible with survival, he was making a concession to a logical tautology, rather than engaging in causal analysis. The unexpressed negative version of the tautology is, of course, that societies whose needs in the aggregate are not compatible with survival will perish.

> If the preponderance of social phenomena had a parasitic character, the budget of the organism would show a deficit, and social life would be impossible.[17]

Elsewhere we find the statement:

> . . . As in the case of the individual type, the collective type is formed under the influence of very diverse causes and even fortuitous circumstances. Produced by historical development, it bears the mark of all sorts of circumstances that the society has encountered in its history. It would be miraculous if everything found in it were adjusted to some useful end.[18]

"Needs," for Durkheim, cannot properly be understood apart from his conception of the autonomous nature of social phenomena—a conception sometimes inappropriately alluded to as his "social realism."[19] Reference has already been made to one example of Durkheim's use of "need" in this sense. The relevant passage reads in French, "La matière dont elle [la société] a besoin ne saurait donc lui manquer, car elle se l'est, pour ainsi dire, preparée de ses propres mains."[20] The "function" of a social phenomenon proves, in the last analysis, to be its causal contribution to the existing state of affairs; the "needs" of the social organism are the effects of the whole complex of its juxtaposed elements on anything contained within it.

Durkheim actually used the term "social needs" only rarely, and few of the contexts in which it appears give us any cogent clue as to precisely what he meant by it. For this reason, one might be tempted to regard his use of it in the example just given as merely figurative. If so, however, the same interpretation would have to be made of the "impersonal character" of social needs—and it is generally agreed that this term should be understood quite literally. Further evidence of what Durkheim designates by "social needs" will have to come largely from what has been referred to as his implicit usage of the term in discussions of the causal inefficacy of individual needs in determining social process. By implication, the efficacious needs involved in the process are society's.[21] Examples of this implicit usage occur in abundance, but a few should suffice to establish the point.

> We arrive, then, at the following rule: *The determining cause of a social fact must be sought among the antecedent social facts, and not among the individual states of consciousness.* Moreover, we can readily see that the preceding applies to the determination of the function as well as to that of the cause. The function of a social fact can only be social; that is, it consists in the production of socially useful effects. But it can no doubt happen and will happen that, consequently, the function will also be of service to the individual. But that fortunate result is not its immediate *raison d'être.* We may now complete the preceding proposition by saying that: *The function of a social fact must always be sought in the relationship the fact sustains with some social end.*[22]

In saying that the function of a social fact may also serve the individual, Durkheim implies that social facts implant in human agents such individual needs as are necessary to serve society's "need" (*fin sociale*—literally, "social end"). Furthermore, since "utility" and "need" are hardly separable, "socially useful effects" imply "social needs." This must be understood in the context of Durkheim's conception of societies *as things,*[23] things that are possessed of a high degree of autonomy or self-determination. In the light of this conception, society's "needs" become the consequences of its immanent development. This is particularly true when society acts to shape the mentalities and influence the conduct of its human agents, who are a necessary but insufficient condition of its existence. To Durkheim, society as *a thing* had attributes which can be ascertained if one knows the patterning of the activities of its human agents and which can be expressed as rates, norms of conduct, and so on. It is these latter, rather than the human agents through whom they are implemented, which constitute the "parts" or elements— the "social facts" characterized by "exteriority and constraint." This is the sum and substance of Durkheim's contention that society is a reality *sui generis*. The needs of the individual members of a society are social needs if, and only if, societal conditions give rise to them. Such an idea is, of course, contrary to the convictions of common sense, as Durkheim himself notes. Stated in another way, social needs are the attributes of a society that are involved, *inter alia*, in the determination of what the members of the society will define as their needs.

The basic thesis of *De la division du travail social* is one exemplification of this idea: An increase in the size and density of a population (these being attributes of the whole whose effects in patterning human activities make them social needs) comprise jointly a precipitating condition of the division of labor, which, in turn, brings about further growth and agglomeration in the population. A few brief passages will serve to illustrate:

> We are not saying that the growth and condensation *permit* a greater division of labor, but that they *necessitate* it. They do not constitute an instrument through which the division of labor is realized; they comprise its cause.[24]
>
> . . . All condensation of the social mass, especially if it is accompanied by an increase in the population, necessarily brings about an increase in the division of labor.[25]

The uses of "necessitate" and "necessarily" in the foregoing passages would seem to imply the active and impersonal nature of social need, as Durkheim conceived it, since there is one sense in which "necessity" may be equated with "need." The following passages from the same work are also relevant:

> In determining the principal cause of the development of the division of labor, we have simultaneously discovered the essential factor in what is called civilization.
>
> Civilization is itself a necessary consequence of changes in the

161

volume and density of societies. If science, art, and economic activity develop, this development follows from a necessity which imposes itself on men. There is no other manner in which they can live in the new conditions in which they are placed.

This is not to say that civilization serves no purpose, but rather that it is not the services it renders that cause it to progress. It develops because it cannot fail to develop. Once that development has taken place, it is found to be generally useful—or, at least, it is utilized. It responds to needs which are formed at the same time because they depend on the same causes. But this is an adjustment after the fact.[26]

Here it is rather the form of the whole that determines that of the parts. The society does not find the bases on which it rests already present in human minds [les consciences]; it puts them there itself.[27]

An additional example is found in another work.

If one can say that collective representations are, in a certain sense, exterior to individual consciences, this means that they do not derive from individuals in isolation but from them in the aggregate, and this is quite another matter. Undoubtedly, in the elaboration of the common result, each contributes his share, but private sentiments become social only under the impetus of *sui generis* forces that the association develops. Because of these combinations and the mutual changes which result from them, *they become something else.* . . . The emergent result [la résultante qui s'en dégage] transcends [déborde] each individual mind, as the whole transcends the part. It is in the whole just as it is for the whole. This is the sense in which the synthesis is exterior to the particulars. No doubt, each contains some of it, but it is not entirely in any one of them. In order to know its true nature, one must consider the aggregate in its totality.[28]

Thus we have the basic context required to understand Durkheim's concept of social need. Since, as we have seen, he did not regard societies as static; since he did not regard adaptive evolution as a sufficient explanation of social change; since he regarded social needs as impersonal and as determined independently of individual needs; and since he conceived those individual needs to be shaped by society for its own needs, social needs must be conceived as immanent tendencies of the social whole to influence its parts. Radcliffe-Brown's definition of "needs" as being the "necessary conditions of existence" presupposes a static or a social-Darwinian context, and Durkheim's conception of society is not either.

It would appear, then, that the social need is an attribute of the whole and is analogous to the function of the part. "Function" refers to the effect of the part on the whole; "social need," to that of the whole on the parts. However, the "parts" in the second half of our proposition appear to be much more explicitly related to human agents than is "part" in the first half; that is, the "whole" seems to work rather directly on individual minds in such forms as collective representations, whereas functions seem to mediate such things as population density, division of labor, social suicide rates, and the like.

We have now reached the point where we may consider the question to which our investigation has been leading: Should Durkheim be classified with any of the major groups who are today regarded as functionalists?[29] On first consideration this would appear to constitute a formidable project involving a rather detailed comparison of Durkheim with leading exponents of the various schools of thought that might lay claim to the title "functionalist." There can be little doubt that such a project, if properly carried out, would be a most instructive and valuable one. For reasons which should soon become clear, however, it is not necessary for the completion of our present task.

We can first eliminate from consideration all those who are called functionalists only because of an overly broad definition, of which Bredemeier's is a notable example: "The functional approach to sociology consists basically of an attempt to understand social phenomena in terms of the relationship to some system."[30] From this statement it would be difficult to discern who in the field of sociology is *not* a functionalist. Bredemeier himself would qualify, however, under a much less inclusive definition in that he appears to fall among the "structural functionalists," whom I shall consider shortly.

We can also quickly dispose of those who might be labeled functionalists by reason of the practical intent of their work.

Publishers, for example, often refer to their "marriage manuals" as "functional." One "reader" in the field is described as "suitable for use with all functional marriage texts." Its Table of Contents lists such topics as "Dating," "Love," "Buying Life Insurance," and so on. Durkheim, so far as I have been able to determine, was never professionally preoccupied with subjects of this nature.

Virtually all other contemporary groups to which the term "functionalist" is normally applied seem to fall into some combination of the following categories:[31] (1) those who, with heavy overtones of social Darwinism, imply adaptive adjustment in terms of the survival of the system; (2) those who stress individual needs, ends, or goals and reject conceptions of them that could not be translated into individual terms; and (3) those who make essentially "static" or "point-in-time" analyses, or at least regard "function" as a concept whose basic importance lies in its relationship to structure. We cannot here attempt a detailed documentation of all who would qualify under one or more of these categories, but a listing would include such anthropologists as Bronislaw Malinowski, A. R. Radcliffe-Brown, Gregory Bateson, and Ruth Benedict, and, in general, those sociologists who are under the influence of Talcott Parsons and who are commonly identified as structural functionalists. Robert K. Merton is a member of this latter group.

The question whether Durkheim can be considered a functionalist in any modern sense of the term finally resolves itself, then, into whether or not he fits into one or more of the categories listed. The answer to this question lies in the fact that his conceptions of function and need are inseparable from his basic conception of society. The key to the answer is supplied by a phrase that he reiterated again and again, namely, that society is a reality *sui generis,* that is, a reality of its own unique kind that cannot be translated into other terms. It is evident throughout his work that he thought of societies as dynamic things that do not change under the impetus of human will or in adjustment to external environment but because of factors within their own nature. For Durkheim functions and needs were not static, nor were social needs transferable to the individual level. It would surely be stretching the point to regard suicide as an individual need, yet Durkheim regarded the fluctuations in the social suicide rate as needs of the society. He believed that virtually any social phenomenon—crime, economic activity, population size and density, suicide, religious ritual, or whatever—ultimately proved to contribute, in one way or another, to the self-realization of the society.

Since I know of no significant contemporary school of sociologists who are regarded as "functionalists" and who share Durkheim's general conception of society or regard social functions and needs as part and parcel of the immanent changes occurring in the society; and since, virtually without exception, these modern functionalists transfer needs to the level of the individual conscious or subconscious, we must conclude that it would be erroneous to regard Durkheim as a functionalist in any of the commonly accepted contemporary meanings of the term.

Talcott Parsons has observed that "it cannot but strike the reader of his [Durkheim's] works how conspicuous by its absence from his thought is any clear-cut theory of social change."[32] An extension of Durkheim's sociology would logically have been the development of such a theory. For whether or not he had a clearly discernable *theory* of the patterns of social change, the *fact* of change itself was an inseparable part of his sociological theorizing. One may well wish that those aspiring to extend Durkheim's thinking had developed in this direction instead of reverting to formalistic structural analysis.

1. I am deeply indebted to Kurt H. Wolff and Roscoe C. Hinkle, Jr., for truly thoughtful and constructive criticisms of an earlier draft of this paper. Neither of them, of course, is responsible for the shortcomings of the present version.

2. That Durkheim is widely regarded as a functionalist seems hardly to require documentation. However, examples chosen at random are: Walter Buckley, "Structural-Functional Analysis in Modern Sociology," in *Modern Sociological Theory in Continuity and Change,* ed. Howard Becker and Alvin Boskoff (New York: Dryden Press, Inc., 1957), pp. 237-38; Lewis A. Coser and Bernard Rosenberg (eds.), *Sociological Theory* (New York: Macmillan Co., 1957), pp. 511-18; and Robert K. Merton, *Social Theory and Social Structure* (Glencoe, Ill.: Free Press of Glencoe, Illinois, 1949), p. 370 n. 66. It may also be noted that the leading figure in the so-called structural-functionalist school specifically acknowledges Durkheim's influ-

ence. See Talcott Parsons, *The Structure of Social Action* (2nd ed.; Glencoe, Ill.: Free Press of Glencoe, Illinois, 1949), *passim,* but especially p. D of the Preface to the second edition, and pp. 301-470, 708-14, and 717-18. We may also mention in passing the acknowledgment of Durkheim's influence made by such anthropologists as Bronislaw Malinowski and A. R. Radcliffe-Brown.

3. Buckley, *op. cit.,* p. 249.

4. Emile Durkheim, *The Division of Labor in Society,* trans. George Simpson (Glencoe, Ill.: Free Press of Glencoe, Illinois, 1947), pp. 45, 49. I assume that the reader is aware that Durkheim sharply distinguished "social needs" from "individual needs." Later we shall dwell on this point at greater length.

5. Emile Durkheim, *De la division du travail social* (5th ed.; Paris: Félix Alcan, 1926), pp. 8, 11.

6. Emile Durkheim, *Les règles de la méthode sociologique* (7th ed.; Paris: Félix Alcan, 1919), p. 64. All translations are my own unless the reference is to a specific one.

7. *Ibid.,* p. 119.

8. *Ibid.,* p. 117.

9. Emile Durkheim, *Le Suicide* (Paris: Félix Alcan, 1930), p. 4. This is an unmodified reprint of the first edition of 1897.

10. *Ibid.,* p. 365.

11. *Ibid.,* p. 366.

12. There will be no further comment here on this matter, but I am currently preparing a paper dealing with Durkheim's "convergence" and his alleged "positivism."

13. *Les règles de la méthode sociologique,* pp. 118-19.

14. *De la division du travail social,* p. 19.

15. Cf. *ibid.,* pp. 343-44.

16. A. R. Radcliffe-Brown, "On the Concept of Function in Social Science," *American Anthropologist,* XXXVII (1935), 394. This interpretation also receives the approval of Harry Alpert, in his book *Emile Durkheim and His Sociology* (New York: Columbia University Press, 1939), p. 107. Although we disagree on this particular point, I regard Alpert's book as by far the most perceptive and accurate of the extended interpretive treatments of Durkheim's work.

17. *Les règles de la méthode sociologique,* p. 119.

18. *De la division du travail social,* p. 75

19. For a discussion of this so-called realism, see Albert Pierce, "The

Scientific Adequacy of the Regional Approach," in Carle C. Zimmerman and Richard E. DuWors, *Graphic Regional Sociology* (Cambridge, Mass.: Phillips Book Store, 1952), pp. 195-99.

20. *Le suicide*, p. 366.

21. The assertion is sometimes made that Durkheim may have been uncertain whether he should assign so inconsequential a role to individual needs. This assertion is generally based on material in his pamphlet *Qui a voulu la guerre?* ("Who Wanted War?" [1915]), and is devoid of merit even when bolstered by its consonance with the specious theory that he had in the course of his life gradually moved from "positivism" to "idealism." In point of fact, he explicitly denies such a transition in his last major work; see *The Elementary Forms of the Religious Life*, trans. Joseph Ward Swain (Glencoe, Ill.: Free Press of Glencoe, Illinois, 1947), p. 208 n. 4. We cannot, in any case, accept as serious evidence for such a change this co-authored pamphlet written in the heat of wartime conditions with an unconcealed propagandistic objective. Durkheim could indeed have used his own involvement with such a pamphlet as evidence of the operation of "social constraint" upon himself.

22. *Les règles de la méthode sociologique*, p. 135. Italics are in the original. All evidence appears to indicate that for Durkheim all "social phenomena" are "social facts."

23. The specious objection to the "illegitimate reification" supposedly involved in regarding societies and other social facts "as things" was anticipated by Durkheim in the Preface to the second edition of *Les règles de la méthode sociologique*, pp. x ff. I have seen no compelling refutation of the position stated there.

24. *De la division du travail social*, p. 244. (Italics in the original.)

25. *Ibid.*, p. 250.

26. *Ibid.*, p. 328.

27. *Ibid.*, p. 342.

28. Emile Durkheim, *Sociologie et philosophie* (Paris: Presses Universitaires de France, 1951), pp. 35-36.

29. As used today, the terms "function" and "functional" have many definitions. A partial listing of those found in modern sociological and anthropological literature and conversation will bear out this claim:

1. "Function": A dependent mathematical variable whose value is determined by the values of one or more independent variables in accordance with a prescribed rule or formula for relating them; for example, $y = f(a, b)$.

2. "Function": An observable condition known to be at least partially predictable from other observable conditions. Human fertility, for example, is a function of religion and income.

3. "Function": A condition of "meaningful" interdependence among concepts or propositions which is such that a change in any one of them will call for changes in the others according to an accepted set of rules— say, the canons of logic. For example, if one changes any term of a valid syllogism, compensating change in at least one other term is called for if the validity of that syllogism is to be preserved.

4. "Function": Reciprocal effects among things (that is, substantive units) conceived within a framework of efficient causality. On the basis of this definition, a given conflict is accounted for by reference to specific acts on the parts of the participants: "I hit him because he hit me."

5. "Function": Reciprocal effects among variable attributes of a thing, such attributes being conceived within a framework of formal causality. This definition is implicit in the use of fluctuations in the "social suicide rate" of a society to predict concomitant fluctuations in other indexes of social solidarity, or vice versa.

6. "Functional": Anything conceived to be practical or useful in terms of some accepted value. When certain authors of textbooks designed to prepare students for married life refer to their approach as "functional," they are using the term in this sense.

7. "Functional": Anything that operates as it was designed to operate, whether or not one regards it as useful; for example, a hydrogen bomb made by an enemy, or a prayer wheel that actually spins.

8. "Functional analysis": Biological or psychological reductionism in which all human behavior is explained in terms of biopsychological "needs" or tensions of individuals.

9. "Functional analysis": Analysis in terms of a means-end schema in which for the purpose of that analysis the ends and norms are taken as constants or givens.

10. "Functional analysis": An analysis made in terms of the "needs" of a system, that is, in terms of the conditions necessary for the continuance of the system as a factually distinct complex. Such needs include the maintenance of security when it is threatened by destructive forces, the preservation of food resources, and so on.

11. "Functional analysis": An analysis of the components which any system must have to qualify as a system of a specified type, that is, to meet the requirements of a definition. Such an analysis would attempt to discover, for example, what characteristics any aggregation of people must have to qualify as a "functional entity."

12. "Functional analysis": An *ex hypothesi* demonstration of the relationships among the elements in an a priori conceptual scheme.

This list is by no means exhaustive, but it covers some of the more common contemporary usages. The complications that would arise in attempting to make such a list complete would come not so much from additional meanings as from ambiguous combinations of the definitions already given and from surreptitious semantic shifts from one meaning to another.

30. H. C. Bredemeier, "The Methodology of Functionalism," *American Sociological Review*, XX (1955), 173.

31. Excellent brief surveys of contemporary functionalist schools of the types to be considered may be found in Buckley, *op cit.*, pp. 240-59; and Nicholas S. Timasheff, *Sociological Theory: Its Nature and Growth* (Garden City, N. Y.: Doubleday & Co., Inc., 1955), pp. 219-29.

32. Parsons, *op. cit.*, p. 448.

DURKHEIM'S POLITICS AND
POLITICAL THEORY

MELVIN RICHTER

From an early date, Durkheim defined the scope of sociology broadly enough to include political theory.[1] In his classification of societies by types, he gave an important place to their political institutions and legal systems. And here, as elsewhere in his "scientific ethics," description led to prescription. Thus in his Introduction to the second edition of the *De la division du travail social* and in the final chapter of *Le suicide,* called significantly "Practical Consequences," he stated what functions the state and organized occupational groups ought to perform in modern society.[2] His advocacy of a syndicalism without violence as the cure for anomie and excessive egoism, along with his lectures on socialism, represented most of what was known about Durkheim's theory of the state until the publication in 1950 of *Leçons de sociologie.* This is a posthumous reconstruction of a course on the science of morals and law which Durkheim gave repeatedly at Bordeaux and Paris.[3] Its importance to his system is described in his pivotal essay of 1906, "La détermination du fait moral."[4] These lectures provide material for an analysis that up to now could only have been inferred, and this conjecturally, from his other works.

Durkheim's political theory would be worth study simply as the work of a powerful and original mind who influenced, in addition to his students, such thinkers as Jean Jaurès, Léon Duguit, and Georges Sorel.[5] And although Durkheim's political thought is surely not his greatest intellectual achievement, neither is it merely a negligible by-product of his sociological analysis. Anyone who seeks to understand Durkheim's work on its own terms, or who would determine what is living and what is dead in that work today, will find it worth while to know just what he wrote about government and what its political significance was at the time he wrote it.

Georges Gurvitch has remarked that Durkheim made his greatest contributions to sociology in the same way Columbus came upon the New World—while pursuing quite another objective.[6] What Durkheim sought was a science of ethics; his empirical studies, his speculative theories, he envisioned as a means to that end. Throughout his life he continued to believe that normative rules could be validly derived from scientific observation. Sociology should determine the normal and the pathological for each type of society.[7] The same procedure used to study how men in fact behave, can and should be applied to judgments of value.

Today even Durkheim's admirers consider as misguided his lifelong quest for a scientific ethic.[8] It is his empirical insights, the problems he posed on that level, and the brilliant hypotheses he suggested which have made much of his work classic. Indeed, his efforts to derive normative prescriptions from social facts have come to appear increasingly curious, a question for the sociology of knowledge.[9] His preoccupation with a secular ethic divorced from religion and identified with science is best explained by his political commitments and the role he played within the state educational system.

Durkheim came of age in the years after the defeat of France in 1871. The future of the new Republic long remained precarious. This young man, having prepared for the rabbinate, now decided that his vocation lay elsewhere.[10] He wanted to be a professor, but no ordinary teacher; he saw himself surrounded by disciples, the founder of a doctrine.[11] When he first came as a student to the Ecole Normale, he did not yet know what form that doctrine would take. Then its outlines began to take shape: although he would teach philosophy, his approach would be scientific and empirical rather than literary and abstract. What the country needed was a strong dose of science and professionalism, a new concern with the harsh facts and urgent necessities of industrial society. He began to formulate a project; it was to become *The Division of Labor in Society*.[12] First conceived as the "relations between individualism and socialism," his subject was subsequently recast as the "relation between the individual and society." After considering what had been said on this traditional subject by political philosophers, he decided that the only way to deal with the problem was to rescue sociology from the discredit in which Comte had left it, and to turn it into a genuinely positive science. But at the same time, sociology was to create a solid base for the Republic. It would indicate what reforms were needed; it would provide principles of order in politics, as well as a moral doctrine on which the country could unite; for he believed that beneath the choppy surface of political and ideological differences, lay a real consensus of values. This belief motivated his effort to discover what the ties are that hold together the members of a society and produce at least that minimum of order and harmony requisite to its maintenance.[13] His sociology of religion grows out of the same concern. It should be noted that both his theory of religion and his treatment of social solidarity found almost immediate applications in the political arena: the first in the state educational system; the second in the *Solidarité* movement, which has been called the official social philosophy of the French government in the decade prior to the First World War.[14]

Durkheim's life and thought take on added significance when they are related to the events and political alignments of the Third Republic. From his student days on, he held with passionate conviction the position that later took the name of *Dreyfusard*: one devoted to republicanism, the rule of law, political liberty, and anticlericalism. Durkheim's sociology originated in his concern for the reconstruction of France; his alliance with the anticlerical Radical Socialists and Socialists, who later comprised the *Bloc des gauches,* led to the establishment of Durkheim's subject within the national university system. As one of the most distinguished members of the "Republic of Professors," he rallied to its support during the Dreyfus Affair, at which time he became an active member of the League for the Defense of the Rights of Man. The sociological morality he formulated in his courses on education received the active support of the state; no one contributed more to the secular ethic of citizenship and patriotism taught in the public schools and teachers' colleges. So great was his influence that one of his critics could say, "The requirement that M. Durkheim's sociology be taught in the two hundred normal schools of France is among the gravest perils to which our country is subjected."[15] His great exertions in propaganda for his country during the First World War and the loss in battle of his gifted son contributed to his death in 1917. And the Nazis who put an end to the Third Republic took their own way of recognizing Durkheim's intimate connection with it by destroying his papers during the Occupation.[16]

Whatever the effect of Durkheim's political affiliations upon the rest of his thought, they are crucial to the development of his political theory. There is much in his theory of obligation, and more in his scheme of social analysis, which has led certain critics to describe his orientation as conservative.[17] Whether that term may be properly applied to Durkheim is something better discussed after, rather than before, the exposition of his political theory. But this much can be said: At a given point in Durkheim's development, he was forced to distinguish his position from conservatism, to make it clear to himself and others that behind his attack on the atomistic individualism of Spencer and the classical economists lay his positive intention of constructing a new and systematic rationale of republican ideals. That point came with the Dreyfus Affair. The battle lines were drawn, the alternatives as starkly defined for him as for the doctrinaires. Either France was to have

a social and political order based upon common citizenship and civilian rights within the Republic; or else it would be replaced by an authoritarian, hierarchic order, dominated by the Church and privileged ruling classes in the Army and civil service. French logic interpreted the conflict in these clear terms, and the battle began.[18]

Few historians now view the Affair as a Manichean conflict between the forces of good and evil.[19] The fate of Dreyfus as an individual and the issues of liberty and justice involved in his case soon became subordinated to a struggle for power between rival absolutisms.[20] Although some took up the cause of Dreyfus because of their principles, there were many on his side, as on the other, who really cared little about Dreyfus' innocence or guilt but were concerned only that their party win.[21] And when the *Bloc des gauches* gained victory, it took reprisals against the Roman Catholic religious orders who had contributed to anti-Semitism and helped lead the anti-

173

Dreyfusard forces. Using its parliamentary majority, the *Bloc* imposed new laws which made teaching illegal for members of those Roman Catholic orders not authorized by law, and the Government did not propose to issue many authorizations. This "created a new class of Frenchmen with fewer rights than any other, a departure from the common law that was justified on the ground that it forbade teaching by orders which were propagandists for the 'Counter-revolution.' "[22] Those who had fought for Dreyfus in the name of impartial law did not believe that the law governing religious orders ought to be impartial.[23] It was this and other uses of the electoral power gained in the name of high principle that disillusioned Charles Péguy and occasioned his famous epigram: "Tout commence en mystique et tout finit en politique."

Like the Dreyfus Affair, the relations of Church and State, of religious to public education, so bitterly contested in Durkheim's day, remain highly controversial matters with which an outsider meddles at his peril. The passions and prejudices on both sides are far from having subsided. Circumstances of ancient origin have disposed both the Church and the anticlericals to consider education as primarily a method of indoctrinating beliefs, religious or secular. The antagonism arose out of the Church's historical alliance with the enemies of republicanism; that policy, although disavowed by Leo XIII, appeared to endanger the Republic, particularly after the violently partisan position taken by the Church during the Affair. The possibility that national unity might be reconciled with two systems of schools, that Catholicism might at last make its peace with Republicanism—these alternatives were brushed aside by the doctrinaire extremists on both sides.

Durkheim had an important place among the anticlerical doctrinaires. This fact must be taken into account in assessing both his thought and the recognition he won for sociology as a subject within a university system notoriously resistant to change. Durkheim, although a partisan of free, public, and secular education, did not believe that the Republic could attain its objectives merely by prohibiting the teaching of revealed religion in its schools. Religion and morality are closely connected, and if religion is removed without putting anything in its place, then morality itself will be destroyed. "In a word, it is necessary to discover rational substitutes for those religious conceptions which have so long served as the vehicle for the most essential ideas of morality."[24] This search for a naturalistic ethic left its mark on his political thought as well as his sociology of religion. It will be seen how his political theory was pushed in the direction of finding a sociological equivalent of natural law. And his ethics and philosophy of history are best understood as a positivist version of liberal, modernist theology which seeks to maintain the morality of the Judaeo-Christian tradition while abandoning all the theological, dogmatic, and hierarchical forms with which it has been associated. These are obsolete survivals of a now transcended type of society. It was this view of hierarchical organization—he described the Roman Catholic Church as "a monstrosity from the sociological point of view"[25]—which may have led him to classify bureaucracy as an abnormal phenomenon.[26] Durkheim's sociology of religion falls outside the scope of this paper, but it is striking how the theory elaborated in *Les formes élémentaires de la vie religieuse*[27] turns up at the very center of the fervent defense, "L'Individualisme et les intellectuels," which Durkheim wrote at the height of the Dreyfus Affair.[28]

Through his enormous and fruitful labors, not the least of which was the establishment of *L'Année sociologique,* Durkheim founded a discipline that had every right to recognition within the French educational system. The merit of this work was indubitable, but merit is not necessarily rewarded. It becomes a question, then, of how sociology was in fact introduced into the university system. In 1882, the Primary Education Law had made education free, obligatory, and non-religious for children aged six to thirteen. But its effectiveness was reduced by the fact that almost fifty thousand brothers and nuns taught in state-supported schools.[29] To make these laws a reality, lay teachers had to be trained; furthermore, they also had to be properly indoctrinated in the Republican creed. A whole series of Radical educators devoted themselves to this task. Among them was Louis Liard, a student of Charles Renouvier, first a professor of philosophy, then in 1884, director of higher education at the Ministry of Higher Education, and finally, rector of the Ecole Normale Supérieure.[30] Another was Ferdinand Buisson, who, as director of primary education, for many years prepared the decrees that gave effect to the new system.[31] When he left the civil service in 1896, he became professor of Education at the Sorbonne; two years later he was elected president of the League for the Defense of the Rights of Man, founded by Clemenceau. In 1902, he entered the Chamber of Deputies. It was the chair that Buisson left that Durkheim was to occupy. A consideration of the careers of Buisson and Liard, together with Durkheim's, may give an indication of what processes caused the government to sponsor sociology.

After graduating from the Ecole Normale in 1882, Durkheim taught philosophy while continuing his study of sociology. In 1886, he had a significant conversation with Liard, who found that the young professor shared his belief that a scientific study of society could provide a secular creed suitable for teaching in the state normal schools.[32] He advised Durkheim to go to Germany to discover what was being done there to develop such an ethic. The next year, 1887, Liard created a course in social science for Durkheim in the Faculté des Lettres at Bordeaux, where Durkheim taught courses in pedagogy as well. After taking his doctorate in 1893, he continued to teach at Bordeaux; three years later he became the occupant of a chair in social science, which was the first in France and was created especially for him. When Buisson entered the Chamber of Deputies, Durkheim became his successor as professor of the Science of Education at the Sorbonne. In 1913, the name of the chair was officially changed to "the Science of Education and Sociology." Durkheim, as a staunch Republican, was also appointed to the faculty of the Ecole des Hautes Etudes Sociales, founded to promote the teaching of social science at the level of higher education.[33] Liard, now rector of the Ecole Normale, brought him to lecture to that elite student body on philosophy and education.[34]

Durkheim, then, was advanced to the highest place available in the University.[35] It is certain that if his views had clashed violently with those of the Ministry of Education, all his achievements, his eloquence, and his industry would not have brought him and his subject to such prominence. Politics and the University were closely linked—too closely, said Charles Péguy, who saw in the triumph of sociology still another proof that the *Dreyfusards* had succumbed to the temptations of power.[36] By putting the enormous force of the state behind a doctrine, they had intruded temporal means and standards into an area where intellect alone should rule. The Republicans wished everyone to conform to their views; promotions and preference depended on compliance. Into the Sorbonne, the Ecole Normale, the national educational system, they had introduced an apparatus to control men's minds. The doctrine it taught was called "pedagogy, sociology . . . or better, 'sociagogy,' an '-agogy' like 'demagogy' and all other '-agogies' which exercise a tyranny, mental, intellectual, moral, civic, over human thought."[37]

Péguy was not deceived about the influence of politics on education. But it would be completely misleading to represent Durkheim as a political appointee, a spokesman for those controlling the state, or for anyone else. It is true that being on the winning side was not altogether a good thing for someone so sure of himself and his cause as Durkheim. He had a faith in the benevolence of history which proved to be a disadvantage to him as a social scientist. But all that he did, once installed in his strategic and prominent place, was to continue the work he had set himself: the construction of a system at once sociological, philosophical, religious, and political. This had always been his ambition; this apparently was what his role prescribed; the man and the situation were well matched. Everything about the condition of France, he thought, predestined it to play a leading part in the development of sociology.[38] More than any other country in Europe, its ancient roots—religious, political, juridical—had been torn up, and nothing had replaced them. Yet France remained the country of Descartes and reason, of the clear ideas fundamental to all science. In Durkheim's classroom, sociology was presented as a mode of thought that corrected the errors of simplistic rationalism without falling into mysticism; that avoided both egoistic individualism and socialism, materialism and idealism. Durkheim felt obliged to fend off pragmatism in a series of lectures just before the

First World War.[39] His work abounds in polemics, because he wished to hold his audience against all rivals. Durkheim's thought forms a system, and as such it was proposed, discussed, and accepted or rejected. Although he denied that anyone should attempt comprehensive treatises on the ambitious scale of nineteenth-century sociologists; although to his immediate disciples he counseled patience, hard work, and monographs, Durkheim had his share of the *esprit du système* he lamented in others.

In the memoirs of his friends and associates, there are constant references to the religious temperament of this enemy of revealed religions.[40] Durkheim once said smilingly to Célestin Bouglé as they passed Notre Dame, "There is the sort of chair I should have held."[41] Another student remarked that Durkheim aspired above all to find a scientific statement of reason that could restore it to its once proud place.[42] Any materialist explanation of morality and social life repelled him. He believed that at the heart of society there is a moral reality *sui generis,* which is capable of rational expression. "He believed in reason, he confessed his faith with the same intransigence and the same passion as his ancestors, the prophets of Israel, confessed their faith in Jehovah."[43]

By all accounts, he created an extraordinary effect with his lectures. "Those who wished to escape his influence had to flee from his courses; on those who remained, he imposed his mastery."[44] His eloquence and ardor, combined with logic and profound originality, made him a great force, first in Bordeaux and then in Paris. Alone among the thinkers of his time, he made and organized disciples (on the principle of the division of labor), thus founding a school which perpetuated his own work and outlook.

Yet serious difficulties in his political theory followed from Durkheim's role as the head of a school, professing his system in eagerly awaited lectures. One of his students recalled how Durkheim would dazzle his audience by reviewing within an hour everything said on a particular topic by all known schools of thought. Then, gathering together their separate contradictions, he would construct out of them "a new synthesis, the sociological solution."[45] This implied a scheme of development among previous theorists, as though they all moved in single file, and all had Durkheim's system for their secret goal. This is the *déformation professionnelle* of the system-builder, the impulse to synthesize contradictions. This trait in Durkheim led him to translate such beliefs and ideas as liberalism and democracy into sociological concepts which quite altered the original meaning of these terms while retaining their familiar names. Were this but an idiosyncratic use of terms, its importance would be slight. But Durkheim tended to assume that he had retained all that was essential and desirable in the political ideal while changing what was inadequate or obsolete in the form of its statement. In this, he sometimes deceived himself; and because he failed to recognize what was novel in his theory, he did not think through all its implications.

This quality of Durkheim's mind at work on the basic problems of moral and political obligation may be conveniently observed in "L'Individualisme et les intellectuels." This essay puts in brief compass his sociological restatement of liberalism. It was occasioned by an article of Ferdinand Brunetière, literary critic, Catholic publicist, and one of the most conspicuous spokesmen for the anti-*Dreyfusards*. Shocked by the fact that a general of the Army had had his word called into question by the partisans of Dreyfus, Brunetière attacked the presumption of these intellectuals who put their private stock of reason above the respect due constituted authority. Their excessive pride, their inveterate rationalism and individualism, were symptomatic of the spiritual decay which had now to be dealt with. Durkheim replied in kind. He proudly accepted the title of intellectual: this term, properly used, he said, does not imply the claim to a monopoly on intelligence. Rather, he goes on, it is the assertion of the right, indeed the obligation, to use intelligence, by those who have demonstrated their capacity to do so. As for rationalism, individualism, liberalism, they are, as Brunetière says, the values held by the *Dreyfusards*. But the conservatives' account of these doctrines is a caricature. True, there is a narrow individualism, the egoistic utilitarianism of Spencer and the classical economists. Their ideal lacks moral grandeur; it reduces society to a shabby commercialism concerned with nothing more than production and exchange. Individualism in this form is about to die a natural death. The individualism which now holds the loyalty of men takes quite another form.

This development, Durkheim claims, is foreshadowed in the ethics of Rousseau and Kant, in the *Declaration of the Rights of Man,* and in the moral catechism taught in the state schools. Moral duty consists in turning our attention away from what concerns us personally to the search for what is demanded of us by our human condition. The integrity of the individual is the basic moral assumption inherent in the very constitution of the type of society in which we live. The human person is considered sacred in a ritual sense, because it has something of that transcendent majesty with which the churches of all ages have surrounded their gods. Thus it is invested with that mysterious property which sets off the sacred from the profane. Whoever attacks the life of a man, his liberty, or his honor, inspires the sense of horror felt by the believer who sees his idol profaned. Reason of state can never justify such an attack; the rights of the human person are above the state. This, then, is the religion of individualism, so called because it has man for its object, and man by definition is an individual.

The cult of man has the autonomy of reason as its dogma, and free thought as its ritual practice. No doubt the adversaries of reason will continue to contend that liberalism leads inevitably to intellectual and moral anarchy. In the name of order, they demand the sacrifice of political liberty and freedom of thought. At this point, Durkheim brushes aside this conservative theory of social order. Triumphantly producing his own sociological work, he claims the sanction of science for his liberal and individualist conclusions. Brunetière is obviously confused about the nature of religion, which he believes alone can produce order. In his mind, religion is identified with the churches and preachers, the rites and symbols, familiar to him. But this is superficial. In reality, religion is a system of beliefs and collective practices that are invested with a special authority. When a goal is pursued unanimously by a people, and becomes recognized as superior to purely private ends, it is properly called religious. The cult of the individual is such a religion.

In our type of society, the division of labor and the increase of population produce so many differences among its members that all they share in common is their humanity. And since each incarnates something of humanity, his person is sacred and inviolate. This is how man has become a god to man, and cannot, without denying himself, worship other gods. The cult of individualism is a religion which, like all others, is a worship of society itself. The progress of individualism could be halted only by preventing the further division of labor, and this in the nature of things is beyond human capacity. It is impossible to return to the conformity found in an earlier type of society.

The problem is not how to achieve social order by restraining or combating individualism, but rather how to complete and extend it. There are still too many liberals whose vision is limited by eighteenth-century theories. This position is too negative, too closely bound to the past, when the rights to think, vote, and write in freedom seemed to be the pinnacle of liberty. These rights must be maintained, but it has now become necessary to extend the spirit of liberty to social and economic arrangements. All artificial obstacles to the development of the individual's capacities must be removed, and society must be made to realize the precept, "To each according to his work."[46]

Together with his *L'Education morale*, this essay provides insight into Durkheim's values and his sociological justifications of them. His restatement of individualism ought to be read beside his better-known polemics against Spencer and the laissez faire economists. His plea that all artificial obstacles to individual development be removed—a formula almost identical with Thomas Hill Green's—reveals a liberal social philosophy justifying state intervention in economic life. But what is most striking is Durkheim's use of his key concepts in sociology to vindicate the values of 1789 and '91, if not '94. Also worthy of notice is the announcement of a historical law that prevents any return of conformity. The philosophy of history, which Durkheim banished from sociology because of Comte's misdeeds, here returns to take an important place in his moral and political theory.

Individualism, rationalism, liberalism—these are said to be rooted in the type of solidarity that holds the society together.

The individual is to be considered sacred because of a social condition, a moral fact, created by the division of labor. The human person has rights above the state; to violate these rights would be to endanger all that is sacred to this type of society. Durkheim has here substituted, article by article, a sociological theory of natural right for the eighteenth-century formulas. He thought that he had set his political and moral values firmly upon the nature of things, upon social facts. How sound was that foundation?

Elsewhere in his work, Durkheim insists that the moral systems of all peoples are a function of their social organization.[47] It is curious how little anxiety he felt as a moralist about the potential implications of this relativism. "History has established that except in abnormal cases, each society has in the main a morality suited to it, and that any other would not only be impossible but also fatal to the society which attempted to follow it."[48] Consequently, individualism could not be considered an ideal adequate to any other type of society. And, if a new type of social solidarity were to arise, there could be no valid moral claim to the values considered sacred in our society. This eventuality he did not anticipate. Like Marx, he would put a brake on the historical process once it had reached the point he desired. There was to be no evolution beyond organic solidarity. And organic solidarity implied his values. This tautology caused him no visible discomfort.

Another problem, in one sense the classic problem of political philosophy, arose out of his "scientific ethic." When, in his terms, does an individual have the right to resist the morality of his group? The details of Durkheim's ethics need not be rehearsed here. It is enough to note that he emphasized two points: the term "moral" has never been applied to actions prompted by purely individual interests; and more important, society is always the end of moral activity, provided that society always be considered as qualitatively different from the individuals who compose it.[49] The objection was raised that Durkheim, who regarded himself as an individualist, left little room for personal judgment. If morality derives from society, how can the individual rightly criticize or rebel against its precepts?

First, he answered, the morality of a society is not to be confused with the social opinion prevalent in it.[50] What has to be discovered is society "as it actually exists or as it can be said to be becoming by virtue of the inevitable causes that govern its evolution."[51] Resistance may be justified when an individual comprehends the reality of his society better than most of its other members. "Socrates expressed more clearly than his judges, the morality suited to his time."[52] Again, rebellion in theory or action may be justified against moral ideas that we know to be out of date and nothing more than survivals.[53] There is a third possibility: Suppose, asks Durkheim, that a society as a whole tends to lose sight of the sacred quality of individual rights.

> Could we not correct it with authority by reminding it that the rights of the individual are so closely bound to the structure of the great European societies and our whole mentality that to deny them, under the pretext of social interests, is to deny the most essential interests of society itself?[54]

The morality of one's society may be resisted only in the name of that morality properly interpreted.

Thus provision is made for certain circumstances in which resistance is morally warranted. Yet in every case, Durkheim's decision is determined by whether the individual in rebellion has identified himself with the direction in which his society is moving. This is a refined form of what Popper has called "moral futurism."[55] Presumably, if Socrates' ethics had looked back to the past rather than forward to the future, his judges would have been right. In his lectures on socialism, Durkheim discusses Saint-Simon's theory of history, which is similar to his, without giving any indication that he saw anything except commendable insight on Saint-Simon's part.[56] Indeed, Durkheim seems to have accepted Saint-Simon's view that in society there is always a system of institutions in the ascendancy and another in decline. The scientific student of society must determine to which of these categories each institution belongs. In all social decisions, the sole question becomes that of choosing the new order over the old. Durkheim, like Saint-Simon, did not waste sympathy upon those who had had judgment passed against them.

Durkheim did not produce an adequate theory of political obligation, but his concern with the actual morality of his society led him to carry on empirical studies that are interesting and valuable. Knowledge of the moral reality that comprises a society can be gained only through a study of its operative rules—domestic, civic, professional, and contractual.[57] Once these rules are determined, their functions must be analyzed and their causes established. The most important rules are those embodied in the law. Every society uses sanctions to secure compliance with its rules; a sanction is the consequence of an act that violates a pre-established rule. Hence to study sanctions is to study the values of a society. Since, in a modern political society, the state by its sanctions enforces certain rules such as contract, family law, and the obligations and rights of its citizens, Durkheim is led to develop his theory of the state.

Durkheim contended that only sociology could make an adequate study of the state. He did not find much to recommend political science as he knew it:

> To the extent that a true sociology is established, it will continue to distinguish itself from what is improperly called political science: bastard speculations—part theoretical, part practical, part science and part art—which are still confused, but wrongly so, with social science.[58]

This judgment was based not only on experience with its practitioners but also on a healthy amount of the imperialistic spirit. Both of Durkheim's university degrees were in philosophy, and he had to work with professors who saw no scope for sociology because in their view its work had been done by Aristotle. Besides, could "sociology"—a neologism, half-Latin, half-Greek—designate a proper university subject? Paul Janet had forced Alfred Espinas to omit an introduction to his dissertation because he refused to delete Comte's name. Janet had himself written a history of political science; and so Durkheim, in his Latin dissertation on Montesquieu, had to use *scientia politica* as an equivalent for sociology.[59]

There were other reasons for Durkheim's antagonism to political science. In addition to the fact that it was a potential rival

184

of sociology, the Ecole Libre des Sciences Politiques, formed after the defeat in 1871, had become the stronghold of forces much more conservative than Durkheim cared for.[60] Besides, both political science and sociology were parricidal offspring of philosophy, history, and law. Durkheim feared competition in the area he had marked out for sociology: a view of collective life that avoided both the nominalism of historians and the extreme realism of philosophers.[61] And as for intellectual imperialism, what should be said about Paul Janet's opening lines on Aristotle: "For him it is political science that is the supreme, the master and architectonic science which, treating the highest good of man, prescribes what ought to be done and what avoided"?[62] But this, by Durkheim's definition, fell within the scope of sociology.

At the beginning of his career, the great figures of political philosophy—Plato, Aristotle, Machiavelli, Hobbes, Rousseau, and Kant—exemplified for him the abstract method and disregard for empirical data which thus far had prevented the development of a true science of society. Durkheim's two doctoral dissertations are closely related. *The Division of Labor in Society* marks his attempt to demonstrate by constructive practice the errors of political philosophy that were carefully catalogued in his study of Montesquieu.[63] *The Rules of Sociological Method* codifies that practice with a dogmatic vehemence that is partially explained by Durkheim's attack upon political science.

His image of political philosophy had an effect on his own work: his too rapid dismissal of political power from his theory of the state perhaps stems from his view of Hobbes's theory of order; his well-known definition of communism reflects his hostility towards Plato.[64] The political philosophers went wrong because they sought to determine neither the origin and operation of institutions nor the laws of actual communal life. Their goal was to ascertain the best form of society through which man might realize his nature.[65] Facts were used only to support the prior conclusions of the author. Even in Aristotle, everything that resembles science is actually psychology or art. By psychology, Durkheim meant the a priori reasoning used by Plato and Aristotle to determine what is human nature. This

185

mode of thought, Durkheim insists, always arrives at teleology and never at scientific laws.

Thus political philosophers have used an abstract morality independent of time and place to create a Utopian ideal. But this is to disregard the fact that human societies fall into different types which vary radically in the social ties that hold them together. It may be said that Aristotle anticipated this concept. No, answers Durkheim, Aristotle took into account only variations in the number of rulers. He thought that other aspects of social organization—morality, religion, economics, family organization—were contingent and hence not subject to systematic study. Until Montesquieu, all political philosophers followed Aristotle's practice. Because of their exclusive preoccupation with the political regime, certain of them, such as Machiavelli and Hobbes, treated law as nothing more than an instrument used by the ruler at his will. Others, though they continued the classical philosophers' neglect of social reality, wanted to correct or reform society. Action was their goal. But the most that can come out of such an enterprise will be art. An art so defined is oriented to action. It is utilitarian and dominated by a sense of urgency.

But this dichotomy between science and art did not mean that the social scientist should play no part in practical affairs. It was Durkheim who wrote:

> Nothing is so vain and sterile as that scientific Puritanism which under the pretext that science is not fully established, counsels abstention and recommends to men that they stand by as indifferent or resigned witnesses at the march of events.[66]

He thought that the student of society should diagnose a situation as scientifically as possible and then issue a general recommendation, the details of which would be filled in by those charged with executing the program. Thus in *Suicide,* after arguing the necessity for giving organized occupational groups a place in the political order, Durkheim stops short of prescribing a detailed program.[67] He warns against the too definite plans proposed by political philosophers. These engage in imaginative flights, too far from the complexity of facts to be

of much practical value; social reality is as yet too little understood to be anticipated in detail. Only direct contact with facts
can give social science the precision it now lacks. "Once the
existence of the evil is proved, its nature and source established,
we know in general what the remedy is and where it ought
to be applied. The important thing is not to draw up a plan
that anticipates everything but to set resolutely to work."[68] Most
of Durkheim's writings on politics are conceived in this spirit;
he sought to be at once scientific and *engagé*.

No other attitude was possible for a professor of social science
hoping to gain an audience and demonstrate the relevance of
his teaching. France had fallen far behind its neighbors in
developing social services and regulating industrial capitalism.
There was much discontent among factory workers who were
then being organized into unions, and socialism was steadily
gaining support. With change of some kind apparently imminent, a great many doctrinal programs competed for public
attention. Every variety of socialism, anarchism, syndicalism,
mutualism found advocates, if not always followers. The last
part of *The Division of Labor in Society,* with its analysis of
industrial crises and the conflict between labor and capital,
carries the stamp of this period. This section of the book,
together with Durkheim's attack upon Spencer and other
theorists of laissez faire, so offended influential economists that
for a time teaching in Paris was closed to him.[69] In fact, Durkheim never identified himself with any party. But he maintained close ties both with the reformist Socialists, led by his
old friend Jaurès, and with the Radical Socialist movement of
solidarism. Of the two, he seems to have preferred Jaurèsian
Socialism.[70] But since the Parliamentary Socialists and Radical
Socialists were united for a time in the *Bloc des gauches,* Durkheim co-operated with both.

Yet he always fought to maintain a separate identity for his
own sociological school. This effort emerges clearly from his
lectures on socialism. Rather less is known about his attitudes
towards solidarism, an adaptation of Radical politics to the
mounting pressure from the left. This movement proposed
a moderate program of state intervention not unlike that
enacted by the British Liberals in the decade before the First

World War. The state was to provide social services such as insurance against old age, infirmity, and unemployment; it was to regulate working conditions, hours and wages, and standards of public health.[71] The philosophers of this movement based their argument on the theory of social solidarity, of which there were many versions, some deriving from Durkheim, others diverging so much that they must have been unacceptable to him. The division of labor in society creates a solidarity that binds men together and makes them interdependent. Thus obligations are created which justify legal intervention by the state on behalf of its poor or oppressed members. Durkheim provided another point to the Solidarists when he argued, against Spencer, that as organic solidarity develops, the rights of the individual and the scope of the state, so far from being mutually exclusive, must expand simultaneously.[72]

From 1900 to 1914, the Solidarist movement received extensive support from the governments in power. An international conference on solidarism, officially sponsored as part of the Exposition Universelle, included Durkheim among the select list of speakers.[73] In the years that followed, the theme of solidarity was developed by politicians such as Léon Bourgeois, jurists such as Léon Duguit, historians such as Charles Seignobos, and economists such as Charles Gide. Although the Solidarists often invoked Durkheim's work, it is certain that some of their theories were incompatible with his. Nevertheless, when the Ecole des Hautes Etudes Sociales was founded to propagate solidarism, Durkheim was named to its faculty. Despite all that was said and written about solidarism in those years, little of its program passed into law. The divisions of the National Assembly prevented action; the left had always said it came to nothing more than a pretentious restatement of the classic slogan, "Neither reaction nor revolution."

Durkheim displayed an ambivalence toward socialism which he never resolved. Although sympathizing with many of the objectives of the Parliamentary Socialists, he nevertheless thought that he detected in many of them a materialism no less offensive than that of the laissez faire economists. Certain concepts of Marxism he flatly rejected, such as the class war and the legitimacy of using violence. Nor did he believe that revolution would bring fundamental changes. France, despite numerous revolutions, had not much altered its social framework since the end of the Old Regime.

But he could not ignore the fact that socialism, like his own sociology, taught a system, a morality, a way of analyzing society. After several of his most brilliant students at Bordeaux had been converted to orthodox Marxism, he began to lecture on socialism "to justify himself in his own eyes, those of his students, and of the public."[74] Unfortunately, he never went beyond Saint-Simon in his lectures, for the effort involved in establishing L'Année sociologique and the pressure of his other scientific work thereafter precluded his return to complete this course. And so there is no record of how he viewed Marx. The course began with a claim of detached objectivity, but it soon began to show an increasing sympathy toward socialism, which he defined so as to emphasize its similarities to his own position. However, he took care to leave for himself important points to criticize. Thus he was able to maintain that everything of value in socialism could be expressed within the terms of his own system.

These lectures hinge on his distinction between communism and socialism, and it must be said that his definitions, although ingenious, are not valuable tools of analysis. Communism is identified with the *Republic* of Plato and the writings of More and Campanella. The work of ascetics, alienated or isolated from their societies and obsessed by their images of human nature, communism is an abstract morality that pays no attention to variations in social type, time, or place.[75] In its view, all wealth and economic activity generate egoism; and egoism, being antisocial, menaces the community.[76] Hence communists would moralize the state by minimizing or excluding economic life. This doctrine Durkheim treats with ill-disguised scorn, attributing to it all the errors he had diagnosed in classical political philosophy.[77]

Socialism, on the contrary, is represented as nearly compatible with Durkheim's own conception of the state which he evolved in the series of lectures he began the next year.[78] So far from being Utopian, socialism is founded on a realistic study of the special economic opportunities offered modern industrial

189

society. Socialism examines present economic arrangements to determine whether or not they are normal. And after having decided that they are not, it proposes to fuse economic interests with the state and thus put under its conscious direction an important area of life not now subject to any set of rules.[79] Socialism may be achieved either by attaching economic functions to the state or by assigning them to secondary centers such as professional groups and corporations.[80] Durkheim has relatively few faults to find with socialism, and these are dictated by the fundamental themes of his impending lectures. Socialism, as he defines it, lacks moral grandeur; its only concern is to increase wealth and distribute it more widely, a materialistic ideal which it shares with the classical economists. And socialism of the type which would have the state control the economy directly is, in Durkheim's views, neither possible nor desirable. It is impossible because the state has demonstrated its incapacity to assume such responsibilities; undesirable, because it would not counter the anomie of modern industrial society by incorporating now isolated individuals into occupational groups. These criticisms of socialism are made to point toward Durkheim's theory of state and society.

In the first half of his scholarly career, Durkheim fitted the modern democratic state into the framework of his sociology. The function of the state is individualist: it should liberate personality, both by removing obstacles to personal development and by calling the individual to a moral existence.[81] Thus the state is to be neither the passive observer of social reality, envisioned by the laissez faire economists, nor the socialist alternative, a mechanism for economic production. Above all, the state is to moralize and organize the society to ensure that each of its members be treated as he deserves, that he be freed of any unjust or humiliating dependence, and, on the other hand, that he maintain his obligations to the other members of his political society.[82]

Durkheim distinguishes between the political society and the state. By political society he means a society comprising a number of secondary social groups which submit to a sovereign authority, not itself subject to any regularly constituted higher authority.[83] The state is the special group of officials who represent the sovereign authority; it is the organ pre-eminent among that collection of groups which is the political society.[84] Using a somewhat obscure organic metaphor, Durkheim finds the distinctive characteristic of the state in its capacity to "think" and "act" for the political society. Such services as are performed by courts and armies do not fall within the state as he defines it. The state elaborates certain of the society's representations and volitions. This is not to say that the state incarnates the *conscience collective*.[85] In every society, there is a widely diffused psychic life which may affect the state. Every state to some extent maintains communication with the members of its political society. But the state thinks for the society in a rational and self-conscious way and makes certain decisions for it; it does not govern directly, but like the central nervous system, it co-ordinates the secondary organs that make up the body politic. This seems to constitute, first, an endorsement of Saint-Simon's belief that the modern state will administer but not govern, and, second, a rephrasing of the ancient constitutional doctrine that the body charged with making law should lay down general principles which other parts of the government will apply to specific cases. The state is not executive but deliberative. The cabinet, the ruler, and the parliament do not themselves act; rather, from them emanate the orders upon which others act.[86]

It may be asked whether Durkheim discusses the state as it is or as it ought to be. This is not a meaningful distinction in his terms. His study of the political philosophers had convinced him that it is futile to search for the best form of state. Instead his interest focused on what Lord Lindsay has called "operative ideals," the study

> of what is actually operative; of the operative ideals which at any time inspire men in their relations to law; of the authorities and obligations which from their belief in those ideals men actually recognize, even though they act only imperfectly in such recognition and the authorities they respect are not all that they are supposed to be.[87]

Durkheim's theory of the state formed an indispensable part of his "scientific ethics." For him, what ought to be is determined by a study of the ideals implicit in the morals and law of a given society at a given time and place. After discussing the individual's relation to himself (subjective moral obligation), to his family, and to his occupational group, Durkheim turns to what he calls *morale civique,* the citizen's rights and duties to his state.[88]

The origin of the state is traced in *The Division of Labor in Society.* As society passes from mechanical to organic solidarity, so the type of law shifts from penal to restitutive sanctions. Society develops specialized functions, subgroups, and individual activities. And along with the predominance of organic solidarity comes the parallel evolution of contract and the state. These produce equality, liberty, and justice in the law.[89] Thus the individual is progressively freed from the mass of his fellows. At the same time as the place of the individual in society becomes greater, the state adds to its functions through public services which administer but do not command. These steadily expanding administrative functions require only restitutive and not repressive sanctions. This is why the state can add to its sphere of action while that of individuals increases simultaneously.[90] Durkheim places the passage from mechanical to organic solidarity within a theory of progress, which attributed higher value to organic solidarity and restitutive law. For him it is no less a law of history that penal law gives way to restitutive law, and punishments become increasingly milder.

Later Durkheim altered his hypothesis of the inverse relation between penal law and organic solidarity. He continued to assert that the lower *(moins élevé)* the form of society, the more savage its punishments. But in "Deux lois de l'évolution pénale," he corrected his hypothesis, declaring that when political power is absolute, punishments become more cruel, regardless of the stage of social development.[91] In short, political power becomes an independent variable that may be more significant than the type of solidarity predominant in a society. This rescinds an earlier generalization that "the force of authoritarian governments does not come from authorities themselves, but from the very constitution of society."[92] The central authority, then, can acquire political force quite apart from the society's structure. It may do so by gathering all the directive functions of society into the same set of hands. This is a possibility whenever the political order contains no effective counterbalance regularly organized to prevent such an occurrence.[93] Durkheim's conclusions on this point could conceivably have led him to modify his emphasis on moral consensus. It might have led him to consider the possibility of authoritarianism in modern society. Yet nothing of the sort happened. This law of penal evolution remained an unexploited insight.

Although the main body of Durkheim's political theory applies modes of thought familiar to those who know the rest of his work, it also introduces new themes and gives unexpected turns to some old ones.[94] In *Leçons de sociologie,* he distinguishes between the narrow and true forms of individualism and between true individualism and mysticism. The narrow individualists see in the individual all that is real and valuable in society; the state, as far as they are concerned, adds nothing. Durkheim answers that this is quite incompatible with the evidence. History proves that rights are acquired only in and through society, which moralizes men and at the same time adds to their material resources. And as the state has gained in power, the liberty and dignity of the individual have increased.[95] In the course of the state's historical evolution, the individual is liberated from all the elementary societies that he once had to obey: patriarchy, the family, the city-state, the feudal system, or the commune.[96] Thus the narrow individualist theory of the state is inadequate. But what is the alternative to it?

Is it Durkheim's contention that every society has an end which transcends the individuals who compose it, that the role of the state is to pursue this end to which individuals are only means? On the contrary, Durkheim rejects this position as a variety of mysticism and identifies it with Hegel.[97] It represents the anachronistic effort to replace the cult of the individual by restoring the cult of the ancient city-state. It is true that at a certain stage of history the principal objective of public activity was to magnify the fame and power of the state. When the public religion and civic morality were in fact the same thing, the individual was completely submerged in his society. And this was necessary, for otherwise these societies could not have existed. But history has transformed this situation: the dignity of the human person has steadily increased, proving that the state must have the individual as its highest value.[98] Once more Durkheim has invoked his philosophy of history.

Having rejected the narrow individualist and mystical views of the state, Durkheim must avoid their respective pitfalls. This he attempts in a way that might have pleased the authors of the Federalist Papers who had also read Montesquieu. The description of the state as a force liberating the individual from tyranny must now be qualified, for it neglects the possibility that the state may become the tyrant in its turn. A situation of this kind may arise if in the political society there are no countervailing forces pitted against the state. Such forces must be provided in the form of secondary groups, professional or occupational. Nor may these secondary groups be left alone to do as they will, for a secondary group may itself tyrannize over its members. Hence there must be a more general power that makes the law for all and reminds them that their unit constitutes but a part of the whole. As such, it may not claim for itself what belongs to the society. Secondary groups should be checked by the state, and the state checked by secondary groups.[99]

This argument is based on an admission which qualifies considerably Durkheim's usual praise of the benefits conferred upon individuals by membership in society. Here, although he will not admit recourse to any morality outside that of the society, he does attempt to establish institutional checks within it. It is true, he says, that through its collective moral and mental life, society enriches and intensifies the resources of those who compose it. But every social group, whether the society as a whole or a secondary unit, tends to impose upon its members certain models of thought and action, any deviation from which is punished. Thus every society is despotic if nothing exterior to it intervenes to restrain its despotism. But if there are competing societies, then from this clash, individual liberties are born.[100] This, then, is another novelty in Durkheim's political thought—he finds a positive function for conflict.

It is from such reasoning that Durkheim's pluralism derives. The political malaise from which France suffers is due to the same causes as its social malaise: the whole weight of society rests upon individuals unprotected by intermediate units.[101] Thus the political function of such units would be to prevent the state from crushing the isolated individual; their social use-fulness would be to provide moral rules and institutions for those areas of life, especially in commerce and industry, that were not subject to effective regulation. No recognized prin-ciples governed the rights and duties of employer and employee, of competitors to each other and to the public. Hence conflict had become characteristic of economic life, but even when the strongest subdued the weak, the truces imposed by violence were only provisional. Such anarchy was abnormal. Any society in a healthy condition suppresses or moderates war among its mem-bers by subordinating the law of the strongest to a higher law. Nor could this chaos be justified by describing it as the condi-tion of individual liberty. Genuine liberty can be guaranteed only by authority, a moral authority.[102] But where is this au-thority to be found and how can it be incorporated into social life?

Durkheim emphasized the urgency of this question in his study of suicide. The family no longer provides cohesion as it used to when most of its members stayed within its orbit from birth to death. Organized religion may confer a relative im-munity to suicide, but it does so only by keeping its communi-cants from thinking freely. And in the present type of society, it cannot long continue to do so because freedom of thought is needed, demanded, and increasingly granted. As for political organization, at least in the form of our great modern states, it is too far removed from the individual to affect him with suffi-cient force and continuity. The state is a cumbersome machine made only for making general decisions rather than for adjust-ing itself to the detailed circumstances of social and economic life.[103]

The only substitute for unilateral state action is for the state to share its power with occupational groups. Although granted considerable autonomy, they would be subject to the state's regulation. The occupational group, Durkheim thought, could attach its members to it much more thoroughly than the family or the church or political society. Such a group is much better fitted to draw its individual members out of their moral isola-tion, and to develop for them a new sort of moral discipline. Each corporation or occupational group would be governed by an elected assembly. This would be made up of representatives of employers and employees, who, although meeting together in their directing council, would be separately organized. Such groups might in time replace territorial groups as the basis of suffrage.[104]

Apparently, Durkheim envisioned that the state would lay down general principles which would be applied to particular cases by the corporations affected. And yet he assigned a surprising number of positive functions to the state. It would legislate standards for social welfare and business competition. It would direct education, for the state must in this way unify the members of different secondary groups. And the state must also adjust the laws of contract and property to the new conditions of organic solidarity, with the equality of opportunity it presupposes. Thus the occupational group is not a panacea for all the problems of government. Durkheim, although not recommending the abolition of private property, nevertheless foresees that the state will refuse to recognize the right to will property to heirs, just as it refuses to recognize certain contracts.[105] As long as people are born rich or poor, there cannot be a just distribution of social goods. This indicates that Durkheim, like many another pluralist, assigned to the state some of the most urgent tasks of industrial society.

Although this emphasis upon corporations bulked large in Durkheim's political thought, events since his time have removed much of the interest that once attached to it. It is his diagnosis of the malaise of modern society that is read rather than his proposed cure for it. Contrary to his predictions, the democratic state has been able to find techniques for extending its influence into those areas he thought it could not control. And the use made of corporations and syndicates by fascist states, although not at all consistent with Durkheim's philosophy, has not encouraged others to keep the concept alive. Pluralism, which as late as the 1920's attracted much attention, is already a curiosity. But its significance for Durkheim's thought is that it places him in the line of Montesquieu and Tocqueville, for like them, his objective was a revised and strengthened liberalism. Just as much of his work is devoted to breaking down what he regarded as a false dichotomy between authority and liberty, so his pluralism represented his attempt to destroy another traditional opposition—that between the individual and the state. The occupational group is Durkheim's version of Montesquieu's *corps intermédiaire*. But Durkheim favored democracy and Montesquieu did not.

The culmination of Durkheim's political thought is his revised version of democracy, which he defines in a highly suggestive and personal way. To prove the utility of his enterprise, he shows its superiority to "direct democracy." Finally, he connects his politics and ethics by depicting democracy as that form of government best suited to the cult of the individual.

His conception of democracy foreshadows some attempts now being made under the influence of cybernetics to study political processes in terms of the communication network that links different parts of a society. The distinctive quality of democracy for Durkheim is the relatively close communication it establishes between the state and its citizens.[106] This is a matter of degree, for no state, however absolute, breaks off all contacts with its subjects. But in this case, degree is all-important, and can be measured by the presence or absence, by the highly developed or rudimentary character, of institutions that allow the public to transmit its opinions to the state, and the state to keep the public fully informed of official acts. Because of such constant exchanges between state and citizens, they become interrelated, and neither regards the other as a stranger.

But this is not to say that democracy is a regime in which society governs itself. That is the theory of direct democracy which proclaims that whatever is willed by the citizens should be translated into law by the state without any additions or modifications. To this concept, Durkheim attributes much of the blame for the political instability of France, its unsatisfactory parliamentary practices, and its incapacity to make the basic decisions required to reform its social and economic system.[107]

Direct democracy is based on an erroneous notion of the state and political society. In fact, democracy presupposes a state, an organ or government, distinct from society although closely linked to it. Direct democracy re-absorbs the state into the political society. The role of the state is not to reflect the unconsidered sentiments of the society but to add to those sentiments a more rational and informed thought. The statistics, the reports, the deliberations of assemblies culminate in a mode of thought qualitatively different from any actually found in the society. The state would not serve its proper function if it did not use its superior resources to determine what is in fact useful to the society. This is literally its *raison d'être*. Since it is a democratic state, it must know what its citizens think; but it cannot abdicate its role to changing currents of opinion. Its citizens have the right to grant or deny confidence to the government, but they do not have the right to usurp its functions. This statement must be put within its context: the political society must not absorb the state; the state must not absorb the political society.[108]

Because this principle is violated, he argues, political life is highly unstable. France, which appears so agitated politically, does not in practice modify its inflexible routine. An enormous, an abnormal gulf exists between the theory and practice of government in France. On the one hand, there is a conception of democracy which is fitted only to a primitive society; on the other, there is the complicated mechanism of a vast administrative system.[109] The state's susceptibility to the currents of popular passion paralyzes its capacity to deal with fundamental issues; to compensate, the bureaucracy stores up powers which may be used oppressively. "A society composed of an infinite number of unorganized individuals that a hypertrophied State is forced to oppress and contain, constitutes a veritable sociological monstrosity."[110] And yet, Durkheim admits, it is the administrative machinery that alone maintains whatever stability there is to be found in the political order. Here the description of the state bureaucracy as abnormal does not fit his empirical observation that the bureaucracy performs an indispensable function. Thus his preconceptions prevented him from recognizing the significance of this phenomenon.

Durkheim explained what was wrong with the actual practice of the Third Republic by this misconception of democracy and the absence of secondary groups. But democracy, properly conceived, is not doomed to futility. In fact, the exchange of ideas between citizens and state provides more information, rationality, and power than were ever known in the absolutist states of the past. And this is why democracy is becoming the typical form of government among large and complex societies which must adjust constantly to new circumstances. Another reason for this acceptance is that democracy is the political regime best fitted to realize the cult of the individual. It is repugnant to human dignity that men should be merely the creatures of their political masters. The moral superiority of democracy stems from the fact that it allows men to be autonomous, to understand their rights and duties, and to execute them as moral agents rather than as passive subjects.[111]

Durkheim criticized the classical political philosophers because they came to the study of politics with a priori conceptions that precluded rigorous empirical investigation. It might be expected that Durkheim's political theory would be a highly specific account of how and why political institutions in a given society operate as they do. This is not the case, and the reasons for it are easily found. Durkheim never investigated political institutions with anything like the attention and care he gave to his work on suicide and religion. Indeed, almost all his political thought is concentrated within the first fifteen years of a career which lasted twice that long. The fact is that after 1895 he became increasingly absorbed by his research in the sociology of religion. This might have been predicted by anyone following the evolution of his political theory.

In this part of his work, he disregarded the principles of method he had himself established, for he dealt with the state in a highly abstract way, producing little evidence for his conclusions. Here he relied too heavily on his definitions of such concepts as socialism and communism, the state and the political society. Harry Alpert has demonstrated that Durkheim extracted rather too much from his definition of socialism.[112] It is no less true that Durkheim's critique of direct democracy depends on his prior definition of the state and political society. From the meaning he assigned them, he drew conclusions which were purely formal but which he represented as substantive. And after he had gained important insights into the nature of absolute power, bureaucracy, and the potential value of conflict in politics, Durkheim failed to incorporate these concepts into his social theory. Once this omission is recognized, an explanation for it must be sought in the dominant tendencies of his thought.

Various attempts have been made to place Durkheim. He has been called an irrationalist;[113] he has been accused of subordinating the individual to the group and to the group mind;[114] he is said to have foreshadowed the integral nationalism of Charles Maurras.[115] Recently, he has been depicted as a conservative opposed root and branch to individualistic rationalism,[116] as nostalgic for preindustrial society and bearing a grudge against modern society because it has destroyed religious belief.[117] Some of these images appear to derive from a selective reading of Durkheim, a procedure always dangerous, but particularly misleading in this case. Few other social scientists of his stature have chosen such ambiguous terms to carry their meaning; few have so often neglected to insert into their major works those qualifications which they concede elsewhere. But it is no longer justifiable to attribute to Durkheim the concept of a group mind that is not embodied in and through individuals.[118] Nor can the identification of Durkheim with integral nationalism stand close scrutiny; his views clearly belong to a common variety of liberal nationalism.[119] And was Durkheim an irrationalist believing that man's conduct stems from forces which he can neither understand nor control? Certainly he attacked what he called "simplistic rationalism," but only to prepare the way for a more complex formulation than that found in Cartesianism and its eighteenth-century applications to social thought.[120] This emerges clearly from his newly published critique of pragmatism;[121] it is even more explicit in his statement that "only one who has great faith in reason would dare to apply its laws to the facts and events of society."[122]

Recently, Robert Nisbet has argued that in the writings of Durkheim, "we find the most important link between conservatism and the contemporary study of human behavior." In a carefully reasoned paper, he contends that conservatism is more than an attitude. "In the contexual terms of history, there are also conservative ideas." Such concepts as status, cohesion, adjustment, function, norm, ritual, and symbol are essentially conservative. Durkheim, then, is to be placed in the tradition diametrically opposed to rationalistic individualism.[123]

"Conservative" is not a pejorative term. The only reason for objecting to its use in connection with Durkheim is that it does not accurately describe his thought. It ignores altogether his political context. Should a *Dreyfusard* and sympathizer with Jaurès be called a conservative? And if some of his concepts derive from thinkers reacting against the Enlightment and the French Revolution, the question remains of what function they served within Durkheim's thought, taken as a whole. Surely, the origin of a concept does not permanently determine its function and meaning; what is conservative within one system may be revolutionary in another. Such transformations of meaning were particularly common among nineteenth-century thinkers using the devices of dialectic (a conservative concept?), Idealistic logic, and positivist sociology.[124] From such sources Durkheim assimilated a mode of thought practiced by Marx as well as by Hegel and Comte: he constantly claimed to have discovered for the first time the essential but latent meaning of doctrines imperfectly understood by their original exponents. Thus he asserted that the concepts described as conservative by Nisbet provide, when properly interpreted, new justifications for rationalism, individualism, and liberalism. Consider his treatment of the Burkean theme of social integration: Durkheim's distinction between mechanical and organic solidarity is heavily laden with liberal values. With organic solidarity, the highest form of social evolution, he associates all the ideals he himself held: equality, liberty, fraternity.[125]

His perspective is dominated by his unquestioning faith in science, freedom of thought, and the reality of progress. His work, when read carefully, reveals no nostalgia for the past; he finds almost nothing commendable about the type of social cohesion characterized by traditionalism and an unquestioned religious authority. Its legal system imposed savage penalties; its members, because of its excessive integration, were exposed to "altruistic" suicide.[126] This condition could scarcely be preferred even to the anomie of modern society, which is but suffering from the pains of transition. Durkheim's contempt for the past is matched by his robust confidence that sociology can provide rational solutions to even the most profound problems revealed by his analysis. He was far from being a radical pessimist in respect to human nature or the condition of his society. All his strictures against egotism, his phrases about the necessity of discipline, reveal the bourgeois citizen, the *Dreyfusard,* not the conservative authoritarian.

Durkheim's strategy, indeed the details of his position, recall that of T. H. Green, who revitalized liberalism in England by incorporating its values within an Idealist framework. The similarity of their views suggests that Durkheim, like Green, should be classified as a liberal.[127] Both writers engage in polemics against favorite dichotomies of the old liberalism: between the individual and the state; between authority and liberty. Durkheim and Green attempt to justify freedom and quality on moral grounds rather than on those of hedonism or material advantage; they prescribe much more activity by the state than was condoned by earlier liberals. But if they believe that the state may use its power to liberate individuals from hindrances, they retain enough of the traditional mistrust of the state to suspect that it may become despotic if left unchecked. For them the function of government is to make men moral, and the condition of morality is spontaneity. Thus the only purpose of state intervention is to free the individual from whatever environmental disabilities may keep him from realizing his potentialities.

Yet this doctrine, liberating and reforming on the one hand, emphasizes self-imposed discipline on the other. It takes very seriously the problem of maintaining order in the self and society. And the source of this concern is not exclusively intellectual. Behind this political liberalism is a species of theological liberalism, the attempt to discover a humanistic creed compatible with science and reason. Such a search may derive from both institutional and personal causes. Durkheim was among the architects of the secular morality required by the anticlerical policy of the Third Republic. But he was also a rabbi's son, as T. H. Green was the son of an Evangelical clergyman. This was more than coincidence. In the nineteenth century, a significant number of clergymen's sons became intellectually prominent as philosophers or professors.[128] Although

rebelling against the orthodoxy of their parents, they nevertheless retained a vague religiosity. They constructed various secular moralities which they thought would fulfill that function in
modern society which the historical religions had fulfilled in
the past. One of the distinguishing characteristics of modern
social science, what Hannah Arendt has called "the functionali-
zation of all concepts and ideas," originated in such surrogate
theologies.[129]

All of Durkheim's work, and not least his political theory,
was affected by his search for a religion without God. He was
driven to find a sociological equivalent of natural law by which
to defend his political values. It is society which, for him,
incarnates the highest good, the principle of individualism.[130]
This in the course of time progressively realizes itself through
the form of organic solidarity. The religious overtones are
unmistakable:

> Individualism, free thought, dates neither from our time, nor
> from 1789, nor from the Reformation, nor from scholasticism,
> nor from the decline of Graeco-Latin polytheisms or oriental
> theocracies. It is a phenomenon which begins in no one place, but
> which develops without cessation all through history.[131]

Society, permeated by this principle, disciplines and moralizes
men by placing common values within their consciences. Thus
between society and man, there can be no fundamental contradiction. The duties of a man to himself are always those of his
duties to society.[132] These theological assumptions of harmony
and moral consensus help explain why Durkheim never again
took up those insights he had gained through his political
thought; that is, that conflict may on occasion serve positive
ends and that absolute political power can quite outweigh the
consequences of social organization. As for his refusal to recognize bureaucracy as part of a normal society, he identified
bureaucracy with hierarchy, and hierarchy with the Roman
Catholic Church. As a "survival" from an earlier stage, this
type of organization was obsolete.

Thus Durkheim's quest for a secular ethic led him into a
typical liberal and idealist theology. "The ideal society is not
outside the real society; it is part of it."[133] This confidence about

the benevolent nature of modern man and his society is at the heart of his theory of progress. Seeing history as the immanent unfolding of institutions which enshrined all the values he held dear, Durkheim never faced the problem of leadership except to deny that it existed. Nor did he confront the possibility of extreme situations in which there is a genuine conflict of moral and political obligations. Thus he did not see the danger of his argument that each society has the morality suited to it. All that he could have said against totalitarian regimes would have come to no more than his attack on Wilhelminian Germany as an abnormal case of hypertrophy of the will.[134] It was his belief that a society that violates the rights of its citizens could be brought up short by "reminding it that the rights of the individual are closely bound to the structure of the great European societies."[135] The danger of this method was that others could derive very different interpretations of that structure and what it implied. The elitist theory of leadership that played so large a role in Fascism is no less, and no more, scientific than Durkheim's generalizations about the values inherent in modern society.

As a political theorist, Durkheim was very much the late nineteenth-century liberal. He did not anticipate the great wars and totalitarian institutions of the twentieth century. He predicted that "a day will come when our societies will know again those hours of creative effervescence, in the course of which new ideas arise and new formulae are found which serve for a while as a guide to humanity."[136] But these new ideas and new formulas were not to be what he anticipated. The limitations of Durkheim's political thought are nowhere more clear than when put in the perspective of twentieth-century totalitarianism.

1. "Les études récentes des sciences sociales," *Revue philosophique,* XXII (1886), 79.

2. Durkheim's theory of the state first appears in *De la division du travail social: Etude sur l'organisation des sociétés supérieures* (Paris: Félix Alcan, 1893). The subject is discussed briefly in the series of lectures given in 1895-96 and published posthumously as *Le socialisme,* ed. Marcel Mauss (Paris: Félix Alcan, 1928). There is an extensive discussion in *Le suicide: Etude de sociologie* (Paris: Félix Alcan, 1893); but the most complete

treatment of the state is to be found in the lectures given in 1898-99 and printed as *Leçons de sociologie: Physique des moeurs et du droit* (Paris: Presses Universitaires de France, 1950), translated as *Professional Ethics and Civic Morals* by Cornelia Brookfield (London: Routledge & Kegan Paul, Ltd., 1957). (References to this work will be to the French edition.) In his paper, "Deux lois de l'évolution pénale," *L'Année sociologique*, IV 1901), 65-95, Durkheim significantly altered some of the conclusions stated in *De la division du travail social*. When the second edition appeared in 1902, he contributed a new preface, "Quelques remarques sur les groupements professionels." This contribution came in the middle of his career. Thereafter, he wrote little about the state until his war pamphlet, *L'Allemagne au-dessus de tout: La mentalité allemande et la guerre* (Paris: Armand Colin, 1915). Thus in the last fifteen years of his life, Durkheim turned away from politics and political theory to the study of religion and ethics. Why he did so may be explained both by the immanent development of his social theory and by the remark he made in 1914: "How petty and mediocre politics have become" (Georges Davy, "Emile Durkheim," *Revue de métaphysique et de morale*, XXVI [1919], 189). This comment indicates how closely Durkheim's political theory was connected to the Dreyfus Affair and its aftermath.

3. This series was given at Bordeaux in 1898-99, and at the Sorbonne in 1904-5, 1910-11, and 1914-15. Cf. Harry Alpert, *Emile Durkheim and His Sociology* (New York: Columbia University Press, 1939), pp. 64-66.

4. *Sociologie et philosophie* ([1925] Paris: Presses Universitaires de France, 1951), pp. 49-90. Translated as *Sociology and Philosophy* by D. F. Pocock (Glencoe, Ill.: Free Press of Glencoe, Illinois, 1953), pp. 35-62.

5. *Le socialisme*, pp. vi-vii, viii.

6. *Essais de sociologie* (Paris: Librairie du Recueil Sirey, 1938), p. 279.

7. *Les règles de la méthode sociologique* ([1896] 10th ed.; Paris: Presses Universitaires de France, 1947), Chaps. iii, iv. *L'Education morale* ([1923] Paris: Félix Alcan, 1934), pp. 91-108.

8. Cf. Talcott Parsons, *The Structure of Social Action* ([1937] Glencoe, Ill.: Free Press of Glencoe, Illinois, 1949), pp. 390-99.

9. Parsons struggles with this as a problem immanent in Durkheim's positivism.

10. Alpert, *op. cit.*, p. 15.

11. Davy, *op. cit.*, p. 183.

12. *Le socialisme*, pp. v-vi.

13. *The Division of Labor in Society*, trans. George Simpson (Glencoe, Ill.: Free Press of Glencoe, Illinois, 1947), p. 409.

14. John A. Scott, *Republican Ideas and the Liberal Tradition in France* (New York: Columbia University Press, 1951), p. 179.

15. Jean Izoulet, as cited in Célestin Bouglé, *Bilan de la sociologie française contemporaine* (Paris: Félix Alcan, 1935), p. 168 n.

16. Durkheim, *Pragmatisme et sociologie,* ed. Armand Cuvillier (Paris: Librairie philosophique J. Vrin, 1955), p. 8.

17. Robert A. Nisbet, "Conservatism and Sociology," *American Journal of Sociology,* LVIII (1952), 167-75.

18. David Thomson, *Democracy in France* (2nd ed.; New York: Oxford University Press, 1954), p. 141.

19. This assumption is made in Alpert's otherwise excellent monograph, *op. cit.,* p. 60. I have followed D. W. Brogan, *The Development of Modern France* (London: Hamish Hamilton, Ltd., 1940); Hannah Arendt, *The Burden of Our Time* (London: Secker & Warburg, Ltd., 1951); Thomson, *op. cit.;* and Joseph N. Moody, "Catholicism and Society in France," in *Church and Society,* ed. Joseph N. Moody (New York: Arts Inc., 1953).

20. Thomson, *op. cit.,* p. 141.

21. Arendt, *op. cit.,* pp. 112-13. Much the same point could be made about the Alger Hiss case.

22. Brogan, *op. cit.,* p. 360.

23. Arendt, *op. cit.,* p. 120.

24. *L'Education morale,* p. 10.

25. Cf. "Associations de culte," in *Libres entretiens* (Première Série; Paris: Bureaux des "Libres entretiens"), p. 369.

26. *The Division of Labor in Society,* p. 28.

27. Paris: Félix Alcan, 1912. Translated as *The Elementary Forms of the Religious Life* by Joseph Ward Swain (Glencoe, Ill.: Free Press of Glencoe, Illinois, 1947).

28. *Revue bleue,* X (1898), 7-13.

29. Brogan, *op. cit.,* p. 153.

30. Scott, *op. cit.,* p. 76 n.

31. *Ibid.,* pp. 185-86.

32. Alpert, *op. cit.,* p. 38.

33. Scott, *op. cit.,* p. 181 n.

34. Marcel Mauss, "In memoriam: L'Oeuvre inédite de Durkheim et de ses collaborateurs," *L'Année sociologique,* Nouvelle Série, I (1923-24), 19.

35. "The University was the name given by Napoleon I to his organization of all levels of French public education from the highest to the lowest" (Brogan, *op. cit.,* p. 146).

36. *Situations* ([1907] Paris: Gallimard, 1940), pp. 161 ff.

37. *Ibid.*, p. 165.

38. "Notre siècle: La sociologie en France au XIX⁰ siècle, Saint-Simon et Auguste Comte," *Revue bleue*, XIII (1900), 651.

39. *Pragmatisme et sociologie.*

40. Célestin Bouglé, Georges Davy, Marcel Granet, Raymond Lenoir, and René Maublanc, "L'Oeuvre sociologique d'Emile Durkheim," *Europe*, XXII (1930), 281-304.

41. *Ibid.*, p. 280.

42. *Ibid.*, p. 299.

43. *Ibid.*

44. *Ibid.*, p. 297.

45. *Ibid.*, p. 298.

46. "L'Individualisme et les intellectuels," p. 12.

47. *Sociology and Philosophy*, p. 56.

48. *Ibid.*

49. *Ibid.*, p. 37.

50. *Ibid.*, pp. 38, 63.

51. *Ibid.*, p. 63.

52. *Ibid.*, pp. 64-65.

53. *Ibid.*, p. 61.

54. *Ibid.*, p. 60.

55. Karl R. Popper, *The Open Society and Its Enemies* (London: George Routledge, 1945), II, 192-95.

56. *Le socialisme*, pp. 155-74. "We must seek in the past the germs of new life which it contained and hasten their development" (*Le suicide*, p. 391).

57. *Sociology and Philosophy*, p. 39, 42-43.

58. "Les principes de 1789 et la sociologie," *Revue internationale de l'enseignement*, XIX (1890), 455.

59. *Montesquieu et Rousseau* (Paris: Marcel Rivière, 1953), p. 25 n.

60. For the "Science Po," cf. Thomson, *op. cit.*, p. 59.

61. *The Rules of Sociological Method*, trans. Sara A. Solovay and John H. Mueller, and ed. G. E. G. Catlin (Chicago: University of Chicago Press, 1938), p. 76.

62. *Histoire de la science politique* (2 vols.; 5th ed.; Paris: Félix Alcan, 1925 [?]), I, 165.

63. *Quid secundatus politicae scientiae instituendae contulerit* (Bordeaux: Gounouilhou, 1892). Translated as "La contribution de Mon-

tesquieu à la constitution de la science sociale," by Armand Cuvillier, in *Montesquieu et Rousseau*, pp. 26-113.

64. *Le socialisme*, pp. 38-60, esp. p. 60.

65. *Montesquieu et Rousseau*, pp. 29-42.

66. *Education and Sociology*, trans. Sherwood D. Fox ([1922] Glencoe, Ill.: Free Press of Glencoe, Illinois, 1956), p. 104.

67. *Suicide*, trans. John A. Spaulding and George Simpson ([1897] Glencoe, Ill.: Free Press of Glencoe, Illinois, 1951), pp. 361-92.

68. *Ibid.*, pp. 391-92.

69. *Le socialisme*, pp. vii-viii.

70. *Ibid.*, p. ix. Hubert Bourgin, *Le socialisme universitaire* (Paris: Stock librairie, 1942), pp. 72-79.

71. Scott, *op. cit.*, pp. 157-92. Francis W. Coker, *Recent Political Thought* (New York: D. Appleton-Century Co., 1934), pp. 408-15.

72. *The Division of Labor in Society*, pp. 219-26.

73. Scott, *op. cit.*, p. 180. Cf. Alpert, *op. cit.*, p. 178.

74. *Le socialisme*, p. ix.

75. *Ibid.*, p. 38.

76. *Ibid.*, pp. 47, 51.

77. *Ibid.*, p. 60. Surely, Parsons is wrong in calling Durkheim a communist rather than a socialist *(Structure of Social Action*, p. 341). Durkheim characteristically locates his own position as avoiding the errors of two opposite and extreme theories, but he is much closer to socialism than communism, as he defines them.

78. Alpert, *op. cit.*, p. 64.

79. *Le socialisme*, pp. 23-24, 51.

80. *Ibid.*, p. 24.

81. *Leçons de sociologie*, pp. 83-84.

82. *Ibid.*, p. 87.

83. *Ibid.*, p. 55.

84. *Ibid.*, p. 59.

85. *Ibid.*, p. 61. This would seem to repudiate his earlier statement that governmental power is "an emanation of the inherent life of the collective conscience" *(The Division of Labor in Society*, p. 195 n.).

86. *Leçons de sociologie*, pp. 60-61.

87. A. D. Lindsay, *The Modern Democratic State* (London: Oxford University Press, 1943), I, 47.

88. *Leçons de sociologie,* p. 52. Cf. the plan of the lectures in Alpert, *op. cit.,* pp. 64-65.

89. Page 388. Cf. Georges Gurvitch, *Sociology of Law* (London: Kegan Paul, 1947), pp. 83-96; and Gurvitch, *Essais de sociologie,* pp. 283-84.

90. *The Division of Labor in Society,* pp. 220, 223.

91. Page 70.

92. *The Division of Labor in Society,* p. 195.

93. "Deux lois de l'évolution pénale," pp. 66-69.

94. That is, the possibility that the group may tyrannize over the individual; that out of conflict, liberties are born.

95. *Leçons de sociologie,* p. 70.

96. *Ibid.,* p. 78.

97. *Ibid.,* pp. 66-67.

98. *Ibid.,* pp. 68-70.

99. *Ibid.,* pp. 74-76.

100. *Ibid.,* p. 78.

101. *Ibid.,* p. 127.

102. *The Division of Labor in Society,* pp. 2-6.

103. *Suicide,* pp. 361-92.

104. *Leçons de sociologie,* pp. 46-51.

105. *Ibid.,* pp. 249-52.

106. *Ibid.,* pp. 99-100, 103-4.

107. *Ibid.,* p. 113.

108. *Ibid.,* pp. 115-16.

109. *Ibid.,* p. 119.

110. *The Division of Labor in Society,* p. 28. For the admission of the bureaucracy's value, cf. *Leçons de sociologie,* p. 120.

111. *Ibid.,* pp. 103-20. For the concept of moral autonomy which Durkheim thought could best be realized in and through democracy, cf. *L'Education morale,* pp. 109-43.

112. Alpert, *op. cit.,* pp. 116-17.

113. William M. McGovern, "Irrationalism and the Irrationalists" (Chap. ix), *From Luther to Hitler* (London: George G. Harrap & Co., Ltd., 1946), esp. pp. 425-26.

114. William Y. Elliott, *The Pragmatic Revolt in Politics* (New York: Macmillan Co., 1928), p. 302. John H. Hallowell, *Main Currents in*

Modern Political Thought (New York: Henry Holt & Co., Inc., 1953), pp. 533-34.

115. M. M. Mitchell, "Emile Durkheim and the Philosophy of Nationalism," *Political Science Quarterly*, XLVI (1931), 87-106. For statements of Durkheim's liberal nationalism, cf. *Leçons de sociologie*, pp. 79-91; *L'Education morale*, pp. 84-89, 322; and "Pacifisme et patriotisme," *Bulletin de la société française de philosophie*, VIII (1908), 66.

116. Nisbet, *op. cit.*

117. Morton Grodzins, *The Loyal and the Disloyal* (Chicago: University of Chicago Press, 1956), pp. 239-40.

118. Cf. *Pragmatisme et sociologie*, p. 196, and the Preface by Cuvillier, pp. 7-26.

119. Cf. n. 117 in this paper.

120. *L'Education morale*, pp. 4, 137, 286-92; and *The Rules of Sociological Method*, pp. xxix-xl.

121. *Pragmatisme et sociologie*, pp. 27-29.

122. "La sociologie en France au XIXe siècle," p. 651.

123. Nisbet, *op. cit.*, pp. 167, 174-75.

124. Cf. F. A. Hayek, "Comte and Hegel," *The Counter-Revolution of Science* (Glencoe, Ill.: Free Press of Glencoe, Illinois, 1952), pp. 191-206.

125. Gurvitch, *Essais de sociologie*, pp. 282-83.

126. *Suicide*, pp. 221, 368, 373-76, 383.

127. Cf. Melvin Richter, "T. H. Green and His Audience: Liberalism as a Surrogate Faith," *Review of Politics*, XVIII (1956), 444-72.

128. Raymond Aron, *German Sociology*, trans. Mary and Thomas Bottomore (London: William Heinemann, Ltd., 1957), p. 114.

129. "Authority in the Twentieth Century," *Review of Politics*, XVIII (1956), 415.

130. "L'Individualisme et les intellectuels."

131. *The Division of Labor in Society*, p. 171.

132. *Ibid.*, p. 399.

133. *The Elementary Forms of the Religious Life*, p. 422.

134. *L'Allemagne au-dessus de tout*, p. 44.

135. *Sociology and Philosophy*, p. 60.

136. *The Elementary Forms of the Religious Life*, pp. 427-28.

DURKHEIM'S CONSERVATISM AND ITS
IMPLICATIONS FOR HIS SOCIOLOGICAL THEORY

LEWIS A. COSER

"A way of seeing is always a way of not seeing."[1] It is clear
that Durkheim saw much, and many writers in this volume will
help to remind us of it. My task, though complementary, is
different: I shall attempt to establish that Durkheim's conservatism significantly limited his perception of society. I would
hold with Max Weber that "the choice of the object of investigation and the extent or depth to which this investigation
attempts to penetrate into the infinite causal web, are determined by the evaluative ideas which dominate the investigator
and his age."[2] Since Durkheim was unusually explicit in stating
his values, it is possible to trace in some detail the manner in
which they limited the extent or depth of his investigation in
certain areas, just as they helped him open up other areas to
fruitful and often entirely new investigation.

In spite of all the adverse criticism which it contains, this
essay is written in praise of Durkheim. I know of no better way
to celebrate the work of a master of the past than to account
for the limitations of his work. No one knew better than Durkheim that progress in science can be achieved only through
the selective elimination as well as the selective preservation of
past contributions.

As one studies the numerous hostile criticisms of Durkheim's
sociology,[3] one is struck by the fact that many, though not all,
of them share a limited number of common themes. It is said
that Durkheim was so fascinated by the study of cohesion that
he neglected to study the phenomena of conflict; that he was
so absorbed in the study of society as a whole that he did not
deal adequately with the subgroups and subdivisions which
make up the total society; that he neglected the individual and
his claims because he concentrated upon the society and its
claims; that he stressed the cohesive function of religion without considering its divisive features; that he did not duly
appreciate the import of social innovation and social change

211

because he was preoccupied with social order and equilibrium; and that he neglected to analyze power and violence in the body politic because he was overly concerned with the factors which make for agreement.

In what follows I shall make an attempt to show that these shortcomings, assuming for a moment that his critics are correct, are not due to fortuitous circumstance, such as the exigencies of a particular research situation, but that they can be accounted for to a large extent in terms of Durkheim's abiding conservatism. To the extent that I can support this interpretation, I may be able to contribute to the sociological interpretation of his sociology.

I shall, of course, not be concerned with Durkheim's conservative ideas as such, but only with the way in which these ideas obscured, for him, certain fruitful sociological problems. Theoretical orientations result from a series of decisions by a theorist concerning what he considers problematical. Such decisions lead him to adopt particular theoretical frameworks and to ignore others. Durkheim's conservatism, accordingly, led him to make a series of decisions regarding theory which crucially influenced the direction of his research.

By conservatism, I mean an inclination to maintain the existing order of things or to re-enforce an order which seems threatened. For the conservative, as Karl Mannheim has argued, "everything that exists has a positive and nominal value merely because it has come into existence slowly and gradually."[5] The conservative does not reject all change; he insists only that change must be slow and gradual and that it must never endanger the social order.

There can be no doubt that Durkheim considered himself a conservative in this sense; he often reiterated his conviction that social reform ought to be introduced with the utmost care so that it does not damage the fabric of society. The science of ethics, he believed, "does teach us to treat [reality] with extreme caution, imparting to us a conservative attitude."[6] There will be times, he wrote, when "everything is not all it ought to be, and that, consequently, will be the time to intervene." But this intervention must always be limited and piecemeal: "It has for its object, not to make an ethic completely different from

212

the prevailing one, but to correct the latter, or partially to improve it."[7]

Before considering in detail the shortcomings of Durkheim's theory, let us recall briefly that his whole contribution to theory was itself a result of his concern as a conservative with the conditions of the French society of his time. The problem of order preoccupied Durkheim from his earliest writings to the last pages of the *Introduction à la morale,* a paper he wrote shortly before his death. Directly or indirectly, all of his writings are related to this problem.

Durkheim wrote during a period of social disorganization. When he was a student, the Third Republic was in its infancy. Deeply attached to the new republican society and yet aware of the weak foundation upon which it rested, Durkheim felt that it was his central task to contribute to the development of a new French republican moral order. Even though he was utterly devoted to the idea of establishing a science of society, Durkheim nevertheless believed that this science would have no value if it did not eventually lend itself to practical application. "We should judge our researches to have no worth at all," he wrote, "if they were to have only a speculative interest."[8] "A science that deserves that name," he stated in his last paper, "must result in an art: otherwise it would only be a game, an intellectual distraction, pure and simple erudition."[9]

There is no need here to document further the well-known connection between Durkheim's program of study and his moral and political orientation. Harry Alpert[10] and several others have shown that Durkheim's thoughts were centered upon the problems of his time; they have shown how close the relationship is between Durkheim the moralist and Durkheim the sociologist. I agree with Robert A. Nisbet, who, after tracing some of the similarities between Durkheim's themes and those of the French conservatives that preceded him, remarks that "what Durkheim did was to take the conservative view of society out of what was essentially a speculative framework of inquiry and translate it into certain hypotheses, which he sought to verify."[11] I shall now show that this led Durkheim to neglect certain other types of hypotheses and in consequence made him unable to account for a wide range of social facts. The discussion must begin with a consideration of Durkheim's views on social order and disorder.

Alfred North Whitehead once wrote that periods of transition, although they manifest "the misery of decay," also show "the zest of new life."[12] Durkheim would have understood only the first part of this statement. He often referred to the Saint-Simonian distinction between critical and organic periods of history, a distinction which in his opinion marked "an important progress in the philosophy of history."[13] But it is remarkable that Durkheim, although his sociology arises out of an awareness of the crises of his age, never really attempts to analyze such crises in their own terms. They are always seen as departures from the expected order and equilibrium; they are pathological, and thus devoid of any inherent worth. Just as to Durkheim any type of nonconformity is criminal by definition, so critical periods, periods of social disequilibrium, are by definition aspects of social pathology. Such a definition prevents the study of these crises in terms of the opportunities they offer for the emergence of alternatives to the existing order. At best, Durkheim believed, the sociologist can only suggest how the patient may be cured by the judicious application of carefully (that is, conservatively) defined remedial action: "The duty of the statesman is no longer to push the patient toward an ideal that seems attractive to him, but his role is that of the physician: he prevents the outbreak of illnesses by good hygiene, and he seeks to cure them when they have appeared."[14]

The liberal or radical thinker contrasts an ideal state with a real state. Durkheim, to the contrary, substituted the distinction between the normal and the pathological for the disjunction between the ideal and the real—a distinction which was not as "scientific" as he thought it was, since normality may itself be considered a fact or a value—and thus introduced bias toward conservatism. This bias predisposed him to consider any attempt to make the world more nearly resemble an ideal world a wanton disregard of the facts of social life. Such a procedure is likely to make the sociologist less able to understand social innovation. It is true, of course, as Gaston Richard and others have pointed out, that Durkheim does not always follow his own prescription.[15] For example, he states in *The Division of Labor* that all generally existing forms of labor division in his times are pathological, even though he considered the general to be the normal. In *The Division of Labor,* the normal turns out to be a utopian fiction and not general at all. Durkheim's very inconsistencies reveal that his method did not permit him fully to understand periods of transition.

Durkheim believed disorder was a special case within a generally ordered system. To him, just as to the classical economists, disequilibrium is only a special instance of a general equilibrium. His commitment to the idea of a state of order prevented him from considering the alternative which obtains in the Keynesian approach in economics—that equilibrium might be a special case of a general disequilibrium. With such an approach, conflict and change would be considered the rule, stability and order the exception, perhaps even the "pathological" exception.[16] "Transitional states" would not be seen as exceptions but, at least in the modern world, the rule. This is not the place to discuss the respective merits of these alternative approaches, but one may at least ask whether an orientation similar to that of Keynes in economics is not likely to reveal elements which the "classical" orientation obscures.

With his ideal of an ordered state of affairs, it is not surprising that Durkheim deals but little with those aspects of social life which concern division, strife, conflict. In this he is clearly within the general conservative tradition: the conservative thinks in terms of the "whole," ignoring antagonisms and struggles between the "parts"; whereas these struggles are central to the thought of the change-oriented radical or liberal.[17] Nor should it surprise us that Durkheim's morphology tends to be a morphology of the total group. Gunnar Myrdal has laid bare the shortcomings of this approach in his well-known criticism of William Graham Sumner's method. Although Sumner's and Durkheim's theoretical orientations are widely divergent, the bias toward conservatism which they share seems to account for similar shortcomings in theory. Myrdal writes:

Sumner's construction contains a valid organization and offers a useful methodological tool for studying primitive cultures and isolated, stationary folk communities . . . . The theory is, however, crude and misleading when applied to a modern Western society . . . it is likely to conceal more than to expose. It conceals what is most important in our society: the changes, the conflicts, the absence of static equilibria, the lability in all relations even when they are temporarily, though perhaps for decades, held at a standstill.[18]

This is a harsh judgment; nevertheless one cannot but feel that by and large it also applies to Durkheim's work. This may help to explain why, though deeply indebted to that work, modern sociology seems to have utilized less of its heritage from Durkheim than has anthropology. (It must be remarked, however, that even nonliterate societies are much less homogeneous than Durkheim had supposed. Conflicts between subdivisions, between age classes, kinship groups, and residential groups are, even there, the rule rather than the exception.[19])

Durkheim's general neglect of conflicting subgroups in modern society is perhaps nowhere as evident as in his neglect of class phenomena. This is especially striking since he wrote extensively on professional groups. Class groupings are of necessity conflict groupings whereas professional groupings are not. Only in the very last pages of his *The Division of Labor*, a subject matter which would seem to require close attention to the sociology of class relations, does Durkheim mention class conflicts—or, for that matter, classes—at all, and then only in order to affirm that when organic solidarity replaces mechanical solidarity there is a diminution of social inequalities and hence a reduction of class differentiation.

Durkheim always rejected socialism, though he knew socialist theory quite well and though a great number of his friends, such as Jean Jaurès, were among the leaders of French socialism. Marcel Mauss, his relative, intimate friend, and collaborator, writes:

All his life he was disinclined to become an adherent of socialism properly speaking because of certain aspects of its activities: its violent character, its class character, its working-class orientation, and also its political and "hack" character. Durkheim was profoundly opposed to any class war . . . he wanted only changes that would profit the total society and not only one of its parts, even if this were a powerful and numerous part.[20]

The point here is obviously not to reproach Durkheim for not having become a socialist, but rather to indicate that his rejection of socialism was based not so much—perhaps not at all—on its economic program, for which he often expressed some sympathy, but rather on the fact that it was the doctrine of a conflict group, benefiting, he believed, a part, not the whole. He found the harmonious socialism of the Saint-Simonians much more attractive. This explains Durkheim's neglect of the study of class phenomena: they appeared to him a priori divisive and disintegrating.

For Durkheim, the "social question" was a moral question, a question that involved the relation of individuals to the social whole, not the contention for power, status, and wealth. The following quotation will provide sufficient evidence:

> It is not a question of putting a new society in the place of that which exists, but to adapt the latter to new social conditions. It is no longer a question of classes, of the opposition of the rich to the poor, of entrepreneurs to workers, as if the only possible solution were to diminish the portion of one in order to increase that of the other. What is needed in the interest of the one and the other is the necessity to contain from above the appetites of both, and thus to put an end to the state of disorganization, of maniacal agitation, which does not stem from social activity, and which makes it suffer. In other words, the social question posed this way is not a question of money or of force; it is a question of moral agents. What dominates it is not the state of our economy, but rather the state of our morality.[21]

We shall have to come back to the insistence on the necessity of containing individual desires which informs so much of Durkheim's writing; at present we need only note his quite explicit refusal to deal with the "social question" in terms of contentions for scarce power and scarce wealth. Durkheim's sociology here closely followed in the path of his moral philosophy. He did not believe that contentions for power and wealth touched upon the significant moral issues that preoccupied him; consequently, his sociology did not in any real sense take cognizance of them. His sociology was the poorer for it.

Durkheim was forced to assume that the major social norms generally express the sentiments of the total society. He never seriously entertained the idea that they might only express the sentiments of a specific stratum within it. If it is affirmed a priori that the major social norms express the sentiments of the total collectivity, then one cannot recognize conflicting norms within a society; one cannot take cognizance of clashing values; one is unable to understand, as Roger Lacombe has pointed out, that certain subordinate social strata may accept a norm only because it is imposed upon them by violence or because they passively submit to it, whereas it is the genuine expression of the moral sentiment of only a superordinate stratum.[22]

All this is not to say, of course, that Durkheim was unaware of the existence of subgroups within a society. His intense concern with professional and family groupings reminds us of this fact. However, and this seems important, he sees the various norms of subgroups only as complementary, as having a specific place in a hierarchy. He did on occasion speak of a "decentralization of moral life," and discussed the fact that "the priest and the soldier have different duties" and that occupational moralities vary in different branches of industry. Yet he was convinced that there existed a hierarchy among the different groups and institutions, and hence among the duties peculiar to them. Thus professional morality was "lower" than state morality, and domestic morality lower than either. This is not the place to discuss the dubious foundation of a "scientific morality" which pretends that it has established scientifically that one's duty to one's family is necessarily inferior to one's duty to the state; one needs only to point out that, here again, Durkheim, though recognizing that there may be a clash of values and norms between various subgroups in a society and that loyalties and allegiances to various institutions may be at variance, dismisses this consideration by affirming that hierarchy is the central scientific fact and that infringements upon the hierarchial principle can be due to pathological factors only.[23] To Durkheim a divided society can be neither normal nor

218

moral. The "good" society is cohesive. There may be deviation and criminality on its fringes, as there are red-light districts within a metropolitan area, but its main constituent groups, far from contending, must complement each other in a disciplined conformity to the overriding norms of the whole. It is not surprising that a postwar generation to whom class divisions, revolutions, and wars had become "normal" social phenomena found that Durkheimian sociology was an unsuitable instrument for the analysis of their social world.[24]

Consideration of a few of Durkheim's definitions may enable us to grasp the relationship between his conservatism and his shortcomings in theory. The matter of initial definitions, as Harry Alpert has remarked, is all-important for Durkheim.[25] It is for him the most indispensable condition of scientific proof and verification. But, as Alpert has also pointed out, it is precisely here that Durkheim's methodological approach is weak indeed. To him definitions were by no means merely tentative working tools to be discarded or changed during the course of research; he assumed, instead, that a definition could disclose a truth rooted in the nature of things. Hence definitions may be considered more important in the assessment of Durkheim's system than in an appraisal of a thinker more adequately aware of their tentative function and of the crucial role of the definer. His definitions may not give us, as Durkheim believed, a "firm foothold on reality," but they can give us a kind of privileged access to his own cast of mind. A few examples may serve to illustrate this.

Let us take Durkheim's famous definition of crime as all acts which present "the external characteristic that they evoke from society the particular reaction called punishment . . . . We call every punished act a crime."[26] Such a definition could have been adopted only by a thinker whose general orientation is fundamentally conservative. For under this definition, as Lucien Goldmann has remarked,[27] is subsumed the action of Jesus in ejecting the merchants from the temple, as well as the activities of a Thomas Münzer and a Lenin, on the one hand, and of a highway robber, on the other. Such subsuming of what would appear to the non-conservative thinker essentially

219

dissimilar phenomena may indeed appear quite natural to a conservative, who places everything which disturbs the social order in the same category. The failure to discriminate between heterogeneous phenomena is not likely to be scientifically productive. I am, of course, aware that Durkheim did not consider crime an abnormal occurrence, and that he did in fact—with rather obvious embarrassment and strained reasoning—attempt in a number of places to distinguish between crime and the intellectual dissent of, for example, Socrates.[28] It is true, nonetheless, that he never departed from his definition of crime, thus maintaining that, in spite of certain difficulties in the application of his concepts, all acts which evoke societal punishment are basically similar. When all forms of dissent are thus criminal by definition, we are in the presence of a system which is ill-equipped to reveal fully the extent to which nonconformity, as distinct from crime, involves the striving toward an alternative moral basis rather than moral deviation.[29]

To Durkheim, "undisciplined and irregular people" were "morally incomplete"; in his belief, "it is impossible to consider moral those practices which are subversive of the society in which they are observed; because it is everywhere a fundamental duty to ensure the existence of the fatherland."[30] Given these premises, the lines that divide genuine pathological failure from nonconformity are, of course, blurred. Thus Durkheim was not able to ask whether a high percentage of conformists may not be pathological failures as well, and whether individuals cannot adhere pathologically to the approved patterns of society as easily as to disapproved patterns. There is, after all, something which might be called the "mad orthodoxy" of the mentally ill, and prison inmates often have quite "proper" political views.

Durkheim's definition of the state affords us another example of the effects of a conservative bias on one's definitions and hence on one's theoretical orientation. I have mentioned Durkheim's reluctance to discuss, or even to take full cognizance of, power and violence. This becomes especially obvious in his definition of the state. While Weber, to whom struggle, conflict, and contention are in the very center of social life, defined the state as a human group "that (successfully) claims the monopoly of the legitimate use of physical force within a given territory,"[31] one finds in Durkheim's definition no reference to the authoritative enforcement of will but rather a curiously abstract and intellectualistic conception of the state. The state is to him "a group of functionaries *sui generis* within which representations and directives which engage the collectivity are being elaborated." Not the whole of the collective consciousness is incarnated in the state; "it is only the seat of a special and delimited consciousness, but a consciousness higher and clearer, having a more lively feeling of itself." It was a mistake, Durkheim believed, to identify the state with the executive power: "The state executes nothing." "All the life proper of the state is not spent in exterior action, in movements, but rather in deliberations, that is, representations." Administrative action must be distinguished from state activity. They differ as the muscular system does from the central nervous system. "The state is, rigorously speaking, the organ of social thought." "Its essential function is to think."[32]

Defining the state as he does, it is not surprising that Durkheim never succeeded in analyzing or even in taking theoretical cognizance of the role of governmental force and violence or of political power and coercion. He relegated all of that to the "muscular system," and it seemed, in a sense, *infra dignitatem*. Being so deeply concerned with buttressing the authority of the secular republican state, he may, in fact, have felt that to pay attention to the mechanics of power might undermine that respect for the state which he attempted to implant. He took the disenchantment with religious symbols in his stride; but disenchantment with the symbols of secular authority, he may have felt, could contribute only to further anomie. He was exclusively concerned with those functions of the state which would make it appear as a kind of brain trust, the special seat of the more rarefied and self-conscious collective ideas. Given Durkheim's initial decision to build a sociology which would help to re-establish the threatened order of the Third Republic, given his lifelong endeavor to elaborate a secular morality which would serve to strengthen the foundations of the republican regime, it was perhaps understandable that he focused attention only on the positive functions of the state.

The fact remains that what may perhaps have been a gain for the political practice of the regime turned out to be a loss for sociological theory. A system of sociology which proved incapable of dealing with the facts of state power, which framed its definitions in such a way that these facts could not be properly identified, was to remain a truncated system. Even though it may have been adequate for a limited understanding of the "Republic of Professors"—as the Third Republic has sometimes been called—it could hardly aid comprehension of the era of the total state which began after Durkheim's death. We cannot reproach Durkheim for lacking the gift of prophecy, but we might reproach him for not having grasped the irreducible facts of power so glaringly obvious in the living past of his own age. If he had had the tough-minded detachment of a Marx or a Weber, his contribution might have been of value to the understanding of an era which was in crucial ways different from his own. As it was, his tender-minded attachment to the institutions of Republican France proved to be a fatal handicap.

Durkheim's definition of the term "society" is closely connected with his definition of the state. Though he customarily used the term with various meanings when speaking of domestic society, professional society, and the like, usually, when he refers to *the* society in the modern world, the term denotes the national political order and becomes almost synonymous with fatherland, nation, or even state. Durkheim was occasionally quite explicit in equating society with the fatherland. He says, for example, "It seems to me quite evident that we cannot live without a fatherland, because we cannot live outside organized society that exists."[33] "We must see in the fatherland *in abstracto* the normal and indispensable milieu of human life."[34]

While the term "society" is used as approximately equivalent to the fatherland and nation of the modern world, it is also used in about the same sense to denote a tribal unit among nonliterate peoples. By thus obscuring the differences between relatively heterogeneous and relatively homogeneous social structures, by making no distinction between structures with differentiated political institutions and structures which lack such institutions, Durkheim made it difficult to develop a comparative sociology of political structures within the framework of his system; and this is especially true since he used the term "society" all too often in an honorific rather than in a factual sense—"the perpetual state of dependence in which we find ourselves vis-à-vis society inspires in us a sentiment of religious respect toward it."[35]

Durkheim's intense patriotism and his intense "religious" devotion to society have often been commented upon; what has perhaps not been sufficiently discussed is the curiously abstract character of his patriotism and his religion of society. Here it would seem appropriate to introduce a consideration of Durkheim's background.

It is customary to find evidence in most patriotic writings of an attachment to particular localities or regions, to particular historical or linguistic traditions. Not so with Durkheim. We encounter in his writings a highly rational, non-emotional attachment to *la patrie*. This intellectualized and abstract relation to his country may well have had its source in his social origin. When this son of a rabbi from the eastern fringes of France came to Paris to develop into one of the guiding spirits of the Third Republic, he did not feel bound to any one subgroup, class, stratum, or region. His loyalty went to France, which became for him the prototype of *the* society. His attachment was not mediated through tradition and history, but was, so to speak, abstractly intellectual.

This may explain why we find in Durkheim's work so little discussion and understanding of the loyalties which men have for different subgroups within a society, and also why Durkheim does not seem to have understood ideological loyalties which cut across national allegiances. This is why he could write that "a class, even an enlarged class, is not and cannot be a fatherland; it is only a fragment of a fatherland, just as an organ is only a fragment of an organism. Because internationalism misunderstands this elementary truth, it is but too often the pure and simple negation of any organized society."[36] Here again, we come upon self-imposed limitations which explain why the investigator of such modern social movements as communism, for example, finds so little aid in Durkheim's sociology. He who tended at times to hypostatize society as the Hegelians before him had hypostatized history left us no instruments with which to understand those ideological movements of the Stalinist variety, for instance, which function, to use a phrase of Léon Blum, as "foreign national parties" within the national polity.

A related shortcoming is apparent in Durkheim's sociology of religion. Perhaps in no area of research was Durkheim so hampered by his initial conservative orientation as in his analysis of religious phenomena. Obsessed with the need to maintain and to re-create the basis for order in society, he wanted to see in religion an exclusively integrating and cohesive force. Ritual and ceremony, to quote Alpert's succinct summary, provide "disciplinary, cohesive, vitalizing and euphoric social forces."[37] The practices of a cult strengthen "the bonds attaching the believer to his god [and] . . . at the same time strengthen the bond attaching the individual to the society of which he is a member, since the god is only a figurative expression of society."[38] Hence "religion has given birth to all that is essential in society."[39]

Durkheim was faced with the fact that religion had declined in France, that religious sanctions and religious symbols had lost much of their efficacy. Consequently, throughout his life he was preoccupied with finding a moral equivalent for religion. But this very fact indicates that to him religion appeared to be invariably productive of social cohesion.[40]

There is no reference in any of Durkheim's writings to the divisive and the dysfunctional aspects of religious practices. This seems almost incredible since Durkheim was, of course, well-read in European history and must have been quite familiar with the divisive effect that, for example, religious wars had had in the history of, say, sixteenth-century France. There is no Frenchman with even a modicum of education who does not know something about the Massacre of St. Bartholomew, the revocation of the Edict of Nantes, the destruction of the flowering culture of the Albigenses, and so on. These events are alive in the collective consciousness of the French. Yet exclusive attention to the demands of the theoretical and moral system which he attempted to build prevented Durkheim from considering any of them. This man, the son of a people which has suffered from religious persecution perhaps more than any other Western people, never allowed knowledge of these events to intrude into his thinking when he constructed his system.

It apparently never occurred to Durkheim that religion may serve as a means of legitimizing and glorifying acts which would not have been perpetrated in good conscience had such legitimation not been available. He was apparently unable to recognize a social fact which appeared so obvious to the ripe wisdom of Gilbert Murray when he wrote, "Probably throughout history the worst things ever done in the world on a large scale by decent people have been done in the name of religion."[41] Nor did Durkheim's theory take cognizance of the historical evidence which indicates that religion, while it may draw men together, may also separate them and set them against each other. To quote Murray again, "I suppose that a thoroughly orthodox member of any of the million religious bodies that exist in the world must be clear in his mind that the other million minus one are wrong, if not wickedly wrong."[42]

It has often been argued that Durkheim's neglect of the divisive function of religion may be accounted for by the fact that his theories were mainly derived from data on non-literate societies. This seems insufficient grounds. The fact is that Durkheim, not an anthropologist by training, deliberately concentrated his attention upon non-literate societies. There were a number of reasons for this choice. For one, the evolutionist tradition played some part: what was "most primitive and simple" might be expected to yield more essential data. In addition, the choice of relatively homogeneous groups as objects of analysis was clearly connected in Durkheim's case with a desire to study those groups in which religious dissension and the possible dysfunctions of religion were minimized. Having asserted that religion was necessarily productive of unity, solidarity, and cohesion, Durkheim turned for verification to those homogeneous societies where it would be easiest to demonstrate this function of religion. Because Durkheim chose tribal society as the unit of analysis, he did not have to consider religious manifestations which militate against attachment to society in the name of a religious ideal. It is difficult to analyze Islam or the Church Militant in Durkheimian terms, just as hard as it is to understand the secularized international religions of our time within the framework of his analysis. To the extent that a religion is subversive of the society in which it is practiced and divides that society, Durkheim's sociology of religion remains unable to cope with it.

Lest this paper degenerate into a wearisome catalogue of all the shortcomings of Durkheim's sociology, it may be advisable to close it with a discussion of two additional aspects of his work which seem to be of special import, since they concern areas in which conservative and liberal or radical thinkers have most often parted company: the question of "human nature" and the related question of education. Traditionally, the conservative has been given to a pessimistic interpretation of human nature, and he has pitted this view against the progressivist belief in the perfectibility of man.[43] Traditionally—though there are exceptions—the conservative has asserted that a more or less authoritarian system of education is needed in order to curb the savage propensities of the young, whereas the progressive has insisted on permissive methods of education designed to lead to the spontaneous emergence of autonomous individuals through the careful cultivation of autonomous moral tendencies. Durkheim, too, was a pessimist about human nature and authoritarian in his educational views. As before, we shall explore these two areas, not to show that Durkheim was a conservative, but rather to indicate how his views influenced his research program and his findings.

Durkheim was strongly convinced that culture and civilization, the maintenance of social order, depend on the ability of society to curb the individual propensities and desires of its members. Like Freud—and the parallelism, we might note in passing, is quite startling—Durkheim believed that social progress depended on the repression of instincts. Freud claimed that "civilization is built upon renunciation of instinctual gratification,"[44] that "civilization consists in an ever increasing subjection of our instincts to repression," that "the process of progress in civilization is paid by forfeiting happiness."[45] Durkheim echoes him almost word for word:

If society were only the natural and spontaneous development of the individual, these two parts of our selves would harmonize and adjust to each other without hurt or friction . . . . But in fact society has its proper nature and hence exigencies which are altogether different from those of individual nature . . . . We must do violence to certain of our most imperious drives. And as the social part of the total being that we are becomes ever greater as we advance in history, it is contrary to all expectations that there should ever come an era where man should be less required to resist himself and could live a less tense and more relaxed life. On the contrary, everything leads one to predict that the place of effort will ever increase with civilization.[46]

Durkheim believed—and passages in his works which confirm this are so well known we can dispense with quotations—that society must control man's desires and appetites, which are potentially boundless and immoderate, and that a most rigorous social discipline is needed to build barriers against the flood of human passion and desires.[47] He saw man as a *homo duplex;* on the one hand, individual, body, desire, appetite; on the other, socialized personality. There is mutual contradiction and antagonism between those two components, and true moral action consists in the sacrifice of certain individual drives and desires in the service of society. An ever watchful superego is needed to keep the threatening id in check.[48] This profound pessimism had important consequences for Durkheim's sociology. Being convinced of the cultural necessity for repression, he was never led to ask himself whether there might not be different degrees of repression in different societies; that is, whether it was not conceivable that though there was an absolute bedrock of instinctual repression without which no society could exist, there were also "surplus-repressions," to use a phrase of Herbert Marcuse,[49] which, far from being inevitable products of all societal arrangements, were functionally required in only some of them. Modern anthropologists have revealed the wide range in degrees of instinctual repressions that exist in non-literate society; historians have pointed out that in Western society the level of repression of instinctual gratification has varied widely among the various strata of the population. Yet Durkheim's general pessimistic philosophical premises led him to ignore almost completely those most promising leads toward a sociology cognizant of differing degrees of repression.

The effects of Durkheim's conservative bias can be more clearly perceived in his writings on education than elsewhere in his work. Here, as Jean Piaget has skillfully pointed out, Durkheim's general conception of the need for social constraint to curb the wickedness of biological propensity led him to a view on education fundamentally at variance with most modern thinking, leaving no place for the idea of co-operation between children or between teacher and pupils.[50] Durkheim conceived of the schoolmaster as a kind of priest who acted as an intermediary between society and the child. As a result, everything depended on the schoolmaster, and moral rules were seen as a kind of revelation which the priest of society reveals to the child. The teacher must have a maximum of authority; he must be a stern disciplinarian. "Life is not all play; the child must prepare himself for pain and effort, and it would therefore be a disaster if he were allowed to think that everything can be done as a game."[51] No wonder, then, that Durkheim was fundamentally opposed to all forms of education which attempted to maximize individual interests and free initiative as well as co-operation. His view of education limits unduly the problems that a full-scale sociology of education has to deal with. Just as in his general sociology he placed such great stress on the antinomy between society and the individual that he was no longer able to perceive the importance of contending subgroups and conflicts within the social system, so his views on education precluded an understanding of the fact that, to quote Piaget, "far from limiting himself to the rules laid down by his parents and teachers, the child ties himself down to all sorts of rules in every sphere of his activity, and especially in that of play. These rules are no less social, but they rest on different types of authority."[52] Durkheim's sociology of education turns out to be a sociology of educational constraints, a sociology which is consequently unable to deal with the facts of educational co-operation, a sociology, moreover, that is unable to account for the complex network of social relations between peers. Here again, Durkheim's general conservatism seriously limited his vision.

In brief, it is impossible to maintain the claims that the Durkheimian system is the all-encompassing system of sociological theory which its founder, and, more particularly, some of his epigones believed it to be: its meshes are much too wide to allow us to catch within it all social reality. This is not a reproach but a simple statement of fact. Only those who still pursue the will-o'-the-wisp of believing that *the* sociological system can be built in our time could thus reproach Durkheim. Those who think that sociology today must set itself the more modest aim of developing theories of the middle range, "theories intermediate to the minor working hypotheses evolved . . . during the day-by-day routines of research, and the all-inclusive speculations comprising a master conceptual scheme,"[53] can rest content with the masterly theories of the middle range which Durkheim has given us and which will remain part of the permanent heritage of sociology. Yet it has seemed necessary to demonstrate why it is that Durkheim, though so superlatively successful in certain areas of investigation, has failed in others to enrich our knowledge. To make this clear, it must be stressed that

> observational discrimination is not dictated by the impartial facts. It selects and discards, and what it retains is rearranged in a subjective order of prominence. This order of prominence in observation is in fact a distortion of the facts . . . . We have to rescue the facts in the discard, and we have to discard the subjective order of prominence which is itself a fact of observation.[54]

To the extent that Durkheim's conservative orientation led him to select some problems and discard others, he attempted to impose on his successors a subjective order of prominence in sociological analysis. This order needs to be discarded. Only by rejecting it can that which is of value in the Durkheimian heritage be fully incorporated into the body of sociology as a cumulation of theoretical interpretation.

1. This is Kenneth Burke's dictum in *Permanence and Change* (New York: New Republic, Inc., 1935), p. 70.

2. *On the Methodology of the Social Sciences,* ed. and trans. Edward A. Shils and Henry A. Finch (Glencoe, Ill.: Free Press of Glencoe, Illinois, 1948), p. 84.

229

3. See, for example, Roger Lacombe, *La méthode sociologique de Durkheim* (Paris: Félix Alcan, 1926); Emile Benoit-Smullyan, "The Sociologism of Emile Durkheim and His School," in *An Introduction to the History of Sociology,* ed. Harry Elmer Barnes (Chicago: University of Chicago Press, 1948); Jules Monnerot, *Les faits sociaux ne sont pas des choses* (Paris: Gallimard, 1946).

4. Of course, what is said here about conservatism would also be true of liberalism or radicalism in other cases.

5. Karl Mannheim, *Ideology and Utopia* (New York: Harcourt, Brace and Co., 1936), pp. 211-12.

6. *The Division of Labor in Society,* trans. George Simpson (Glencoe, Ill.: Free Press of Glencoe, Illinois, 1948), p. 35.

7. *Ibid.,* pp. 35-36.

8. *Ibid.,* p. 33.

9. "Introduction à la morale," *Revue philosophique,* LXXXIX (1920), 84.

10. Harry Alpert, *Emile Durkheim and His Sociology* (New York: Columbia University Press, 1939).

11. "Conservatism and Sociology," *American Journal of Sociology,* LVIII (1952), 165-75.

12. *Adventures of Ideas* (New York: Mentor Books, 1955), p. 15.

13. *Le socialisme* (Paris: Félix Alcan, 1928), p. 312.

14. *The Rules of Sociological Method,* ed. George E. G. Catlin (Glencoe, Ill.: Free Press of Glencoe, Illinois, 1950), p. 75.

15. Gaston Richard, "La pathologie sociale d'Emile Durkheim," *Revue internationale de sociologie,* XXXVIII (1930), 123; see also Achille Ouchy, "Les sociologies et la sociologie," *Revue internationale de sociologie,* XLVII (1939), esp. pp. 482-84.

16. Cf. Ralf Dahrendorf, "Struktur und Funktion," *Kölner Zeitschrift für Soziologie,* VII (1955), 491-519, esp. 510-14. See also the author's *The Functions of Social Conflict* (Glencoe, Ill.: Free Press of Glencoe, Illinois, 1956), and "Social Conflict and the Theory of Social Change," *The British Journal of Sociology,* VIII (1957), 197-207.

17. Cf. Karl Mannheim, *op. cit., passim,* and "Conservative Thought," *Essays on Sociology and Social Psychology* (New York: Oxford University Press, 1954), pp. 74-164.

18. *An American Dilemma* (New York: Harper & Bros., 1944), II, 1032.

19. Cf. Max Gluckman, *Custom and Conflict in Africa* (Glencoe, Ill.: Free Press of Glencoe, Illinois, 1956). See also Armand Cuvillier, "Durkheim et Marx," *Cahiers internationaux de sociologie,* IV (1948), 75-97, esp. 79.

20. Introduction to Durkheim, *Le socialisme*, p. viii.

21. *Ibid.*, p. 297.

22. Lacombe, *op. cit.*, p. 73.

23. For Durkheim's main discussion in this connection, see *L'Education morale* (Paris: Félix Alcan, 1925), esp. pp. 83 ff., and "Morale professionelle," *Revue de métaphysique et de morale*, XLIV (1937), 527-44, 711-38, esp. 535-36. See also the excellent essay by Georges Gurvitch, "La morale de Durkheim," in *Essais de sociologie* (Paris: Recueil Sirey, 1939).

24. Cf. Monnerot, *op. cit.*, esp. pp. 75-76, 88-91.

25. Alpert, *op. cit.*, esp. pp. 114 ff.

26. *The Rules of Sociological Method*, pp. 35-36.

27. *Sciences humaines et philosophie* (Paris: Presses Universitaires de France, 1952), pp. 21-22.

28. Cf., for example, *L'Education morale*, pp. 60-61, and *Sociology and Philosophy*, trans. D. F. Pocock (London: Cohen and West, 1953), pp. 64-65.

29. This is, of course, not meant to deny that it might not be necessary for the purpose of a particular study to distinguish between crime and conformity, but only to indicate that failure to distinguish between them on the conceptual level prevents the sociologist from perceiving their distinctive functions. Cf. for the above distinction Robert K. Merton's lucid discussion in his *Social Theory and Social Structure* (rev. ed.; Glencoe, Ill.: Free Press of Glencoe, Illinois, 1957), pp. 360-68. See also Roger Nett, "Conformity-Deviation and the Social Control Concept," *Ethics*, LXIV (1953), 38-45; L. G. Brown, *Social Pathology* (New York: F. S. Crofts Co., 1942), esp. pp. 70 ff.; and Lewis A. Coser, "Social Conflict and the Theory of Social Change."

30. *De la division du travail social* (Paris: Félix Alcan, 1893), p. 21. All translations are the work of the author unless reference is made to a specific translation.

31. *From Max Weber*, ed. H. H. Gerth and C. Wright Mills (New York: Oxford University Press, 1953), p. 78.

32. *Leçons de sociologie* (Paris: Presses Universitaires de France, 1950), pp. 61-63.

33. *Bulletin de la société française de philosophie*, VIII (1908), 45.

34. *Ibid.*, p. 52.

35. "De la définition des phénomènes religieux," *L'Année sociologique*, II (1898), 23.

36. *Ibid.*, p. 52.

37. *Op. cit.*, p. 202.

38. Durkheim, *The Elementary Forms of the Religious Life,* trans. Joseph Ward Swain (Glencoe, Ill.: Free Press of Glencoe, Illinois, 1954), p. 226.

39. *Ibid.,* p. 419.

40. Many of the contemporary debates aroused by Durkheim's sociology of religion seemed to have involved a rather curious misunderstanding. While Durkheim's antagonists felt that he attempted to discredit religion by pointing to its elementary totemic forms, Durkheim had actually intended to show the eminently positive role of religion in the creation of social cohesion. Since social cohesion was to him supremely important— perhaps the most important factor—he thought that he had in fact contributed a thoroughgoing defense of religion. His adversaries, however, were concerned with a concrete religion, not with religion *in abstracto.*

41. *Five Stages of Greek Religion* (New York: Doubleday & Co., Inc. [Anchor Books], 1955), p. 8.

42. *Ibid.,* p. 7.

43. "Coming from the hand of the author of all things," begins Rousseau's *Emile,* "everything is good; in the hand of man, everything degenerates." Bonald answers, "We are bad by nature, good through society. The savage is not a man, he is not even a childish man, he is only a degenerate man." *Recherches philosophiques (Oeuvres,* Vol III [Paris: J. P. Migne, 1864]), pp. 360-61.

44. Sigmund Freud, *Civilization and Its Discontents* (London: Hogarth Press, 1946), p. 63.

45. Quoted in Ernest Jones, *The Life and Works of Sigmund Freud* (New York: Basic Books, Inc., 1957), III, 336-37, 342.

46. "Le Dualisme de la nature humaine et ses conditions sociales," *Scientia,* XV (1914), 220-21.

47. See *L'Education morale,* pp. 46-47.

48. Durkheim was wont to stress that repression of instincts redounded to the benefit not only of society but also of the individual. He apparently never entertained the idea that a repressive society might frustrate the individual, or rather he rejected such consideration as "utopian thinking."

49. *Eros and Civilization* (Boston: Beacon Press, 1955).

50. *The Moral Judgement of the Child* (Glencoe, Ill.: Free Press of Glencoe, Illinois, 1948), Chap. iv.

51. *L'Education morale,* p. 183.

52. *Op. cit.,* p. 364.

53. Merton, *op. cit.,* pp. 5-6.

54. Whitehead, *op. cit.,* p. 159.

THE INFLUENCE OF DURKHEIM AND
HIS SCHOOL ON THE STUDY OF RELIGION

PAUL HONIGSHEIM

The influence of Durkheim and the Durkheimians on the study of religion is reflected, in large part, in the writings of Henri Berr, Marcel Mauss, and Lucien Lévy-Bruhl, who were the editors of important series of sociological, religio-historical, and ethnological monographs. Among these collections are two of special importance: *Travaux et mémoires de l'Institut d'Ethnologie* (abbreviated hereinafter as *Travaux et mémoires*), which was edited by Lévy-Bruhl and published in Paris by Félix Alcan beginning in 1926; and *L'Evolution de l'humanité* (abbreviated *L'Evolution*), which was edited by Berr and was published originally by La Renaissance du Livre and later by Albin Michel. Berr's forewords are often especially significant; some of them were collected in his *En marge de l'histoire universelle,* published in two volumes in the Séries Complémentaires of the same collection. Some of the works in these series are available in English in *The History of Civilization,* a series edited by C. K. Ogden, and published in London by Kegan Paul, Trench, Trubner and Co., and in New York by Alfred A. Knopf.

The following is a list of the bibliographic sources for the present paper. When translated works are cited in the notes of this paper, page references are to the English version.

ALPHANDÉRY, PAUL. *La chrétienté et l'idée de Croisade.* (*L'Evolution,* Vol. XXXVIII.), 1954. Translated as *Christendom and the Crusades (The History of Civilization.).*

BERR, HENRI. *La synthèse en histoire.* (*L'Evolution,* Séries Complémentaires.), 1911. (2nd ed., 1953.)

BLOCH, MARCEL. *La société féodale.* (*L'Evolution,* Vol. XXXIV.), 1939.

BOUGLÉ, CÉLESTIN. *Essai sur le régime des castes.* Paris: Félix Alcan, 1908. (2nd ed., 1927.)

BRÉHIER, LOUIS. *Le monde byzantin: La civilisation byzantine.* (*L'Evolution,* Vol. XXXII.), 1940. (2nd ed., 1950.)

DELAPORTE, LOUIS. *La Mésopotamie.* (*L'Evolution,* Vol. VIII.), 1922. Translated as *Mesopotamia* by V. GORDON CHILDE. *(History of Civilization.)*, 1926.

DUPRAT, G. L. "Auguste Comte et Emile Durkheim," *Gründer der Soziologie.* Jena: Gustav Fischer, 1932.

DURKHEIM, EMILE. *Les règles de la méthode sociologique.* Paris: Félix Alcan, 1895. (7th ed., 1919.) Translated as *The Rules of Sociological Method* by SARAH A. SOLOVAY and JOHN H. MUELLER. Glencoe, Ill.: Free Press of Glencoe, Illinois, 1947.

———. *Les formes élémentaires de la vie religieuse.* Paris: Félix Alcan, 1912. (2nd ed., 1925.) Translated as *The Elementary Forms of the Religious Life* by JOSEPH WARD SWAIN. Glencoe, Ill.: Free Press of Glencoe, Illinois, 1947.

FEBVRE, LUCIEN. *Le problèm de l'incroyance au XVIᵉ siècle. (L'Evolution,* Vol. LII.), 1942.

GERNET, LOUIS, and BOULANGER, ANDRÉ. *Le génie grec dans la religion. (L'Evolution,* Vol. XI.), 1932. Translated as *Religious Thought of Greece. (The History of Civilization.)*

GLOTZ, GUSTAVE. *La cité grecque. (L'Evolution,* Vol. XIV.), 1928. Translated as *The Greek City* by N. MALLISON. *(The History of Civilization.)*, 1929.

———. *La civilisation égéenne. (L'Evolution,* Vol. IX.), 1932. Translated as *The Aegean Civilization* by M. R. DOBIE and E. M. RILEY. *(The History of Civilization.)*, 1935.

GRANET, MARCEL. *La pensée chinoise. (L'Evolution,* Vol. XXV bis.), 1934.

———. *La civilisation chinoise. (L'Evolution,* Vol. XXIII.), 1948. Translated as *Chinese Civilization* by K. E. INNES and M. R. BRAILSFORD. *(The History of Civilization.)*, 1951.

———. *Catégories matrimoniales et relations de proximité dans la Chine ancienne.* Paris: Félix Alcan, 1939.

———. *Etudes sociologiques sur la Chine.* Paris: Presses Universitaires de France, 1953.

GRENIER, ALBERT. *Le génie romain dans la religion, la pensée et l'art. (L'Evolution,* Vol. XVII.), 1925. Translated as *The Roman Spirit in Religion, Thought and Art* by M. R. DOBIE. *(The History of Civilization.)*, 1926.

GUIGNEBERT, CHARLES ALFRED HONORÉ. *Des prophètes à Jésus: Le monde juif vers le temps de Jésus. (L'Evolution,* Vol. XXVIII bis.), 1935. Translated as *The Jewish World in the Time of Jesus* by S. H. HOOKE. *(The History of Civilization.)*, 1939.

———. *Jésus. (L'Evolution,* Vol. XXIX.), 1938. Translated as *Jesus* by S. H. HOOKE. *(The History of Civilization.)*, 1935.

———. *Le Christ. (L'Evolution,* Vol. XXIX bis.), 1943.

HOUSE, FLOYD N. *The Range of Sociological Theory.* New York: McGraw-Hill Book Co., 1936.

HUBERT, HENRI. *Les Celtes depuis l'époque de la Tène et la civilisation celtique. (L'Evolution,* Vol. XXI.) , 1932. Translated as *The Greatness and the Decline of the Celts* by M. R. DOBIE. *(History of Culture.),* 1934.

HUBERT, HENRI, and MAUSS, MARCEL. *Mélanges d'histoire de religion.* Paris: Félix Alcan, 1909.

———. "Esquisse d'une théorie générale de la magie," *Année sociologique,* VII (1904) .

JARDÉ, AUGUSTE. *La formation du peuple grec. (L'Evolution,* Vol. X.), 1923. Translated as *The Formation of the Greek People* by M. R. DOBIE. *(The History of Civilization.),* 1936.

LABOURET, HENRI. *Les tribus du Rameau Lobi. (Travaux et mémoires,* Vol. XV.) , 1931.

LEENHARDT, MAURICE. *Notes d'ethnologie néo-calédonienne. (Travaux et mémoires,* Vol. VII.) , 1930.

———. *Documents néo-calédoniens. (Travaux et mémoires,* Vol. XI.) , 1930.

LÉVY-BRUHL, LUCIEN. *La mentalité primitive.* Paris: Félix Alcan, 1922.

———. *La mythologie primitive.* 2nd ed. Paris: Félix Alcan, 1935.

LODS, ADOLPHE. *Des prophètes à Jésus: Les prophètes d'Israël et les débuts du Judaisme. (L'Evolution,* Vol. XXVIII.) , 1935.

LOT, FERDINAND. *La fin du monde antique et le début du Moyen Age. (L'Evolution,* Vol. XXXI.) , 1927. Translated as *The End of the Ancient World and the Beginning of the Middle Ages* by P. LEON and M. LEON. *(The History of Civilization.),* 1931.

MARICA, GEORGE M. *Emile Durkheim.* Jena: Gustav Fischer, 1932.

MASSON-OURSEL, PAUL, WILLMAN-GRABOWSKA, HELENA, and STERN, PHILLIPE. *L'Inde antique et la civilisation indienne. (L'Evolution,* Vol. XXVI.) , 1933. Translated as *Ancient India and Indian Civilization* by M. R. DOBIE. *(The History of Civilization.),* 1934.

MAUSS, MARCEL. "Essai sur le don," *Année sociologique,* Nouvelle Série, I (1923-24) . Translated as *The Gift* by IAN CUNNISON. Glencoe, Ill.: Free Press of Glencoe, Illinois, 1954.

———. "Fragments d'un plan de sociologie descriptive," *ibid.,* Série A, Fascicule 1, 1934.

MORET, ALEXANDRE. *Le Nil et la civilisation égyptienne. (L'Evolution,* Vol. VII.), 1920. Translated as *The Nile and Egyptian Civilization* by M. R. DOBIE. *(The History of Civilization.),* 1927.

MORET, ALEXANDRE, and DAVY, GEORGES. *Des clans aux empires. (L'Evolution,* Vol. VI.) , 1923. Translated as *From Tribe to Empire* by V. GORDON CHILDE. *(The History of Civilization.),* 1926.

The authors of these studies were professors of philosophy, sociology, statistics, ethnology, history, and oriental philology; colonial officials; and, in one case (Leenhardt) , a Protestant missionary. In their works, they often refer to English Darwinists and evolutionists, such as Edward B. Tylor, Herbert Spencer, Baldwin Spencer, and F. J. Gillen; to German ethnologists, such as Heinrich Schurtz and Karl von den Steinen; to German Biblio-critical theologians, such as Hugo Gressmann and Gunkel; and to German historians of the religions of antiquity, such as Hermann Karl Usener and his school.[1] Along with all of these scholars, the Durkheimians believed that the study of religion must be based on the comparative history of religions, including preliterate ones.[2] This is evident when we look at the sociological analyses undertaken by them.[3] In Section I which follows, I shall classify the pertinent propositions and concepts that are contained in these studies according to the contributions they have made to the analysis of particular religions; and, in Section II, I shall classify them according to their significance for our understanding of religio-sociological phenomena. I shall then, in Section III, compare their contributions with Durkheim's. Finally, in Section IV, I shall indicate the significance of the Durkheim school for the history of sociology. It is perhaps not necessary to point out that I shall make no attempt to determine the truth or falsity of the tenets of the Durkheimians, but shall merely describe the contributions which they have made to the history of social thought.

I. The types of religions studied by the Durkheimians

   A. In preliterate cultures

      1. Totemism:[4] According to Durkheim, totemism is one of the earliest forms of group life, a form in which religious functions are undifferentiated from others, and by which the whole of life is regulated. Totemism among Negroes was analyzed by Labouret, that among Melanesians by Leenhardt, and that which occurred during the transitory epoch from preliterate to literate culture and in early Egypt by Moret.

      2. Magic:[5] Durkheim believed that magic differed basically from religion since it was of an individualistic and anti-collectivistic character. Mauss and Hubert studied the magic of preliterate cultures, Granet that of China, and Gernet and Boulanger that of Greece. In contrast to these men, Berr, Lévy-Bruhl, and Delaporte argued that there were cultures in which magic and religion overlapped.

3. The matrilinear society:[6] Labouret, Leenhardt, Granet, and others mention the matrilinear society but they do not analyze it in its relation to religion, as do other scholars.

4. The over-god:[7] Leenhardt only mentions the concept of an over-god or father of the gods occasionally.

5. Prelogical thinking:[8] Lévy-Bruhl used this term to denote a specific kind of reasoning that differed from the occidental (it did not know, for example, the conception that the individual was identical only with itself). By recourse to it, he tried to explain many religious phenomena. The idea of prelogical thinking was opposed by Berr, among others.

B. In literate cultures

1. China:[9] Granet in particular observed the following features of Chinese culture: (a) Almost all religious and apparently non-religious social functions are performed by the same institutions. (b) Marriage is non-individualistic; spouses are selected on the basis of their family membership. (c) Confucianism is non-magical in character. (d) Religious leaders vary from the wise man at the court of a ruler of a small state, to the diplomat, jurist, and casuist at the court of a large empire. (e) The Taoistic sect is the religion of particular lower strata.

2. India:[10] Masson-Oursel pointed out the magical element in the beginnings of the Hindu religion, and emphasized the importance of the expectation of worldly success. Bouglé observed the non-economic element in the beginnings of the caste order, and stressed the importance of Buddhism as a bridge between caste differences.

3. Mesopotamia:[11] Delaporte emphasized the importance of the role of priestesses and—in a departure from Durkheim —of magical functions which were performed by priests.

4. Egypt:[12] Moret insisted that totemism was important in this culture; that the religions of peoples subjugated to the rule of Egypt persisted beneath the official religion; that the worship of Osiris, restricted, at first, to an esoteric cult, later became a mass religion; and that there was a difference between the priest and the magician.

5. Hebrews:[13] According to Lods, the Hebrew prophets orig-

inally came from particular social strata and were professionals who received money as compensation. They sometimes used narcotics to achieve ecstasy and performed magical acts by which they expected to influence the future. They desired to return to a simple, rural life, advocating, in some instances a reversion to animal husbandry and nomadism. Later, the so-called great prophets protested the receipt of monetary compensation and the use of narcotics, but they continued to practice magic. Guignebert analyzed the interrelationship between later Jewish sects and certain social groups; that is, between the Pharisees and the artisans who opposed Hellenism, between the Sadducees and the fashionable bourgeois, and between the Essenes and the esoterics who sought to escape the world.

6. Antiquity: Glotz's[14] ethnological interest in Aegean culture as the background of Greek culture is not particularly relevant (except for the emphasis which he gives to the existence of priestesses). More important are three observations on the religions of antiquity:[15] The life in the city-state, which was based on families considered as sacred entities, and was, therefore, non-individualistic, changed so that the individual was liberated and the power of the city was undermined through the individual. This development led eventually to the rise of large imperialist states such as Alexander the Great's (Glotz), the expansion of esoteric cults into popular movements (Gernet and Boulanger); and the emergence of augurs, who were magicians of a sort, but different from other religious leaders.

7. Celts:[16] Hubert stressed the existence of three different kinds of religious leaders in this culture—druids, who represented a religio-political power; bards, who were popular as prophets; and *vates* who were religious poets.

8. Christian religions:[17] Six points were stressed in this connection: (a) Guignebert pointed out that Jesus was unique and independent of the surrounding world—independent, particularly, of the Jewish sects. (b) He saw the apostles as an example of a small group of disciples united among themselves and with their master in an intimate relation. (c) He discussed the propaganda for

Christianism made by Hellenistic Jews. (d) Lot commented on the distinction between priests, who are concerned with the souls of others, and monks, who normally have no such ministerial concern but live isolated lives, a distinction seen among Irish and Scottish-Gaelic Christians. (e) Alphandéry observed the antagonism between ecstatic masses and the leaders who have incited, but can no longer master them—such as that between Bernard of Clairvaux and the crusaders. (f) Bloch discussed the religious justification of feudal segregation in medieval society. (g) Febvre analyzed the sociopsychological foundation of modern occidental incredulity.

II. Durkheimian studies classified according to the religio-sociological phenomena they investigated

(The religio-sociological phenomena surveyed in the preceding section—totemism, magic, the religion of the matrilinear society, and the concept of the over-god—do not occur in preliterate cultures only; they are characteristic of societies in general, and were treated as general phenomena by the Durkheimians. Others which were also the objects of their investigations follow.)

A. Discipleship: treated by Guignebert in his study of Jesus' apostles.[18]

B. Caste: described by Bouglé as being primarily non-economic in character.[19]

C. Cult: defined by Moret and Gernet and Boulanger as a small esoteric group that became the religion of a larger group; examples were found in Egypt and Greece.[20]

D. Sect: studied among the Chinese by Granet and among the ancient Hebrews by Guignebert, and defined as a group composed of persons coming from a particular social background.[21]

E. Feudal segregation: an institution that was justified on religious grounds, was investigated as a phenomenon of early medieval French society by Bloch.[22]

F. The religion of the masses: the mass ecstasy of the crusaders, in contrast to the moderation of some of their leaders, was discussed by Alphandéry.[23]

G. The religions of specific social strata: that of the Chinese Taoists was studied by Granet, that of the peoples subjugated by Egypt by Moret, that of the Jewish sectarians by Guignebert, and that of the Greek townspeople by Jardé.[24]

H. Propaganda: the Christian propaganda disseminated by Hellenistic Jews was investigated by Guignebert.[25]

I. Religion in its relation to the surrounding world: the comparison between the religion that identifies itself with the state and that whose cults and sects diverge from the state was drawn by Granet, who observed the latter variety in China, and by Gernet and Boulanger, who saw it in antiquity.[26]

J. Religious leadership in its various aspects: (1) the independence of the leader from his environment: Jesus (Guignebert) ; (2) the antagonism between leaders and the masses that follow them: Bernard of Clairvaux and the crusaders (Alphandéry) ; (3) the existence of various types of leaders within the same culture: among the Chinese (Granet) and among the Celts (Hubert) ; (4) priests who are at the same time magicians: in Mesopotamia (Delaporte) and in antiquity (Grenier) ; (5) the special function and position of priestesses: in Mesopotamia (Delaporte), Aegean culture (Glotz), and Greece (Jardé) ; (6) monks, as differentiated from the clergy proper: among Celtic-speaking Christians (Lot) ; (7) prophets in their various forms and activities: Hebrews (Lods) .[27]

K. The individual: Granet pointed out how insignificant he is shown to be by Chinese marriage customs, and Gernet and Boulanger discussed his function in undermining the power of the group in antiquity.[28]

III. The Durkheimians compared with Durkheim

A. Contributions which illustrate Durkheim's theories

1. Concerning preliterate cultures

   a) Totemism: Labouret; Leenhardt; Moret and Davy

   b) Magic: Granet; Hubert and Mauss

   c) The matrilinear society: Granet, Labouret, Leenhardt, and others (there is, however, no analysis of the religio-sociological ramifications of this type of organization)

   d) The over-god: Leenhardt (but without such analysis)

2. Concerning literate cultures

a) China: non-individualistic and non-magical character (Granet)

b) Egypt: continuance of totemism; difference between priests and magicians (Moret)

c) Antiquity: difference between priests and magicians in Rome (Glotz) ; the function of the individual in undermining the group (Gernet)

d) Christianism: the structure of the group of Apostles (Guignebert)

B. Contributions which represent enlargements on Durkheim

1. Concerning preliterate cultures: prelogical thinking (Lévy-Bruhl)

2. Concerning literate cultures

a) China: typology of leaders; relation between social strata and sects (Granet)

b) India: Bouglé, Masson-Oursel

c) Mesopotamia: role of priestesses (Delaporte)

d) Egypt: none

e) Hebrew: function of prophets and sects (Lods, Guignebert)

f) Antiquity: priestesses in the Aegean culture; changes in relation between individual and group (Glotz)

g) Celts: classification of religious leaders (Hubert)

h) Christianism: propaganda made by Hellenistic Jews (Guignebert) ; differentiation between priests and monks (Lot) ; antagonism between leaders and masses (Alphandéry) ; religious justification of feudal segregation in medieval society (Bloch) ; sociopsychological foundation of modern occidental incredulity (Febvre)

C. Contributions which represent direct deviations from Durkheim

1. Prelogical thinking (Lévy-Bruhl)

2. Interrelationship of magic and religion (Berr, Delaporte, Grenier, Hubert, Lévy-Bruhl, Lods, Mauss)

3. Independence of the leader from the group (Guignebert)

D. Objects of controversy among the Durkheimians: The problems of prelogical thinking and of magic, just referred to.

IV. The significance of the contributions of the Durkheim school in the history of sociology

A. Concerning preliterate cultures

1. Totemism: Durkheim and his followers emphasized more than did others the antiquity of totemism, its religious character, and the fact that it is one of the most pronounced instances of the control of the individual by the group. While in more recent years, other problems have become more prominent in the discussion of totemism— for example, the controversy over whether it originated independently in a number of cultures or has spread from one center—the Durkheimian conception has remained indispensable to any discussion of the topic.

2. Magic: The theory that magic is basically different from religion is much older than Durkheim, but it was he who gave it a complete formulation. It has adherents not only among his followers but also among others who are largely or completely independent of him—scholars such as Henri Bergson, Georges Gurvitch, Richard Thurnwald, Ruth Benedict, and Bronislaw Malinowski. However, magic has been considered the beginning of, or as a special kind of, religion by such otherwise heterogeneous authors as Roberton Smith, Max Weber, Lucien Lévy-Bruhl, Robert H. Lowie, and Florian Znaniecki. The discussion is not over, and the ideas of Durkheim and the Durkheimians are still involved in it.

3. Prelogical thinking: Lévy-Bruhl's theory has been much discussed. It has become a conspicuous concept in the "philosophical anthropology" and social philosophy of Max Scheler, but has been rejected by Father Schmidt and his diffusionist school, as well as by his antagonists, the American positivists.

B. Concerning literate cultures

1. China: Granet's scheme of the stages of social history is much more elaborate than that of Max Weber, especially his treatment of the various types of leaders.

2. India: Max Weber presented a more complete system than Bouglé, but Masson-Oursel and his collaborators provided new viewpoints from which to evaluate magic and the importance of the expectation of earthly success.

3. Mesopotamia: International Assyriology has paid little attention to Delaporte's study.

4. Egypt: There has been an uninterrupted interest in Egyptology in France ever since Jean François Champollion. The contributions of Moret are not of great consequence, however, when compared with the later and much more elaborate ones of Jaroslav Černý and Henry Frankfort.

5. Hebrews: Lods's studies on the prophets are part of the vast literature on the Old Testament. They represent a much more detailed description of the various social types of prophets than do Max Weber's. Guignebert's statements on the Jewish sects may or may not be confirmed by further study of the Dead Sea scrolls.

6. Antiquity: Glotz's analysis of the changes in the relations among the individual, the family, and the state was elaborated more systematically than any made before him.

7. Celts: Hubert's classification of religious leaders goes further than earlier ones—Heinrich Zimmer's, for example.

8. Christian religions: Jesus' independence from Jewish sects may or may not be confirmed by future investigations of the Dead Sea materials. Febvre's view of the socio-psychological foundation of modern occidental incredulity was new.

In sum, the Durkheimians have made noteworthy contributions to our understanding of many particular religions—the Chinese, Hindu, Hebrew, and Celtic—and to our knowledge of more general religio-sociological phenomena—totemism, magic, and the interrelationship of magic and religion. The discussion of these phenomena, discussion which the Durkheim school has done so much to stimulate, is still going on.

1. Mauss, "Fragments d'un plan de sociologie descriptive," pp. 2, 8-10, 51; and Moret and Davy, *op. cit.*, pp. 22-54. See also the bibliographies in

Berr, *Travaux et mémoires de l'Institut d'Ethnologie*, Vols. VI and XII, and in the books of Delaporte, Gernet, Glotz, Granet, Grenier, Guignebert, Jardé, Lods, and Moret. Cf. Duprat, *op. cit.*, p. 131, and Marica, *op. cit.*, pp. 22, 133.

2. Durkheim, *The Rules of Sociological Method;* Berr, *En marge de l'histoire universelle*, II, 147; Berr, *La synthèse en histoire*, pp. 156-224; Berr, Introduction to Guignebert, *Le Christ*, p. viii; Bouglé, *op. cit.*, pp. 82-84; and Mauss, "Fragments d'un plan de sociologie descriptive," pp. 2, 8-10, 51 n. 2.

3. For information on the Durkheim school in general, see especially Emile Benoit-Smullyan, "The Sociologism of Emile Durkheim and His School," in *An Introduction to the History of Sociology*, ed. Harry Elmer Barnes (Chicago: University of Chicago Press, 1948), pp. 520-27; Harry Elmer Barnes and Howard Becker, *Social Thought from Lore to Science* (2nd ed.; Washington, D. C.: Harren Press, 1952), II, 839-50; Jean Stoetzel, "Sociology in France," in *Modern Sociological Theory in Continuity and Change*, ed. Howard Becker and Alvin Boskoff (New York: Dryden Press, 1957), pp. 630-46; Paul Honigsheim and Gottfried Eisermann, "Geschichte der Soziologie," in *Die Lehre von der Gesellschaft*, ed. Gottfried Eisermann (Stuttgart: Ferdinand Enke, 1958). All of these contain bibliographical references.

In this paper, the dispute between those who argue that religious ideas, customs, and institutions develop simultaneously and independently in all cultures, and those who maintain that they are diffused from culture to culture, will not be discussed; for this problem—in spite of its complex history—did not play an important part in the development of Durkheim's thought or in that of his followers. Cf. Lévy-Bruhl, *La mythologie primitive*, pp. 132-47, 252; Moret, *op. cit.*, pp. 355-56; Grenier, *op. cit.*, p. 96; Gernet and Boulanger, *op. cit.*, Part I, Chap. iii; Part II, Chap. iii; Part III, Chap. ii. See also Marica, *op. cit.*, p. 105.

4. Durkheim, *The Elementary Forms of the Religious Life;* Duprat, *op. cit.*, p. 121; Marica, *op. cit.*, pp. 22, 130; Moret and Davy, *op. cit.*, pp. 11-54; Moret, *op. cit.*, pp. 49, 121-23, 362-68; and Glotz, *The Aegean Civilization*, pp. 227-42, 252-54.

5. Durkheim, *The Elementary Forms of the Religious Life*, pp. 42-47; Berr, *En marge de l'histoire universelle*, II, 193; Granet, *Etudes sociologiques sur la Chine*, p. 259; Delaporte, *op. cit.*, pp. 150-52; Moret, *op. cit.*, pp. 403-10; Lods, *op. cit.*, pp. 58, 188; Grenier, *op. cit.*, pp. 101-5; and Hubert, "Esquisse d'une théorie générale de la magie," p. 134. See also House, *op. cit.*, p. 127.

6. Berr, *En marge de l'histoire universelle*, II, 155-57; Granet, *Chinese Civilization*, Part II, Book I, Chap. ii; Leenhardt, *Documents néo-calédoniens*, p. 214; and Labouret, *op. cit.*, p. 239. See also Paul Honigsheim, "Altamerikanische Kultur, primitive Kunst und Naturvölker

im heutigen französischen soziologischen Schrifttum," *Kölner Vierteljahrshefte für Soziologie*, XII (1932-33), 78-79.

7. Leenhardt, *Notes d'ethnologie néo-calédonienne*, p. 221.

8. Lévy-Bruhl, *La mentalité primitive;* Lévy-Bruhl, *Primitives and the Supernatural*, trans. Lilian A. Clare (New York: E. P. Dutton & Co., Inc., 1935) ; Berr, *La synthèse en histoire*, pp. 187-90; and Berr, Introduction to Moret and Davy, *op. cit.*, p. xxi.

9. Berr, *En marge de l'histoire universelle*, II, 155, 203; Granet, *La pensée chinoise*, pp. 507-83; Granet, *La civilisation chinoise*, pp. 165-517; and Granet, *Etudes sociologiques sur la Chine*, pp. 3-62.

10. Berr, *En marge de l'histoire universelle*, II, 193; Bouglé, *op. cit.*, pp. 33, 66, 89, 94; and Masson-Oursel, *op. cit.*, Part III, Chap. i.

11. Delaporte, *op. cit.*, pp. 149-57.

12. Moret, *op. cit.*, pp. 49, 121, 234, 355, 362-68, 403.

13. Lods, *op. cit.*, pp. xii-xvi (in the Foreword by Berr), 56-72, 88-153; Guignebert, *The Jewish World in the Time of Jesus*, Book III, Chap. ii; and Guignebert, *Jesus*, Part II, Chaps. iv and xi.

14. Glotz, *The Aegean Civilization*, pp. 227-56, 265-76.

15. Berr, *En marge de l'histoire universelle*, II, 22-24; Jardé, *op. cit.*, Part IV, Chap. i; Glotz, *The Greek City*, pp. 3-5; Grenier, *op. cit.*, pp. 96-102; and Gernet and Boulanger, *op. cit.*, esp. Part I, Chap. iii; Part II; Part III, Chaps. i and ii.

16. Berr, *En marge de l'histoire universelle*, II, 94-96; Hubert, *The Greatness and the Decline of the Celts*, pp. 228-37.

17. Guignebert, *Jesus*, pp. xv (in the Foreword by Berr), 64-66, 130, 146-58, 188-89; Guignebert, *Le Christ*, p. 130; Bréhier, *op. cit.*, pp. 279-313; Lot, *op. cit.*, pp. 445-49; Bloch, *op. cit.*, pp. 191-428; Alphandéry, *op. cit.*, pp. 127-29, 183-85; and Berr, Introduction to Febvre, *op. cit.*, pp. xxvii ff.

18. Guignebert, *Jesus*, pp. 219-23.

19. Bouglé, *op. cit.*, pp. 82 ff.

20. Moret, *op. cit.*, pp. 253-60. Gernet and Boulanger, *op. cit.*, Part I, Chap. iii; Part II, Chap. iii; Part III, Chaps. i, iii, iv.

21. Granet, *La pensée chinoise*, pp. 502-52; Guignebert, *Jesus*, pp. 140-42; 145-58, 163, 400; and Bréhier, *op. cit.*, Book IV, Chap. ix.

22. Bloch, *op. cit.*, pp. 191-428.

23. Alphandéry, *op. cit.*, pp. 127 ff., 183 ff.

24. Granet, *Chinese Civilization*, Part II; Granet, *La pensée chinoise*, pp. 425-71, 554; Moret, *op. cit.*, pp. 355-57; Lods, *op. cit.*, pp. xii-xvi (in

the Preface by Berr), 63-72; Jardé, *op. cit.*, pp. 285-89; and Gernet and Boulanger, *op. cit.*, p. 34.

25. Guignebert, *Le Christ*, Part I, Chap. iv.

26. Granet, *Chinese Civilization*, pp. 165-517; Gernet and Boulanger, *op. cit.*, pp. 318, 350.

27. Berr, *En marge de l'histoire universelle*, II, 94-96; Granet, *La pensée chinoise*, pp. 419-21, 552-78; Delaporte, *op. cit.*, pp. 149-57; Glotz, *The Aegean Civilization*, pp. 265-67; Lods, *op. cit.*, pp. xvi (in the Foreword by Berr), 56-72, 88-153, 188; Grenier, *op. cit.*, p. 101; Hubert, *op. cit.*, pp. 228-37; Guignebert, *Jesus*, pp. xv (in the Foreword by Berr), 64-68, 139, 187-89, 399-405; and Lot, *op. cit.*, Part III, Chap. xiv.

28. Granet, *Etudes sociologiques sur la Chine*, pp. 3-62; Gernet and Boulanger, *op. cit.*, p. 470.

SOME ASPECTS OF THE LEGACY OF DURKHEIM

ALBERT SALOMON

Of those thinkers who, in the history of sociology, have given new directions and perspectives to a discipline in the making, only Emile Durkheim organized a school made up of the creative minds of a younger generation who were able to carry sociology forward. Vilfredo Pareto contributed to depth sociology, Georg Simmel to the epistemology of sociology, Max Weber to the development of sociology as comparative history; but although the ideas of these men were constructive and far-reaching, they did not train students to continue and expand their work.

Durkheim conceived of sociology as a new method, a scientific device for demonstrating the forces of attraction and coercion exerted by collective representations in all fields of thinking, feeling, and conduct. The method was revolutionary in that it rigorously applied scientific principles to the study of the concrete situation of man, and attempted to find rules which would enable sociologists to discover the laws of social behavior in typical situations found in life. The method found both enemies and enthusiastic disciples.

The enemies fell into two groups: the first was composed of representatives of traditional social science—historians who relied on the guesswork of subjective interpretation, and psychologists who were concerned with the behavior of individuals; the second, of theologians and metaphysicians who repudiated a science that rejected all ontological or spiritual assumptions in explaining the natural process of human coexistence in social institutions. Among the followers were students of philosophy who were attracted by a concrete theory and a philosophy of immanence; students of psychology who were convinced that the collective representations conceived by Durkheim provided the necessary complement to individual representations; and historians and social scientists who, in an age of mass societies, understood the value of discovering scientific rules, of setting up classifications of social phenomena,

247

of developing quantitative methods, and of making morphological studies. These followers became members of a new school in sociology—the Durkheim school.

Durkheim's students were fascinated by his passionate belief in the efficiency of his method. They were attracted by his Platonic love of finding higher truths in a search shared with his students: for Durkheim, dedication to his disciples was one with dedication to his cause. The common enterprise, Durkheim's students felt, was in the French humanistic tradition.

Durkheim hoped that his theoretical studies might help to raise human and social standards. He believed in scientific enlightenment. He knew of human suffering, of death and coercion; and he was grimly aware of the inertia of society that results from the false security of its prejudices. He believed in the potential blessings of solidarity, in spite of the trends of his time toward new patterns of despotism. He was convinced that science could give men courage to condition and control their world.

The work carried on by Durkheim with his students has left as its monuments the *Année sociologique* and the publications of his students. Our awareness of Durkheim's greatness increases when we examine his ideas as they were applied by his disciples. When we study his *Le suicide,* we should also consult Maurice Halbwachs' *Les causes du suicide;*[1] in it we see that Halbwachs retained the general pattern of Durkheim's method, although there had been improvements in statistics, and social and economic changes in the thirty years between the two books. The reader of *Les règles de la méthode sociologique* and *Les formes élémentaires de la vie religieuse* should also study Marcel Mauss's theory of total sociology, which he presented in an address on sociology and psychology delivered in 1924, "Rapports réels et pratiques de la psychologie et de la sociologie," and in "Essai sur le don"[2] of 1923, a work that is one of the few great pieces in the field of total sociology.

Many remarkable men in the fields of economics and sociology have been students of Durkheim's; they have worked in the areas of social organization, legal and moral institutions, sociology of religion, statistics, technology, theory of civilization, social psychology, and cultural anthropology. In co-operating with the master, these men became the builders of the first series of the *Année sociologique,* which, between 1896 and 1913, served to express the Durkheim spirit. The volumes of this periodical make exciting reading for the historian of ideas and the student of sociology. For seventeen years, Durkheim and his group collected literature from all the fields that were concerned with the problems of man in his social aspects. The twelve volumes that resulted reflect the sociology of the time, containing analyses of the works of Lester F. Ward, Albion W. Small, Georg Simmel, and Ferdinand Tönnies. The masters of the English and American schools of cultural anthropology were subjected to methodological and substantive critiques, and the German literature in the areas of economics, social history, moral statistics, and the social organization of the family was explored.

In compiling material for *Année sociologique,* Durkheim directed his students to do specialized research. He was convinced that the main task of the sociologist was to penetrate the diverse areas of social action and thought. He knew that methods do not develop in a vacuum and that problems entail their own specific methods according to the requirements of the fields in which they occur. For this reason, he urged his fellow workers to gain a thorough knowledge of specific areas. Marcel Mauss, Robert Hertz, and Henri Hubert became experts in the large field of religion, where they made studies of cult, ritual, prayer, and dogma. In social economics, François Simiand and Maurice Halbwachs specialized in making comparative studies of the family budgets of workers in Europe and the United States; Simiand also studied the sociological aspects of the setting of prices and the distribution of economic goods.

The Durkheim group used the literature in all of these fields as a testing ground for applying and verifying their method. From authors in the humanities and the social sciences, they learned what the substantive problems of their disciplines were, and they measured the value of their works according to the contributions they made to sociology. They found some whose ideas made it possible to form sociological hypotheses, and others who disregarded sociological methods entirely but who would have profited from applying them in their work. They were convinced that unless these methods were used no comprehensive analysis of social facts was possible; and in their critical evaluations, they stressed the problems of comparative methods.

Durkheim and other contributors to the *Année sociologique* were concerned with constructing classifications which were sufficiently flexible and dynamic to accommodate the infinite variety of human social situations. They remembered the dictum which Durkheim had expressed in the Preface to the first volume of their periodical: Only a thorough acquaintance with the humanities, psychology, and the social sciences would enable sociologists to develop a general theory of civilization. They advanced the methods of social-functional and social-causal analysis, although they were not always careful to distinguish their specific characteristics.

In 1908, Durkheim announced that in the future the periodical would appear only every third year. He pointed out that contributors had become so dedicated to their assignments that many of them had had to neglect their own work. This was especially true of Marcel Mauss.

Although Mauss directed the publication's section on religion, his articles also contributed a great deal to general theory. He worked constantly to devise new classifications for the study of religion and to reorganize the field. Thus, when new material on totemism appeared, he found it necessary to form a new subdivision. He also had some noteworthy ideas on the classification of myths. In addition, he wrote a number of illuminating pages on the sociological evolution of prayer from a collective to an individual phenomenon.

Mauss enjoyed a unique relation with Durkheim, who was his uncle as well as his master. As a young man, he worked with him on the final versions of *Le suicide* and *Les formes élémentaires de la vie religieuse*. The latter appeared at the same time as Sir James Frazer's *Totemism and Exogamy*,[3] and Durkheim and Mauss wrote a comparative analysis of the two studies, which showed the differences between the theories of totemism of the two men. This analysis was Durkheim's final statement concerning the relevance of totemism in explaining the social organization of the Australian tribes. In his most important books, Mauss often paid tribute to the inspiration which he had received from Durkheim, giving him the credit for the work that he himself did in sociology—work which turned a method of research into a theory of total sociology.

One article written jointly by Durkheim and Mauss in 1901, was of special importance to both of them. It is "De quelques formes primitives de classification,"[4] a contribution to the study of collective representations, and the foundation of a sociology of knowledge and religion. The authors explain that the patterns of logic which operate among the Australian tribes are the result of their having experienced the divisions of their own tribal organization. Durkheim and Mauss reject Lucien Lévy-Bruhl's idea of prelogical thinking and develop a theory which demonstrates that logical patterns reflect social experiences. According to them, the Australians constructed concepts of genera and species from the reality of phratries and clans. The modes of social cohesion, such as homogeneity and hierarchy, were transferred, in a logical sequence, to the categories of the mind. The bonds that united all beings were conceived of as social bonds.

Collective representations, which give cohesion to society, are, at the same time, collective affections. For this reason, logical and affective categories merge; value attitudes and logical procedures are intertwined. The Australians, for example, divide everything into sacred and profane, pure and impure. They conceive of a whole, for example, as a dual structure of positive and negative elements.

Collective representations are the basis for classifying the world, which is a totality of the divine and the demonic, and men, who are part of this totality. Man is by nature sociocentric: society is the center of all early conceptions of nature. The Sioux and Zuni Indians, the early Greeks, and others held that their land was the center of the world; they referred to other parts only in relation to themselves. The primary dualism of the social world—which is typified by the divisions into we and they, Greeks and barbarians, friends and enemies, and I and thou—is reflected in early conceptual systems. Durkheim and Mauss went so far as to assert that all diversities in primitive classifications could be explained on the basis of physiological differences.

This study by Durkheim and Mauss was the first effort ever made to conceive the social phenomenon as a totality in which the physiological, psychological, and social elements in the constitution of man in society are interdependent and interact with one another. The authors themselves noted that this discovery was the beginning of a new road—one which implied the possibility of error. Ultimately, it led to the idea of total sociology. For Mauss, it became the basis of his essay, *The Gift,* a masterpiece of analysis and synthesis in scientific sociology, in which he shows that in primitive societies exchange more frequently consists in reciprocal gifts than in economic transactions. Such gifts have a much more important function in archaic societies than in our own. Primitive exchange is a total social fact; at one and the same time, it has social and religious, magical and economic, utilitarian and sentimental, and legal and moral significance. In many of the societies found among the Indians of the American Northwest, and in many of those in Alaska, New Zealand, and Australia, the nobles or the whole tribe offered gifts to other groups on all solemn public and private occasions. Usually, gifts of equal value were exchanged simultaneously by both parties. Or, if the second group reciprocated later, the gifts they rendered had to be more precious than the ones they received earlier—in order to pay interest, as it were. These ceremonies had still other functions: to establish publicly the claim of a group or family to a title or privilege, and to surpass a rival in generosity or crush him under the burden of overwhelming obligations.

The goal of this exchange of gifts is social prestige rather than economic advantage. The leitmotiv of Mauss's work is that giving-receiving and rendering are the main patterns of social behavior by which lasting human peace can be established and the possibilities of humaneness in the routine of economic or political institutions can be maintained. It is a universal pattern all over the world, one that transcends the artificial distinction between primitive and historical societies. Mauss gave ample proof of the fact that people everywhere are moved by the same desire for power, prestige, and social position, and by the same fear of losing all three. For this reason, they offer gifts to one another, and it does not matter whether the giving is called presentation, potlatch, or contract. Mauss opens our eyes to the fact that in its everyday routine and on its great occasions —both public (the making of peace, the declaration of war, the punishing of an outlaw, the re-admission of a repentant sinner) and private (birth, marriage, death)—the life of man is a series of rituals. The rituals in which gifts are exchanged are the bonds which make for the integration of the diverse interests, tensions, and affections that are indispensable factors in the coexistence of human beings with, for, or against one another. Rituals are more than habits since they are accompanied by the ambiguity of our affections. Gifts can be received and given with good will and friendship or with fear and resentment. They can be the expression of pride or humility, despair or ambition. The German *sich revanchieren,* which means both "to return a gift or favor" and "to take revenge," preserves this ambiguity.

Mauss did not share Durkheim's gloomy view of capitalist society. Rather he saw in capitalism corporate elements which created mutual responsibilities for both management and labor, and transformed the revolutionary relationship between these classes into a variety of exchanges that were made in the spirit of giving, receiving, and rendering.

The Gift found its counterpart in theory in the previously mentioned address on sociology and psychology that Mauss delivered in 1924, seven years after Durkheim's death. In this paper, he refers to specific investigations being conducted by the Durkheimians as constituting the fundamental elements from which a theory of the totality of social facts could be derived, and establishes the rules of total sociology. Mauss begins his speech by insisting on a point on which psychologists and sociologists agree: they share the attitude of the scientist and employ a method that is experimental and empirical but have different subject matters. Psychology is concerned with the individual conscience, sociology with the natural history of man in society and the manifestations of the *conscience collective.* However, both sciences are, according to Mauss, part of a larger complex which he calls anthropology—a combination of the sciences dealing with man as a living, conscious, and social being. It was Mauss's conviction that the co-operation of psychologists, biologists, and sociologists would make possible the creation of a sociology that could develop as a theory of the totality of social facts.

In logical sequence, the elements of total sociology are (1) social morphology, (2) mass phenomena, (3) social facts, and (4) collective representations, affections, and recollections. "Social morphology"—a term coined by Durkheim in 1900 to designate a classification that he added to a new division in social research—is the original sphere of the study of man in a social perspective. It deals with the relation between social behavior, collective representations and affections, and the substratum of group life. "Substratum" refers to the material and external conditions under which societies live. As they change, according to Durkheim's theory, so do intellectual, social, and emotional factors. Collectivities create specific modes of behavior and action in order to establish a sensible way of meeting and controlling their life conditions. In penetrating and organizing their substrata, they build up intelligible and subjectively meaningful social contexts.

Mauss pays particular attention to the substrata that are composed of climatic and geographic conditions, analyzing their presence or absence within particular political frontiers, and determining the effect they have on the size and density of the population and the system of communication that is used. And in his essay on the seasonal variations found in Eskimo societies, "Essai sur les variations saisonnières des sociétés eskimos,"[5] which he subtitled "An Essay in Social Morphology," he demonstrates the truth of the theory concerning the effect of the substratum on the way of life of the collectivity. The scientist, Mauss says, is not bound to apply quantitative methods only; the thorough qualitative analysis of phenomena can be equally evident and conclusive. Thus, in a paper that is as penetrating and comprehensive as the work on the gift, Mauss introduces the possibility of describing phenomena completely. Dwelling briefly on what is constant in Eskimo behavior throughout the year, Mauss analyzes the different substrata of the winter and summer settlements and the different ways of life that each represents; the religious and legal norms which are operative during the winter when the population is concentrated in a small area vary from those of the summer when the population is widely dispersed.

The second of Mauss's divisions of total sociology, mass phenomena, designates a subject matter that requires statistical treatment. The quantitative measurement of social traits is, indeed, fundamental to the scientific explanation of all societies, whether modern or archaic. It is concerned, among other things, with birth and mortality rates and the movement of populations—both under ordinary circumstances and under the pressure of war, famine, or revolution. Durkheim's *Le suicide* is a famous example and model of the use of statistical methods.

Social facts, the third division, deals with the total complex of such historical phenomena as traditions, mores, habits, rituals, language, religion, art, technology, philosophy, and poetry.

The last, but most important, division is the study of collective representations, affections, and recollections. The study consists of two parts: the collection and systematization of the ideas that constitute the collective representations, and the examination of the collective behavior patterns that correspond to these representations. Societies are united more closely by common ideas and values—economic, religious, or political— than by the pressures of the substratum that is studied by social morphology. Mauss states emphatically that the explanation of collective representations and affections is the task of the sociologist, not the psychologist; for the sociologist can penetrate to the deep layers of social cohesion, which results from the density and intensity of the collective recollections and affections. This penetration is valuable to the sociological analysis of social and historical time, an analysis that is of importance to the political scientist and the sociologist who studies revolutions.

In constructing the rules of total sociology in this fourfold program, Mauss followed Durkheim's suggestions and expanded his investigations. In addition, he saw the significance of physiology for sociology, a consideration which Durkheim had ignored. Mauss's investigations concerning the techniques used in performing certain physical activities have provided new insights for the theoretical sociologist, the teacher of physical education, and the health officer. In his early life, Mauss had observed variations in the techniques used in swimming, and during the First World War he had studied the various ways in which soldiers in different armies walked and marched. These observations prompted him to inquire into the extent to which collective norms produced such variations; and he found that they were indeed conditioned by the social norms of the education promulgated by specific institutions, and that the techniques of marching, jumping, and running that were used by the different armies were the result of authoritarian decisions. His investigation uncovered further examples of collective education—examples such as that girls educated in convents often walk with closed fists. In addition, he sought to determine the influence of motion pictures on the techniques of bodily activity. While convalescing in a hospital, he noticed that the nurses had a peculiar way of walking, which he could not account for until he realized that they were copying the manner of walking of American movie stars. Many other physical mannerisms can also be attributed to the influence of the motion picture.

The techniques of the body are socially conditioned habits; and these habits produce our social nature (an idea that was first established by Montaigne) and demonstrate the reality of the human being as a totality in which physiological, psychological, and sociological elements merge. Mauss defined a technique as a traditional, efficient act. Techniques form a part of magical, religious, and symbolic behavior. There can be no technique without a means of transmitting it, such as tradition.

Mauss and his disciples disagreed with Durkheim's definition of the relationship between the sociologist and the psychologist. Durkheim had been a student of Théodule Ribot and Wilhelm Wundt, but he maintained that psychology could not contribute to the solution of the problems of the collectivity. Mauss, however, specified three ways in which the psychologist can be of value to the sociologist.

First, the psychologist's concept of mental vigor and weakness (this is related to William James's tough and tender-mindedness) is implicit in the sociologist's idea of anomie. Mauss contributed a case study of anomie—or, more particularly, of thanatomania or the lust to die. Among the Maori, individuals have been known to abandon the will to live and subsequently to die, not because of any physical ailment or act of suicide, but simply because of the pressure of collective recriminations. Such a phenomenon presents a problem to the sociologist which, since it is centered in an individual conscience, the psychologist can help him to solve.

Second, sociologists apply the category of psychosis, and they need the enlightenment which psychiatrists can provide concerning hallucinations, the frenzy of the vendetta, the amok (common among Polynesians and Malayans), and so on. Mauss had the opportunity of witnessing the collective hysteria which swept over Europe after 1933.

Third, the psychologist can help the sociologist in his study of the symbol-constructing activity of the mind. Mauss could not admit the validity of such a claim in its entirety, however, for he saw that the activities of the collective conscience are more symbolic than are those of the individual mind. Indeed, one of the characteristic features of the social fact is its symbolic aspect. Furthermore, the notion of the symbol is a sociological conception derived from the study of religion, law, language, and politics. Durkheim and his students demonstrated that one communicates through symbols. Therefore, although they are ambiguous in their meanings, symbols are easily identified with verities.

Mythical and moral symbols are the manifestations of the effects of the *conscience collective*. They permanently influence the behavior both of the group and of the individuals who compose it. Mauss, then, here saw another meeting ground for the psychologist and the sociologist. And, in this case, Durkheim would not have objected, for he had explicitly stated that the individual, as part of the whole and in performing his social roles, retains various possibilities for realizing himself. Within the limits set by social coercion, human beings are astoundingly alert to loopholes that enable them to indulge their subjective interests. Most individuals are fifth columnists within the *conscience collective*.

The work of another of Durkheim's disciples, Maurice Halbwachs, demonstrates the lasting value and the constructive truth of Durkheim's greatest book, *Le suicide,* which appeared in 1896. Halbwachs published his own *Les causes du suicide* in 1930. A generation had elapsed between the two works, new material had been collected, and new refinements in statistical methods had been developed. But, in spite of all this, Durkheim's theses remained valid. Halbwachs verified and amended them but did not change their basic conceptions. Durkheim's book opened with some chapters on methodology which demonstrated that non-sociological factors were irrelevant to a sociological explanation of suicide rates. Halbwachs praised the sound methodology of the master, who had refused to be concerned with the subjective motivations of the individuals who committed suicide. Motives, he argued, are either subjective ideological constructs or arbitrary definitions laid down by the police or by coroners. He rejected any concern with them as unscientific.

According to Durkheim's fundamental conception, suicide and crime are normal social facts. They become pathological only when they increase at an accelerated tempo. Furthermore, they are subject to causal investigation, and there is a basic correlation between tendencies to suicide and other social patterns. Durkheim made the profound observation that every group and society has a specific scale of values which has its foundation in the evaluation of life and death. Military and commercial societies differ in the evaluations that they make, as do spiritual and secular, and industrial-urban and agricultural–pre-industrial ones.

The social causes of suicidal tendencies can be derived from the diverse social roles which men play in the total social context. Men live in domestic, religious, professional, social, political, and occupational groupings which condition them positively and negatively. Durkheim showed that the suicide rate varies inversely with the degree to which these collective bodies are internally integrated. The more the rules of these groups disintegrate, the more the individual detaches himself from them. His goals and aspirations prevail over those of the group; the individual ego becomes stronger than the social ego.

Egoistic suicide results, then, from the excessive individualism or egoism that is caused by the deficient authority of a *conscience collective* that is disintegrating.

For Durkheim, man is dual. He aspires to be safe, protected, and obedient, and is therefore willing to submit to the moral coercion exerted by society. At the same time, he desires to unfold his personality, and thus he revolts against the necessity of conforming with the collective imperatives. For this reason, societies are dual, as the individual human being is, and are both shelter and barracks, waiting room and prison. This duality results from the fact that civilized men are concerned with more than satisfying their organic needs, and the life of society is a process in which the vital forces are constantly being organized in behalf of social needs. The roles of art, science, morality, and religion, however, transcend the lowest level of social control and establish the higher level of social institutions. The influence of society is paramount in education, which is the socialization of man, the process by which society arouses the sentiments of sympathy and solidarity so as to fashion the young in its image and inculcate in them the beliefs and convictions concerning the good, the beautiful, and the true which it takes for granted. Education is the socialization of man on the basis of the ideals of the older generations of society.

Durkheim's view of man is Machiavellian: man's greeds, lusts, and needs are infinite, and they must be controlled. Machiavelli made the state the humanizing agency; Durkheim made it the moral authority of the *conscience collective*. Society must set the goal for the group and invent the modes of social relations by which human urges and passions are channeled and directed in a way that is favorable to the whole.

If society loses its regulating vitality, anomie arises. This state is further heightened by the passions that are unleashed when men are denied discipline and social authority. Such a situation promotes anomic suicide, which differs from egoistic suicide. The latter results from the release of radical self-centeredness that occurs when the social bonds and collective obligations have grown so weak that they have lost the power to act as integrating forces. Anomic suicide, on the other hand, results when

259

there are no social imperatives because there is no collective integration, a situation that leaves men suffering and forlorn.

In spite of their differences, both egoistic and anomic suicides spring from the fact that society is not present in the necessary amounts in the individual egos. But this absence is not the same in the two cases. In egoistic suicide, the collective power is not sufficiently attractive and constructive to appeal to the vital and strong individual so that he is deprived of goals and directions. In the society in which there is a high incidence of anomic suicide, no creative strength comes from the collectivity. In the social roles he is supposed to perform, the individual does not receive moral direction and meaning from a constructive *conscience collective;* and men are exposed to passions within themselves which are not channeled by common goals and values. Egoistic and anomic suicides do not occur in the same human groups. Egoistic suicide prevails in the professional and intellectual worlds; anomic suicide, in the worlds of industry and finance, among workers and managers alike. Indeed, Durkheim saw a definite correlation between anomic suicide and the free capitalistic society with its grim and unregulated competition, its crises and depressions; for him, this kind of human tragedy expressed the moral vacuum of the contemporary economic and social world.

Before discussing Durkheim's third category of suicide—altruistic—it is important to understand his general definition of the phenomenon and the way in which Halbwachs modified it. Durkheim defined a suicide as a death which results—directly or indirectly—from an act accomplished by the victim who has full knowledge of what the result will be. Durkheim did not say that it is an act committed with the intention of killing oneself, and this was consistent with his belief that "motives" are not relevant for the scientist. Furthermore, the definition he did *not* choose would have excluded many acts which he wished to include.

Halbwachs suggested a modified version. For him, a suicide is a death which results from an act committed by the victim with the intention of causing his own death. It is an act of which society disapproves, although the *conscience collective* does approve of certain suicides of expiation. This modification contains an implicit criticism of Durkheim's conception of altruistic suicide. According to Durkheim, this third type results from an individual's total identification with the commands of the collectivity, as when men die as heroes for their country in war, or permit themselves to be killed as sacrificial victims or as martyrs for their creeds when they have been forced to convert to the religion of a majority.

Halbwachs saw that Durkheim was victimized by his own definition, which made it possible to identify as suicides acts that are incompatible. For this reason, Halbwachs made a distinction between sacrifice and suicide. He defined sacrifice as a death that results from an act based on the decisions and duties emanating from the *conscience collective*. Such an act involves the volition of the sacrificial victim and his recognition of an obligation to the values of the collectivity: a human being who sacrifices himself for the sake of his platoon or becomes a martyr for his conviction meets death voluntarily because he is fulfilling his obligation to the collective institutions to which he belongs. Halbwachs reserves the term "suicide" to designate the voluntary act of a person emancipating himself from the bonds of the collectivity.

This distinction forced Halbwachs to reflect on the ambiguous attitudes which societies disclose in their judgments on death. They condemn suicide, but they strongly approve of it under certain circumstances. This means that, strictly speaking, there is no such thing as suicide as such: there are only types of suicide. Halbwachs distinguishes three: the expiatory, the imprecatory, and the disillusioned.

Expiatory suicide may result from a homicide or from sins committed against the social codes of honor in business or in the military or medical professions. The expiatory suicide kills himself in an act of self-condemnation and atonement. The imprecatory type, illustrated by Anna Karenina's suicide, is inspired by defiance of the collectivity. Here an individual's killing herself is an act against society. Anna hates society's hypocrisy and collective judgment; she is disgusted with life. She kills herself in defiance of a group that has no understanding of the sufferings of a human being; she disputes the right of the collective conscience to act as a moral authority. In the case of the suicide that results from disillusionment, the cause is a profound disenchantment with the place of man in society which is the consequence of the victim's not receiving from the collective structures the protection and guidance he needs. Halbwachs' is a most valuable and constructive critique of Durkheim's conception of altruistic suicide. In addition, his methods were more refined, for he applied microsociological devices that made Durkheim's broad generalizations specific. Durkheim had worked largely with national data, while Halbwachs made greater use of regional figures in drawing comparisons of the social facts in metropolitan, urban, and rural areas.

Halbwachs' re-examination of religion as a protective collective force confirmed Durkheim's thesis concerning the integrating power of Catholicism and the disintegrating tendency in Protestantism. Halbwachs' figures on Jewish suicides show a rapid increase all over Europe between 1891 and 1900; in Amsterdam, for instance, the Jewish suicide rate between 1905 and 1914 was the highest of all religious groups. In general, the suicide rates of various religious groups depend on the faith confessed, but they are also determined, in part, by social conditions. Thus one must know whether a religious group is a majority or a minority, whether it is urban or rural, and whether it is politically conservative, liberal, or radical. For instance, there is a rather high suicide rate among Catholics when they are isolated and dispersed, but it becomes lower when they live in compact enclaves.

Halbwachs discovered an aspect of Catholic suicides which Durkheim had not realized: he found an exact correspondence between the number of mixed marriages and the suicide rate among Catholics. Mixed marriages are an index of Catholic disintegration; and in proportion to their increase, the Catholic suicide rate grows. Halbwachs refined Durkheim's thesis on Catholicism as an integrative force. Although the customs of Catholicism are *religious* customs, it is as customs that they are of interest to the sociologist; for it is as customs that they secure the unity of the group—through the authority of traditions and the traditions of authority. Catholicism is more than an ecclesiastical institution: it is a way of life, a pattern of civilization. Religious and traditionalist motives merge with the mores of the people; Catholic peasant societies are often identical in France, Italy, and the countries of Central Europe. Halbwachs concluded that it is not the religious unity of the Catholics, but the social cohesion produced by their traditions, habits, and customs, that explains why their suicide rate is lower than that of urban and Protestant milieus.

In this discussion, "rural" and "urban" refer not to geographic areas but to segments of the social structure. The high suicide rate among the urban population cannot be explained by assuming that city dwellers are more morbid; actually, native urban inhabitants are relatively secure. Rather the high over-all suicide rate of the city derives from the large number of maladjusted persons, who, after they have migrated from the country to the town or from the town to the metropolis, have found the ways of life and the patterns of work, sociability, and entertainment completely bewildering—a situation that produces anomic suicide.

One of the most impressive among Halbwachs' contributions is his re-examination of Durkheim's theory of the protective character of the family. Durkheim's thesis, he found, had remained valid: the husband is more protected than the wife, and the widower more than the widow. Halbwachs added the observation that as the number of children increases, the protective force exercised by the integrated family grows.

Halbwachs praised Durkheim for his keen analysis of the future of the family. Durkheim had foreseen that what had been the structure of the family for the last three hundred years was going to change because of changes in technology and morals. The technological revolution would free individual members of the family from the obligation to contribute to its maintenance; and the disappearance of the moral and spiritual meaning of the family—together with its function as the model of sympathy, intimacy, and mutual responsibility—would come about, he predicted, with the transfer of allegiances and affections to the collective institutions of totalitarian societies.

Halbwachs accepted Durkheim's statement that the suicide rate is lower in time of war and political crisis, but he modified his analysis of the causes that explain this reduction. Durkheim believed that war and crisis stir the collective affections which

263

unify and integrate otherwise antagonistic groups. Halbwachs did not reject this thesis but added his own observation that wars and crises produce a general simplification of all patterns of life. The limitations placed on all societal relationships and social intercourse by a common danger restrict the possibilities of suicide. When the shadow of death threatens the whole community, the tendency to suicide in the individual is reduced.

Although Durkheim's theory of anomic suicide refers specifically to the nineteenth century, it is confirmed by Halbwachs' analysis of the phenomenon in modern capitalist society; the analysis also substantiates Durkheim's prediction that economic institutions would undergo a transformation, and that, possibly, new patterns of anomie would emerge. Halbwachs points out, however, that Durkheim should have connected the higher suicide rate with the rapid industrialization that was taking place in Germany and France during the second half of the nineteenth century rather than with capitalism in general. Halbwachs makes a distinction between the industrial expansion and the financial expansion of Germany and France; and he shows that, because it was new and revolutionary, it was the former that created maladjustment on all levels of society—a maladjustment that necessitated physiological, psychological, intellectual, and moral changes, and contributed to a rise in the suicide rate.

Halbwachs does well to stress the importance of the particular character of this period: the suicide rate decreased when dynamic capitalism became relatively stable before the First World War, and again following the postwar inflation. He corrects Durkheim when he observes that the suicide rate increases in the depression that follows an economic crisis rather than during the crisis itself. Durkheim's conviction was that capitalistic societies lack the regulatory powers of the *conscience collective,* and, for this reason, anomic suicide has become a feature of modern social pathology.

Halbwachs modifies Durkheim's prediction concerning the anomic state of modern economic societies; for, he maintains, as capitalism develops into a rationally planned society, capitalist and socialist elements merge. Therefore, it becomes possible to inject notions of government-planning and state interference into free economic institutions, so that governments are given the power to control crises and unemployment and to regulate segments of the economy. Halbwachs foresees the general trend to be toward a corporate capitalism that permits the use of socialist devices. Such a development would entail the re-examination of anomie and anomic suicide.

The new corporate state of society envisioned by Halbwachs is not, however, the corporate society in which Durkheim had seen the solution to the moral problem of capitalism. On the contrary, it is characterized by the tendency toward a new monopolistic capitalism, with all the political and moral implications of such a system. Halbwachs saw the trend of the economy moving toward a state of affairs which Durkheim could not have foreseen, but he did not realize that this new type of social organization, with its mammoth institutions and its total rationalization of social behavior, would create new patterns of anomic suicide, and that social stereotypes and the production of technological patterns of culture would throw surviving human beings into total anomie in a world that had become a vacuum ruled by the norms of anonymous efficiency.

Finally, to Halbwachs goes the credit for reconciling the sociologist's position on suicide with that of the psychiatrist—who too often assigned pathological suicides to himself and normal ones to the sociologist. Actually, the interaction of the two disciplines is indispensable for both theoretical and practical purposes.

Halbwachs saw that there is a reciprocal relationship between anomie and neurosis. All social catastrophes—such as loss of a loved one, economic failure, continuous lack of success, cultural and social displacement, exile, and disgrace—produce *déclassés:* men who are removed from their accustomed groups and are discriminated against by the codes of honor or the *conscience collective* of those groups. This feeling of being outside the social framework—a framework that has been taken for granted—produces a consciousness of isolation and loneliness; and men who become aware of solitude in a social vacuum are driven to suicide.

Durkheim did not see that because social facts cause anxieties and depressions it is necessary to use sociological method in psychiatry. Halbwachs and some of his contemporary psychiatrists did. Anarchy in the sphere of values and chaos in moral codes create anomie as a social condition of suicide, but the elements of depression and insecurity and other pathological features are never absent. Halbwachs held that no neurotic is adapted to his social environment, and that every mental illness is an element of social disequilibrium and must be explained by the interpenetration of social and organic causes.

One of the greatest French psychiatrists, Charles Blondel, was a sociologist *because* he was a psychiatrist. He wrote:

> What we call "will" exists merely by the fact that systems of collective imperatives are present in the individual conscience. When we do not conform in our conduct to the collective duties, our will has to justify our behavior before society. The very presence of collective representations suffices to turn our activities into acts of will. We human beings are within ourselves and outside ourselves. So are the reasons for the different patterns of suicide. They can be caused by external coercion and by psychic inner causes, the two most of the time being interdependent.[6]

This synthesizing procedure, which analyzes both the sociological aspects of neuroses and the pathological aspects of social catastrophes, marks genuine progress beyond Durkheim. It constitutes another of the achievements of his disciples in developing his method into a theory of the totality of social facts.

1. Paris: Félix Alcan, 1930.

2. *Année sociologique,* Nouvelle Série, I (1923-24). Translated as *The Gift* by Ian Cunnison (Glencoe, Ill.: Free Press of Glencoe, Illinois, 1954).

3. 4 vols.; London: Macmillan & Co., Ltd., 1910.

4. *Année sociologique,* VI (1901), 1-72.

5. *Année sociologique,* IX (1906), 39-132.

6. Maurice Halbwachs, *Les causes du suicide* (Paris: Félix Alcan, 1930), p. 473.

DURKHEIM IN AMERICAN SOCIOLOGY

ROSCOE C. HINKLE, JR.

Despite their commonly acknowledged indebtedness to Sigmund Freud, Vilfredo Pareto, Max Weber, and Emile Durkheim, American sociologists have just begun actual study of these European influences on their discipline in this country.[1] Recently, investigations of the impact of Freud and Weber have been reported.[2] In turn, this paper attempts to redress the neglect of Durkheim. It examines the role of changing intellectual orientations in the varying reactions of American sociology to Durkheim, just as the previously noted inquiry did for Freud.

The original plan for a comprehensive study of all published statements about Durkheim which can be found in the history of the discipline in the United States was altered only because the proliferation of the literature since the Second World War would have required a paper of excessive length. Consequently, analysis has been confined to three periods prior to 1940: 1890-1917, 1918-29, and 1930-39.[3] Despite this delimitation, the inquiry should be significant to sociologists who share the current interest in Durkheim, which appears to have developed in the 1930's, along with many of the prevailing theoretical and methodological trends.

During the period 1890-1917, few European sociologists were more generally disregarded and less enthusiastically received by American sociology than Durkheim. Of his major studies, only the second edition of *De la division du travail social* and *The Elementary Forms of the Religious Life* were reviewed in the *American Journal of Sociology,* then the sole periodical in the field.[4] Although he was among its foreign editors, he never contributed an article—in conspicuous contrast to Georg Simmel. His participation was limited to a letter to the editor protesting Tosti's misinterpretation of his position, and the abstract of a paper which he delivered at the London School of Economics in 1904.[5] Furthermore, only three articles primarily devoted to analyses of Durkheim were published between 1895 and 1917, and not one was written by an American sociologist.[6] None of the major theorists—including William Graham Sumner, Lester F. Ward, Franklin Henry Giddings, Albion W. Small, Charles Horton Cooley, and Edward Alsworth Ross—extensively treated Durkheim. Sumner's *Folkways* and *Science of Society* (written in collaboration with A. G. Keller) confine references to bibliographic citations. Cooley's works contain only a single allusion to *Le suicide*.[7] Ward is unique among these six sociologists in specifically recognizing Durkheim's endeavor to establish the independence and distinctiveness of social phenomena *sui generis*.[8] Giddings merely notes that Durkheim studies social causes.[9] For him, as for Small and Ross, the emphasis on constraint in the conception of the social fact appears to be the principal distinguishing feature of Durkheim's position.[10] Only Giddings directly confronts the question of the objectivity of the social fact.[11] Although the controversy between Gabriel Tarde and Durkheim was probably widely known, it was mentioned or alluded to only in the major publications of Giddings and Ross.[12] They and Ward also evidence concern with Durkheim's interpretation of social evolution in *De la division du travail social*. Giddings and Ross analyze the implications of the theory of mechanical and organic solidarity.[13] However, Ward confines comment to an appraisal of the appropriateness of the horde, simple segmental (or unsegmented) and polysegmental (or segmented) structures, and the notion of dynamic density in the study of social change.[14] *Le suicide* is the only one of Durkheim's inquiries whose importance for research is noted: to Small, it signifies the possibility of obtaining relatively exact knowledge by using valid methods of research.[15]

On the whole, the judgments which these early theorists passed on Durkheim seem to be negative rather than positive. Cooley's one, limited, incidental, and possibly insignificant reference to Durkheim does appear to be favorable, however. He suggests that the "idea of 'altruistic' suicide . . . enables us to understand how a disgraced army officer, for example, might be driven to . . . [self-destruction] by social pressure."[16] Ward disagrees somewhat with Durkheim, but not in a fundamental or comprehensive way. He proposes certain alterations in terminology and rejects what he believes is Durkheim's idea that sociology is a science devoid of purpose.[17] Although Giddings commends *Les règles de la méthode sociologique* for its "excellent suggestions on the scientific observation of fact," he maintains that the basis of the argument for the exclusive, independent, objective reality of the products of association is fallacious.[18] Ross's evaluation is direct and unmistakable: Durkheim is a "thinker who realized vividly the constraint exercised upon the individual by the plexus of social forms, yet stands helpless before the task of explaining just how these forms came to be."[19] Small apparently was not inclined to extend his endorsement of *Le suicide* to Durkheim's general orientation. His reviews of *Année sociologique* betray some reservations at first, and finally express exasperated incomprehension: the judgments of the *Année* circle, he declares, "do not place themselves in easily definable relations with those of any other group of scholars in the same field."[20]

These reactions to Durkheim on the part of the major theorists of the formative period of American sociology are disconcertingly brief and at best suggestive. The only inclusive analyses of Durkheim are contained in the doctoral dissertations of Lucius Moody Bristol and Charles Elmer Gehlke, both of which were published in 1915.[21] These studies differ in that Bristol is interested in only one aspect of Durkheim's work, his interpretation of social evolution or adaptation, and Gehlke is preoccupied with the entire range of his approach. Although Bristol endeavors to delineate social realism as Durkheim's sociological orientation and offers an introductory summary of Durkheim's basic intellectual antecedents, he is primarily concerned with giving an exposition of *De la division du travail social* and the theory of social solidarity. Criticism is only incidental,[22] but he does dispute Durkheim's claim that men normally achieve a functional position in the division of labor corresponding to their natural capacities. He accuses Durkheim of considering normal only what is morally ideal and of rejecting as abnormal what is factually frequent or normal on a frequency or normal distribution curve. Durkheim

seems to have been misled by Comte's theory of society as a developing personality, by the general organic analogy and by

Galton's theory of natural ability. The law of adaptation does not work so rigidly in social evolution at present as to bring about the survival of those societies only where division of labor is based on natural capacity to the degree assumed by our author. Indeed, . . . we have no data available which afford proof of such differences in ability as assumed by Galton and Durkheim.[23]

Bristol also objects to the view that a group reacts only "passively to its social environment."[24] To "succeed in the greatest degree it must *take thought*. . . . It must, too, not only find its place but *make* its place by seeing a social need as yet unrealized by others."[25]

Although Gehlke provides a more extensive formulation of his fundamental objections to Durkheim's thought than Bristol, his major indictments—apart from Chapter iv, "The Major Premise in Durkheim's Thinking"—are scattered throughout the book. At the end of Chapter v, Gehlke censures Durkheim's sociology for being ideological because it derives logically from his definition of a social fact, which is, in turn, "a concise statement of an elaborate system of psychological metaphysics."[26] He deprecates the Durkheimian social taxonomy for lacking a "basis in ascertained fact" (the horde, for instance, may not be studied objectively since it does not have an independent empirical existence), for requiring too many qualifications to be of much use, and for presupposing the validity of uniform, unilinear social evolution.[27] Gehlke impugns Durkheim's theory of causation on two counts: (1) "Internal necessity cannot be objectively determined," and (2) Durkheim's own procedure appears to be inconsistent with his argument (directed against John Stuart Mill) that a given social phenomenon is the result of one and only one social cause.[28] Gehlke implies that the method of proof is defective, relying as it does on the use of the simple mathematical form of concomitant variation which "does not seem to have kept up with progress in this field."[29] He also objects to certain alleged discrepancies between Durkheim's methodological prescriptions and concepts, on the one hand, and the implications of empirical data, on the other. For example, the social conditions which Durkheim terms abnormal forms of the division of labor are actually found in every advanced country of European civilization. To say that they are abnormal is to deny the likeness of . . . European countries; and this would be an assertion difficult to prove without the use of a much finer scheme of classification than that which Durkheim has put forward.[30]

However, these criticisms are secondary to Gehlke's basic objection to Durkheim's sociology, which is directed against his realist conception of the group. In the chapter on "The Major Premise in Durkheim's Thinking," Gehlke delineates four principal arguments against Durkheim's social realism. First, he maintains that the notion that the group emerges from the compounding or recombining of individual psychic states is either figurative or metaphysical.[31] Second, he reproves Durkheim for resorting to inappropriate analogies in order to justify his social realism. He criticizes his assertion that there is a similarity between the individual minds in a group and the elements in a chemical compound or the cells in a living organism, for this assertion ignores the dissimilarity between knowledge of mind and matter—the former is direct, the latter indirect—and implies "a materialistic conception of the origin of mental processes."[32] Third, he finds Durkheim's conception of the group intellectualistic to the point of disregarding the proper role of the emotional and volitional.[33] Fourth, he argues that his social realism demeans and destroys the role of the individual in social causation. Gehlke insists that Durkheim's position implicitly denies the fact that genius and other innate individual mental differences are operative as causal factors in social life.[34] The Durkheimian theory of social causation presupposes an "intellectual equality of an unreal and impossible kind."[35] For Gehlke, inherited variations in the mental structures of individuals and such other attributes of individuality as consciousness, the "power of choice (whether scientifically or pragmatically verifiable)," and intent are ineluctably important in "that fusion out of which comes the social state of mind."[36] This conviction is an expression of the individualism, nominalism, and voluntarism that are so characteristic of American sociology and so antithetical to social realism.

The same fundamental premise is basic to Bristol's implicit

criticism of Durkheim's social realism. It is expressed, however, as opposition to his attributing "some kind of objective reality,—whether phenomenal or ontological is not discussed," to social consciousness.[37] For Bristol, social self-consciousness, which is the simultaneous recognition that there is a corporate or sociopsychic continuity and a unity in the acceptance of a common end or purpose, "is temporary."[38] Nowhere in the social order can one find "a consciousness of socio-personal continuity,—of identity persisting in change,—such as characterizes the personal ego."[39] The individual's intermittent consciousness of "his organic relation to the various groups to which he belongs"—a relation which involves an extension of his self-consciousness and self-regard so that they include the group, and a feeling or belief that others have a similar experience—has no counterpart in the group; for the group is not conscious of a persisting core within the social personality such as that found by the individual within his own ego.[40] Thus "the individual personality [apparently] has some kind or degree of ontological reality not possessed by any group."[41] Bristol applies the term "group" to an aggregate of individuals only when all of them are conscious simultaneously of a common unity and accept a common end and work toward it voluntarily.

Like other sociologists, Bristol and Gehlke recognize that their individualism and Durkheim's social realism are contradictory. Consequently, they reject Durkheim's conception of the group. Their objection is based on their adherence to the fundamental individualism of American sociology, which is also displayed by both Michael M. Davis, Jr., and Charles A. Ellwood when they criticize Durkheim as an exponent of medieval realism and sociological objectivism.[42]

Another important feature differentiating American from Durkheimian sociology, one which is not specified or articulated, is the deductive, rationalistic formulation of theory in the United States. This practice stems from the assumption that the group must be conceived as deriving, in some sense, from the properties of the constituent individuals. The early American sociologists constructed theoretical systems which explain social structure and change by making logical inferences from an a priori characterization of the nature of the human individual (for example, Sumner's four instincts, Ward's three divisions of social forces, and Small's six categories of innate interests). These systems can be termed rationalistic, for they presuppose the universality of natural laws, appeal to sense perceptions for particulars that illustrate such laws, and use logical consistency as the criterion of truth. In contradistinction, Durkheim does not formally present his sociology as a deductive structure, though his theoretical and methodological apparatus can readily be formulated as a set of logical propositions. Not one of his major works constitutes a system in the sense that Ward's *Pure Sociology* and *Applied Sociology* and Small's *General Sociology* are systems. From the perspective of early American sociology, Durkheim probably seemed to be much more inductive and empirical than deductive and rationalistic. Thus the very formulation and exposition of his sociology are at variance with some of the basic intellectual traditions of the discipline as it developed in this country before the First World War.

Durkheim never experienced the popularity and acceptance enjoyed by such foreign scholars as Auguste Comte, Herbert Spencer, Gustav Ratzenhofer, Ludwig Gumplowicz, Albert Schäffle, or Gabriel Tarde. The systems of these men were used as points of departure for the construction of American sociological theory, but the position of Durkheim served, more often than not, only as the occasion for criticism. His orientation was not given a sympathetic exposition in the journals or major theoretical works of the first period of American sociology.

During the second period of American sociology which lasted from the end of the First World War to the beginning of the depression in 1929—the so-called Chicago era—the construction of large-scale theoretical systems virtually ceased, and European sociologists, including Durkheim, were largely ignored in discussions of the major sociological issues. The few articles in professional sociological periodicals in which Durkheim was considered an important figure were primarily contributed by intellectuals outside America. In 1921, the philosopher J. E. Boodin discussed Durkheim and Lucien Lévy-Bruhl in "The Law of Social Participation."[43] In 1923, an English translation of the Introduction to Durkheim's *Education et Sociologie*, by the French sociologist Paul Fauconnet, was published as "The Pedagogical Work of Emile Durkheim."[44] A year later, Clarence Marsh Case reviewed the entire volume.[45] In 1926, Arthur F. Bentley, the author and journalist, contributed a brief comparative study, "Simmel, Durkheim, and Ratzenhofer,"[46] and Cecil Clare North invoked Durkheim's *De la division du travail social* to document his own argument in *Social Differentiation*, which is couched within the framework of social evolution and progress.[47] However, as is evident from the series of monographs published by the University of Chicago Press in the late 1920's, Durkheim exerted no perceptible influence on the newer movement in empirical research in Chicago. Ruth Shonle Cavan's investigation, *Suicide*, for instance, cites Durkheim's research on the subject only once and entirely ignores his theoretical argument.[48] Occasionally, he was even ignored in the field of theory. Ellwood's apparent protest at Lichtenberger's neglect of Durkheim in the *Development of Social Theory* does not mitigate the fact that he was widely neglected.[49] Indeed, Durkheim's lowly position in Hornell Hart's rating of theorists seems to be an accurate index of the minor significance which American sociologists attributed to him.[50] And this assessment was not the result of ignorance, for as Ellsworth Faris pointed out, "Durkheim has been familiar to American scholars for a generation,"[51] a claim that is certainly true in respect to sociologists—including those of the 1920's. However, Faris' additional allegation that no "European author is more frequently quoted and referred to by our writers" is at best equivocal and at worst erroneous.[52] Even if the meaning of this declaration is narrowly confined, it appears to be incorrect. Obviously, the ultimate test of its validity would involve a laborious—and, from the standpoint of other problems, quite profitless—enumeration of all the references made to European sociologists in American publications. The impression that I gained from an examination of the periodical literature for the present study is that Faris is in error. The same verdict is warranted if Faris' assertion was intended to imply that Durkheim exerted a strong influence on the theory of American sociology.

Objections to the fundamental features of Durkheim's sociology persisted throughout this period. The primary opposition was directed against his social realism. The famous methodological dictum of Thomas in the "Methodological Note" of *The Polish Peasant in Europe and America* was explicitly an attack upon Durkheim's notion of social causality.[53] Thomas' formula that the cause of a social or individual phenomenon (or of a value or an attitude) is never another social or individual phenomenon alone (or exclusively a value or an attitude) but always a combination of a social and an individual phenomenon (or of a value and an attitude) retains the voluntarism and nominalism that are characteristic of American sociology. Other sociologists objected to Durkheim's social realism because it appeared to be metaphysical or mystical.[54] Elsewhere, he was indicted for particularism, premature generalization, or over-simplification.[55] In addition, unrecognized and unarticulated obstacles may have been important. It seems likely that the development, of an a- or anti-theoretical empiricism during the 1920's helped to prevent his being accepted. His insistence on research which is conceived strategically in terms of theory could have had paradoxical consequences: before the First World War, some sociologists may not have liked his stress on research, but in the decade following the war others may have taken exception to his emphasis on theory.

Misunderstanding is scarcely an adequate explanation for this continuing rejection of Durkheim. Park, for example, seems to have adequately comprehended him. His article, "Sociology and the Social Sciences," which constitutes the introductory chapter of *Introduction to the Science of Sociology,* contains the first extensive, lucid, perceptive, and sympathetic interpretation of Durkheim's place in the history of American sociological theory.[56] Park discusses the contrast between Durkheim's social realism and the nominalism of Tarde and Giddings; argues for the real existence of the group; analyzes the distinction between like (individual) purpose and the common (social) purpose that is generated by the association of individuals and is something new, objective, and public which is not merely the sum of, or even like, the particular sentiments and opinions of individuals; describes the external and constraining (or controlling) qualities of the social fact; and states that collective representations conventionalize or symbolize common purposes. Basically, however, Park's theory and the methods of his research are not indebted to Durkheim, despite his occasional references to social solidarity, collective representations, and the dichotomy between the sacred and the secular.[57] Indeed, Park's theory of human association, with its two aspects of community and society (which derive from the traditions of Spencer's individualist and utilitarian competition and Comte's traditionalist and organic consensus) really compromises Durkheim's position. When he declares that man "has never quite succeeded in practice and for long in treating other men as . . . mere physical objects in the landscape," he seems to imply a pan-human sympathetic "consciousness of kind"—man "recognizes that other individual as human like himself"—which is the basis of normative social order.[58] Park proposes that societies "grow up in the efforts of individuals to act collectively."[59] He employs phrases such as "wherever and whenever individuals come together to carry on a common life," and "ever since men first consciously united their common efforts to improve and conserve their common life."[60] In brief, his endeavors to account for society suggest his adherence to an individualism, a voluntarism, and a contractualism that are inconsistent with Durkheim.[61]

It is clear, therefore, that American sociologists of the 1920's did not radically or substantially revise the earlier appraisal of Durkheim. His basic assumptions about the nature of social behavior were at variance with those of American sociology.

In the decade which followed the First World War, however, there were intellectual changes which prepared the way for and facilitated the re-orientation and re-evaluation of Durkheim that came in the 1930's. These modifications came about —directly or indirectly—from disputes concerning methodology. In the course of these controversies, sociologists were led toward, rather than away from, Durkheim's methodological conceptions. Although they affirmed their adherence to a pluralistic approach as opposed to what they believed to be his particularistic (or monistic) conviction, they redefined and restricted the range of the variables which they conceived to be directly and immediately relevant to the explanation of social behavior. Because sociologists of this period came to reject instinct as an explanation of social conduct, to accept the concept of culture of cultural anthropology, to understand George Herbert Mead's conception of the role of the symbol in social conduct, and to insist on inductive, objective research, their ideas tended to converge with those of Durkheim.

By the end of the 1920's, sociologists had generally concluded that the innate features of human nature could not explain the distinctive characteristics of human social conduct. They refused to accept any idea that the human psyche was either innately rational or irrational. The First World War had undermined faith in the inevitability of progress and the underlying postulates concerning man's natural psychic disposition to be rational. Lamarckianism had become suspect even earlier. During the first years of the 1920's, L. L. Bernard and Ellsworth Faris had effectively disputed the role of instincts in social behavior. This de-emphasis of nature was accompanied by an increased emphasis on nurture. Sociologists came to recognize the organic plasticity (or biological elasticity) of man. They conceived human social behavior to be acquired rather than innate. Although many of them refused to accept the deterministic implications of behaviorism, they did not ignore or reject the relevance for sociology of conditioning, the formation of habits, and the processes of learning.

Perhaps the most important factor in delimiting the variables in human behavior and in subtly re-orienting sociologists to Durkheim and especially to his conception of the autonomous character of social phenomena, was the notion of culture that was gained from cultural anthropology. Sociologists had always had contacts with anthropologists, for they had been colleagues in joint departments. But in the 1920's their associations increased in frequency, directness, and scope. Such figures as Ruth Benedict, Margaret Mead, Alexander Goldenweiser, Robert Lowie, Ralph Linton, Melville Herskovits, and Wilson Wallis published papers in the sociological periodicals and appeared at the meetings of the American Sociological

Society. Their arguments on the pertinence of culture for human social behavior has had a permanent impact on sociology. For several years, "cultural sociology" even appeared as a specialty within the discipline. It was especially the concept of culture as something *sui generis*, explicable only in terms of itself, which sociology imported from cultural anthropology, that led sociologists to a re-evaluation of Durkheim. Not all anthropologists subscribed to this definition of culture without qualification. Nor did all sociologists accept the thesis and all of its implications. What is important is that this notion of culture was introduced, intentionally or unintentionally, into deliberations with anthropologists. As a consequence, sociologists were made conscious of the problems involved in interpreting group phenomena individualistically, subjectively, nominalistically, or voluntaristically. Dorothy P. Gary's chapter, "The Developing Study of Culture," in *Trends in American Sociology* is notable in this respect because she views culture as a phenomenon of group (or collective) behavior, the explanation of which on the basis of individual behavior "is not only an inadequate but an irrelevant procedure."[62] As a group phenomenon, culture is objective, shared, or public. The similarity between this conception of culture and Durkheim's views can readily be seen, for his general notion of social fact includes the cultural realm, and his collective representations are specifically cultural.[63] Gary herself refers to Durkheim, among others, as exhibiting "a marked tendency to treat culture as a collective social process."[64] But Gehlke was perhaps the first sociologist to note that "Durkheim . . . aligns himself with those who are emphasizing the explanation of cultural facts . . . by antecedent culture-facts, not by appeal to some posited human trait."[65] Later, Ellsworth Faris characterized Durkheim as a contributor to the knowledge of the nature and growth of mores, and as one who, with his colleagues, has shown "that cultural products exercise a coercive influence over the individual members of a society."[66]

George Herbert Mead's conceptions of the linguistic symbol, meaning, and the social act provided a valuable intellectual vehicle for understanding Durkheim's collective representation. Indeed, the Meadian "verbal symbol" and the Durkheimian "collective representation" are virtually synonymous. Both refer to a separate, objective level of phenomena. Ultimately, each is maintained and re-enforced by a set of public, shared, commonly understood, and conventionalized responses or actions. For Mead, the prototype of the linguistic symbol is the gesture and its meaning in the social act. Meaning is indicated by the gesture of one person oriented to another, by the response of the second individual, and by the subsequent conduct of these or other participants—each of whom plays a part in completing the action and among whom consensus exists. Common social participation and communication are the necessary context. "Meaning is implicit—if not always explicit—in the relationship among the various phases of the social act."[67] It is given or stated in terms of responses referring to or completing a given act or action. This Meadian interpretation makes comprehensible the collective representation as the public symbol or meaning of a shared experience derived from and maintained by common social participation. The import of the collective representation obtains within a social matrix entailing a specific sequence of social acts. When the Meadian doctrine of symbols and symbolic behavior was joined to the anthropological notion of culture, they comprised a body of intellectual conceptions which were congenial to the understanding of Durkheim's views on ideas, meanings, social participation, and social structure.[68]

When American sociologists came to demand careful description, exact comparison of concrete behavior, and inductive empirical study rather than a priori deductive speculation, they were able to appreciate Durkheim's endeavors to formulate canons of sociological research.[69] With the emergence and ascendance of statistics, *Le suicide* assumed a new relevancy. Sociologists began to insist on value-objectivity or impartiality in research, and, in so doing, they were in agreement with Durkheim's contention that a normative or evaluative approach must be rejected as inconsistent with the mandates of science.[70]

It may be said, therefore, that during the 1920's the response of American sociologists to Durkheim was both like and unlike earlier reactions. It was similar in that his orientation was generally disregarded and commonly rejected. It was dissimilar

in that intellectual changes within the discipline were producing a climate that was favorable to an acceptance of his ideas.

The sudden increase of literature on Durkheim during the
late 1920's and the decade of the 1930's—the last years of the
second and the first years of the third periods in American
sociology—are indicative of a new orientation toward him.
Robert K. Merton's article, "Recent French Sociology," and
Mabel A. Elliott and Francis E. Merrill's chapter "Social Disorganization in Contemporary French Thought," informed
sociologists in this country of the persistence of the Durkheimian tradition in France.[71] Almost simultaneously, two of the
three major monographs that had not yet been translated
appeared in English.[72] Merton's and Benoît-Smullyan's reviews
of these translations were valuable analyses in their own right.[73]
Several histories of sociological thought and articles in scholarly
journals also contributed to the exposition of Durkheim's
sociology.[74] Of signal importance in this elucidation and ampli-
fication of Durkheim's intellectual orientation were several
doctoral dissertations of the period: Benoît-Smullyan's "The
Development of French Sociologism and Its Critics in France"
(Harvard, 1938); Harry Alpert's *Emile Durkheim and His
Sociology* (Columbia; published as a book in 1939) ; and John
Foskett's "Emile Durkheim and the Problem of Social Order"
(California, Berkeley, 1939) . The research conducted in preparation for these dissertations prompted the authors to deal
further with Durkheim in subsequent articles.[75] Wilson's early
synoptic presentation, "Durkheim's Sociological Method," appears to be another work which was inspired by doctoral
research.[76]

These articles are unmistakably symptomatic of an emergent
interest in Durkheim, but they do not provide so valuable a
clue to the nature and scope of this interest as do Parsons'
The Structure of Social Action and Merton's "Social Structure
and Anomie."[77] Parsons' 150-page analysis of Durkheim is
undeniably a milestone in the scholarly interpretation of the
steps in Durkheim's intellectual development. It is also important as a source of leads in the search for an explanation of
Durkheim's growing relevancy for American sociology. *The*

Structure of Social Action aligns Durkheim with the pervasive, continuous voluntarism, and Merton's article construes anomie within the same Parsonian theory of action and, in effect, orients Durkheim toward the recurrent preoccupation with social disorganization and social change. Thus Parsons and Merton do explicitly and directly what Everett Hughes did implicitly and indirectly some ten years earlier in his inquiry, "Personality Types and The Division of Labor":[78] they apply Durkheim's concepts and theories to theoretical concerns and problems in an American setting.

In seeking to account for the unprecedented attention paid to Durkheim during this period, we must not ignore the impact of the larger social context. The instrumentalist sanction of the discipline has always demanded a constant sensitivity to the events in American society. The fact that the proliferation of the literature on Durkheim coincides generally with the years of the depression poses the question whether a connection exists between the economic crisis and the new interest in Durkheim.

Apparently, the paroxysm in the economy re-articulated the problem of social order with unparalleled urgency. American intellectuals as a whole became apprehensive about the state of the American social structure. With the complacency of prosperity shattered, sociologists were compelled to recognize that the conditions of social order could no longer be assumed. The crisis raised the question of social integration, solidarity, unity, or order as a crucial, central problem. Sociologists scrutinized the intellectual resources of their discipline for clues and turned to theory, especially foreign systematic theory, for formulations of the nature and conditions of social order.

Since Durkheim had made social order his fundamental theoretical problem, his works were germane to the concerns of American sociologists. He regarded the establishment of a positive science of morals as a means of attacking social disorganization or disorder—particularly in his own France, then so recently defeated in the Franco-Prussian War. His analysis seems to imply that a study of "what is" can divulge "what ought to be." In Foskett's words, Durkheim's morality did not involve "some metaphysical or absolute criteria of right and wrong, of good and bad, but [aimed at] the conditions of social order, harmony, and solidarity."[79] The "ought" or moral rule entails that "type of conduct which contributes to the integration of human behavior and produces social order."[80] And social order itself is made possible by the existence of a body of common and accepted modes of thought and action, by commitment to a set of common, ultimate values.

In 1934, Elliott and Merrill referred to French sociologists, inspired largely by Durkheim, as being the only European group which was "consistently interested in the theoretical aspects of social disorganization."[81]

> Following the tradition of Durkheim, the French have consistently interested themselves in problems of social "normality" and "abnormality," in social solidarity and its opposite, social disorganization. With singular insularity, American writers have neglected to inform themselves concerning these foreign developments in the field of social disorganization. The present chapter ["Social Disorganization in Contemporary French Thought"] attempts to remedy, in confessedly slight measure, this lamentable vacuity.[82]

Although Elliott and Merrill present the theories, concepts, and research of Paul Lilienfeld, Paul Fauconnet, Charles Blondel, G. L. Duprat, and Pierre Janet, they devote about one quarter of the chapter solely to Durkheim. Nevertheless, a systematic account of the implications of Durkheim's arguments for the re-establishment of social order is not offered. Instead, the authors are preoccupied with his statement of the conditions of social disorganization which are exhibited in the abnormal—anomic and coerced—forms of the division of labor, and with his criteria for distinguishing the normal from the abnormal or pathological. They also summarize Gaston Richard's criticisms of Durkheim's social pathology.

The actual exploration of the possibilities of Durkheim's theory of social disorganization did not begin until 1938, when Merton's analytical essay, "Social Structure and Anomie," was published. Accepting Parsons' means-ends action schema, Merton examines organization and disorganization in terms of the relationships of cultural goals and institutional norms. He does not explicitly define anomie, but it seems to be a condition in which either goals or normative means are disproportion- ✓ ately emphasized. Therefore, it obtains in any one of several types of underemphasis or overemphasis of the institutional rules in relation to ends or goals—for example, innovation, ritualism, retreatism, and rebellion.

This developing concern with general theory was found primarily in the work of sociologists who had no connection with the systematic theory of the earlier era in American sociology. Among those active in the revitalization of theory were Robert M. MacIver and Talcott Parsons. Both had been trained abroad and both actively promoted the interest of graduate students in European sociology. Although preoccupation with Durkheim was scarcely confined to Columbia and Harvard, many of the most active figures were students of MacIver (Simpson and Alpert for example) and Parsons (Merton and Benoît-Smullyan).

However, the acceptance of Durkheim was qualified by opposition, objection, criticism, exception, and reservation of such sizable proportions as to preclude an adequate summary here. The criticisms in Merton's review of *The Division of Labor in Society* and Alpert's study, *Emile Durkheim and His Sociology,* are illustrative of the range and depth of the strictures against him:[83]

1. In his work, such basic methodological notions as "thing," "fact," "mechanical," "objective," "natural," "individual," and "constraint" have varied or ambiguous meanings.

2. Positivism requires that Durkheim ignore the "fact that the concept of causation, more markedly perhaps in the social sciences than in the physical, is an epistemological assumption, a matter of imputation and not of observation."

3. Durkheim fails to recognize the role of the *capta* (that is, indirectly, the investigator) and is exclusively preoccupied with the data (the object investigated).

4. His method of deriving definitions ignores the a priori assumptions of the inquirer and fails to offer criteria for deciding how a class should be defined.

5. He does not distinguish properly between his abstract conceptions, which are ideal constructions, and the concrete, empirical situations in all of their variety.

6. He employs concepts as they have been defined in a polemic so that he is compelled to accept the terms set by his opponent.

7. His indexes are deficient in systematic rationales and narrowly limited by his principle of the objectivity of data.

8. The resort to the method of elimination is methodologically fallacious.

9. He adheres to an unverified conception of unilinear social evolution.

10. His schema of analysis is defective because it omits a *verstehen* and means-ends type of inquiry.

However, this criticism, unlike that of the earlier period, was accompanied by a recognition of Durkheim's accomplishments. Emergence of a favorable disposition seems to have been a concomitant of four developments in the treatment of Durkheim.

First, his methodological canons—despite acknowledged defects—were sympathetically explored. After the vigorous disputes over methods in the late 1920's and early 1930's, Durkheim's statement became more meaningful. Ethel Wilson summarized his method for the sociologists of the early 1930's.[84] Later, Alpert devoted about one fifth of his volume to elucidating Durkheim's procedure for making scientific inquiries and giving scientific explanations. In his account of Durkheim's conception of sociology, he adverts to Durkheim's conviction that sociology can prosper only as it confronts specific problems, accumulates relevant facts, and uses "the methods of accurate observation, logical validation and systematic generalization that are characteristic of the scientific approach."[85] Alpert's concise, lucid exposition of Durkheim's schema of analysis—which is perceptively illustrated by concrete cases—specifies seven basic procedural operations: (1) "Define the problem to be analyzed." (2) "Subject existing theories to critical review." (3) "Posit a tentative causal nexus on the basis of firmly grounded correlations." (4) "Demonstrate the intelligibility of the causal nexus . . . by placing it in a given axiological system." (5) "Establish the operative secondary factors." (6) "Treat each of them in the same manner as one has analyzed the causes." (7) "Derive and critically review the consequences of the established propositions and laws."[86] This simple outline of Durkheim's methodological schema increased sociologists' understanding of the French scholar and enhanced their respect for him.

Second, a critical review and redefinition of Durkheim's position on the group, the individual, human nature, and psychology helped to elicit a more positive reaction. Earlier sociologists were repelled by what they regarded as his social realism and his antipsychological animus. Admittedly, this reappraisal did not occur immediately. George Simpson's "Emile Durkheim's Social Realism" can scarcely be said to represent any substantial modification of the older, prevailing conception.[87] But Alpert's designation of realism as a relational or associational social realism did mitigate, if it did not entirely remove, the onus of the "group mind" label. Alpert explicitly differentiates Durkheim's notion of the group from both social nominalism and substantialist social realism:

> In contradistinction to the former, it [relational social realism] insists that "society" does not refer to a plurality of independent beings who are complete in and by themselves and who derive nothing from their "pluralitiness," but rather that it is a term connoting a distinctive reality: a plurality of associated individuals who are in reciprocal relationship, who are bound to one another in an organization of interrelations, and whose characteristics and behavior are directly affected by the fact that they constitute a network or reticulum of relationships. Relational realism is also opposed to substantialist realism, for unlike the latter, it refuses to accord transcendent reality to the whole as against the parts, and conceives society as being in its members, not over and above them. Associational realism, as here defined, is the only kind of realism that Durkheim ever espoused.[88]

In declaring that social facts exist independently, Durkheim means simply that social phenomena are qualitatively different from the characteristics of the members of the group as separate personalities. Association and communication create a new level of phenomena, the social.

Although it is distinctive, the group does not have a separate ontological existence. Durkheim does not hypostatize society. Collective representations and consciousness can "exist nowhere else than in individual minds and individual consciousnesses."[89] In expanding on Durkheim's notion of the whole, Alpert observes that

> a whole cannot be an existential reality apart from, or outside of, its parts. Water doesn't exist in one place, and its constituent elements in another, nor does a painting exist somewhere other than where the brush strokes that comprise it are; and neither does society have a location in time and space different from that of its individual components. Durkheim asked his critics to spare him the humiliation of even suspecting him of such a manifest absurdity.[90]

In effect, Alpert's analysis of Durkheim also suggests that the earlier charges of the alleged anti-individualism and antipsychological orientation in his sociology were exaggerated. Durkheim *is* subject to censure on the count of tending "to adopt or invent psychological principles *ad hoc.*"[91] However, he does not ignore "the biological basis of human nature" and does not reduce "the individual to a mere automaton impassively receiving and conforming to his social heritage."[92] Alpert notes that Durkheim unmistakably recognizes "resistances" and "conflicts between our biological and our social selves" and the divergent directions in which our

> social and organic natures . . . tend to orient us. . . . Such thoughts could hardly be expressed by one who ignored the organic rootings of human life, or who saw in the individual only a passive, psittaceous product of his social milieu.[93]

Third, Durkheim's acceptability was substantially increased by a theoretical association with the voluntarism of American sociology. Alpert's study only implies that Durkheim, near the end of his career, moved vaguely in that direction; but Parsons explicitly lists Durkheim as one of four contributors to his action theory and argues that Durkheim's notion of constraint and the functioning of ritual presuppose a discernible voluntarism. Alpert's inference is based on the implications of the views endorsed in Durkheim's pamphlet *Qui a voulu la guerre?* ["Who Wanted War?"]. Alpert hazards the guess that if Durkheim had lived to fully appreciate his position in this work, "he would have been led to perceive the incompleteness of the type of sociological analysis which deals exclusively with causes and functions," and, presumably, to supplement this deficiency by resorting to motivational and means-ends inquiries.[94]

In *The Structure of Social Action*, Parsons involves Durkheim in his account of the formal derivation of the analytical components of the action system. Durkheim is brought into direct relation with the schema of means, conditions, ends, norms, and the premise that choice in some form is omnipresent in social conduct. He contributes substantially to the specification and conceptualization of ends and institutional norms. The nature of these two components is referable to the body of common ultimate values, the foundation of social order. The common system of ultimate values defines the direct ends of specific acts of persons and their interrelations and provides a set of institutional rules for ascertaining which immediate ends or means to ends are appropriate in specific social contexts.

According to Parsons, a more direct commitment to a voluntaristic view of conduct is to be found in Durkheim's study of constraint and the role of ritual. As he pursues the problem of social control, Durkheim shifts the basis of his conception of constraint. At first, he sees it as resulting from subjection to naturalistic causation, then from the avoidance of sanctions, and finally from the subjective awareness of moral obligation.[95] Since norms enter directly into the constitution of the actor's ends, the rules to which persons orient their conduct are not external but internal. Thus Durkheim comes to conceive of constraint as the voluntary acceptance or self-imposition of the moral obligation to obey a norm. Durkheim's theory of ritual does not regard values as capable of automatic self-realization in the sense that a cognitive understanding or moral acceptance is sufficient for their realization. The functions of ritual demand the exercise of "what is generally called will or effort."[96] Since "the realization of ultimate values is a matter of active energy, of will, of effort, . . . a very important part may be played empirically by agencies which stimulate this will."[97] Parsons offers several quotations which represent

Durkheim as admitting that just as "the main function of ritual is to stimulate faith," so "that of faith, in turn, is to stimulate will."[98] In brief, in these arguments Parsons achieves a strategic accommodation, if not assimilation, of Durkheim to the pervasive voluntarism of American sociology.

Fourth, the ascendancy of functionalist theory during the 1940's has provided another source for a more favorable evaluation of Durkheim.[99] Alpert's article, "Durkheim's Functional Theory of Ritual," seems to have been the first study to link Durkheim prominently with functionalism. By the mid-1940's, Parsons was using functionalism to modify and extend his action theory so as to account for social action systems. In 1945, he cited the work of Durkheim and his followers as one of four important intellectual antecedents of modern structural functionalism. Parsons avers that "a genuine structural-functional treatment of the social system . . . gained increasingly in strength in the course of his [Durkheim's] career."[100] In his essay, "Manifest and Latent Functions," Merton includes references to Durkheim along with an extended analysis of the three basic types of functional postulates found in the work of British and American anthropologists and sociologists, one of whom was Radcliffe-Brown who had been inspired by Durkheim.[101] Merton construes his earlier inquiry, "Social Structure and Anomie," which combines the means-ends-norms action schema of his mentor Parsons with Durkheim's concept of anomie, as providing a functionalist approach for investigating social change.[102] On the whole, the action-predicated functionalism of Parsons and his students has been the most significant factor, perhaps, in stimulating interest in Durkheim among contemporary American sociologists.

The part played by American anthropology in introducing Durkheim to American sociology cannot be disregarded, however. It is part of what Howard Becker has characterized as Durkheim's "hop-skip-and-jump" effect.[103] Durkheim stimulated British anthropologists, especially Radcliffe-Brown, who influenced American anthropology through such figures as W. Lloyd Warner, who, in turn, has had an appreciable impact on the training of several sociologists. Warner's explicit identification with Durkheim is reflected in the works of some of his students who are sociologists, works such as Charles War-riner's recent article, "Groups Are Real," and Leo Srole's study, "Social Integration and Certain Corollaries."[104]

The interest in Durkheim in the 1940's and 1950's, which apparently originated in the 1930's, has become so extensive and diversified—especially since 1945—that it warrants a separate study. Durkheim has become a central figure in a number of specialized fields. It seems likely that his impact could be observed in such specialties as the sociologies of values, knowledge, law, religion, industry, communications, crime, small groups, formal organization, social change, and, perhaps, collective behavior.

At the present time, Durkheim's theories, approach, methods, and research are incontrovertibly relevant and important to American sociology. However, his central methodological principle which entails relating social facts etiologically to other social facts "has fallen," as Harry Alpert has argued recently, "for the most part, on deaf ears."[105] To a considerable extent, "American sociologists have been unwilling to accept this [basic] Durkheimian tenet" because it would entail a serious modification of the prevailing voluntaristic nominalism.[106]

1. Talcott Parsons' *The Structure of Social Action* (2nd ed.; Glencoe, Ill.: Free Press of Glencoe, Illinois, 1949) focuses generally on the action frame of reference rather than specifically on American sociology.

2. Gisela J. Hinkle, "Sociology and Psychoanalysis," *Modern Sociological Theory,* ed. Howard Becker and Alvin Boskoff (New York: Dryden Press, Inc., 1957), pp. 574-603; Guenther Roth and Reinhard Bendix, "Max Weber's Einfluss auf die amerikanische Soziologie," *Kölner Zeitschrift für Soziologie,* XI (1959), 38-53. Elton F. Guthrie's "Historical Materialism and Its Sociological Critics," *Social Forces,* XX (1941), 172-84, is a pertinent study.

3. This periodicization is an adaptation from Roscoe C. Hinkle, Jr., and Gisela J. Hinkle's *The Development of Modern Sociology* ("Studies in Sociology," No. 6 [New York: Random House, 1954]).

4. Albion W. Small, review of Durkheim's *De la division du travail social,* in *American Journal of Sociology,* VII (1902), 566-68; and U. G. Weatherly, review of *The Elementary Forms of the Religious Life, ibid.,* XXII (1917), 561-63. Small also commented on some of the volumes of *Année sociologique, ibid.,* III (1898), 700; V (1899), 124; VI (1900), 276-77; VIII (1902), 277-78; and XI (1905), 132-33. Anthropologist Hutton

Webster reviewed the French edition of *Les formes élémentaires de la vie religieuse, ibid.,* XVIII (1913), 843-46.

5. Letter to the editor on Gustavo Tosti's "Suicide in the Light of Recent Studies," *ibid.,* III (1898), 848-49; and "On the Relation of Sociology to the Social Sciences and to Philosophy," *ibid.,* X (1904), 134-35.

6. Two were the work of the Italian Tardean, Gustavo Tosti, "Suicide in the Light of Recent Studies," *ibid.,* III (1898), 464-78, and "The Delusions of Durkheim's Sociological Objectivism," *ibid.,* IV (1898), 171-77. The first of these articles is primarily a critical analysis of Durkheim's *Le suicide.* Note also: James H. Leuba, "Sociology and Psychology: The Conceptions of Religion and Magic and the Place of Psychology in Sociological Studies; A Discussion of the Views of Durkheim and of Hubert and Mauss," *ibid.,* XIX (1913), 323-42. Two pages of James H. Tufts, "Recent Sociological Tendencies in France," *ibid.,* I (1896), 448-50, are devoted to Durkheim.

7. Charles Horton Cooley, *Social Process* (New York: Charles Scribner's Sons, (1918), p. 400.

8. Lester F. Ward, *Pure Sociology* (New York: Macmillan Co., 1907), p. 80.

9. Franklin Henry Giddings, *Inductive Sociology* (New York: Macmillan Co., 1901), p. 17.

10. Giddings, *Readings in Descriptive and Historical Sociology* (New York: Macmillan Co., 1906), p. 5; Albion W. Small, *General Sociology* (Chicago: University of Chicago Press, 1905), pp. 512, 564; Edward Alsworth Ross, *The Foundations of Sociology* (New York: Macmillan Co., 1905), p. 92.

11. Giddings, *The Principles of Sociology* (New York: Macmillan Co., 1896), pp. 146-47.

12. *Ibid.,* p. 15; Ross, *op. cit.,* p. 275.

13. Giddings, *Studies in the Theory of Human Society* (New York: Macmillan Co., 1922), p. 62; Ross, *op. cit.,* pp. 268, 274.

14. Ward, *op. cit.,* pp. 200, 213, 273-74; see also his *Applied Sociology* (Boston: Ginn & Co., 1906), pp. 171-72.

15. Small, *op. cit.,* p. 642.

16. Cooley, *op. cit.,* p. 400.

17. Ward, *Pure Sociology,* p. 274; and *Applied Sociology,* pp. 193, 290.

18. Giddings, *The Principles of Sociology,* pp. 60, 146-47.

19. Ross, *op. cit.,* p. 92. Ross's endorsement of Tarde, to whom he was indebted, is obvious in his writings. The fact that American sociology was, in general, favorably disposed to Tarde should obviate the inclination to

attribute the opposition to Durkheim to the conversance of Americans with German academic attainment and intellectual life in the decades around the turn of the century.

20. Small, review of *Année sociologique,* in *American Journal of Sociology,* XI (1905), 132. It may be significant that following this declaration no subsequent volumes of the *Année* were reviewed.

21. Bristol, *Social Adaptation* ("Harvard Economic Studies," Vol. XIV [Cambridge, Mass.: Harvard University Press, 1915]) ; Gehlke, *Emile Durkheim's Contributions to Sociological Theory* ("Studies in History, Economics and Public Law," Vol. LXIII, No. 1 [New York: Columbia University, 1915]).

22. Bristol, *op. cit.,* p. 143.

23. *Ibid.*

24. *Ibid.,* p. 144.

25. *Ibid.,* pp. 144-145, *passim.*

26. Gehlke, *op. cit.,* p. 148.

27. *Ibid.,* pp. 137, 138, 141-2.

28. *Ibid.,* p. 144.

29. *Ibid.,* pp. 144-45.

30. *Ibid.,* p. 179.

31. *Ibid.,* p. 94.

32. *Ibid.,* pp. 94, 95, 96.

33. *Ibid.,* p. 96.

34. *Ibid.,* p. 98-99.

35. *Ibid.,* p. 99.

36. *Ibid.,* pp. 100, 101.

37. Bristol, *op. cit.,* p. 146.

38. *Ibid.,* p. 148.

39. *Ibid.*

40. *Ibid.,* pp. 148-49.

41. *Ibid.,* p. 149.

42. Davis, *Psychological Interpretations of Society* ("Studies in History, Economics and Public Law," Vol. XXXIII, No. 2 [New York: Columbia University, 1909]), p. 50; and Ellwood, "Objectivism in Sociology," *American Journal of Sociology,* XXII (1916), 291. In the present paper, the term "individualism" has been used as a correlative of "voluntaristic nominalism," as it is in "Social Stratification in Perspective," *Modern Sociological*

EMILE DURKHEIM

Theory, pp. 374-94, and *The Development of Modern Sociology* (the term is defined on pages v and 73 of the latter work). As used in American sociology, "individualism" does not carry the implications of economic individualism and laissez faire. It does not refer to calculated, unremitting, unrestricted aggrandizement and the indulgence of the ego. Rather individualism in American sociology is close to, if not actually identical with, Morris Ginsberg's concepts of "sociological individualism" and "methodological individualism." These two types of individualism involve a theory of society and a method for studying it. "Sociological individualism" designates the theory that society is to be conceived as "an aggregate of self-determining individuals who remain self-determining despite their relations with others." "Methodological individualism" advises that social units be studied as "complexes of social relationships, arising out of the behavior of individuals in so far as this is directed towards or away from other individuals." See Morris Ginsberg, "The Individual and Society," *International Social Science Bulletin,* VI, No. 1 (1954), 147.

43. *American Journal of Sociology,* XXVII (1921), 26-33.

44. *Ibid.,* XXVIII (1923), 529-53.

45. "Durkheim's Educational Sociology," *Journal of Applied Sociology,* IX (1924), 30-33.

46. *American Journal of Sociology,* XXXII (1926), 253-54.

47. Chapel Hill, N. C.: University of North Carolina Press, 1926, pp. 15, 272, 274, 315.

48. Cavan, *Suicide* (Chicago: University of Chicago Press, 1928), p. 289.

49. Ellwood, review of James P. Lichtenberger's *Development of Social Theory,* in *American Journal of Sociology,* XXIX (1923), 104.

50. "The History of Social Thought: A Consensus of American Opinion," *Social Forces,* VI (1927), 190-96.

51. In his review of Durkheim's *The Division of Labor in Society,* trans. by George Simpson, in *American Journal of Sociology,* XL (1934), 376-77.

52. *Ibid.,* p. 377.

53. William I. Thomas and Florian Znaniecki, *The Polish Peasant in Europe and America* (Boston: Richard G. Badger, 1918), 1, 44 n.

54. Gehlke, "Social Psychology and Political Theory," in *A History of Political Theories: Recent Times,* ed. Charles Edward Merriam and Harry Elmer Barnes (New York: Macmillan Co., 1924), p. 414; Kimball Young, "Social Psychology," in *The History and Prospects of the Social Sciences,* ed. Harry Elmer Barnes (New York: Alfred A. Knopf, Inc., 1925), p. 161.

55. Read Bain, "Trends in American Sociological Theory," in *Trends in American Sociology,* ed. George A. Lundberg, Read Bain, and Nels Anderson (New York: Harper & Bros., 1929), p. 80.

56. Robert E. Park, "Sociology and the Social Sciences," *American Journal of Sociology*, XXVI (1921), 11-13, 15-17. See also Robert E. Park and Ernest W. Burgess, *Introduction to the Science of Sociology* ([1921] Chicago: University of Chicago Press, 1924), pp. 33-40.

57. It is impossible within the limits of this paper to attempt to assess the relative importance of the intellectual antecedents of the dichotomy between the sacred and the profane. True, Park does refer to *De la division du travail social* in an early usage of the dichotomy, but Ferdinand Tönnies' *Gemeinschaft und Gesellschaft* exercised a conspicuously greater influence. Significantly, Park does not cite the distinction made by Durkheim in *The Elementary Forms of the Religious Life*. See Robert E. Park, *Race and Culture* (Glencoe, Ill.: Free Press of Glencoe, Illinois, 1950), pp. 12-13.

58. Park, *Human Communities* (Glencoe, Ill.: Free Press of Glencoe, Illinois, 1952), p. 182; and *Race and Culture*, p. 180.

59. Park, *Human Communities*, p. 181.

60. *Ibid.*, p. 260; Park and Burgess, *Introduction to the Science of Sociology*, p. 953.

61. See Milla Aissa Alihan, *Social Ecology* (New York: Columbia University Press, 1938), pp. 94, 95, 96.

62. P. 176 n.

63. Talcott Parsons' more recent exposition of culture as a kind of object is indebted to this intellectual development. See, for example, *Toward a General Theory of Action*, ed. Talcott Parsons and Edward A. Shils (Cambridge, Mass.: Harvard University Press, 1954).

64. Gary, *op. cit.*, p. 186.

65. Gehlke, "Social Psychology and Political Theory," in *A History of Political Theory: Recent Times*, p. 415.

66. Faris, *The Nature of Human Nature* (New York: McGraw-Hill Book Co., 1937), pp. 134, 197.

67. Mead, *Mind, Self, and Society* (Chicago: University of Chicago Press, 1934), p. 76.

68. Note the presence of the Durkheimian tradition and the anthropological notion of culture in the modern Meadian textbook by Alfred R. Lindesmith and Anselm L. Strauss, *Social Psychology* (rev. ed.; New York: Dryden Press, 1956), especially Chap. iii, "Groups, Language, and Symbolic Environments," and Chap. viii, "The Social Bases of Thought."

69. Floyd N. House, "Topical Summaries of Current Literature: The Logic of Sociology," *American Journal of Sociology*, XXXII (1926), 277.

70. See Pitirim A. Sorokin, "Sociology and Ethics," in *The Social Sci-*

ences and Their Interrelations, ed. William Fielding Ogburn and Alexander Goldenweiser (New York: Houghton Mifflin Co., 1927), p. 316.

71. *Social Forces,* XII (1934), 537-45; Elliott and Merrill, *Social Disorganization* (New York: Harper & Bros., 1934), pp. 735-65.

72. *The Division of Labor in Society,* trans. George Simpson (New York: Macmillan Co., 1933); *The Rules of Sociological Method,* trans. Sarah A. Solovay and John H. Mueller (Chicago: University of Chicago Press, 1938).

73. Robert K. Merton, "Durkheim's Division of Labor in Society," *American Journal of Sociology,* XL (1934), 319-28; Emile Benoît-Smullyan, review of *The Rules of Sociological Method,* in *American Sociological Review,* III (1938), 577-79.

74. Sorokin, *Contemporary Sociological Theories* (New York: Harper & Bros., 1928); House, *The Development of Sociology* (New York: McGraw-Hill Book Co., 1936); Harry Elmer Barnes and Howard Becker, *Social Thought from Lore to Science* (2 vols.; Boston: D. C. Heath & Co., 1938); George Simpson, "Emile Durkheim's Social Realism," *Sociology and Social Research,* XVIII (1933), 3-11; Ethel M. Wilson, "Emile Durkheim's Sociological Method," *ibid.* (1934), 511-18; and Robert Marjolin, "French Sociology: Comte and Durkheim," *American Journal of Sociology,* XLII (1937), 693-704.

75. See Emile Benoît-Smullyan, "The Sociologism of Emile Durkheim and His School," in *An Introduction to the History of Sociology,* ed. Harry Elmer Barnes (Chicago: University of Chicago Press, 1948); Harry Alpert, "France's First University Course in Sociology," *American Sociological Review,* II (1937), 311-17; Alpert, "Durkheim's Functional Theory of Ritual," *Sociology and Social Research,* XXIII (1938), 103-8; Alpert, "Emile Durkheim and Sociologismic Psychology," *American Journal of Sociology,* XLV (1939), 64-70; Alpert, "Explaining the Social Socially," *Social Forces,* XVII (1939), 361-65; and John Foskett, "Emile Durkheim's Contribution to the Problem of Social Order," in *Research Studies of the State College of Washington* (Pullman, Washington: The College, 1940), Vol. VIII.

76. Wilson, *op. cit.,* p. 511.

77. New York: McGraw-Hill Book Co., 1937, pp. 301-450; *American Sociological Review,* III (1938), 672-82.

78. *American Journal of Sociology,* XXXIII (1928), 754-68.

79. John M. Foskett, "Emile Durkheim and the Problem of Social Order" (Ph.D. dissertation, Department of Sociology and Social Institutions, University of California, Berkeley, 1939), p. 50.

80. *Ibid.,* p. 51.

81. Elliott and Merrill, *op. cit.,* p. 735.

82. *Ibid.*

83. For discussions of these points, see Alpert's dissertation (Point 1, pp. 85-86, 111-13, 133, 135, 135-42, 191; for Point 3, pp. 114, 116; Point 4, pp. 114, 117; Point 6, pp. 145-46; Point 7, pp. 124, 127; Point 8, p. 88; Point 10, pp. 109-11) and Merton's review (Point 2, p. 320; Point 5, pp. 323-24; Point 8, p. 328; Point 9, pp. 324-25; Point 10, pp. 321-22, 323).

84. Wilson, *op. cit.*, pp. 511-18.

85. Alpert, *Emile Durkheim and His Sociology*, p. 80.

86. *Ibid.*, pp. 95, 97. For an analysis, see pp. 86-108.

87. *Sociology and Social Research*, XVIII (1933), 3-5.

88. Alpert, *Emile Durkheim and His Sociology*, pp. 156-57.

89. *Ibid.*, p. 161.

90. *Ibid*, p. 157.

91. Alpert, "Emile Durkheim and Sociologismic Psychology," *American Journal of Sociology*, XLV (1939), 70.

92. *Ibid.*, p. 68.

93. *Ibid.*, pp. 68-69, *passim.*

94. Alpert, *Emile Durkheim and His Sociology*, p. 111.

95. Parsons, *The Structure of Social Action*, p. 385.

96. *Ibid.*, p. 440.

97. *Ibid.*

98. *Ibid.*, p. 440 n.

99. This does not necessarily mean that Durkheim's views may simply be equated with contemporary functionalism. See Albert Pierce's "Durkheim and Functionalism" in this volume.

100. Parsons, *Essays in Sociological Theory: Pure and Applied* (Glencoe, Ill.: Free Press of Glencoe, Illinois, 1949), p. 31.

101. Merton, *Social Theory and Social Structure* (Glencoe, Ill.: Free Press of Glencoe, Illinois, 1949), p. 27.

102. *Ibid.*, pp. 115-17.

103. "Anthropology and Sociology," in *For a Science of Social Man*, ed. John Gillin (New York: Macmillan Co., 1954), pp. 112-13.

104. Charles K. Warriner, "Groups Are Real: A Reaffirmation," *American Sociological Review*, XXI (1956), 549-54; Leo Srole, "Social Integration and Certain Corollaries: An Exploratory Study," *ibid.*, pp. 709-16.

105. Alpert, "Emile Durkheim: Enemy of Fixed Psychological Elements," *American Journal of Sociology*, LXIII (1958), 662.

106. Hinkle and Hinkle, *op. cit.*, p. 51.

DURKHEIM'S INFLUENCE ON JAPANESE SOCIOLOGY

KAZUTA KURAUCHI

Nearly a century has elapsed since the science of sociology, which developed in Europe, was introduced into Japan. A review of its history there is a necessary preliminary to any survey of Durkheim's influence upon Japanese sociological thought, for although the Japanese sociological output has been large, foreign scholars are comparatively unfamiliar with it.

Sociology was introduced into a Japan which was socially and culturally ready to receive it, even though the content of the discipline was fundamentally foreign to Japanese civilization. Japan underwent tremendous political reforms at the time of the Meiji Restoration in 1868. Political supremacy was transferred from the shogun—the feudal ruler or overlord—to the emperor, until then only the nominal head of the nation. With this change, the hierarchical distinctions between warriors, peasants, artisans, merchants, and tradespeople were abolished. Japan abandoned her isolationist foreign policy and adopted modern political principles. The large-scale westernization of Japan in the political, legal, economic, and cultural fields began. Japan was strongly conservative in religion and public morality, but she enthusiastically welcomed Western learning, arts, and technology. Japanese scholars had to acquaint themselves with foreign literature, to catch up with developments in their respective sciences, and to communicate what they had learned to those within their own country.

Here was the same eagerness with which Japan had imported the Indian and Chinese civilizations in the early Middle Ages. This attitude has always characterized the Japanese approach to foreign civilizations. Generally, a few select Japanese come into contact with such civilizations; they transmit what they have learned about these foreign cultures to the rest of Japan. Unfortunately, such an approach to a foreign culture does not afford an opportunity for observing and evaluating it against its native background; and, unlike direct, personal, daily contact, which provides an opportunity for cultural exchange on the part of two nations, it may result in wholesale imitation.

The chief concern of Japanese scholars with respect to European and American sociology has been to disseminate their knowledge of that sociology to the rest of the nation. This has led to a rather peculiar situation in which a great number of foreign theories are expounded by Japanese sociologists. There are numerous Japanese studies in sociology (witness the current UNESCO catalogue of sociological publications in Japan), but although Japanese scholars are ready to accept all schools of sociological theory, they are reluctant to publish the results of their research in languages other than their own. It was only a short time ago that Japanese monographs began to appear accompanied by résumés written in European languages. Nearly the whole of Japanese sociological literature, except for studies by Yasuma Takata and a few others, has been inaccessible to scholars overseas. Because Japanese scholars find it much more difficult to write a European language than to read it and because their publications in Japanese have a large sale among Japanese readers, they have published little in foreign languages.

For a time after the Meiji Restoration, Japanese science turned from its native traditions and looked to the West. Natural science, philosophy, and the social sciences all made a new beginning. In philosophy and the social sciences, however, each nation always has its own peculiar problems and areas of interest which—though crude and unsystematized—remain worth restudying. Indeed, any people reveals its national character unconsciously through its acceptance or rejection of particular foreign theoretical views. The intellectual level of the people at large, the focal point of their attention in response to foreign matters, the nation's pattern of thinking—all these act as a priori factors in the acceptance or rejection of another nation's intellectual resources.

An analysis of the Japanese conception of society before the introduction of the social sciences, especially sociology, is complicated because of the many currents of social thought which had existed previously—few of which were compatible with modern sociological notions. Take, for instance, the attitude of some classical Confucian scholars who assumed the historical development of a nation to be of a dialectical nature. In examining a historical event, they analyzed the relation between the effects of spontaneous social forces or trends and those of a consciously held ideal. This mode of thinking was very important in the system of sociology of the late Tongo Takebe, who occupied the chair of sociology at Tokyo Imperial University from 1901 to 1922.

Another way of interpreting the culture of a people focused on geographical factors, a method which was adopted by a group of Japanese scholars during the *ancien régime*. Japanese military tacticians contributed a great deal to this undertaking. They systematically and objectively observed the habits and group behavior of the people of a particular local community. One may assume that training in such observation contributed greatly to the development of the social sciences in Japan.

The effects of Western social science were felt in three stages. In the first, the Japanese learned to look with detachment and discernment at their own social life; they began to compare Japanese and European societies, although their knowledge of the latter was modest. For example, in 1798, the year marked by the publication of Malthus' *An Essay on the Principle of Population,* Toshiaki Honda wrote his *Tales of the Western Lands (Seiiki Monogatari)* in which he hinted that the government's closed-door policy toward foreign nations ran counter to the natural law governing the increase of population. The second stage was reached when the Japanese began to look upon social phenomena as resulting from causal laws, an attitude stimulated by their studies of Western natural sciences. This attitude bore fruit in the thought of Yukichi Fukuzawa, the great intellectual leader in the days immediately following the Meiji Restoration. The third stage was marked by the actual entry of Western social science into Japan. Dutch geography was introduced in the latter part of the Yedo period (1603-1867) and was followed, just before the Meiji Restoration, by the introduction of the sciences of statecraft, economics, and sociology.

The first Japanese introduced to sociology were a number of students—the first group of Japanese to study in Europe—

who were sent to the Netherlands in 1861 by the Tokugawa shogunate. One of them, Amane Nishi, frequently referred to Auguste Comte in his lectures—particularly to Comte's classification of the sciences. At about this time, Shoichi Toyama, who returned to Japan from the United States in 1876, and the American, Ernest Francisco Fenollosa, who came to Japan in 1878, began to lecture on Herbert Spencer's sociology at Tokyo Imperial University.

Because of the social needs of Japan at that time, Spencer's sociological ideas were especially attractive. After scrapping the feudal social structure dominated by the samurai class, Japan stood on the threshold of modern capitalism and was about to participate in a world economy. This exemplified what Spencer described as the change from the "militant" to the "industrial" society. It was soon felt that Japan, which had belatedly entered the arena of international rivalry, would be well advised to adopt modern social institutions and industrial techniques under the aegis of nationalism. This made Japanese scholars more willing to accept German thought. The first Japanese scholar to study the German language was Hiroyuki Kato, who became an exponent of social Darwinism. In 1893, he wrote a book which appeared simultaneously in German and Japanese, *Kampf ums Recht der Stärkeren* ("The Struggle for the Right of the Stronger"), urging that human rights were nothing but the recognized rights of the strong. At the same time he admitted that even the weak can become strong as human civilization advances and that mutual recognition of rights is possible between the strong and the weak. The same is true, he argued, of international relations, and he envisaged the possibility of a world commonwealth. Ludwig Gumplowicz objected to Kato's contention on the latter point.

In time, sociology as an academic science began to attract students in Japanese universities, and numerous sociological theories from Europe and America began to flow into Japan, including, in roughly this order, psychological sociology, German formal sociology, Marxian socialism, and Durkheim's sociology. As a result of all this, a great deal of sociological writing was done in Japan.

The introduction of the new science of sociology in Japan

did not meet with resistance from the sciences that were already established. Georg Simmel's efforts in Europe to establish the validity of sociology as a science may have been necessary because of strictly European circumstances; in Japan, however, interest in the nature of that science was purely academic—that is, theoretical and methodological—and sociology took its place among the regular subjects of study at Tokyo Imperial University as early as 1881 without opposition from the Japanese public. It was, however, often mistaken for socialism and was consequently frowned upon for political reasons. This was especially true during the Second World War, when rabid nationalism created a climate unfavorable to sociology.

Japanese culture was amenable to Durkheim's thought. The Japanese tend to think of individuals and their actions in relation to the community. This conception can be traced historically to a merger of Buddhism, which found its way into Japan in the sixth century, and pre-Buddhist elements of the Japanese ethos. The Japanese emphasis on the contentment of the individual mind in relation to the continuity of the social community, which is superior to the individuals composing it, made Durkheim's way of thinking attractive. Durkheim aroused the interest of Japanese scholars who sought to give a sociological interpretation of Japanese behavior and the structure of Japanese society. Indeed, as we know, Durkheim held that the pattern of our idea of God is to be found in human society; that the essential nature of society consists in the moral constraint it puts upon the individual; and that the individual's mental stability depends upon the social cohesion of his community.

Nearly half a century has passed since Japanese scholars began to treat Durkheim's sociological theories in detail. Probably Enku Uno (afterward professor at Tokyo Imperial University) and Chijo Akamatsu (late professor of Seoul Imperial University) were the first to expound Durkheim's views on the sociology of religion. Uno urged the necessity of approaching religion through many channels, but his chief concentration upon ethnological studies was certainly due to Durkheim's influence.[1] Akamatsu showed special interest in Durkheim. His studies in collaboration with Takashi Akiba of Korean Shamanism are highly appreciated for their scholarly qualities.[2]

The Japanese scholar who did most to introduce Durkheim to Japan was Juri Tanabe. He translated *De la division du travail social* and *Education et sociologie* in 1932, and *Les règles de la méthode sociologique* in 1942; he also wrote monographs on various Durkheimian ideas. He discussed the French sociology of language and traced the history of the ideas of progress and positivism from Condorcet to Comte and Durkheim, elucidating the thought of these and other French philosophers and sociologists.[3]

Another notable Durkheimian is Kiyoto Furuno, translator of *Les formes élémentaires de la vie religieuse*. Sochu Suzuki and Kenichi Tobizawa translated *Le suicide* in 1928; Gentaro Ii, like Tanabe, translated *De la division du travail social* in 1932; and Yoshihiko Yamada, better known by his pseudonym "Minoru Kida," translated *Philosophie et sociologie* into Japanese in 1943. It should be noted that in 1927 the tenth anniversary of Durkheim's death was observed in speeches by Enku Uno, Shukei Akamatsu, Juri Tanabe, and Sylvain Levi, professor at the Collège de France.

An outstanding representative of the Japanese preoccupation with the nature of sociology as a science is Junichiro Matsumoto. He wrote a triology—*Introduction to Sociology (Shakaigaku Genron)*, *Principles of Group Sociology (Shudanshakaigaku Genri)*, and *Principles of Cultural Sociology (Bunkashakaigaku Genri)*—which deals with social relationships and social groups, the process of growth of human society, and culture. Matsumoto believed that he had done full justice to Durkheim's work on culture.[4]

Matsumoto traced Durkheim's conception of sociology in detail. He agreed with Durkheim that sociology is a science which holds, from a fixed point of view, a mirror to social phenomena. At the same time, however, he pointed out that there is a discrepancy between Durkheim's method of objective, positivistic cognition and the objects of cognition which are mental by nature; and he criticized Durkheim's definition of "collective representation." He showed that Durkheim's dictum, "Society is to be explained by itself," and his emphasis upon cultural factors have in effect received extended application in American cultural anthropology.

Looking at cultural phenomena as "things" did not violate

Japanese sentiment. No religious body strongly opposed this scientific attitude because Japan has no tradition of a metaphysical philosophy of history. There was no inclination to regard sociology as "a science of resignation" or as a science dealing with the interference of the dark realities of the actual world with the operation of reason.

Although Durkheim's way of thinking was sometimes questioned on theoretical grounds, it never provoked negative feelings. Rather, his manner of explaining social phenomena by reference to collective representations induced many scholars to engage in sociological studies of cultural problems.

Durkheim's pre-eminent influence upon Japanese sociology evolved from his views on the sociological meaning of population. Since the Meiji Restoration, the population of Japan has been increasing rapidly, and the problem of population has aroused much attention. Tongo Takebe, who studied in France at the close of the nineteenth century, gave a prominent place to this problem in his system of sociology and in his theory of social dynamics.[5]

Takebe's contemporary, Shotaro Yoneda, professor of sociology at Kyoto Imperial University, directed his attention to population pressure in Japan. He was influenced not only by Durkheim but also by Franklin H. Giddings and Gabriel Tarde. Yasuma Takata, now professor emeritus of the universities at Kyoto and Osaka and a leading figure in Japanese sociology, shows, especially in his theory of social change, an unmistakable indebtedness to Durkheim.[6] He is one of Yoneda's disciples and his theoretical position is that of formal sociology.

In his monumental *Principles of Sociology,* Takata treats three topics which remind us of Célestin Bouglé and Durkheim: the constitution of society, forms of association, and effects of social changes. He had previously made a sociological study of the division of labor. In this book—in which Takata made his debut as a sociologist—he tried to synthesize Simmel's theory of social differentiation with Durkheim's theory of the division of labor. While obviously influenced by Durkheim's interpretation of the increase in population, it was here that he first developed his theory of the desire for power, the central idea underlying his system of sociology. But Takata's position most closely resembles Durkheim's in respect to his social dynamics, or what he calls the "third" interpretation of history (the first two are the spiritualistic and materialistic interpretations): neither the human soul nor the productive power of society is the independent variable in social change. Instead, Takata sees the self-changing and self-moving social force in population. While population is affected by the productive power of a particular society, its increase is decisive in determining the quantitative and qualitative constitution of that society, its stratification, and other social phenomena. In taking this position, Takata admits the influence of Durkheim's views on population, as well as Eugène V. De Roberty's biosocial hypothesis.

Takata has played a leading role in Japan in the critical analysis of Marxist economic theories and has pioneered in the field of mathematical economics. His position as a critic of Marxist views on history is related to Durkheim's on social morphology. The sociologies of Durkheim and Takata were subjected to countercharges from the Marxist camp, particularly on the ground that Durkheim's morphology did not take due notice of the fact that hitherto human society has been composed of different social classes.

Another of Durkheim's studies which has been highly esteemed in Japan is the one on suicide. His excellent methodology appealed to Japanese sociologists and stimulated them to give increased attention to this phenomenon. Takata studied suicides committed by couples in particular, giving an interpretation of them which was criticized by Koshin Iguchi, who was then a professor at Kyushu Imperial University. According to Iguchi, this type of suicide was not, as Takata held, attributable exclusively to a unique emotionality of the Japanese, because it could be found in other countries as well. Iguchi tried to elucidate his theory by comparative analyses.[7] Recently, Keiichi Chikazawa has sought an explanation of suicide by examining several potential causal factors, including psychological ones, and has thus modified Durkheim's exclusively sociological position.[8] This modification resembles that which has occurred in France, notably through the work of Maurice Halbwachs.

The work of Durkheim and his disciples in the field of social psychology has greatly influenced Japanese scholars. Tetsuo Watanuki, a professor at Chuo University in Tokyo, who lectured on social consciousness and social constraint at Tokyo Imperial University from 1923 to 1939, came to sociology from history. Following Durkheim's methodology, in large part, he has devoted many years to the study of the social aspects of the Meiji Restoration. He has also been influenced considerably by Charles Horton Cooley, especially by his illumination of social phenomena through introspection. Watanuki's inquiries into the Meiji Restoration are not yet complete; but he has studied, among other things, the social consciousness which may have actuated the reactionary fanatics, indicted as traitors, who were active after the Restoration.[9] He postulated two types of social consciousness which were in conflict in the minds of these people: a sense of duty to family and native place, and an allegiance to sovereign and state.

Durkheim's method of analyzing social facts has exerted a wide influence upon Japanese students of religion and ethics. The most eminent of these students is Kiyoto Furuno, president of North Kyushu University. Furuno's range of interest is wide. He has done research on the religious beliefs of the aboriginal tribes of Formosa. He has studied the spiritual life of the secret Christians living in sequestered places on Kyushu, who have developed a transformed and degenerate cult in their three hundred years of isolation, which began with the persecution of their ancestors by the Tokugawa government. He has investigated the nature of religious ecstasy, pointing out the workings of social factors even in apparently non-social phases of the individual's life, thus showing himself to be a remarkable Durkheimian sociologist of religion.[10]

Durkheim's concept of the religious cult as a system of beliefs and rituals lent itself to the over-all interpretation of the religious and social rites of the Orient, especially those of ancient China. Chinese rituals are thus analyzed in Joken Kato's *The Origin of Rituals and Their Development (Rei no Kigen to Sono Hattatsu)*.[11] Kato holds that the Confucian system of moral doctrines was derived from the social rites which were taught and directed by tribal elders. These rites arose from the taboos concerning sacred things and from the worship of the mana, with its mystic power. The rites are of two kinds. One kind requires fasting and abstinence from certain foods in order to purify the mind and body in preparation for approaching the sacred object; the other requires the consumption of certain foods and drinks, the tasting of which has a similar preparatory function. Starting with this distinction of the two types of ritual, Kato ventured on to a consistent interpretation of the complex religious rituals of ancient China. This is a conspicuous example of Durkheim's influence upon a certain group of Japanese sociologists of religion. Kato's work was inspired by Chijo Akamatsu's studies of Durkheim in this field.

More recently, Japanese students of religion have given a good deal of attention to Max Weber's sociology of religion, as well as Joachim Wach's systematic attempt to bridge the gap between Weber and Durkheim. At the present time, both are highly respected. For example, Togo Mori of Osaka University observed (in a paper read at the 1957 congress of the Kansai Sociological Society) that in treating dysfunctional aspects of religious rites, we should start from Weber's sociological views.

In the concluding part of *Les formes élémentaires de la vie religieuse,* Durkheim contended that the formation of the cognitive categories is explicable by the fact of collective representation. In contrast to this conception of the sociology of knowledge, Max Scheler and Karl Mannheim developed one oriented to the analysis of historical modes of thought. By the 1920's and 1930's, these developments had interested several Japanese sociologists and a number of books were written in this new field, including my own studies of the development of the sociology of knowledge and of the Japanese pattern of thinking.[12]

Durkheim's handling of non-literate societies and religions has produced similar investigations by numerous Japanese scholars. Pre-eminent among them are students of Chinese social institutions. Tatsumi Makino at Tokyo University and Morimitsu Shimizu at Kyoto University have done distinguished work in this field.[13] They were influenced more or less by Durkheim's comparative and historical method. Durkheim's views of primitive society are also given much weight in the books of the distinguished moral philosopher Tetsuo Watsuji, who bases ethics on a philosophy of human relationships, much of which he derives from Durkheim and Bronislaw Malinowski.[14]

Finally, there is the influence of Durkheim's thought on educational sociology. Because of the need to reform Japan's educational system after the Second World War, investigations in the field of educational sociology have been carried on with enthusiasm, and American theories of democratic education, which have brought great advances in the United States, have been zealously studied by many Japanese scholars. But the way for such new theories had been prepared since the 1920's by Japanese sociologists who were impressed by Durkheim's views on education. Recently, problems of moral education have loomed large, and because of this, Durkheim's ideas on the subject will surely receive new attention.

Japan's defeat in the Second World War shattered the nation's faith in the state as the highest authority. The sudden and radical political and social changes that occurred during and after the war have produced many "marginal men" and have bred tendencies which Durkheim called anomie. It is very difficult for a nation, as well as for individuals, to discard old ideas and to form new ones commensurate with the new order of things. However, owing to the relatively quick economic recovery of the country and the time-honored willingness of the Japanese to co-operate in maintaining the social order even amidst turmoil, Japanese society has been stabilized and the confusion which was dreaded after the war has been averted.

But in view of the great increase of population among those who grew up during the postwar period, the need for moral education has made itself felt more and more. Moral lessons, deprecated since the end of the war because of the danger that they might rekindle nationalist fervor, are now likely to be re-introduced, though with a new content, into the curriculum of the public schools. This movement is opposed, however, by a large section of the Japanese intelligentsia, especially elementary-school teachers.

Durkheim had shown great interest in education as early as *De la division du travail social*. He considered education to be

306

a social fact which can be studied by scientific methods. A prominent advocate of secularism in education and of secular rationalism in ethics, he thought that secular morality was theoretically possible and historically inevitable, and that it would become practically possible because the intensification of individualism in modern society would awaken a consciousness of man's dignity and evoke a sense of justice.

Unlike Europe and America, Japan has no church with the power of moral instruction, but Japan's secular education in morality is centuries old. During the Yedo period (beginning in the seventeenth century), Confucian moral doctrines formed part of orthodox education. With the Meiji Restoration, when the present educational system was adopted in Japan, secularism in public education was established. There was almost no need for those advocating secular moral education to combat a church. Until the end of the late war, however, this moral education was primarily designed to bring the people into absolute obedience to the state. This is the major reason why today many persons are in doubt about the real effects of the contemplated revival of moral education in Japan. Moreover, a large number of its opponents contend that morality can only be learned by experience; it cannot be imposed as a subject of school instruction.

It should be noted that there was a controversy on the same subject in Japan toward the end of the Yedo period. The Confucian method of education then current involved instruction in discipline and the inculcation of individual virtues. Its opponents took the position of psychological naturalism. Among them was Mitsuye Fujitani, who asserted that moral education was calculated to intensify the conflict between reason and impulse and that it would make men dispute with each other over moral questions, and thus produce more ill will than good.

The question of the method seems less serious than that of the content of the new moral education. We should try to find a practical way of giving a beneficial moral education within a secular framework by reconciling democratic and traditional ideals. To find a solution to the problem is a formidable challenge, but Durkheim's suggestions may prove to be of great assistance.

307

EMILE DURKHEIM

1. *Shukyogaku* ("Science of Religion"), Tokyo, 1931.

2. *Chosen-Fuzoku no Kenkyu* ("Studies in Korean Shamanism"), 2 vols., 1937-38.

3. *Gengo-Shakaigaku* ("Sociology of Language"), Tokyo, 1936; *Furansu Shakaigakushi Kenkyu* ("Studies in French Sociology"), Tokyo, 1931.

4. *Shakaigaku Genron,* Tokyo, 1935; *Shudanshakaigaku Genri,* Tokyo, 1937; *Bunkashakaigaku Genri,* Tokyo, 1938; *Gendai Shakaigakusetsu Kenkyu* ("Studies in Contemporary Sociological Theories"), 2nd ed., Tokyo, 1948.

5. *Futsu Shakaigaku* ("General Sociology"), 4 vols., Tokyo, 1904-18.

6. *Bungyoron* ("On the Division of Labor"), Kyoto, 1913; rev. ed., Tokyo, 1927. *Shakaigaku Genri* ("Principles of Sociology"), Tokyo, 1919. *Kaikyu oyobi Daisan-Shikan* ("Social Classes and the Third Interpretation of History"), Tokyo, 1925. "Eine dritte Geschichtsauffassung," in *Reine und angewandte Soziologie: Eine Festgabe für Ferdinand Tönnies* (1936), pp. 309-20.

7. Iguchi, *Jisatsu no Shakaigakuteki Kenkyu* ("Sociological Studies in Suicide"), Tokyo, 1934.

8. *Jisatsu no Kisetsuteki Hendo* ("Seasonal Fluctuation of Suicide"), Bungakukai-Shi (Yamaguchi University), Vol. VI, No. 1.

9. *Ishin Zengo ni Koeru Kokujihan* ("Political Criminals before and after the Restoration"), *Kokkagakkai Zasshi,* Vol. XLVI, Nos. 9-10.

10. *Shukyoshakaigaku* ("Sociology of Religion"), Tokyo, 1938.

11. Tokyo, 1943.

12. *Chishiki-Shakaigaku* ("Sociology of Knowledge"), Tokyo, 1932; *Bunka-Shakaigaku* ("Cultural Sociology"), Tokyo, 1943.

13. Makino, *Shina Kazoku Kenkyu* ("Studies on the Chinese Family"), Tokyo, 1944; Shimizu, *Shina Kazoku no Kozo* ("The Structure of the Chinese Family"), Tokyo, 1942.

14. *Rinrigaku* ("Ethics"), 3 vols., Tokyo, 1937-49.

REMINISCENCES OF THE DURKHEIM SCHOOL

PAUL HONIGSHEIM

My memories of France center around my contacts with the Durkheim school, but before I describe some of the most vivid and significant of them I must say a few words about my own background. My father's ancestors were German peasant folk, and my mother was French. I spoke French as my first language, and always considered myself a link between the French and the German peoples. During the First World War, I was critical of the German invasion of Belgium; indeed, my parents and I were in continual difficulties with the German war authorities. I was drafted as an interpreter with the rank of corporal in a camp of French and Belgian prisoners, among them Paul-Henri Spaak. Like Ernst Troeltsch, I had predicted the inevitable collapse of the Kaiser's Germany. Upon the desertion of Wilhelm II, Ludendorff, and other authors of the defeat, the soldiers took over, and I was unanimously elected to represent sixteen thousand revolutionary soldiers in the provisional government.

After the establishment of the German Republic, I supported it actively as a member of the socialist party, for which I was later to be persecuted by both National Socialists and Communists. In the field of adult education, I participated in international holiday courses and was a leader in international youth movements and meetings; I was active in many pacifist organizations; I acted as German-French interpreter at peace conferences in Geneva and elsewhere. As a German delegate to the League of the Rights of Man, notably at its meeting in Metz, I insisted that since the people of Alsace-Lorraine had clearly shown their wish to belong to France rather than to Germany, their decision must be respected by everyone, especially by the Germans. In the course of my work, I often met and collaborated with Frenchmen.

When Hitler came to power in 1933, I immediately resigned my positions as director of the people's university (Volkshochschule) and member of the faculty of the University of Cologne. Despite censorship, I succeeded in corresponding with my French friends, who worked through the French consulate in Cologne to help me escape. Moreover, they gave me rooms in the building of the Ecole Normale Supérieure in Paris to establish a branch office of the Institute of Social Research, whose headquarters had been removed from Frankfurt to Geneva. I became the director of the Paris branch. Most of the men who helped me, and with whom I was later associated, had started as pupils of Durkheim or shared his views. I shall now attempt to describe briefly some of the members of this group.

First I must mention Célestin Bouglé, who was descended from Breton Celtic-speaking ancestors, and who retained his Breton accent. When he was a young teacher in southern France, although his students often complained of being unable to understand his speech, he was very well liked. Even as director of the Ecole Normale, he maintained the role of older brother in his relations with students. He was seldom upset except when one of his colleagues wrote badly. On such occasions he would exclaim, "Ça, ce n'est pas de français!"

Marcel Mauss, a perfect gentleman and a considerate friend, was Durkheim's nephew, but he had great difficulty living up to the relationship. Perhaps the fact explains many of his oddities. Until he married at the age of sixty-one, he maintained that a woman might properly become president of the Republic or of a university, but no female was suited to the task of buying food or preparing meals. Often when Mauss was walking home in the winter rains of Paris, his arms full of groceries, he would stop anyone who crossed his path and explain his newest anthropological theories. If the listener was ignorant of the civilization he was discussing or had erroneous conceptions of it, he was likely to remark, "Here again you show how stupid you are." Soon after I had escaped from Germany he wrote to ask me to call on him at eight o'clock one Sunday morning. In his nightshirt when I arrived, he ordered me to take a seat and excused himself to look after some beans that were boiling on the stove. Presently, he welcomed me with these words: "You have been a contributor to the reviews of

Leopold von Wiese and Max Horkheimer and now you will have to work with Bouglé. That is very appropriate because all of you are equally stupid." In desperation Bouglé referred to him as "un homme bizarre."

In addition to Bouglé and Mauss, I must briefly mention others in the Durkheim group. Among them was Paul Fauconnet, a fine scholar but, unfortunately, by that time a very sick man. Gaston Richard lived in the south of France and therefore entered the picture to a lesser extent. Then there was Marcel Granet, a first-class Sinologist and director of the Institut de Chine. There was also Lucien Lévy-Bruhl, the well-known ethnologist, then an old man but still very productive. Finally, I must mention René Maunier. Maunier was a man of universal knowledge. He had lived in Africa and was one of the first in the field of colonial sociology. Though deadly serious in his scientific convictions, he was at the same time a typical French joker.

These men usually congregated at the periodical meetings of the Sociological Society. This long-established organization published the *Année sociologique*. In accordance with the rather sweeping concept of sociology in France at that time, the Society had a vast range of interests. Foremost among them were ethnology and oriental problems.

The so-called *dinées Proudhon* offered another opportunity for gatherings. One may wonder how men who had started as adherents of Durkheim, a "group metaphysician," could have become interested in Proudhon, an extreme individualist. For one thing, almost all the Durkheimians had to some extent shifted away from the group metaphysic of their master. For another, Proudhon, though almost an anarchist with regard to the state, emphasized the importance of the family even more than Durkheim did. Finally, Marx may never have played as great a role in France as elsewhere, but the so-called pre-Marxian's emphasis on voluntary co-operation was not forgotten. Thus the memory of Charles Fourier was still green enough to warrant the publication of a Fourier dictionary in the 1890's. Proudhon was another pre-Marxian; and it was to discuss plans for a definitive edition of his work that Bouglé, Maunier and others met. As French professors they were not

311

accustomed to doing much work in their offices; as fathers they were not supposed to bring many men into their homes for fear the reputations of their wives and daughters might be damaged. So, like true Frenchmen, they met in private rooms in one of the countless small Parisian restaurants. In rotation, the members selected a restaurant where the food was first class. Needless to say, dinner included hors d'oeuvres, wines, and liqueurs. Of the gourmets in the group, Maxime Leroy, the well-known historian of seventeenth-century social ideas, was without peer.

Much more important were the activities of these men in three other organizations. Some of them, such as Mauss and Fauconnet, belonged to one of the seven different socialist parties. Few, if any, of the Durkheim group had much in common with Marxism. Other Durkheimians, like Bouglé, belonged to the radical socialists. The term is a misnomer, for members of the party were neither radical nor socialist. In fact, they were less radical than any of the Socialist parties in France. Especially after the Dreyfus Affair, the word "radical" in France implied unconditional opposition to the Catholic Church on the assumption that it was an enemy of the French Republic. "Socialist" connoted opposition to laissez faire and unrestricted competition. The radical socialist party was made up of middle-class farmers in the South who hated Catholicism and practiced birth control, and of lower-middle-class people in small towns. There and in the village, the radical socialists were led by the primary-school teacher. He was the representative of the secular (laïque) government and the traditional antagonist of the village priest. The priest held forth in one, the teacher in the other, of the two village restaurants. In matters of paternal authority and family life, they were equally conservative; and both were the object of jokes in motion pictures such as *La femme du boulanger* and in novels like *Clochemerle*. Leadership in the radical socialist party also came from lycée professors—often productive scholars—and from university professors. The latter, who taught even fewer hours in France than in Germany, had plenty of time for both their scholarship and their political activities. Bouglé and his associates in the radical socialist party were among them.

The third organization, closely connected with this party and sometimes even overlapping it, was one of the most characteristic French institutions, the *League des Droits de l'Homme*. It came into being in connection with the Dreyfus Affair, and Lévy-Bruhl, one of the most independent pupils of Durkheim, was chief among its founders. Bouglé himself was noted for his struggles in behalf of all those who were persecuted for their convictions. In the mid-1920's, shortly after my speech at the Metz meeting, one of Bouglé's friends became president of the League. He was Victor Basch, a professor of aesthetics and literary history. The French government, spurred on by the nationalism of the secretary of war, Paul Painlevé, was beginning to persecute teachers suspected of being Communists. The League protested; Basch declared that although it struggled implacably against sovietism because that system hindered free individual expression through governmental interference, it stoutly defended every Communist who was prevented from freely expressing himself by the government.

It is obvious that these men did not help me merely because of personal friendship: they were fighting for principle when the threat of Hitlerism became apparent. In 1923, Bouglé had come to Berlin in the interest of French-German rapprochement and had expressed his admiration for German culture and science. In 1933, after Hitler's rise to power, a dinner was organized in Geneva in honor of Bouglé, the protector of refugees. In his address, Bouglé defined Hitlerism as "une des choses les plus exécrables qui existent." In both cases he was completely sincere, and he revealed himself as a man of courage. In the atmosphere of postwar hatred of things German, it took courage for a man to say anything in favor of Germany. But after the rise of Nazism the classical individualism of the French Enlightenment turned into an individualism of the *petit bourgeois*. The typical French intellectual, who wanted security and a predictable future for himself and his family, found his way of life threatened by those damned German intellectuals, who did not spend their time drinking aperitifs with their friends but worked twice as hard as the Frenchman. They worked for the sake of God or, if they were not religious believers, for work's sake, which for a true German scholar is almost the same. Accordingly, in contrast to the sympathetic attitude in the United States, the French did not welcome the appointment of German scholars in their midst. Thus it took courage to work openly on behalf of German refugees.

Nevertheless, these men did so. One went even further, and his attitude may be described because it is so typical of one kind of French mentality. I refer to Paul Rivet, a notable investigator of pre-Inca culture. He was somewhat different from the men I have discussed. Politically, he belonged to the left wing of the socialist parties; as an anthropologist, he incorporated some elements of Father Schmidt's diffusion theory into his system. In a remarkable anticipation of the future, Rivet said to me that after the collapse of Hitlerism, many German scientists who supported Hitler might be obliged to flee Germany and must be given a place of refuge and an opportunity to work in France. The majority of Durkheimians did not go so far in their humanitarianism. But they helped the enemies of the Nazis when they could, more than once successfully.

Although I disagreed with them on many religious and philosophical points, I am proud to have participated in the life of the Durkheim group, and especially to have been Bouglé's friend. In their vigorous defense of the right of the individual conscience, they had some kinship with Max Weber. To be sure, there were differences, for Weber had a strong religious background and a concept of the tragic aspect of life. But this is not the place to discuss Weber, for the purpose of this paper is simply to shed some light on a group of men who, aside from their scientific importance, deserve to be remembered.

TRANSLATIONS

DURKHEIM'S LETTER
TO RADCLIFFE-BROWN

J. G. PERISTIANY

Transcript

9 Nov. 1913
4, Avenue d'Orléans. XIVe.

Cher Monsieur,

Absent de Paris depuis le mois d'août, je/ n'ai trouvé votre brochure qu'en rentrant/ il y a quelques jours: elle m'avait attendu/ chez moi comme tous les livres et imprimés./ C'est ce qui vous explique le retard bien/ involontaire que j'ai mis à vous en accuser/ réception et à vous en remercier ainsi/ que de l'aimable lettre qui l'accom-/ pagnait.

Je me felicite de l'occasion que vous m'/ avez ainsi offerte d'entrer directement/ en rapport avec vous et j'ai eu le/ plus grand plaisir d'apprendre de vous/ que nous nous entendions sur les principes/ généraux de la science. Rien ne pouvait/ me donner plus de confiance dans/ la méthode que j'essaye d'employer.

J'ai lu votre travail avec le plus/ vif intérêt. Sans parler de nombre de/ faits de détail que j'ai notés, ce que/ vous dites sur les règles matrimoniales/ en Australie est certainement de nature/ à me faire réflechir et à hésiter. Pour/ savoir si je dois abandonner complétement/ l'explication que j'avais autrefois proposée/ de l'organisation en huit classes, il me faudrait/ faire une étude nouvelle des faits que/ je ne puis songer à entreprendre pour/ l'instant; car tout mon temps est pris [par]/ mon enseignement qui vient de recommencer./ Mais je reconnais très nettement que/ l'objection est très forte et je vous suis/ reconnaissant de me l'avoir signalée./ La question est à reprendre./ Je vous renouvelle tous mes remercie-/ ments pour votre obligeante communi-/ cation et je vous prie de croire à mes/ plus devoués sentiments

E. DURKHEIM

Translation

November 9, 1913

Dear Sir,

Absent from Paris since the beginning of August, I found your booklet only on my return some days ago; it waited for me at home like all books and printed matter. This explains to you my involuntary delay in acknowledging its receipt and in thanking you for the kind letter which accompanied it.

I am grateful for the opportunity that you have thus offered me of entering into direct relations with you and I am extremely glad to learn from you that we are in agreement concerning the general principles of the science [sociology]. Nothing could have given me greater confidence in the method that I am trying to apply.

I read your work with the greatest interest. Without mentioning numerous points of detail which I have noted, what you say about matrimonial rules in Australia is certainly such as to make me reflect and hesitate. In order to know whether I should completely abandon the explanation which I had previously put forward concerning the organization in eight classes, it would be necessary for me to carry out a new study of the facts, which I cannot contemplate doing at the moment; for all my time is taken by my teaching which has just started again. But I recognize very clearly that the objection is a very strong one and I am grateful to you for having pointed it out to me. The subject has to be investigated anew.

I give you once again all my thanks for your kind communication and I beg you to believe in my devoted sentiments.

E. DURKHEIM

This letter was given to me by A. R. Radcliffe-Brown shortly before his death. The booklet that he had sent to Durkheim was clearly a reprint of his article "Three Tribes of Western Australia,"[1] which contains a direct reference to, and criticism of, Durkheim's contribution to *Année sociologique*, "Sur

318

8 Nov. 1913
4, Avenue d'Orléans. XIVe

Cher Monsieur,

Absent de Paris depuis le mois d'Août, je n'ai trouvé votre brochure qu'en rentrant il y a quelques jours : elle m'avait attendu chez moi comme tous les livres et imprimés. C'est ce qui vous explique le retard bien involontaire que j'ai mis à vous en accuser réception et à vous en remercier ainsi que de l'aimable lettre qui l'accompagnait.

Je me félicite de l'occasion que vous m'avez ainsi offerte d'entrer directement en rapports avec vous et j'ai eu le plus grand plaisir d'apprendre de vous que nous nous entendions sur les principes généraux de la science. Rien ne pourrait me donner plus de confiance dans la méthode que j'essaye d'employer.

J'ai lu votre travail avec le plus
vif intérêt. Sans parler de nombre de
faits de détail que j'ai notés, ce que
vous dites sur les règles cérémoniales
en Australie est certainement de nature
à me faire réfléchir et à hésiter. Pour
savoir si je dois abandonner, ou plutôt corriger
l'explication que j'avais autrefois proposée
de l'organisation en huit classes, il me faudrait
faire une étude nouvelle des faits que
je ne puis songer à entreprendre pour
l'instant; car tout mon temps et presque
mon [courage?] que je viens de recouvrer.

Mais je reconnais très nettement que
l'objection est très forte et je vous suis
reconnaissant de me l'avoir signalée.
La question est à reprendre.

Je vous renouvelle tous mes remercie-

ments pour votre obligeante communication je vous prie de croire à mes
plus dévoués sentiments

E. Durkheim

l'organisation matrimoniale des sociétés australiennes."[2] I have been unable to trace this controversy further. Professor E. E. Evans-Pritchard, who is Radcliffe-Brown's literary executor, kindly gave me access to Radcliffe-Brown's papers, but there was no copy of this letter and no further letter from Durkheim among them. This is an indication that the correspondence was discontinued, since Radcliffe-Brown carefully preserved all letters received from Marcel Mauss and other eminent sociologists. In any event, the First World War broke out the next year, and Durkheim's death before the war ended prevented him from carrying out the "new study of the facts," which he could not "contemplate doing at the moment." Radcliffe-Brown did not refer to this letter in his article "The Social Organisation of Australian Tribes,"[3] but all those who have come into close contact with him know that he considered Durkheim one of his masters, and this is certainly apparent in the best of his writings. The care with which this letter was preserved in his annotated copy of Durkheim's *Le suicide* shows his reverence for the older man. At the same time, however, Radcliffe-Brown knew that the interest of anthropologists had shifted to topics other than origin and evolution. Therefore, in a sense, this short discussion between these two eminent representatives of the outgoing and incoming generations of anthropologists may be regarded as both a landmark and a turning point.

The article which Durkheim contributed to the first number of *Année sociologique* (1896-97) was concerned with the prohibition of incest, primarily among the Australian aborigines. It was followed, in the fifth volume (1900-1901), by an article on totemism which discussed both phratry and totemic exogamy. The last article in the series on the matrimonial organization of Australian societies is the subject of this brief correspondence with Radcliffe-Brown. These three articles propound Durkheim's ideas on exogamy. As discussions of origins and evolutionary stages, they are of little interest to anyone except the historian of ideas. But if Durkheim's hypotheses are of little value, his treatment of them—especially his demonstration of the logical consistency of the *hypothèse explicative* (which seemed to fascinate him)—and the way in which he used facts to substantiate them (a process which Radcliffe-Brown brushed aside) may interest the present-day anthropologist.

Both Durkheim and Radcliffe-Brown are interested in drawing comparisons and making classifications, but they do not have quite the same objectives in mind. In "The Social Organization of Australian Tribes," Radcliffe-Brown is concerned with ordering individual observations, with creating a typology which would enable the anthropologist to see a common pattern in what are, apparently, discrete and unrelated facts. In his own words, he wishes to use his types as "norms with which to compare others."[4] Durkheim's classification of Australian marriage rules should have the utility of both a structural typology and an evolutionary ladder, but the modern reader is, at times, aware that the questions asked concerning the social typology are so conditioned by the evolutionary scheme that the typology is but the "child of the larger growth," and when used for making a simple comparison, it is awkward and outside its element, as it were.

Although the problems of origins and evolution which are basic to the three Durkheimian articles should be seen in a universal framework, the changes in the structure of institutions—in this case, of marriage regulations—are not discussed *in abstracto*. They refer not to the abstraction *society* but to specific societies; the Australian ones are discussed in detail. In typical fashion, Durkheim does not think of the changing institutions as constituting merely a configuration in a vacuum, but attempts to relate their changing forms—and, sometimes, their changing functions—to each other and to an evolving principle of social organization. In the third article, he explains that the change from a system of four, to one of eight matrimonial classes was caused by the new practice of transmitting the totem through the paternal rather than the maternal line. His hypothesis does more than state the existence of paired variations (in radical form: matrilineal totemic descent=four-class system; patrilineal totemic descent=eight-class system); it also offers a causal analysis in which patrilineality—which itself emerged from matrilineality—determined the change from a four- to an eight-class system.

Durkheim's argument[5] found its ethnographic point of departure in Baldwin Spencer and F. J. Gillen's *The Northern Tribes of Central Australia.*[6] The following is an outline of this argument: Spencer and Gillen's evidence shows that each society was divided into two phratries, each of which comprised a number of "totemic groups or clans."[7] In the examples that Durkheim discusses, the boundary of the phratry generally also marked the limit of the totem since each clan was associated exclusively with one or the other of the two phratries. Furthermore, it appears that the clans were localized whenever the totem was transmitted in the paternal line. The major segment, the phratry, "in many Australian tribes . . . is divided into two sections or classes."[8] As a result of this division, the entire tribe was segmented into four parts. The main principles involved in the constitution of these "sections or classes"—or, as they are later styled by Durkheim, "matrimonial classes"[9] were the following: children (1) did not belong to the same class as either of the two parents, and (2) could not marry into either of the classes to which their parents belonged. Since the phratry was exogamous, the result of the combination of these two rules in a four-class system was that children could marry into only one matrimonial class.

Spencer and Gillen give an extensive description of societies which, like the previous example, are divided into two phratries, but in which each phratry is subdivided into four, instead of two, matrimonial classes. Since Durkheim believes that the organization of matrimonial classes is inextricably interwoven with the rules of descent, he considers it essential to the study of the evolution of the rules of exogamy to discover why this eight-class system came into being.[10]

Setting aside for the moment the question whether one may marry into the maternal or the paternal phratry, we see that in the four-class system one could only marry a member of one's own generation who was in the class opposite one's own. One married, that is, into the class of that phratry of which one was not a member. In the eight-class system, however, it is impossible for an individual to marry into a class made up of members of the generation that follows that of either parent. Why, then, did the eight-class system come into being? What is the reason for this new prohibition?

Since the terminology of the eight-class system bears traces of that of the four-class one, it may be assumed that the four-class system is of greater antiquity. Some new factor, then, must be responsible for this change in systems. For Durkheim, the crucial question involved in determining what this factor is, concerns the line of transmission of the totem. His argument is based mainly on the internal logic of the system itself and an analysis of the different alternatives the system offers.

Up to this point, Durkheim's argument is clear in intention—if not always in exposition. What he wishes to convey is this: According to the lines of phratry descent under both the matrilineal and the patrilineal systems, the children of the father's brother and those of the mother's sister are in the same phratry as Ego, while those of the father's sister and of the mother's brother are in the opposite phratry, into a class of which Ego marries. (All kinship terms are used *lato sensu*.) When totem descent was in the maternal line, the mother and the mother's brother's children could not possibly have shared the same totem; but when the totem is transmitted in the paternal line, the mother, the mother's brother, and the mother's brother's children do have the same totem. Since cross-cousins find themselves in opposite phratries—no matter what the line of transmission of the phratry is—changing the totem's line of descent from a matrilineal one to a patrilineal one meant that the individual found members of the mother's totem in the opposite phratry (into the proper class of which he had to marry in the four-class system). It is possible that under a patrilineal system of clan descent, marriage into the mother's clan did not appear so repulsive; but Durkheim assumes that the horror which was felt for this type of marriage under the matrilineal system of clan descent survived when the totem was being transmitted patrilineally. And since the horror of marrying into the mother's totem was associated particularly with marriage into the class to which the mother's brother's children belonged, the change from a matrilineal to a patrilineal method of totem transmission closed the only avenue of endotribal marriage.

After the adoption of the patrilineal method of transmission of the totem, it was necessary that any system that replaced the four-class one be so structured that marriage with the mother's brother's children, or into the class of which these children were members, was impossible. This requirement was met by duplicating the four classes in two separate ways. The first was to pattern the line of phratry descent on that of totemic descent —that is, the phratry was transmitted patrilineally; to duplicate the two existing classes of each phratry; and to separate the clans in such a way that each phratry had two sets of alternating generations (instead of the previous one), and each clan was associated with one alternation and not with the others. In this way, marriage with the mother's brother's children was prevented. The second way—which Durkheim considers a case of arrested development[11]—was to make the clan patrilineal and the phratry matrilineal. The four classes of each phratry were not divided into pairs but could be seen as a sequence of successive matrilineal generations, A containing the mother of A_1, A_1 of A_2, A_2 of A_3, A_3 of A, and so on. This example, the "Chingalee" one, was important to Durkheim since in it he found proof that (1) the line of transmission of the totem changed before that of the phratry, (2) this change was, in itself, sufficient to transform a four-class into an eight-class system, and (3) the system of marriage classes was patterned on the system of clan descent. "It is as though we were following the discussion of a mathematical problem."[12]

In "Three Tribes of Western Austrialia," Radcliffe-Brown asserts that (1) the number of marriage classes cannot serve as an indication of the marriage law of the tribe; and (2) he had found a type of marriage in which patrilineal descent of the totem was coupled with marriage of the mother's brother's daughter, and also one in which matrilineal descent of the totem was coupled with marriage with the mother's mother's brother's daughter's daughter.[13] The fact that in the paper published in 1913 Radcliffe-Brown refers to Type I as first-cousin marriage and to Type II as marriage with the second cousin, is less relevant here than the fact that in Type I he points to a type of marriage in which patrilineal descent is found together with marriage to the mother's brother's daughter. Durkheim claims that changes in the class system take place in such a way as to prevent this from happening.

1. *Journal of the Royal Anthropological Institute,* XLIII (1913), 143-94.

2. Vol. VIII (1903-4), pp. 118-48.

3. *Oceania* I (1930-31), 34-63, 206-46, 322-41, 426-56.

There is one reference to Durkheim in this work, however. It runs as follows: "Practically all the theoretical discussion of Australian social organization has been directed towards providing hypothetical reconstructions of its history. Even Durkheim, though approaching the subject as a sociologist, devoted his attention to questions of historical development. The more modest but really more important task of trying to understand what the social organization really is and how it works has been neglected." (p. 426 n. 12).

4. *Ibid.,* p. 46 n. 5.

5. Durkheim, *op. cit.,* pp. 116-47.

6. London: Macmillan & Co., Ltd., 1904.

7. Durkheim, *op. cit.,* p. 120.

8. *Ibid.,* p. 121.

9. Cf. Radcliffe-Brown, "The Social Organization of Australian Tribes," p. 37, where he calls them "marriage classes."

10. Durkheim, *op. cit.,* p. 122.

11. *Ibid.,* p. 141.

12. *Ibid.,* p. 147.

13. "The fact that a tribe has two or four named divisions tells us nothing whatever about the marriage law of the tribe, which can only be ascertained by a careful study of the system of relationship." To this he adds: "It may also be worth while to note, in connection with the theory that the prohibition of the marriage of first cousins (and the origin of the relationship system of Type II) is due to the change from maternal to paternal descent of the totem (Professor Durkheim, *Année sociologique,* Vol. VIII), that in the Kariera tribe, Type I (with the marriage of first cousins) exists together with paternal descent of the totem, and that in many tribes of New South Wales and Victoria, Type II exists together with maternal descent of the totem. The theory is therefore not supported by the facts" (pp. 193-94).

In "The Social Organization of Australian Tribes," Type I is called the Kariera Type, and Type II the Aranda Type. In "Three Tribes of Western Australia," he describes the marriages belonging to Type I as being those in which a man marries his mother's brother's daughter. In the later work, he adds marriages to one's mother's brother's or father's sister's daughter to this category. A Type II marriage is one in which a man marries his mother's mother's brother's daughter's daughter.

THE DUALISM OF HUMAN NATURE AND ITS SOCIAL CONDITIONS[1]

EMILE DURKHEIM

Although sociology is defined as the science of societies, it cannot, in reality, deal with the human groups that are the immediate object of its investigation without eventually touching on the individual who is the basic element of which these groups are composed. For society can exist only if it penetrates the consciousness of individuals and fashions it in "its image and resemblance." We can say, therefore, with assurance and without being excessively dogmatic, that a great number of our mental states, including some of the most important ones, are of social origin. In this case, then, it is the whole that, in a large measure, produces the part; consequently, it is impossible to attempt to explain the whole without explaining the part—without explaining, at least, the part as a result of the whole. The supreme product of collective activity is that ensemble of intellectual and moral goods that we call civilization; it is for this reason that Auguste Comte referred to sociology as the science of civilization. However, it is civilization that has made man what he is; it is what distinguishes him from the animal: man is man only because he is civilized. To look for the causes and conditions upon which civilization depends is, therefore, to seek out also the causes and conditions of what is most specifically human in man. And so sociology, which draws on psychology and could not do without it, brings to it, in a just return, a contribution that equals and surpasses in importance the services that it receives from it. It is only by historical analysis that we can discover what makes up man, since it is only in the course of history that he is formed.

The work that we recently published, *The Elementary Forms of the Religious Life*,[2] offers an example of this general truth. In attempting to study religious phenomena from the sociological point of view, we came to envisage a way of explaining scientifically one of the most characteristic peculiarities of our nature. Since the critics who have discussed the book up to the present have not—to our great surprise—perceived the principle upon which this explanation rests, it seemed to us that a brief outline of it would be of some interest to the readers of *Scientia*.

The peculiarity referred to is the constitutional duality of human nature. In every age, man has been intensely aware of this duality. He has, in fact, everywhere conceived of himself as being formed of two radically heterogeneous beings: the body and the soul. Even when the soul is represented in a material form, its substance is not thought of as being of the same nature as the body. It is said that it is more ethereal, more subtle, more plastic, that it does not affect the senses as do the other objects to which they react, that it is not subject to the same laws as these objects, and so on. And not only are these two beings substantially different, they are in a large measure independent of each other, and are often even in conflict. For centuries it was believed that after this life the soul could escape from the body and lead an autonomous existence far from it. This independence was made manifest at the time of death when the body dissolved and disappeared and the soul survived and continued to follow, under new conditions and for varying lengths of time, the path of its own destiny. It can even be said that although the body and the soul are closely associated, they do not belong to the same world. The body is an integral part of the material universe, as it is made known to us by sensory experience; the abode of the soul is elsewhere, and the soul tends ceaselessly to return to it. This abode is the world of the sacred. Therefore, the soul is invested with a dignity that has always been denied the body, which is considered essentially profane, and it inspires those feelings that are everywhere reserved for that which is divine. It is made of the same substance as are the sacred beings: it differs from them only in degree.

A belief that is as universal and permanent as this cannot be purely illusory. There must be something in man that gives rise to this feeling that his nature is dual, a feeling that men in all known civilizations have experienced. Psychological analysis has, in fact, confirmed the existence of this duality: it finds it at the very heart of our inner life.

Our intelligence, like our activity, presents two very different forms: on the one hand, are sensations[3] and sensory tendencies; on the other, conceptual thought and moral activity. Each of these two parts of ourselves represents a separate pole of our being, and these two poles are not only distinct from one another but are opposed to one another. Our sensory appetites are necessarily egoistic: they have our individuality and it alone as their object. When we satisfy our hunger, our thirst, and so on, without bringing any other tendency into play, it is ourselves, and ourselves alone, that we satisfy.[4] [Conceptual thought] and moral activity are, on the contrary, distinguished by the fact that the rules of conduct to which they conform can be universalized. Therefore, by definition, they pursue impersonal ends. Morality begins with disinterest, with attachment to something other than ourselves.[5] A sensation of color or sound is closely dependent on my individual organism, and I cannot detach the sensation from my organism. In addition, it is impossible for me to make my awareness pass over into someone else. I can, of course, invite another person to face the same object and expose himself to its effect, but the perception that he will have of it will be his own work and will be proper to him, as mine is proper to me. Concepts, on the contrary, are always common to a plurality of men. They are constituted by means of words, and neither the vocabulary nor the grammar of a language is the work or product of one particular person. They are rather the result of a collective elaboration, and they express the anonymous collectivity that employs them. The ideas of *man* or *animal* are not personal and are not restricted to me; I share them, to a large degree, with all the men who belong to the same social group that I do. Because they are held in common, concepts are the supreme instrument of all intellectual exchange. By means of them minds communicate. Doubtless, when one thinks through the concepts that he receives from the community, he individualizes them and marks them with his personal imprint, but there is nothing personal that is not susceptible to this type of individualization.[6]

These two aspects of our psychic life are, therefore, opposed to each other as are the personal and the impersonal. There is in us a being that represents everything in relation to itself and from its own point of view; in everything that it does, this being has no other object but itself. There is another being in us, however, which knows things *sub specie aeternitis,* as if it were participating in some thought other than its own, and which, in its acts, tends to accomplish ends that surpass its own. The old formula *homo duplex* is therefore verified by the facts. Far from being simple, our inner life has something that is like a double center of gravity. On the one hand is our individuality—and, more particularly, our body in which it is based;[7] on the other is everything in us that expresses something other than ourselves.

Not only are these two groups of states of consciousness different in their origins and their properties, but there is a true antagonism between them. They mutually contradict and deny each other. We cannot pursue moral ends without causing a split within ourselves, without offending the instincts and the penchants that are the most deeply rooted in our bodies. There is no moral act that does not imply a sacrifice, for, as Kant has shown, the law of duty cannot be obeyed without humiliating our individual, or, as he calls it, our "empirical" sensitivity. We can accept this sacrifice without resistance and even with enthusiasm, but even when it is accomplished in a surge of joy, the sacrifice is no less real. The pain that the ascetic seeks is pain nonetheless, and this antinomy is so deep and so radical that it can never be completely resolved. How can we belong entirely to ourselves, and entirely to others at one and the same time? The ego cannot be something completely other than itself, for, if it were, it would vanish—this is what happens in ecstasy. In order to think, we must be, we must have an individuality. On the other hand, however, the ego cannot be entirely and exclusively itself, for, if it were, it would be emptied of all content. If we must be in order to think, then we must have something to think about. To what would consciousness be reduced if it expressed nothing but the body and its states? We cannot live without representing to ourselves the world around us and the objects of every sort which fill it. And because we represent it to ourselves, it enters into us and becomes part of us. Consequently, we value the world and are attached to it just as we are to ourselves. Something else in us besides ourselves stimulates us to act. It is an error to believe that it is easy to live as egoists. Absolute egoism, like absolute altruism, is an ideal limit which can never be attained in reality. Both are states that we can approach indefinitely without ever realizing them completely.

It is no different in the sphere of our knowledge. We understand only when we think in concepts. But sensory reality is not made to enter the framework of our concepts spontaneously and by itself. It resists, and, in order to make it conform, we have to do some violence to it, we have to submit it to all sorts of laborious operations that alter it so that the mind can assimilate it. However, we never completely succeed in triumphing over its resistance. Our concepts never succeed in mastering our sensations and in translating them completely into intelligible terms. They take on a conceptual form only by losing that which is most concrete in them, that which causes them to speak to our sensory being and to involve it in action; and, in so doing, they become something fixed and dead. Therefore, we cannot understand things without partially renouncing a feeling for their life, and we cannot feel that life without renouncing the understanding of it. Doubtless, we sometimes dream of a science that would adequately express all of reality; but this is an ideal that we can only approach ceaselessly, not one that is possible for us to attain.

This inner contradiction is one of the characteristics of our nature. According to Pascal's formula, man is both "angel and beast" and not exclusively one or the other. The result is that we are never completely in accord with ourselves for we cannot follow one of our two natures without causing the other to suffer. Our joys can never be pure; there is always some pain mixed with them; for we cannot simultaneously satisfy the two beings that are within us. It is this disagreement, this perpetual division against ourselves, that produces both our grandeur and our misery: our misery because we are thus condemned to live in suffering; and our grandeur because it is this division that distinguishes us from all other beings. The animal proceeds to his pleasure in a single and exclusive movement; man alone is normally obliged to make a place for suffering in his life.

Thus the traditional antithesis of the body and soul is not a vain mythological concept that is without foundation in reality. It is true that we are double, that we are the realization of an antinomy. In connection with this truth, however, a question arises that philosophy and even positive psychology cannot avoid: Where do this duality and this antinomy come from? How is it that each of us is, to quote another of Pascal's phrases, a "monster of contradictions" that can never completely satisfy itself? And, certainly, if this odd condition is one of the distinctive traits of humanity, the science of man must try to account for it.

The proposed solutions to this problem are neither numerous nor varied. Two doctrines that occupy an important place in the history of thought held that the difficulty could be removed by denying it; that is, by calling the duality of man an illusion. These doctrines are empirical monism and idealistic monism.

According to the first of these doctrines, concepts are only more or less elaborate sensations. They consist entirely of groups of similar images, groups that have a kind of individuality because each of the images that comprise the group is identified by the same word; however, outside of these images and sensations of which they are the extension, concepts have no reality at all. In the same way, this doctrine holds, moral activity is only another aspect of self-interested activity: the man who obeys the call of duty is merely pursuing his own self-interest as he understands it. When our nature is seen in this way, the problem of its duality disappears: man is one, and if there are serious strains within him, it is because he is not acting in conformity with his nature. If properly interpreted, a concept cannot be contrary to the sensation to which it owes its existence; and the moral act cannot be in conflict with the egoistic act, because, fundamentally, it derives from utilitarian motives.

Unfortunately, however, the facts that posed the question in the first place still exist. It is still true that at all times man has been disquieted and malcontent. He has always felt that he is pulled apart, divided against himself; and the beliefs and practices to which, in all societies and all civilizations, he has always attached the greatest value, have as their object not to suppress these inevitable divisions but to attenuate their consequences, to give them meaning and purpose, to make them more bearable, and at the very least, to console man for their existence. We cannot admit that this universal and chronic state of malaise is the product of a simple aberration, that man has been the creator of his own suffering, and that he has stupidly persisted in it, although his nature truly predisposed him to live harmoniously. Experience should have corrected such a deplorable error long ago. At the very least, it should be able to explain the origin of this inconceivable blindness. Moreover, the serious objections to the hypothesis of empirical monism are well known. It has never been able to explain how the inferior can become the superior; or how individual sensation, which is obscure and confused, can become the clear and distinct impersonal concept; or how self-interest can be transformed into disinterest.

It is no different with the absolute idealist. For him, too, reality is one; but for him it is made up entirely of concepts, while for the empiricist it is made up entirely of sensations. According to the idealist, an absolute intelligence seeing things as they are would find that the world is a system of definite ideas connected with each other in relationships that are equally definite. To the idealist, sensations are nothing by themselves; they are only concepts that are not clear and are intermixed. They assume the particular aspect in which they are revealed to us in experience only because we do not know how to distinguish their elements. If we knew how, there would be no fundamental opposition between the world and ourselves or between the different parts of ourselves. The opposition that we think we perceive is due to a simple error in perspective that needs only to be corrected. However, if this were true, we should be able to establish that this error diminishes to the degree that the domain of conceptual thought is extended and we learn to think less by sensation and more in concepts; to the degree, that is, that science develops and becomes a more important factor in our mental life. But, unfortunately, history is far from confirming these optimistic hopes. It seems that, on the contrary, human malaise continues to increase. The great religions of modern man are those which insist the most on the existence of the contradictions in the midst of which we struggle. These continue to depict us as tormented and suffering, while only the crude cults of inferior societies breathe forth and inspire a joyful confidence.[8] For what religions express is the experience through which humanity has lived, and it would be very surprising if our nature became unified and harmonious when we feel that our discords are increasing. Moreover, even if we assume that these discords are only superficial and apparent, it is still necessary to take this appearance into consideration. If the sensations are nothing outside of concepts, it is still necessary to determine why it is that the latter do not appear to us as they really are, but seem to us mixed and confused. What is it that has imposed on them a lack of distinctness that is contrary to their nature? Idealism faces considerable difficulty in trying to solve these problems, and its failure to do so gives rise to objections that are precisely the opposite of those that have so often and so legitimately been made against empiricism. The latter has never explained how the inferior can become the superior—that is, how a sensation can be raised to the dignity of a concept while remaining unchanged; and the former faces equal difficulty in explaining how the superior can become the inferior, how the concept can wither and degenerate in such a way as to become sensation. This degeneration cannot be spontaneous; it must be determined by some contradictory principle. However, there is no place for a principle of this kind in a doctrine that is essentially monistic.

If we reject the theories which eliminate the problem rather than solve it, the only remaining ones that are valid and merit examination are those which limit themselves to affirming the fact that must be explained, but which do not account for it.

First of all, there is the ontological explanation for which Plato gave the formula. Man is double because two worlds meet in him: that of non-intelligent and amoral matter, on the one hand, and that of ideas, the spirit, and the good, on the other. Because these two worlds are naturally opposed, they struggle within us; and, because we are part of both, we are necessarily in conflict with ourselves. But if this answer—completely metaphysical as it is—has the merit of affirming the fact that must be interpreted without trying to weaken it, it does confine itself, nevertheless, to distinguishing the two aspects of human nature and does not account for them. To say that we are double because there are two contrary forces in us is to repeat the problem in different terms; it does not resolve it. It is still necessary to explain their opposition. Doubtless, one can admit that because of the excellence that is attributed to it the world of ideas and of good contains within itself the reason for its existence; but how does it happen that outside of it there is a principle of evil, of darkness, of non-being? And what is the function of this principle?

We understand even less how these two worlds which are wholly opposite, and which, consequently, should repulse and exclude each other, tend, nevertheless, to unite and interpenetrate in such a way as to produce the mixed and contradictory being that is man; for it seems that their antagonism should keep them apart and make their union impossible. To borrow the language of Plato, the Idea, which is perfect by definition, possesses the plenitude of being, and is, therefore, sufficient in itself, and needs only itself in order to exist. Why, then, should it lower itself toward matter when contact with it can only alter its nature and make it sink below its former level? But, on the other hand, why should matter aspire to the contrary principle—a principle that it denies—and permit itself to be penetrated by it? And, finally, it is man that is the theatre par excellence of the struggle that we have described, a struggle that is not found in other beings; according to the hypothesis, however, man is not the only place where the two worlds ought to meet.

The theory that is most widely accepted at present offers an even less satisfactory explanation of human dualism: it does not base it on two metaphysical principles that are the basis of all reality, but on the existence of two antithetical faculties within us. We possess both a faculty for thinking as individuals and a faculty for thinking in universal and impersonal terms. The first is called sensitivity, and the second reason. Our activity can, therefore, manifest two completely opposed characters depending on whether it is based on sensory or on rational motives. Kant more than anyone else has insisted on this contrast between reason and sensitivity, between rational activity and sensory activity. But even if this classification is perfectly legitimate, it offers no solution to the problem that occupies us here; for the important thing to determine from our consideration of the fact that we have aptitudes for living both a personal and an impersonal life, is not what name it is proper to give to these contrary aptitudes, but how it is that in spite of their opposition, they exist in a single and identical being. How is it that we can participate concurrently in these two existences? How is it that we are made up of two halves that appear to belong to two different beings? Merely to give a name to each being does nothing toward answering the fundamental question.

If we have too often been satisfied with this purely verbal answer, it is because we have generally thought of man's mental nature as a sort of ultimate given which need not be accounted for. Thus we tend to believe that all has been said and done when we attach such and such a fact, whose causes we are seeking, to a human faculty. But why should the human spirit, which is—to put it briefly—only a system of phenomena that are comparable in all ways to other observable phenomena, be outside and above explanation? We know that our organism is the product of a genesis; why should it be otherwise with our psychic constitution? And if there is anything in us that urgently requires explanation, it is precisely this strange antithesis which is involved in this constitution.

The statement made previously that human dualism has always expressed itself in religious form is sufficient to suggest that the answer to our question must be sought in a quite different direction. As we have said, the soul has everywhere been considered something sacred; it has been viewed as a bit of divinity which lives only a brief terrestrial life and tends, as if by itself, to return to its place of origin. Thus the soul is opposed to the body, which is regarded as profane; and everything in our mental life that is related to the body—the sensations and the sensory appetites—has this same character. For this reason, we think that sensations are inferior forms of our activity, and we attribute a higher dignity to reason and moral activity which are the faculties by which, so we are told, we communicate with God. Even the man who is most free of professed belief makes a distinction of this kind, attributing an unequal value to our varying psychic functions, and giving to each, according to its relative value, a place in a hierarchy, in which those that are most closely related to the body are at the bottom. Furthermore, as we have shown,[9] there is no morality that is not infused with religiosity. Even to the secular mind, duty, the moral imperative, is something august and sacred; and reason, the indispensable ally of moral activity, naturally inspires similar feelings. The duality of our nature is thus only a particular case of that division of things into the sacred and the profane that is the foundation of all religions, and it must be explained on the basis of the same principles.

It is precisely this explanation that we attempted in the previously cited work, *The Elementary Forms of the Religious Life,* where we tried to show that sacred things are simply collective ideals that have fixed themselves on material objects.[10] The ideas and sentiments that are elaborated by a collectivity, whatever it may be, are invested by reason of their origin with an ascendancy and an authority that cause the particular individuals who think them and believe in them to represent them in the form of moral forces that dominate and sustain them. When these ideals move our wills, we feel that we are being led, directed, and carried along by singular energies that, manifestly, do not come from us but are imposed on us from the outside. Our feelings toward them are respect and reverent fear, as well as gratitude for the comfort that we receive from them; for they cannot communicate themselves to us without increasing our vitality. And the particular virtues that we attribute to these ideals are not due to any mysterious action of an external agency; they are simply the effects of that singularly creative and fertile psychic operation—which is scientifically analyzable—by which a plurality of individual consciousnesses enter into communion and are fused into a common consciousness.

From another point of view, however, collective representations originate only when they are embodied in material objects, things, or beings of every sort—figures, movements, sounds, words, and so on—that symbolize and delineate them in some outward appearance. For it is only by expressing their feelings, by translating them into signs, by symbolizing them externally, that the individual consciousnesses, which are, by nature, closed to each other, can feel that they are communicating and are in unison.[11] The things that embody the collective representations arouse the same feelings as do the mental states that they represent and, in a manner of speaking, materialize. They, too, are respected, feared, and sought after as helping powers. Consequently, they are not placed on the same plane as the vulgar things that interest only our physical individualities, but are set apart from them. Therefore, we assign them a completely different place in the complex of reality and separate them; and it is this radical separation that constitutes the essence of their sacred character.[12] This system of conceptions is not purely imaginary and hallucinatory, for the moral forces that these things awaken in us are quite real—as real as the ideas that words recall to us after they have served to form the ideas. This is the dynamogenic influence that religions have always exercised on men.

However, these ideals, these products of group life, cannot originate—let alone persist—unless they penetrate the individual consciousness where they are organized in a lasting fashion. Once the group has dissolved and the social communion has done its work, the individuals carry away within themselves these great religious, moral, and intellectual conceptions that societies draw from their very hearts during their periods of greatest creativity. Doubtless, once the creativity has ceased and each individual has again taken up his private existence, removing himself from the source of his inspiration, the vitality of these conceptions is not maintained at the same intensity. It is not extinguished, however; for the action of the group does not cease altogether: it perpetually gives back to the great ideals a little of the strength that the egoistic passions and daily personal preoccupations tend to take away from them. This replenishment is the function of public festivals, ceremonies, and rites of all kinds.

In mingling with our individual lives in this way, however, these various ideals are themselves individualized. Because they are in a close relation with our other representations, they harmonize with them, and with our temperaments, characters, habits, and so on. Each of us puts his own mark on them; and this accounts for the fact that each person has his own particular way of thinking about the beliefs of his church, the rules of common morality, and the fundamental notions that serve as the framework of conceptual thought. But even while they are being individualized—and thus becoming elements of our personalities—collective ideals preserve their characteristic property: the prestige with which they are clothed. Although they are our own, they speak in us with a tone and an accent that are entirely different from those of our other states of consciousness. They command us; they impose respect on us; we do not feel ourselves to be on an even footing with them. We realize that they represent something within us that is superior to us.

It is not without reason, therefore, that man feels himself to be double: he actually is double. There are in him two classes of states of consciousness that differ from each other in origin and nature, and in the ends toward which they aim. One class merely expresses our organisms and the objects to which they are most directly related. Strictly individual, the states of consciousness of this class connect us only with ourselves, and we can no more detach them from us than we can detach ourselves from our bodies. The states of consciousness of the other class, on the contrary, come to us from society; they transfer society into us and connect us with something that surpasses us. Being collective, they are impersonal; they turn us toward ends that we hold in common with other men; it is through them and them alone that we can communicate with others. It is, therefore, quite true that we are made up of two parts, and are like two beings, which, although they are closely associated, are composed of very different elements and orient us in opposite directions.

In brief, this duality corresponds to the double existence that we lead concurrently: the one purely individual and rooted in our organisms, the other social and nothing but an extension of society. The origin of the antagonism that we have described is evident from the very nature of the elements involved in it. The conflicts of which we have given examples are between the sensations and the sensory appetites, on the one hand, and the intellectual and moral life, on the other; and it is evident that passions and egoistic tendencies derive from our individual constitutions, while our rational activity —whether theoretical or practical—is dependent on social causes. We have often had occasion to prove that the rules of morality are norms that have been elaborated by society;[13] the obligatory character with which they are marked is nothing but the authority of society, communicating itself to everything that comes from it. In the book that is the occasion of the present study but which we can only mention here, we have tried to demonstrate that concepts, the material of all logical thought, were originally collective representations. The impersonality that characterizes them is proof that they are the product of an anonymous and impersonal action.[14] We have even found a basis for conjecturing that the fundamental and lofty concepts that we call categories are formed on the model of social phenomena.[15]

The painful character of the dualism of human nature is explained by this hypothesis. There is no doubt that if society were only the natural and spontaneous development of the individual, these two parts of ourselves would harmonize and adjust to each other without clashing and without friction: the first part, since it is only the extension and, in a way, the complement of the second, would encounter no resistance from the latter. In fact, however, society has its own nature, and, consequently, its requirements are quite different from those of our nature as individuals: the interests of the whole are not necessarily those of the part. Therefore, society cannot be formed or maintained without our being required to make perpetual and costly sacrifices. Because society surpasses us, it obliges us to surpass ourselves; and to surpass itself, a being must, to some degree, depart from its nature—a departure that does not take place without causing more or less painful tensions. We know that only the action of society arouses us to give our attention voluntarily. Attention presupposes effort: to be attentive we must suspend the spontaneous course of our representations and prevent our consciousness from pursuing the dispersive movement that is its natural course. We must, in a word, do violence to certain of our strongest inclinations. Therefore, since the role of the social being in our single selves will grow ever more important as history moves ahead, it is wholly improbable that there will ever be an era in which man is required to resist himself to a lesser degree, an era in which he can live a life that is easier and less full of tension. To the contrary, all evidence compels us to expect our effort in the struggle between the two beings within us to increase with the growth of civilization.

Translated by Charles Blend

1. "Le dualisme de la nature humaine et ses conditions sociales," *Scientia,* XV (1914), 206-21. Used by permission of Paolo Bonetti, editor of *Scientia* (Asso-Como, Italy).

2. *Les formes élémentaires de la vie religieuse* (Paris: Félix Alcan, 1912). [Translated as *The Elementary Forms of Religious Life* by Joseph Ward Swain ([1915] Glencoe, Ill.: Free Press of Glencoe, Illinois, 1947).]

3. To sensations, one should add images, but since images are only sensations that survive themselves, it is useless to mention them separately. The same is true for those conglomerations of images and sensations which are called perceptions.

4. No doubt there are egoistic desires that do not have material things as their objects, but the sensory appetites are the type par excellence of egoistic tendencies. We believe that desires for objects of a different kind imply—although the egoistic motive may play a role in them—a movement out of ourselves which surpasses pure egoism. This is the case, for example, with love of glory, power, and so on.

5. Cf. our communication to the French Philosophical Society, "La détermination du fait moral," *Bulletin de la Société française de philosophie,* VI (1906), 113-39. [Translated as "The Determination of Moral Facts," in Durkheim, *Sociology and Philosophy,* trans. D. F. Pocock, with an Introduction by J. G. Peristiany (Glencoe, Ill.: Free Press of Glencoe, Illinois, 1953), pp. 35-62.]

6. We do not mean to deny the individual the capacity to form concepts. He learns to form representations of this kind from the collectivity, but even the concepts he forms in this way have the same character as the others: they are constructed in such a way that they can be universalized. Even when they are the product of a personality, they are in part impersonal.

7. We say our individuality and not *our personality.* Although the two words are often used synonymously, they must be distinguished with

the greatest possible care, for the personality is made up essentially of supra-individual elements. Cf., on this point, *Les formes élémentaires de la vie religieuse,* pp. 386-90.

8. Cf. *ibid.,* pp. 320-21, 580.

9. Cf. "La détermination du fait moral," p. 125.

10. Cf. *Les formes élémentaires de la vie religieuse,* pp. 268-342.

11. *Ibid.,* pp. 329 ff.

12. *Ibid.,* pp. 53 ff.

13. Cf. *De la division du travail social* ([1893] 3rd ed.; Paris: Félix Alcan, 1907) , *passim* and esp. pp. 391 ff. [Translated as *The Division of Labor in Society,* by George Simpson ([1933] Glencoe, Ill.: Free Press of Glencoe, Illinois, 1947) .]

14. *Les formes élémentaires de la vie religieuse,* pp. 616 ff.

15. *Ibid.,* pp. 12-28 ff., 205 ff., 336, 386, 508, 627.

PREFACES TO *L'ANNÉE SOCIOLOGIQUE*[1]

EMILE DURKHEIM

Preface to Volume I[2]

Neither the sole, nor even the chief, objective of the *Année sociologique* is the presentation of an annual survey of the state of properly sociological literature. Such a task would be too restricted and of little utility, for properly sociological studies are not yet numerous enough to call for a bibliographic periodical. We believe, however, that sociologists have a real need for regular information concerning studies which are being carried on in the special sciences—the histories of law, culture, and religions; moral statistics; economics; and so on—for it is these special sciences that offer the materials out of which sociology must be built. It is the primary aim of the present publication to meet this need.

It seems to us that, at the present stage of our discipline, to provide such regular information is the best way to hasten its progress. In fact, the knowledge a sociologist needs—if he does not want to abandon himself to a vain exercise of dialectics—is so extended and varied, and the facts are so numerous and are scattered in so many quarters, that one has great difficulties in assembling them and always risks omitting important items. It is therefore desirable that a preliminary survey put these facts at the disposal of interested persons. No doubt, to the extent that sociology becomes specialized, scholars will find it easier to acquire the competence and erudition necessary for the particular class of problems to which they devote their labors. But this stage has yet to be reached. There are still too many sociologists who daily dogmatize on law, morals, or religion; and there are still scholars who have only random information or who proceed exclusively by the lights of natural philosophy, without suspecting, it would appear, that a considerable body of documents bearing on these questions has been assembled in recent times by the historical and ethnographic schools of Germany and England. It is thus not a useless task to undertake a periodic inventory of all these sources and to indicate, at

341

least summarily, what profit sociology may derive from them. But aside from expressing views and suggesting lines of inquiry, can these methodical analyses of specific and mutually supplementary works not give a livelier impression, even a fairer notion, of the nature of collective reality than do the generalities that are characteristic of treatises in social philosophy? At any rate, we hope to succeed in interesting not only professional sociologists but all enlightened readers who are concerned with these problems. It is surely necessary that the public take a fuller account of the preparation needed to embark on these studies so that it will become less complacent when faced by facile constructions and will be more demanding of proof and information.

Our enterprise can be useful in still another respect. It can serve to draw together sociology and certain special sciences which keep themselves too removed from us, much to their own detriment, as well as to ours.

In saying this, we are thinking particularly of history. Even today, historians who take an interest in the research of sociologists and feel that it is of concern to them are rare. The too-general character of our theories and their inadequate documentation cause them to be thought of as something negligible; they are conceded hardly more than philosophical importance. Yet history can be a science only to the extent that it explains, and explanation cannot proceed except through comparison. Otherwise, even simple description is hardly possible; one cannot adequately describe a unique fact, or a fact of which one has only rare instances, *because one does not see it adequately.* It is for this reason that Fustel de Coulanges, in spite of his profound insight into historical matters, came to erroneous conclusions regarding the nature of the *gens,* in which he saw nothing but a large agnatic family: he was not acquainted with ethnographical analogies to this type of family. The true character of the Roman *sacer* is very difficult to grasp and, above all, to understand, if one does not see it in relation to the Polynesian *taboo.* We could give other examples without number. We actually serve the cause of history, therefore, if we persuade the historian to go beyond his customary vantage point, to look beyond the country and the period which are the objects of his special studies, and to examine general questions raised by the particular facts which he observes.

As soon as history takes on the character of a comparative discipline, it becomes indistinguishable from sociology. Sociology, in turn, not only cannot do without history but it needs historians who are, at the same time, sociologists. As long as sociology has to sneak like an alien into the historical domain in order to steal from it, in some fashion or other, the facts in which it is interested, it cannot get much out of it. Finding itself in a milieu in which it has no roots and to which it is not accustomed, it is almost inevitable that sociology not notice, or notice only vaguely, that which in reality it has the greatest stake in observing with the utmost clarity. The historian, however, is sufficiently familiar with history to use it with the greatest of ease. Thus, however antagonistic they may be, these two disciplines naturally tend to veer toward one another, and everything suggests that they will be called upon to fuse into one common study, which recombines and unifies elements of both. For it appears equally impossible either that the historian —the student whose role it is to discover facts—ignore the comparisons into which the facts must enter, or that the sociologist, who compares them, ignore how they have been discovered. To produce historians who know how to see historical facts as sociologists do, or—and this amounts to the same thing —to produce sociologists who master all of the techniques of history, is the goal which must be striven for from both ends. In this manner, the explanatory formulas of sociology will progressively extend to the whole complexity of social facts, instead of reproducing only their most general outlines; and, at the same time, historical erudition will become meaningful because it will be employed to resolve the gravest problems with which mankind is faced. Fustel de Coulanges was fond of repeating that true sociology is history: nothing is more incontestable provided that history is carried on sociologically.

Is not the only means sociologists have to attain this result to go spontaneously to history, get in touch with it, show it what role the materials it accumulates can play, become permeated with its spirit, and permeate it with the spirit of sociology? This is what we have tried to do in the analyses found in this volume. When and if one realizes that sociology is far from implying any contempt for facts, that it does not recoil even when faced with details, but that, on the other hand, facts have no significance for our insight unless they are grouped in terms of types and laws, one will certainly better understand the possibility—no, the necessity—of a new conception in which the sense of historical reality at its most concrete does not exclude the methodical research into similarities, a research which is the precondition of any science. If the *Année sociologique* is able to contribute, however little, toward orienting some serious students in this direction, we shall not regret our labors.[3]

The definition of our aim determines, at the same time, the organization of our periodical.

If our chief objective is to assemble the materials necessary to our discipline, it has also seemed useful to us to show through examples how these materials can be put to work. We have therefore reserved the first part of the *Année* for original papers (*Mémoires originaux*). We do not ask that the studies which we shall publish under this heading conform to a clear-cut formula of "originality"; it is sufficient for us if they have a definite object and are done methodically. By imposing on ourselves this twofold condition, we by no means exclude general sociology—the reader may convince himself of this later on. General sociology as a branch of sociology is not less useful than other branches; if it lends itself more readily to abuse for making generalities and fabricating fantasies, this is not due to its nature. We do confess, however, that our efforts here will lean especially in the direction of studies dealing with more restricted subjects and concerning special branches of sociology. For inasmuch as general sociology can be nothing but a synthesis of these particular sciences and can consist only in the comparison of their most general results, it is possible only to the extent that these special disciplines themselves are advanced. We must therefore apply ourselves, above all, to their development.

The second and longest part of the work is dedicated to analyses and bibliographical notes. But since the domain of sociology is as yet defined only poorly, we have had before everything else to delimit the range of studies with which the *Année sociologique* intends to concern itself in order to prevent arbitrary choices and exclusions. In one respect, all that is historical is sociological. In another respect, philosophical speculations on morals, law, and religion are of interest to the sociologist. Thus it was necessary to draw a double demarcation line.

For philosophy, this line was easy to lay down. All doctrines dealing with customs, law, and religious beliefs concern us, provided they admit the postulate which is the condition of any sociology, namely, that laws exist which reflection, carried out methodically, enables us to discover. We do not want to imply by this statement that in order to be a sociologist one must deny all contingency: sociology, like all other positive sciences, need not pose this metaphysical problem. Sociology merely assumes that social phenomena are tied together through relations which are intelligible and accessible to scientific investigation. Consequently, sociology does not have to take into account systems which are based on the opposite hypothesis. The periods when it might have been useful to refute such systems have passed; however little advanced our science is, it has in recent times produced enough results to do without a perpetual justification of its right to exist.

As for history, the line of demarcation is more fluid. It can be laid down only provisionally and will very probably have to be shifted in accordance with the development of sociology. Nevertheless, one rule, at least, may be stated. The only facts which we must collect in the *Année* are those which, it appears, will be susceptible, in the rather near future, to incorporation into sociology—facts, that is, which can enter into comparisons. This principle is enough to eliminate those studies in which the role of historical individuals (legislators, statesmen, generals, prophets, innovators of all kinds, and so on) is the chief object of the research. The same goes for works which are exclusively engaged in retracing in their chronological order the sequence of particular events, the succession of superficial manifestations which constitute the apparent history of a given people (sequences of dynasties, wars, and negotiations;

and parliamentary histories) . In a word, all that is biographical, either of individuals or of collectivities, is actually without utility to the sociologist. It is for this reason, incidentally, that the biologist does not pay much attention to the external history of the vicissitudes through which each individual organism passes in the course of its existence. To be sure, nobody can say that such various details are forever intractable to scientific treatment, but the time when it will be possible to attempt their explanation—or even a partial one—is so remote that it would be wasting one's efforts to engage in it now. In short, what is called a scientific fact is quite simply a fact that is ready to be treated scientifically. Obviously, the conditions of this readiness vary with the state of development of a particular science. This explains why at any given moment not all facts have this character and why the scientist is obliged to choose and abstract those which he thinks it is useful to observe.

After delimiting the materials for our analyses, we had to establish a critical method which was in line with the aim we have in mind. We could not subscribe to the current conception which makes the critic a sort of judge who pronounces sentence and ranks abilities. Posterity alone is competent to proceed to such classifications, which are, besides, of no value to science. Our role as critics must be to extract from the works we study the objective residue, that is, the suggestive facts and the fruitful views—whether they be interesting for their intrinsic value or because of the discussions they evoke. The critic must be the collaborator of the author, his grateful collaborator; for whatever little remains of a book after critical evaluation, that much is gained for science. Such collaboration is made still more important and necessary to us by the character of the works with which we have to deal. Since many of them are not explicitly sociological, we could not be satisfied with giving their contents, with merely expounding, as it were, the materials they contain; as far as was possible, we had to submit them to a preliminary elaboration which would indicate to the reader what information contained in them is useful to the sociologist. For the sake of greater plausibility, all analyses of works which refer to the same question have been grouped together in such a way that they complement and illuminate each other. By themselves, these groupings already constitute comparisons which may be useful.

Such is our program. To execute it, a certain number of workers have united their efforts after reaching an understanding regarding the principles which have just been expounded. And perhaps this spontaneous unity for a common enterprise is itself a fact that is not without significance. Up to now, sociology has generally been an eminently personal undertaking; its teachings have been closely related to the personalities of particular scholars and could not be separated from them. Yet science, because it is objective, is an essentially impersonal affair and cannot progress except through collective labor. For this reason alone, and irrespective of what useful results it may have, our attempt, we believe, deserves to be received with interest by all those who are anxious that sociology leave its philosophical phase and take its rank among the sciences.[4]

Preface to Volume II[5]

A year ago we stated our program; there is, consequently, no need for expounding it again. Moreover, the very favorable reception which our attempt has met proves that we have been generally understood.

Yet there are some points on which an additional explanation might be useful.

Depending upon one's preference, one may reproach us either with not being complete enough or with being too complete, that is, with expanding the fields of sociology beyond measure. If, as still happens all too often, one sees in sociology nothing but a purely philosophical discipline or metaphysic of the social sciences, the very specialized studies we analyze may seem out of place. But our chief objective is to react precisely against this conception and practice of sociology. We are far from denying the existence of a general sociology, which would be the philosophical part of our science; we even grant gladly that in its beginning sociology could not and ought not to have had any other character. But the moment has come for sociology to step out of these generalities and to specialize. By so doing, sociology does not become identical with special techniques which have long been in existence—or, at least, it will not identify itself with these techniques until it transforms them, for it is bound to imbue them with a new spirit. Above all, it is the notion of types and laws which is still too often absent from these techniques. Many of them, in fact, end up in mere literature and erudition rather than in science, for these disciplines aim, more than anything else, at counting and describing particular facts rather than at constituting genera and species and at establishing relationships. Yet one of the main contributions of sociology is the awareness that there is a close kinship among all these highly diverse facts, which have up to now been studied by specialists in complete mutual independence. These facts are interrelated not only in that they cannot be understood in isolation from one another, but in that they are, fundamentally, of the same nature: they are nothing but various manifestations of the same reality—social reality. It is for this reason that the jurist must be familiar with the science of religion and the economist with that of customs, and so on; furthermore, it is for this reason that all these different sciences, inasmuch as they have phenomena of the same species for their subject matter, must practice the same method.

The principle underlying this method is the principle that religious, juridical, moral, and economic facts must all be treated in conformance with their nature as social facts. Whether describing or explaining them, one must relate them to a particular social milieu, to a definite type of society; and it is in the constitutive characteristics of this type that one must search for the determining causes of the phenomenon under consideration. The majority of these sciences are still closed to this approach. The science of religion speaks in the most general terms of religious beliefs and practices, as if these were not related to any social system. The laws of political economy are of so general a nature that they are independent of all conditions of time and place and are disconnected from any collective form; exchange, production, value, and so on, are seen as products of very simple forces common to all mankind. Comparative law is perhaps the only science which is oriented in a different sense; here attention has been called, for example, to the relations between certain domestic institutions and certain forms of social organization. Still, these relations have remained quite fragmentary and have been traced without much consistency or method.

We are challenged, then, by an urgent and truly sociological task: we must labor to make of all these special sciences as many branches of sociology. But to do this it is indispensable that we enter into close contact with them and interpenetrate with them so that they may be renewed. It is necessary to investigate facts in detail, not in an effort to gain a summary view which might be suggestive of philosophical hypotheses, but in order to study them in themselves, to seek to understand them, to reduce them to types and laws which express them as adequately as possible—and it is necessary to do all this in a sociological spirit. In this way, the nature—the often very special nature—of the works covered in our analyses explains and justifies itself. Yet because of this objective of ours, we cannot even think of being complete in the absolute sense of this term. Particular techniques have the habit of enlisting facts in which they are interested and of paying little attention to the properly scientific interest of these facts—little attention, that is, to the extent to which these facts may contribute toward the formulation of a general law. The investigation of specialists does not always lead toward the matters which have the greatest explanatory value, precisely because explanation is not the decisive goal of their studies. It would thus be useless and painful to give here a complete survey of all studies which appear each year in these different fields; the only ones that deserve to be singled out are those dealing with questions which already engender sociological reflection. Even so, since any selection makes for regrettable exclusions, we are generally inclined to extend the circle of our choice rather than to restrict it unduly; since it is impossible to keep to the line, it is better to sin somewhat on the side of generosity.

Under the influence of sociology, the classification of the special sciences and their interrelations must be transformed along with the transformation of the spirit and method of each of them. Up to now, they have developed independently of one another. Consequently, social phenomena have not been distributed among them in a methodical manner or according to a well-reasoned plan: the mutual boundaries separating these special sciences have been determined by the most uncertain, sometimes the most fortuitous, principles. The result has been a number of confusions and distinctions which are equally irrational. Quite different phenomena are often assembled under the same heading, and phenomena of the same nature are divided up among different sciences. What is called in Germany by the untranslatable name of *Völkerkunde* lumps together studies of customs, religious beliefs and practices, habitats, the family, and certain economic facts; and *Kulturgeschichte* is no less comprehensive. Inversely, demography and geography, which are so intimately related to one another, are only now beginning to come together. It is therefore important that new divisions replace the customary ones. To this purpose, however, we must bring together and put into reciprocal contact all these particular disciplines, so that it may become clear which ones among them need one another and tend to converge, and which ones are better left separate. Thus sociology may be expected to bring about a new and more systematic redistribution of the phenomena with which all these various studies are concerned; and this is not one of the lesser services it is destined to render. For nothing is more of an obstacle to the advances of science than a bad classification of the problems it deals with. It should be pointed out, however, that this situation produces one more difficulty for the organization of the *Année*. For inasmuch as the studies which we shall examine have not at present been made to fit divisions in a rationally organized sociology, it is impossible to arrange them in an order which would be perfectly satisfactory. Such inconvenience can be reduced, but it cannot be eliminated altogether.

This year, as well as last, our analyses are headed by those concerning the sociology of religion. The according of the first rank to this sort of phenomenon has produced some astonishment, but it is these phenomena which are the germ from which all others—or at least almost all others—are derived. Religion contains in itself from the very beginning, even if in an indistinct state, all the elements which in dissociating themselves from it, articulating themselves, and combining with one another in a thousand ways, have given rise to the various manifestations of collective life. From myths and legends have issued forth science and poetry; from religious ornamentations and cult ceremonials have come the plastic arts; from ritual practice were born law and morals. One cannot understand our preception of the world, our philosophical conceptions of the soul, of immortality, of life, if one does not know the religious beliefs which are their primordial forms. Kinship started out as an essentially religious tie; punishment, contract, gift, and homage are transformations of expiatory, contractual, communal, honorary sacrifices, and so on. At most one may ask whether economic organization is an exception and derives from another source; although we do not think so, we grant that the question must be kept in abeyance. At any rate, a great number of problems change their aspects completely as soon as their connections with the sociology of religion are recognized. Our efforts must therefore be aimed at tracing these connections. Besides, there is no social science that is more capable of rapid progress, for the materials that have already been gathered are quite considerable and are ready to be elaborated sociologically. This is the reason why the two papers which follow belong to this very science. [Emile Durkheim, "De la définition des phénomènes religieux," pp. 1-28, and Henri Hubert and Marcel Mauss, "Essai sur la nature et la fonction du sacrifice," pp. 29-138.] This is not a fortuitous coincidence. It appeared to us useful to call these studies to the attention of sociologists so as to give them a glimpse of the wealth of this material and of all the results they may expect of it.

To be sure, sociologists pressed for time may find our procedure needlessly complicated. If we want to understand contemporary social phenomena so as to be able to guide their development, is it not enough to observe them as they are given to us in our everyday experience? Is embarking on researches into their remotest origins not merely a work of vain erudition? This last method, it must be pointed out, is full of illusions. One does not know social reality if one has seen it only from the outside and has ignored its foundations. In order to know how it is constituted, one has to know how it has constituted itself; that is, one must have followed historically the way in which it has developed. In order to be able to say, with even a slight chance of success, what will be, or what the society of tomorrow will be like, it is indispensable that one study the social forms of the most distant past. In order to understand the present, one must step out of it.[6]

But if on this point we cannot yield to the observations which have been made to us, there are others from which we have been happy to profit. Hence we think we are correct in saying that the present volume is considerably better than its predecessor. The number of studies analyzed is much larger. We tried our best to make their classification as rational as possible. We even instituted an entirely new section (social morphology) and we take the liberty of calling the reader's attention to its importance. Finally, an alphabetical index has been added which will make for greater convenience in the use of the work. Other improvements are no doubt possible in the future. We shall not fail to strive for them and we shall eagerly receive the suggestions which our readers are good enough to submit.

Translated by Kurt H. Wolff

1. Used by permission of Presses Universitaires de France.

2. *L'Année sociologique* (Paris: Félix Alcan, 1898), I (1896-97), i-vii.

3. All the foregoing could be applied equally well to statistics—both economic and moral—which, like history, is instructive only if it is comparative. If we speak especially of history, it is because at the present stage history is the chief source of sociological investigations, and also because history offers particular resistance to the use of the comparative method.

4. [This note deals with the period covered in each volume of the *Année;* it is omitted here.—Ed.]

5. *L'Année sociologique* (Paris: Félix Alcan, 1899), II (1897-98), i-vi.

6. But it must be understood that the importance we thus attribute to the sociology of religion does not in the least imply that religion must play the same role in present-day societies that it has played at other times. In a sense, the contrary conclusion would be more sound. Precisely because religion is a primordial phenomenon, it must yield more and

more to the new social forms which it has engendered. In order to understand these new forms, one must connect them with their religious origins, but without thereby confusing them with religious phenomena, properly speaking. Similarly, for the individual, it does not follow from the fact that sensation is the primitive fact from which superior intellectual functions develop by means of combinations, that the mind of a cultured adult consists, especially today, only of sensations. On the contrary, the importance of their role decreases to the degree to which intelligence develops.

SOCIOLOGY AND ITS SCIENTIFIC FIELD[1]

EMILE DURKHEIM

A science which has barely begun to exist has, and initially is bound to have, only an uncertain and vague sense of the area of reality that it is about to approach, and the extent and the limits of that area. It can gain a clearer picture only to the degree that it proceeds wth its studies. And the heightened awareness of its subject matter that it acquires in this way is of the greatest importance; for the path of the scientist is the more secure the more orderly it becomes; and the more methodical it is, the more exact is the account that he can render of the territory he is invading.

Sociology has reached the point at which it is opportune to make every effort to bring about such progress. If some reactionary critics, unwittingly under the influence of the prejudice which always militates against the formation of new sciences, reproach sociology for not knowing the precise subject matter with which it intends to deal, they can be told that such ignorance is inevitable in the first stages of study and that our science came into being only yesterday. It must not be forgotten, especially in view of the favorable reception that sociology is given now, that, properly speaking, Europe did not have as many as ten sociologists fifteen years ago. To this must be added that it is asking too much of a science that it define its subject matter with excessive precision, for the part of reality that it intends to study is never neatly separated from other parts. In fact, in nature everything is so connected that there can be neither a complete break in continuity nor any too exact boundaries between the various sciences. Nevertheless, it is urgent that we obtain, if we can, a clear idea of what constitutes the domain of sociology, where this domain is found, and what signs serve us in recognizing the complex of the phenomena with which we must deal—even if we neglect to fix boundaries, which are necessarily indeterminate anyway. This problem is all the more urgent for our science, because if we do not attend to it, its province may be extended to infinity: there is no phenomenon—from physicochemical ones to properly social facts—which does not take place in society. Hence we must accurately isolate social facts and must show what it is that forms their unity in order to avoid reducing sociology to nothing but a conventional label applied to an incoherent agglomeration of disparate disciplines.

Georg Simmel has made a notable, an almost violent, effort to trace the limits of the subject matter of sociology.[2] The basis of his argument is the idea that, if sociology is to be, it must constitute a particular system of investigations that are perfectly distinct from those of the sciences which have long existed under the names of political economy, history of civilization, statistics, demography, and so on. The difference lies in the fact that these other sciences study what occurs in society, not society itself. The religious, moral, and legal phenomena which they treat occur within particular groups; but these groups must themselves be the object of a different inquiry, one which is independent of these others; and it is precisely this independent study that constitutes sociology. With the help of the very society which they form, men living in society achieve many kinds of different ends—some religious, others economic, still others aesthetic, and so on; the special sciences have as their subject matter the particular processes by which these ends are attained. But these processes are not in themselves social—at least, they have a social character only indirectly and only in so far as they develop in a collective environment. These sciences, therefore, are not properly sociological. In the complex usually called society, there exist two kinds of elements which must be clearly distinguished: there is the content, the diverse phenomena that occur among the associated individuals; and there is the container, the association itself, within which such phenomena may be observed. Association is the only truly sociological thing, and sociology is the science of association in the abstract.

Sociology must not seek its problems in the material of social life, but in its form. . . . It is on this abstract consideration of the social forms that the entire right of sociology to exist is founded, just as geometry owes its existence to the possibility of abstracting pure forms from material things.

But by what means is this abstraction given concrete form? If every human association develops with particular ends in view, how can one isolate association in general from the varied ends which it serves, and ascertain its laws?

By putting together associations devoted to the most diverse purposes and eliminating what they have in common . . . the differences, presented by the particular ends around which societies form, mutually cancel each other out, and the social form alone appears. A phenomenon—the formation of parties, for instance—may be observed in the world of art as well as in those of politics, industry, or religion; if we trace what occurs in all these milieus, irrespective of the diversity of ends and interests, it will be possible to determine the laws of this particular manner of grouping. The same method will allow us to study domination and subordination, the formation of hierarchies, the division of labor, competition, and so forth.[3]

It seems that in this fashion sociology is furnished with a clearly defined subject matter. We think, however, that in reality such a conception serves merely to keep it tied to metaphysical ideology when it actually shows an irresistible need to emancipate itself from this sphere. We do not contest the right of sociology to constitute itself by means of abstractions because there is no science that could be established otherwise. The abstractions must be methodically disciplined, however, and must separate the facts according to their natural distinctions; otherwise, they are bound to degenerate into fantastic constructions and vain mythology. The old political economy also claimed the right to make abstractions, and, in principle, it cannot be denied this right; but the use it made of it was vitiated because the basis of every one of its deductions was an abstraction that it had no right to make, that is, the notion of a man who in his action was moved exclusively by his personal interest. This hypothesis cannot be determined at first sight from the beginning of the investigations; we are able to evaluate the impulsive force which personal interest can exercise on us only after repeated observations and methodical comparisons. Without them, there is no way of ascertaining whether there is in us something definite enough that it can be isolated from the other factors of our conduct and be considered apart from them. Who can say that between egoism and altruism there is the decisive separation which common sense unreflectively erects between them?

To justify the method advanced by Simmel, more is needed than to refer to the sciences that proceed by abstraction—namely, proof that the abstraction espoused is undertaken according to the principles with which every scientific abstraction must conform. By what right are the container and the content of society separated, and separated so radically? Only the container is claimed to be of a social nature; the content is not, or only indirectly so. Yet there is not a single proof to confirm such an assertion which, though far from being accepted as a self-evident axiom, may yet overwhelm a student.

To be sure, not all that happens in society is social; but this cannot be said of all that occurs *in* and *through* society. Consequently, in order to eliminate from sociology the various phenomena which constitute the web of social life, one has to demonstrate that they are not the work of the collectivity, but come from wholly different origins to place themselves within the general framework constituted by society. We do not know whether this demonstration has been attempted or whether the research that such a demonstration presupposes has been initiated. Yet it is immediately clear that the collective traditions and practices of religion, law, morality, and political economy cannot be facts less social than are the external forms of the collectivity; and if one deepens the study of these facts, one's first impression is confirmed: everywhere we find society at work elaborating them, and their effect on social organization is evident. They are society itself, living and working. What a strange idea it would be to imagine the group as a sort of empty form of trivial cast that can indifferently receive any kind of material whatever! The claim is that there are arrangements which are encountered everywhere, whatever the nature of the ends attained. But clearly, all these ends, despite their divergences, have characteristics in common. Why should only these common characteristics, and not the specific ones, have social value?

Such abstraction is not only unsystematic in that its effect

357

is to separate things that are of the same nature, but the result of it, which is intended to be the subject matter of sociology, lacks all specificity whatever. Indeed, what are the meanings of the expression "social forms" and "forms of association in general"? If one wanted to speak only of the manner in which individuals are placed in contact with one another in association, of the dimensions of association, of its density—in a word, of its external and morphological aspect—the notion would be definite; but it would be too restricted to constitute, by itself alone, the subject matter of a science. For it would be equivalent to reducing sociology to the exclusive investigation of the substratum on which social life rests. As a matter of fact, however, our author attributes to the term "social forms" a much more extended significance. By it he understands not only the modes of grouping, the static condition of association, but also the most general forms of social relations. The term refers to the largest forms of relations of every kind that mesh in society and to the nature of the phenomena with which we are presented as being directly pertinent to sociology—the division of labor, competition, imitation, or the state of the individual's liberty or dependence vis-à-vis the group.[4] Between these relations and the other, more special ones, however, there is only a difference of degree. How can a simple difference of this sort justify so definite a separation between two orders of phenomena? If the former constitute the subject matter of sociology, why must the latter, which are of the same kind, be excluded from it? The basis which the proposed abstraction seems to constitute when the two are opposed as container and content disappears once the significance of those words is more exactly specified, and it becomes clear that they are no more than metaphors, inexactly applied.

The most general aspect of social life is not, for that matter, either content or form, any more than it is any one of the special aspects which social life shows us. There are not two kinds of reality which, though intimately connected, are distinct and separable; what we have instead are facts of the same nature, examined at different levels of generality. And what, incidentally, is the degree of generality that such facts need in order to be classified among sociological phenomena? We are not told; and the question is one to which there is no answer. This suggests how arbitrary such a criterion is and how it gives us free rein for extending the boundaries of the science. While pretending that it defines research, it actually leaves it to the fancy of the individual. There is no rule for deciding in an impersonal manner where the circle of sociological facts begins and where it ends; not only are the boundaries mobile, which is quite legitimate, but it is not clear why they should be located at this point rather than at another. It must be added that in order to study the most general types of social actions and their laws, one has to know the laws of more special types, since the former cannot be investigated and explained without systematic comparison with the latter. In this respect, every sociological problem presupposes a profound knowledge of all those special sciences that should be placed outside sociology but which sociology cannot do without. And since such universal competence is impossible, one has to be satisfied with summary knowledge, which is rapidly gathered and cannot be subjected to any control.

These are the characteristics of Simmel's investigations. We appreciate their subtlety and ingenuity, but we think it impossible to trace the main divisions of our science as he understands it in an objective manner. No connection can be discovered among the questions to which he draws the attention of sociologists; they are topics of meditation that have no relation to an integral scientific system. In addition, Simmel's proofs generally consist only of explanations by example; some facts, borrowed from the most disparate fields, are cited but they are not preceded by critical analysis, and they often offer us no idea of how to assess their value. For sociology to merit the name of a science, it must be something quite different from philosophical variations on certain aspects of social life, chosen more or less at random according to the leanings of a single individual. What is needed is the formulation of the problem in a way that permits us to draw a logical solution.

We do not wish to imply that there are not two elements in society that must be distinguished, but we insist that the distinction must be made differently: its aim must be to divide the domain of sociology, rather than to restrict it arbitrarily.

Social life has various manifestations, the nature of which we shall indicate presently. All of them, however, have this in common: They emanate from a group, simple or complex; the group is their substratum. Obviously, the study of the social substratum belongs in sociology. Furthermore, it is the object most immediately accessible to the sociologist because it takes on material forms that we can perceive with our senses. The composition of society consists in certain combinations of people and things which by necessity are connected in space. The explanatory analysis of this substratum, however, should not be confused with that of the social life which builds on it. The way in which society *emerges fully formed* is one thing; the manner in which it *acts* is another. These are realities of two kinds, so different that they cannot be treated by the same procedures but require separate investigations. Consequently, the study of the first forms a special, though fundamental, branch of sociology. We have here a distinction that is analogous to that which can be observed in all the sciences of nature. Chemistry, the study of the manner in which bodies are formed, stands beside physics, the study of the phenomena that are enacted by various bodies. Next to physiology, which seeks the laws of life, stands anatomy or morphology, which investigates the structure of living things, the manner of their formation, and the conditions controlling it.

The main points concerning the domain of sociology which now arise are the following: The social substratum must, above all, be determined in its external form. This external form is chiefly defined by (1) the size of the territory; (2) the space which the society occupies, that is, its peripheral or central position in regard to "continents," and the way it is enclosed by other societies, and so on; and (3) the form of its frontiers. As Friedrich Ratzel has demonstrated, the nature and aspects of frontiers change according to the countries involved: in one instance, they may be represented by more or less extensive surfaces; in another, by geometrical lines; in a third, they enter like wedges into contiguous countries or fold and thrust themselves back into the interior.

In addition to the external form, there is the content, which is, first of all, the total mass of the population in its numerical size and density. Furthermore, there are within society secondary groupings which have a material basis, such as villages, cities, districts, and provinces of varying importance. In respect to each of them, there arise various questions which need to be studied in respect to the given collectivity: extension of habitations, size of cities and villages, water courses, external enclosures, size and density of population, and so on.

Finally, every group, as a whole or in part, makes use, according to its needs, of the soil or that part of it that it occupies. Nations surround themselves with fortresses or fortified cities, and roads for communication are constructed. The disposition of streets and squares, the architecture of the houses, and the structure of things made vary from village to town and from the large city to the small one, and so on. Man modifies the social substratum in a thousand ways, and the resultant differences have great sociological significance because of both the causes on which they depend and the effects that they produce. The presence or absence of enclosures and markets, the construction of public buildings and their great variety as compared to that of private establishments—together these facts amount to what is most essential in collective life, and they work together to give it its peculiar stamp.

But the task of the sociologist is not simply to describe these diverse phenomena (the preceding enumeration of which does not claim completeness). He must want to explain them, that is, connect them with their causes and determine their functions. He will ask himself, for instance, why societies, depending on the stage of development they have reached, prefer central to peripheral sites; what significance the territory has in the life of the state; why frontiers tend to acquire one form rather than another; what circumstances give birth to villages and then to cities; and from what the development of urban centers derives. By necessity, all these causes, as well as all these effects, occur in the form of movements. Under the influence of active forces, the various social elements gradually dispose themselves in one form or another. External migrations determine the location of states and the nature of their functions; in fact, in every society, they stand in direct relation to its movement of expansion. The currents of internal migration determine the respective importance of urban and rural populations; they are the factors on which depend the natality and mortality that cause variations in the number of the general population. The tendency of the society to live in a crowded or dispersed condition explains its density.

This branch of sociology is, therefore, not purely a science of statics. Consequently, we do not think it proper to use this word: "static" poorly describes the view of society which is considered here. It is not a question of looking at society arrested at a given moment by abstraction (as has sometimes been said), but of analyzing its formation and accounting for it. Undoubtedly, the phenomena that have to do with structure have something more stable about them than have functional phenomena, but there are only differences of degree between these two orders of fact. Structure itself is encountered in *becoming,* and one cannot illustrate it except by pursuing this process of becoming. It forms and dissolves continually; it is life arrived at a certain measure of consolidation; to disconnect it from the life from which it derives or from that which it determines is equivalent to dissociating things that are inseparable.

We propose to call the science that has for its object the study of the material forms of society "social morphology." The term "form," which, as used by Simmel, has only a metaphorical significance, is here used in its proper sense. In this view, every morphological phenomenon consists of material adaptations that acquire a definite form, which can always be represented graphically.

Yet the substratum of collective life is not the only thing of a social character that exists in nature; the life that flows from it or is sustained by it necessarily has the same character and belongs in the province of the same science. Beside the social ways of being, there are the social modes of doing; beside the morphological phenomena, there are the functional or physiological phenomena. It is easy to foresee that the latter must be more numerous than the former, for the vital manifestations are by far more varied and complex than are the morphological combinations which are their fundamental conditions.

Let us begin by laying down a proposition that should be considered axiomatic: *For sociology, properly speaking, to exist, there must occur in every society phenomena of which this society is the specific cause, phenomena which would not exist if this society did not exist and which are what they are only because this society is constituted the way it is.* A science can be established only when it has for its subject matter facts *sui generis,* facts that are different from those of the other sciences. If society did not produce phenomena which are different from those observable in the other realms of nature, sociology would be without a field of its own. Its existence can be justified only if there are realities which deserve to be called social and which are not simply aspects of another order of things.

A corollary of this proposition is the position that social phenomena do not have their immediate and determining cause in the nature of individuals. If they did, if they derived directly from the organic or physical constitution of man without any other factor intervening in their development, sociology would dissolve into psychology. It is certainly true that all functional phenomena of the social order are psychological in the sense that all constitute a way of thinking or acting. But if sociology is to have its own field, collective ideas and actions must be different in nature from those that have their origin in the individual consciousness and must be subject to laws of their own. Social physiology may be said to be psychology, but only if the proviso is added that it must in no way be confused with the science usually so designated, which aims exclusively at studying the mental constitution of the individual.

But this very simple proposition clashes with an ancient sophism which still influences some sociologists who do not realize that it negates sociology itself. This sophism says that society is formed only of individuals, and that, since the whole can only contain what is found in the parts, all that is social can be reduced to individual factors. On this basis, one would have to say that there is nothing in the living cell outside of that which exists in the hydrogen, carbon, and nitrogen atoms that together form it; yet, evidently, these atoms are not alive.

This way of arguing is thus fundamentally erroneous; it is not true that the whole is always equal to the sum of its parts. When elements combine, a new reality derives from their combination which has entirely new characteristics, characteristics that are sometimes even opposed to those observable in the component elements. Two soft bodies, copper and tin, unite to form bronze, one of the hardest materials known. Perhaps it will be objected that the properties manifest in the whole pre-exist in the parts in a germinal state. A germ is something which is not yet everything that it will be but which already exists, although its existence has reached only the first stage of its evolution. It is actual, nonetheless, and its specific characteristics attest to its existence. But what is there that betrays the slightest germ of life in the mineral atoms which compose the living substance? If they had remained isolated from one another, if something unknown had not closely conjoined them, not one of them would ever have manifested any quality whatever that could be called biological, except metaphorically or by analogy. Thus, if non-living particles can unite to form a living being, it is not extraordinary that an association of individual minds becomes the field of action of phenomena *sui generis* which these minds could not have produced by the strength of their nature alone.

Having laid down this principle, we are in a position to determine a criterion for identifying social phenomena of a physiological nature. These phenomena cannot be recognized in the same manner as individual phenomena because they do not reveal themselves merely by developing their intrinsic properties. They cannot, in other words, pervade the individual except by imposing themselves from without. There must be a pressure on us which drives us out of our nature. We do not notice it, any more than we are aware of the pressure of the atmosphere on our bodies; to it too, perhaps, we yield without resistance. Yet, unconscious or no, freely accepted or passively borne, social pressure is no less real. This is what we meant when we identified the characteristic feature of social phenomena as being this quality of imposing themselves on the individual and, if necessary, constraining him.[5] We do not intend to say that collective practices or beliefs must be inculcated in men by violence and coercion. That force by virtue of which we bow to them and conform with them is not material, or not necessarily material. If we docilely submit to the directive impulses of society, we do not do so only because society is a more powerful being than we are. Normally, a moral authority invests all the products of its activity and bends our spirits and wills; and whatever comes from it is endowed with a prestige that in various degrees inspires us with sentiments of deference and respect. When we find ourselves faced by these forms of conduct and thought which we have not made and which are the results of collective, usually secular, experiences, we pause, realizing that there is something in them that transcends the ordinary power of our individual intelligence, something on which we cannot easily lay our hands. And this impression is all the more intensified by what happens to us when we want to pass beyond it or rebel against it. Individual efforts directed against social facts with the intent to destroy or change them always meet with lively resistance. Whether moral or not, the forces against which the individual rises react against him and demonstrate their superiority by the energy, usually the irresistible energy, of their reaction.

The preceding analysis has been chiefly dialectical, and we have conducted it for the reason stated. We felt the need of clarifying from the beginning the characteristic feature of social facts; we took as our point of departure the axiom that they are social and, for this reason, not individual. The reader, however, who has followed our reasoning must have been aware of the facts which have served us as guide. There is one imposing complex of beliefs and practices which have the features just indicated to the highest degree—the beliefs and practices of the religious, moral, and legal life. Both beliefs and practices are by nature imperative. Normally, they impose themselves by the veneration they inspire, by the obligation to respect them by which we feel ourselves held, and, whenever we tend to rebel, by the coercion they exercise in the form of sanctions. This appears even more evident in the case of religious facts because the very fashion in which we understand them proves that they derive their reality from a source that is above the individual: we conceive of them as the emanation of an authority other than man's, and more elevated than man's, in so far as he is man. Law and morality are no different; since they derive from religion, they cannot have a different nature, and both require our strict obedience. In order to comprehend the authoritative stress on duty, the popular imagination likes to see in it the word of a being superior to man, a divinity. The believer takes this symbolic manifestation literally and, quite logically, explains the religious or moral imperative by reference to the eminent nature of the divine personality. For the scientist, however, a question of this sort does not arise since the domain of science does not extend beyond the empirical world. Science does not ask whether some other reality might exist. What it considers certain is that there are simply manners of acting and thinking that are obligatory and are therefore different from all other forms of actions and ideas. And since every obligation presupposes an authority that obliges and is superior to the subject obliged; and since, on the other hand, we empirically know no moral authority that is superior to the individual except that of the collectivity, every fact of such an obligatory character must be considered social.

Consequently, even if these phenomena were the only ones that presented this distinctive feature, they would still have to be separated from those studied by individual psychology and assigned to another science. In this manner, sociology would acquire an area that—though it might appear restricted —would at least be definite. In reality, however, there are other phenomena that are distinguished by the same characteristic, though to a minor degree. Does our language not oppose bold innovators with a resistance equal to that which religious rites and legal and moral maxims use in opposing those who would violate them? Language has something which inspires respect in us. Traditional usages, though they may have nothing religious or moral about them, festivities, practices of courtesy, even fashions, are protected by a large variety of sanctions against individual attempts at rebellion. Economic organization, too, imposes itself on us with imperative necessity. When we try to rebel against it, we are certainly not blamed for our rebellion alone; such innovations often awaken resistances of a moral character. However, we must keep in mind not only the impossibility of not conforming almost completely with the rules of the *technica consacrata* but also the fact that "consecrated" is not a vain word. In industrial life as well as in other everyday relations, traditional practices that are respected in our milieu cannot help but exert an authority on us that is sufficient to contain our divergencies; an authority, however, which, being minor, controls them less efficiently than does moral discipline. Still, between the two, there is only a difference of degree—and, at this point, we need not go into its causes.

In short, social life is nothing but the moral milieu that surrounds the individual—or, to be more accurate, it is the sum of the moral milieus that surround the individual. By calling them moral we mean that they are made up of ideas; their relation to individual ideas is like that of physical milieus to organisms. Both poles of these contrasts are independent realities, but only in the way in which there can be independent things in this world where everything is connected. We must adapt ourselves to both. Yet the reality, the coercive force, to which we submit our bodies, and the reality to which we submit our wills, are not of the same nature nor are they connected with the same causes. One of them derives from the rigidity of the molecular dispositions that constitute our physical core and to which we are forced to adapt ourselves as a matter of course; the other consists in that prestige *sui generis* which is the privilege of social facts and which protects them from threats by individuals.

We do not mean to assert, incidentally, that social practices or beliefs enter into individuals without undergoing variations —to say this would be to deny the facts. When we turn our thoughts to collective institutions—or rather, when we assimilate them—we individualize them, just as when we think of the sensible world, each of us colors it according to his gifts so that we see a great many different subjects, differently expressed and adapting themselves differently to the same physical milieu. This is why every one of us, up to a certain point, forms his own religious faith, his own cult, his own morality, and his own technology. There is no social uniformity which does not accommodate a whole scale of individual gradations;

there is no collective fact which imposes itself on all individuals uniformly.

Nevertheless, the area of variations that are possible and tolerated is always and everywhere more or less restricted. Almost absent in the religious and moral sphere, where innovation and reform are for all practical purposes always called delinquent or sacrilegious, this area is more extensive in the sphere of economic phenomena. But sooner or later, we encounter, even here, a limit that we cannot transcend. Hence the characteristic feature of social facts lies in the ascendancy which they exert over the minds of individuals.

In regard to the outward signs of social facts, there are at least two which seem to us especially symptomatic and rather easily applied. One is the resistance with which the social group opposes individual deviations from certain ways of doing or thinking. It is very easy to observe such resistance when it takes on the form of exact sanctions—religious, legal, or moral. In all these cases, society directly obligates the individual to behave or think in a certain way, and this demonstrates the social character of all obligatory rules in religion, law, and morality. Sometimes, however, social resistance is less conscious and patent, and thus more difficult to perceive. The resistance to excessively radical innovations in the matter of economic practice is a case in point. Consequently, it is useful to adopt another criterion that can be more easily applied in all instances. Such a criterion is the special manner in which social facts individualize themselves. Since society imposes them on its members, social facts must have a certain generality within the group to which they apply; yet since they derive from society, they cannot pervade individuals except by a process that moves from the outside to the inside. The rules of morality, the practices of courtesy, and the traditional opinions and usages of our milieu reach us by means of common education; the rules of professional practice, by means of technical education; the articles of faith, through religious education, and so on. And what of legal rules, whose outward part is such that throughout our lives we do not know most of it but must make a special effort to study it when the need arises? Therefore, generality by itself is not a sufficient criterion, as we have just

368

demonstrated. On the other hand, mere knowledge of the processes by which social phenomena are actualized in the individuals is no more precise as a distinctive criterion, for others can suggest ideas and actions to us which come from the outside but are not collective. Together, however, these two criteria exhaustively characterize social facts. Ways of acting and thinking which are general in a given society, but which are merely drawn from the outside by the individuals, cannot attain the particular generality of social facts except by the exclusive action of the moral milieu, that is, the social milieu, which alone determines them. It is these impersonal norms of thought and action that pre-eminently constitute the sociological phenomenon. They stand in relation to society as the vital functions do in relation to the organism: they tell the manner from which derive collective intelligence and will. Thus they are the proper subject matter of social physiology.

In delimiting the area of research, this definition also serves to orient it. If one labors to reduce social phenomena to phenomena of a psychological sort in various stages of development, one is condemned to the advocacy and practice of a sociology that I venture to call facile and abstract. If he advocates such a practice, the task of the sociologist is, indeed, rather easy: since society has no laws of its own, he has nothing to discover. All that remains for him to do is to borrow from psychology the laws which it thinks it has formulated and to see how the facts he studies can be deduced from them. The only problem that can still arise is this: What becomes of the general faculties of human nature in the many kinds of relations that men can have with each other? And all the minute, concrete manifestations of social facts, all that constitutes their wealth and specificity, escapes him by necessity. The salient features of the individual mind are too simple, too general, too indeterminate to account for those of social practices and beliefs, the variety of their forms, and the complexity of their characteristics. Such systems of sociology thus limit themselves to the developing, with more or less subtlety, of highly schematic views and wholly formal concepts which in their indeterminateness are removed from any control. But if a social realm really exists that is as different from the individual realm as the biological one is from the mineral, then sociology has a domain which covers a whole world, immense and unexplored, in which forces not yet imagined are at work and where, consequently, many discoveries are to be made. We find ourselves confronted by an unknown magnitude that we must conquer and subject to human intelligence. This conquest is not easy. We cannot move across so virgin a territory except slowly and cautiously. In order to discover the laws of this complex reality, we must adopt procedures that are suited to penetrating such a complexity of facts. It is not enough to observe, to classify, and to compare; in addition, the methods of observation, classification, and comparison must be appropriate to the nature of our particular study.

Understood in this way, sociology still remains vulnerable, however, to the reproach made against it by Simmel. The facts with which sociology is concerned are already pre-empted by sciences that have existed for a long time: population, movements and states, by demography; religious beliefs and practices, by the comparative history of religions; moral ideas, by the history of civilization, and so on. Is sociology, therefore, nothing but a label placed on a more or less coherent collection of extant disciplines? Is there nothing new about it except its name?

In answer to this charge, we must recall, in the first place, that even if this reproach were well founded, it would not constitute a good reason for the arbitrary restriction of the term "sociology" to an indeterminate category of studies which cannot be delimited with any measure of exactitude, and which has no right to any such privileged status anyhow. In the second place, it is wholly wrong to call the assemblage of these different special disciplines under the same rubric merely a simple reform of terminology: in actuality, the change in name involves and translates into visible signs a profound change in substance.

Indeed, until now, all these special sciences—political economy, comparative history of law, comparative history of religions, demography, and political geography—have been conceived and applied as if each of them constituted an independent whole, whereas the facts with which they deal are only the various manifestations of one and the same activity, collective activity. The result has been that the ties which unite these sciences have remained unobserved. Who, until quite recently, could have supposed that there are relationships between economic and religious phenomena, between demographic adaptations and moral ideas, between geographic forms and collective manifestations, and so on? An even graver consequence of the traditional isolation is that each individual science has studied the phenomena of its particular competence as if they were unconnected with any social system. Look at the laws of political economy—or, to be more exact, at the propositions that the economists elevate to the dignity of law: independent of time and space, they seem unrelated to any form of social organization. There is no inkling that there might be definite economic types that are associated with equally determinate social types, just as there are different digestive and respiratory systems depending on the nature of animal species. All economic phenomena are believed to proceed from rather simple, quite general impulses, common to all mankind. Similarly, the comparative history of religions studies religious beliefs and practices as if they merely expressed certain internal conditions of the individual mind—the fear that the great forces of nature inspire in man, for instance, or the reflections suggested to him by certain phenomena of life, such as dreams, sleep, and death. It has only been recently that the comparative history of law has tried to establish some rapprochement between certain domestic institutions and certain forms of social organization; but how timid, embryonic, and unsystematic these rapprochements have been so far, even though they have been tried by Albert Hermann Post and his school, in particular, and Post is a sociologist! Who, prior to Ratzel, thought of seeing in political geography a social science or, to be more general, an explanatory science in the proper sense of the term?

This observation may be broadened: many of these studies not only have nothing sociological about them, they are not—or are only imperfectly—scientific. In not connecting in a scientific manner social facts with the social milieu in which they have their root, these studies remain suspended in mid-air, with

371

no relation to the rest of the world and without any possibility
of becoming aware of the connection which ties them together
and makes them into a unity. Under such conditions one can
do nothing but expound facts without classifying or explaining
them (in the manner of pure historians), or make, from a
schematic point of view, a wholesale collection of their most
general features, a process by which they naturally lose all
their individuality. Following such a method, it is impossible
to establish definite relations among definite classes of facts—
relations which are exactly what the word "laws" refers to in
its most general sense. And where there are no laws, can there
be science?

It is unnecessary to describe in any detail the elimination of
such a difficulty which follows the realization that these different sciences are branches of one science that embraces them
all and is called sociology. From this moment on, whoever
practices one of them cannot remain unfamiliar with the others;
for the facts they study together mesh and are closely connected
with each other like the functions of the same organism. In the
light of this realization, the facts reveal an entirely new aspect.
As the products of society, they present themselves as functions
of society and not as those of the individual; and they can be
illuminated as such. It is the way in which society is constituted,
not the way in which we are constituted individually, that explains why these facts appear in one, rather than another, form.
For this reason, they stop undulating in that dance by which
they managed to escape scientific research, and become a substratum that once more connects them with the rest of human
facts. This is the social substratum—and now we can fix definite
relations among those facts and can establish laws, properly
speaking.

There is another cause which has contributed to this change
of orientation. In order to conceive of searching for the laws
of social phenomena, it was necessary first to know natural laws
and the methods by which they are discovered, and such knowledge could be acquired only by practicing the sciences in which
such discoveries are made every day—the natural sciences.
However, the writers who dedicated themselves to special social
studies—economists and historians—had a literary, rather than

a scientific, education. Generally, they had only the vaguest notion of what constitutes a law. Historians systematically deny the existence of laws in the social world, and as for the economists, it is well known that by "laws" they mean abstract theorems that only express ideological possibilities and have nothing in common with the laws of physics, chemistry, or biology. By contrast, the thinkers who first used the word "sociology" (Comte and Spencer), anticipating the affinity of all those phenomena which until then had appeared to be independent of one another, were well grounded in the methods used in the natural sciences and the principles on which they are founded. Sociology had its origin in the shadow of these sciences; and, being in intimate contact with them, it draws into its orbit all those special social sciences which were originally included in it but which now are imbued with a new spirit. To be sure, one of the first sociologists made the mistake of exaggerating this close connection to the point that he ignored the originality of the social sciences and the autonomy which they must enjoy vis-à-vis the sciences that preceded them. But such excesses must not make us forget how much there is that is fruitful in the natural sciences, those principal forges of scientific thought.

Thus this term "sociology," in the meaning we have given it, must not simply provide an enrichment of the vocabulary. It must be and remain the sign of a profound innovation in all sciences whose subject matter is the human realm,[6] an innovation which represents the task of sociology in the contemporary scientific movement. Under the influence of the ideas which this term summarizes, all studies which up to now have usually come from literature and erudition, show that their true affinities lie elsewhere, and that they must look for their model in a wholly different direction. Instead of stopping at the exclusive consideration of events that lie at the surface of social life, there has arisen the need for studying the less obvious points at the base of it—internal causes and impersonal, hidden forces that move individuals and collectivities. A tendency to this sort of study has already been manifested by some historians; but it is up to sociology to increase consciousness of it, to illuminate and develop it. To be sure, at present, the

373

movement is only in its beginning. But it is a great deal that it exists at all. It remains only to speed it up and give it a clear direction.

This does not mean, however, that sociology must be forever limited to being a system of special sciences. If all the facts that these sciences observe are related to one another, if they are species of the same genus, it is proper to explore what it is that forms the unity of the genus itself; and a special branch of sociology must undertake such an investigation. Society, social life in the whole range of its evolution, forms a whole, and the science of society is not fully developed if it studies the elements of this whole only by themselves. After analysis, there is need for synthesis, showing how those elements unite in a whole. Here is the justification of general sociology. If all social facts have common features, it is because they all derive from the same stem, or from stems of the same genus. It is the task of general sociology to find them.

In respect to morphology, sociology must seek the elementary group which gave rise to ever more compound groupings; in respect to physiology, it must trace the elementary functional phenomena which, in combining with one another, have formed the progressively more complex phenomena that have developed in the course of evolution. But the value of the synthesis obviously depends on the value of the analyses performed by the special sciences. We must therefore apply ourselves to building and advancing these sciences. Today, this appears to be sociology's most urgent task.

Translated by Kurt H. Wolff

1. Emilio Durkheim, "La sociologia ed il suo dominio scientifico," *Rivista Italiana di Sociologia,* IV (1900), 127-48. Used by permission of Fratelli Bocca, Editori, Rome.

2. See his paper on "Le problème de la sociologie," *Revue de métaphysique et de morale,* II (1894), 497-504; and his memoir, "Comment les formes sociales se maintiennent," *Année sociologique,* I (1896-97), 71-109.

3. "Comment les formes sociales se maintiennent," p. 72. [Cf. Simmel, "The Persistence of Social Groups," trans. Albion W. Small, *American Journal of Sociology,* III (1898), 663.—Tr.]

4. "Le problème de la sociologie," p. 499.

5. Durkheim, *Les règles de la méthode scientifique* (Paris: Félix Alcan, 1895) , Chap. i.

6. Psychology, too, is destined to renew itself, in part, under this influence. For if social phenomena penetrate the individual from the outside, there is a whole realm of individual consciousness that depends partially on social causes, a realm which psychology cannot ignore without becoming unintelligible.

SOCIOLOGY[1]

EMILE DURKHEIM

To set forth the role which belongs to France in the establishment and development of sociology is almost tantamount to writing the history of this science; for it was born among us, and, although there is no country today where it is not being cultivated, it nevertheless remains an essentially French science.

Because societies consist of people, it has long been held that they derive their character completely from the human will. As evidence, it has been pointed out that societies are nothing but what the people want them to be, and that they have no character other than that which people confer upon them by an act of their will. On the basis of this assumption, it is out of the question to make societies a subject matter of science. And, indeed, as long as societies were considered indefinitely plastic and without determinate characteristics, there was no way to describe them, analyze them, seek the causes and conditions upon which they depend, and so on. The only problem that could arise in respect to them was to discover which form would be best for a given society. In order to have a true science of social facts, it was necessary to gain the insight that societies are realities comparable to those which constitute the other realms of scientific investigation, the insight that societies have a character which we cannot change arbitrarily, and are governed by laws which necessarily derive from this character. In other words, sociology could not emerge until the idea of determinism, which had been securely established in the physical and natural sciences, was finally extended to the social order.

This extension occurred in the eighteenth century under the influence of the philosophy of the Encyclopédie. For the Encyclopedists, science is one because the world is one. Determinism, therefore, could not be permitted to be any less true in the social realm than in the other realms of nature. It is this feeling which inspired Montesquieu and Condorcet. Yet, although these thinkers cleared the way for sociology, they had a rather vague idea of the laws of social life. It was only at

376

the beginning of the nineteenth century that the new conception was definitely asserted.

Saint-Simon was the first to formulate it, the first to declare that human societies are surely realities in their own right, different from those found in the rest of nature but subject to the same determinism. Social organisms, therefore, ought to be the object of a science comparable to that which deals with individual organisms; and for this reason, he suggested that this science be called Social Physiology. The most striking evidence of the necessity with which social phenomena occur is progress. "It is no more in our power to remove ourselves from its influence or to control its action than to change by our will the initial impetus which makes our planet revolve around the sun." Since progress is not *our* product, the only way to discover the law according to which it proceeds is by observation. We have to block out series of historical facts, as vast as possible, and through these series we shall be able to discover the direction in which mankind has evolved. Thus the method of the new science must be essentially historical, except that history itself must change in order to serve this purpose: instead of being a mere collection of facts, it must become truly scientific.

But Saint-Simon formulated the program of this science more than he tried to put it into practice. There is nothing in his work which could be regarded as a systematic effort to discover that law of progress which he conceived as the law of gravitation of the social world. The great project conceived by him began to become a reality only with Auguste Comte.

In one sense, all the fundamental ideas of Comtean sociology can be found in Saint-Simon; Comte took them from his master. But he did not limit himself to insisting that they could serve as the basis of a new science: he undertook to create this science. He defined its method and established its framework. Some of the divisions he introduced have survived him. In the science of societies, he distinguished two great subdivisions: statics and dynamics. Statics has as its object to determine the relations that are sustained among the diverse elements of a single social milieu considered somehow in repose at a state in its evolution. Social dynamics inquires into the law according to which the sequence of human societies has evolved in time. After conceiving this plan for sociology, Comte wished to execute it completely and by his own efforts alone. With respect to statics, he did hardly more than indicate the problem and outline solutions; but with respect to dynamics, he meant to give us a complete and, he believed, definitive treatise: the two last volumes of the *Cours de philosophie positive* are dedicated to this purpose.

Today, little remains of the various features of his doctrine. The law of the three stages has only a historical interest. The very terms in which Comte posed the problem rendered it insoluble. He believed in the existence of a unique law according to which human society in general has developed, and that it is the task of the sociologist to discover it. He thus admitted that mankind in its totality constitutes a single society which always and everywhere evolves in the same manner. Actually, however, humanity as a whole exists as a unit only in the mind. What exists in reality are particular societies (tribes, nations, cities, states of all kinds, and so on), which are born and die, progress and regress, each in its own manner, pursuing divergent goals. These various evolutions do not always follow one another, continuing as if they were sections of the same straight line. Human development has a complexity that Comte did not suspect.

However, although the positive conclusions at which he believed he had arrived can only rarely be accepted today, the grandeur of his work is nonetheless incontestable. A new science was joined to the complete system of the sciences. Saint-Simon had been its harbinger; but Comte is its father, for through him it received the beginning of its existence. He also gave it the name "sociology," which may be considered a poor name, but which is irreplaceable because it designates not any study of social matters but those studies which are conducted in a spirit analogous to that governing the other natural sciences. Moreover, regardless of the reservations the doctrine of Comte calls forth, a very vivid feeling of what social reality is permeates it throughout. There is no better initiation to the study of sociology.

Yet this considerable work had no immediate consequences.

Neither the July Monarchy [1830-48] nor the Second Empire [1852-70] produced any new contribution to the science which Comte had just founded. To be sure, in his *Essai sur le fondement de nos connaissances* [1851] and in the second volume of his *Enchaînement des idées fondamentales* [1861], Antoine-Augustin Cournot touches questions of interest to sociologists, but he certainly was not concerned with adding a new positive science that would treat of social matters to the physical and biological sciences. He discussed history as a philosopher.

Sociological thought was revived only after the war of 1870. In the meantime, Comte's endeavor had been resumed in England by Herbert Spencer. In order to confirm the hypothesis that societies are natural phenomena, as Comte had held, Spencer undertook to demonstrate that the laws according to which social institutions evolve are only special forms of the more general laws that govern cosmic evolution. He insisted, in particular, on the similarities between social organization and biological organization and thus made societies into a species of the genus "organism." It was this conception which Alfred Espinas undertook to confirm and to illustrate through a study of animal societies (*Les sociétés animales*, Paris, 1877). In order to fill the gap which had so long been felt to exist between societies and the rest of the universe, the author showed, in this very suggestive work, that even animals constitute societies of living elements which are physically associated with one another, and that there is a gradual transition from these simple societies to more complex ones, which are formed by higher animals that are no longer united by material ties but by psychological ones. Thus the social realm appeared as a sort of efflorescence of the biological realm to which it was attached without any break in continuity.

Up to this time, however, sociology had not yet gone beyond philosophical generalities. The thinkers of which we have just spoken had in fact reduced it to one single problem: the point was to find the law which dominates social evolution in general (Comte), or to discover whether or not the law of universal evolution also applies to societies (Spencer). Comte, therefore, was not far from thinking that he had not only founded sociology but had also completed it at the same time. But a science is never completed. It consists of particular, restricted questions which bear on specific objects. Although these questions are interrelated, they must be treated separately; indeed their very interdependence appears only in so far as the science advances and to the extent to which it does. Consequently, sociology could not really become a positive science until it renounced its initial and over-all claim upon the totality of social reality. It had to introduce analysis and had to distinguish ever more among parts, elements, and different aspects which could serve as subject matters for specific problems.

It is to this task that the author of the present note has devoted himself with the help of a whole group of workers who have joined their efforts with his. Our ambition is to initiate for sociology what Comte called the era of specialization. A true division of labor has been instituted. Three groups of facts have been studied in particular: religious, moral and legal, and economic facts. And instead of carrying on general sociology, some of us have devoted ourselves to the sociology of religion, others to the sociology of morals and of law, and still others to the sociology of economics. But even this division was much too general: within each of these special sociologies, particular problems have been taken up—those of sacrifice and of magic by Henri Hubert and Marcel Mauss; *Les formes élémentaires de la vie religieuse* and *Le suicide* by Durkheim; *La prohibition de l'inceste* and various studies of primitive marriage by the same author; *Le régime des castes* by Célestin Bouglé; *Le salaire des ouvriers des mines* by François Simiand; and *La classe ouvrière et les niveaux de vie* by Maurice Halbwachs. More recently, an effort has been made to determine the social conditions upon which certain logical operations or certain forms of thought depend: we refer to the *Essai sur certaines formes primitives de classification* by Durkheim and Mauss, and the *Etude sur la représentation du temps* by Hubert. The book by Lucien Lévy-Bruhl, *Les fonctions mentales dans les sociétés inférieures,* must be seen as a part of this same development.

It is true that these topics of study had already emerged, at least in part, in disciplines which preceded sociology or which had been constituted outside sociology: comparative history of religion, law, and moral ideas; moral statistics; and political economy. But because these studies had not been exposed to the influence of sociology, they fell somewhat short of their goal; for losing sight of what constitutes the very nature of the phenomena of which they treat—that is, their social character—they approached them without knowing whence they came, whither they went, or upon which social milieus they depended; and thus by leaving them suspended in the void, they also left them without explaining them. Indeed, it is impossible to understand them unless they are seen in their relations to each other and to the collective milieu in the midst of which they develop and whose expression they are. Moreover, the very concept of law was too often absent from these studies, which belonged more to literature and scholarship than to science. The totality of the studies of social phenomena thus appeared in the following fashion: On the one hand, there was a rather incoherent multitude of sciences which, despite their identical subject matter, ignored their own kinship, as well as the profound unity of the facts they studied, whose rational structure they were only dimly aware of; and, on the other hand, there was sociology, which was conscious of this unity and of the profound order concealed by the apparent contingency of the facts, but which soared far too high above social reality to have any influence upon the method of its study. The most urgent reform, therefore, was to bring sociology and these other special techniques closely together, to unite them in a fertile marriage, so as to give sociology the data it lacked, and, inversely, to bring the sociological idea down into these disciplines in such a manner as to make true social sciences of them. In order to assure this rapprochement and to make it more intimate, a periodical was established in 1896 under the name *Année sociologique,* whose aim it is to glean from studies in the history of religion, the history of moral and legal institutions, moral statistics, and economic history, the facts that appear to be of particular interest to sociologists.

All the writings mentioned above derive directly from Comte; they are different aspects of the same evolution. It only remains to speak of two important works whose inspiration is very different.

First, there is the work of Gabriel Tarde. The scholars discussed thus far all proceed on the idea that social phenomena are connected with each other according to definite relationships called laws and that to inquire into these laws is the aim of the science of society. Tarde does not go so far as to say that there is no order in the succession of historical facts—this would amount to denying the possibility of a scientific study of societies—but he considers this order so contingent and variable that it is impossible to approach it by methodical procedures and with any precision. All social facts are actually due to individual inventions which are diffused and generalized from place to place by way of imitation. But it must be noted that invention is the product of genius, and genius is "the supreme accident" which resists all prediction, as well as all scientific explanation. It emerges, here or there, by chance. Therefore, Tarde placed chance at the very origin of social life. No doubt, imitation has the laws which Tarde was trying to determine, but these laws are extremely general; being purely formal, they cannot explain any social fact in particular. The forms of institutions and the order in which they have developed in the course of history depend, according to Tarde, upon fortuitous causes and escape the grasp of science.

Thus, in a sense, the work of Tarde appears to be a reaction against the very principle upon which Comtean sociology rests. But in order to understand its full significance, it is necessary to place it in the epoch in which it was conceived. This was the time when the Italian school of criminology exaggerated positivism to the point of making it into a kind of materialistic metaphysics which had nothing scientific about it. Tarde demonstrated the inanity of these doctrines and re-emphasized the essentially spiritual character of social phenomena.

But if Tarde opposed Comtean sociology, he intended to work, and in fact did work, as a sociologist. By contrast, it might be asked whether Frédéric le Play's studies of *Les ouvriers européens* should properly be mentioned here. Le Play, to be sure, was not opposed to this or that sociological conception, but he was completely outside the movement of ideas which gave birth to sociology. His concerns were not even entirely scientific but, in large part, apologetic. Nevertheless, since he dealt with social matters and since a whole school is connected with him (whose mediums are *La réforme sociale* and *La science sociale*) , his name and his work deserve their place in the picture we have outlined.

In this exposition, we have been dwelling on the most characteristic works, on those which may be considered as marking a more or less important phase in the development of sociology. But in order to have a proper idea of the sociological movement in France, one must not lose sight of a great number of works which, though without particular influence, testify nevertheless to the very vivid interest which sociological research has inspired in France. Among them are the writings of Charles Letourneau on the evolution of the family, law, property, education, and literature; Arsène Dumont's studies of *La dépopulation;* or Adolphe Coste's on *Sociologie objective.* There is also the anthropological sociology of G. Vacher de Lapouge, whose bold theses perhaps need more solid confirmation and who wishes to see anthropology re-absorb sociology. An intellectual movement has grown among us, notably during the past twenty-five years, which in its intensity and direction resembles the trend which at the beginning of the nineteenth century determined the appearance of sociology.

In view of the fact that this science was born only yesterday, one can judge the importance of the part which France has taken in its formation and progress. Everything, for that matter, predestined our country to play this role: its native qualities, as well as the difficulties we have had to face. In fact, sociology could have been born and developed only where the two conditions which follow existed in combination: First, traditionalism had to have lost its domain. Among a people who consider their institutions everything they ought to be, nothing can incite thought to apply itself to social matters. Second, a veritable faith in the power of reason to dare to undertake the translation of the most complex and unstable of realities into definite terms was necessary. France satisfies this double condition. There is no country where the old social organization has been uprooted more completely and where, consequently, in order to remake it, there is greater need for thought, that is, for science. On the other hand, we are and shall remain the country of Descartes; we have a passion for clear ideas.

No doubt, today we know the excessively simplistic element in Cartesian rationalism; but if we feel the necessity of going beyond it, it is on the condition that we retain its fundamental principle.

BIBLIOGRAPHY

SAINT-SIMON. *Oeuvres choisies.* 3 vols. Paris: Castel, 1861.

COMTE. *Cours de philosophie positive.** 6 vols. Paris: Rouen frères, 1830-42.

———. *Système de politique positive.* 4 vols. Paris: Dalmont, 1854.

LE PLAY. *Les ouvriers européens: Etude sur les travaux, la vie domestique et la condition morale des populations ouvrières en Europe.* 5 vols. Paris: Mame, 1855.

ESPINAS. *Les sociétés animales: Etude de psychologie comparée.* Paris: Germer-Baillière, 1877.

LETOURNEAU. *L'Evolution du mariage et de la famille.** Paris: Vigot, 1888.

———. *L'Evolution politique dans les diverses races humaines.** Paris: Vigot, 1890.

———. *L'Evolution de la morale.** Paris: Vigot, 1894.

TARDE. *Les lois de l'imitation: Etude sociologique.** Paris: Félix Alcan, 1890.

———. *La philosophie pénale.* Paris: Masson, 1890.

———. *La logique sociale.** Paris: Félix Alcan, 1894.

DE ROBERTY. *La sociologie de l'action.** Paris: Félix Alcan, 1890.

DURKHEIM. *De la division du travail social.** Paris: Félix Alcan, 1893.

———. *Les règles de la méthode sociologique.* Paris: Félix Alcan, 1895.

———. *Le suicide: Etude de sociologie.** Paris: Félix Alcan, 1897.

———. *Les formes élémentaires de la vie religieuse.* Paris: Félix Alcan, 1912.

ANDLER. *Les origines du socialisme d'état en Allemagne.** Paris: Félix Alcan, 1897.

LÉVY-BRUHL. *La morale et la science des moeurs.** Paris: Félix Alcan, 1903.

———. *Les fonctions mentales dans les sociétés inférieures.* Paris: Félix Alcan, 1910.

SIMIAND. *Le salaire des ouvriers des mines de charbon en France.** Paris: Cornély, 1907.

HUBERT and MAUSS. *Mélanges d'histoire des religions.** Paris: Félix Alcan, 1909.

Journals

La réforme sociale. Founded by Le Play in 1881. Paris.

La science sociale, suivant la méthode de Le Play. Published since 1886 by Edouard Demolins. Paris. Firmin-Didot.

Annales de l'Institut international de sociologie. Published since 1894 under the direction of René Worms. Paris. Giard et Brière.

Revue internationale de sociologie. Published since 1896. Paris: Giard et Brière.

L'Année sociologique. Published since 1898 by Durkheim. Paris: Félix Alcan.

*The works marked by an asterisk were exhibited, in part or in their entirety, at the Library of French Science at the San Francisco Exposition.

Translated by Jerome D. Folkman

1. "La sociologie," in *La science française* ("Exposition universelle et internationale de San Francisco" [Paris: Librairie Larousse, 1915]), Vol. I. Used by permission of Larousse, Editeurs.

PRAGMATISM AND SOCIOLOGY[1]

EMILE DURKHEIM

FIRST LECTURE[2]

INTRODUCTION

What are the reasons that lead me to choose the subject of this course? Why have I given it the title *Pragmatism and Sociology?* First of all, it is because of the contemporaneity of pragmatism, which is almost the only theory of truth that exists at present. It is also because pragmatism contains a sense of life and of action that it has in common with sociology. The two are children of the same period.

However, I am far from accepting the conclusions of pragmatism. It is interesting, therefore, to characterize the respective positions of the two doctrines. The problem raised by pragmatism is, in fact, a very serious one. In our time we are witnessing an attack on reason; actually it is an all-out assault.[3] Thus the interest of the problem is three-fold.

1. It is, first of all, of general interest. More than any other doctrine, pragmatism is capable of making us aware of the necessity for renovating traditional rationalism, for it shows us the inadequacies of rationalism.

2. Next, it is of national interest. Our whole French culture is at bottom essentially rationalistic. The eighteenth century is an extension of Cartesianism. Therefore, a total negation of rationalism would constitute a danger: it would upset our entire national culture. The whole French mind would have to be transformed if it were necessary to accept the form of irrationalism that pragmatism represents.

3. Finally, it is of specifically philosophic interest. Not only our culture but the whole of the philosophic tradition, including the first stages of philosophic speculation (with one exception, with which we shall deal shortly), tends to be rationalistic. If pragmatism were valid, we should have to proceed by completely reversing this whole tradition.

In the philosophic tradition, two currents are generally dis-

386

tinguished: the rationalist and the empiricist. But it is easy to see that empiricism and rationalism are only two different ways of affirming reason. Both maintain a cult that pragmatism tends to destroy—the cult of truth: both admit the existence of necessary judgments. The difference lies in the ways this necessity is explained. Empiricism bases its explanation on the nature of things; rationalism, or reason itself, on the nature of thought. Both of them, however, recognize the obligatory and necessary character of certain truths, and the differences between the two are secondary to this fundamental identity. It is precisely this obligatory force of logical judgments, this necessity of true judgments, that pragmatism denies. It affirms that the mind remains free in the face of what is true.

In this, pragmatism resembles the one exception referred to before: sophism. Sophism, too, denied all truth. Nor is this resemblence arbitrary; it is admitted by pragmatists themselves. Thus Schiller proclaims himself a "Protagorean" and recalls the axiom, "Man is the measure of all things."[4]

Let us not forget that sophism played a useful role in the history of philosophical doctrines. In a manner of speaking, it produced Socrates. In the same fashion, pragmatism can serve to awaken philosophic thought from the new "dogmatic slumber" in which it has tended to sleep ever since it received the blow that Kant's criticism inflected on it. As has been said, the value of pragmatism is that it shows up the weaknesses of the old rationalism. Rationalism must be renovated in order to satisfy the exigencies of modern thought, and to take account of certain new points of view that have been introduced by contemporary science. The problem is to find a formula that will preserve the essentials of rationalism and, at the same time, answer the valid criticism that pragmatism makes of it.

THE ORIGINS OF PRAGMATISM[5]

I. Nietzsche

In a recent book,[6] René Berthelot argues that the first form of pragmatism is to be seen in Nietzsche—that, in fact, Nietzsche represents radical and integral pragmatism. In this way, the author believes that he can connect pragmatism with German romanticism and establish that its inspiration was German.

As for us, we prefer relating it to the tradition of Anglo-Saxon thought.

First of all, what are the points that Nietzsche's thought has in common with pragmatism? Nietzsche denies an absolute character, a character of universal truth, to moral ideals of every kind. According to him, the ideal is beyond the true and the false: " 'This—is now *my* way—' " says Zarathustra,[7] " 'where is yours?' Thus did I answer those who asked me 'the way.' For the way—it doth not exist!" As Nietzsche saw it, the matter of logical or moral norms is an inferior concern. He strives for the total liberation of both conduct and thought. Speculative truth can be neither impersonal nor universal. We can know things only through processes that distort them, that transform them, to a greater or lesser degree, into our own thoughts. We construct them in our image: we locate them in space, we classify them by types and species, and so on. But not any of this exists, not even the cause-effect relation. We substitute for reality a whole system of symbols and fictions— in short, illusions: "How could we ever explain! We operate only with things which do not exist, with lines, surfaces, bodies, atoms, divisible times, divisible spaces—how can explanation ever be possible when we first make everything a *conception, our conception?*"[8]

But why do we establish such fictions? Because they are useful to us for living, Nietzsche answers. They are false but they must be believed to be true so that the members of our species can preserve themselves. What has helped us to live has survived; the rest has disappeared:

> No living being might have been preserved unless the contrary inclination—to affirm rather than suspend judgment, to mistake and fabricate rather than be in the right—had been cultivated with extraordinary assiduity.— The course of logical thought and reasoning in our modern brain corresponds to a process and struggle of impulses, which singly and in themselves are all very illogical and unjust; we experience usually only the result of the struggle, so rapidly and secretly does this primitive mechanism now operate in us.[9]

For Nietzsche, therefore, it is *utility* that determines which judgments are to be held as true, and which ones are to be eliminated as false. And the true as the useful is the very principle of pragmatism.

Yet there are some profound differences between Nietzsche's thought and pragmatism. We should note that Nietzsche does not say that what is useful is true but rather that what *seems* true has been established because of its usefulness. In his opinion, the useful is false. According to him, there exists a form of truth other than that which is qualified as true by the men of the "herd," a morality other than the "slave morality," a logic other than common logic. There is a truth that only free spirits can attain. It is the artist who is the spirit free of all rules and capable of adapting himself to all forms of reality, of grasping by intuition that which is hidden under appearances and fiction.

There is nothing like this in pragmatism. For it, there is no surface of things that is distinct from the basis on which they rest. The surface is the things as they appear to us. This is what we live on; this is what constitutes reality. There is no reason to look beneath appearances. We must limit ourselves to the world as it appears to us without worrying about knowing whether or not there is anything else. William James presents his doctrine as *radical empiricism,* and his method of argument often consists of ridiculing reason and logic. The only thing that is important for him is what appears in immediate experience: thought never moves on more than a single plane, not on two different planes.

The proof is that even when pragmatism seems to admit something that surpasses experience, something beyond the world of phenomena, in reality, it does not leave this world. This is what is manifested in James's *religious tendencies,* which are very real. For him, supernatural beings, the gods, are in nature. They are real forces which are near to us, which we never contact directly, but whose effects are revealed to us at certain moments, in certain experiences. Therefore, little by little, we can discover them, just as we have discovered many other physical forces (electricity, and so on), which were unknown for a long time, but which existed nevertheless. Everything takes place on the phenomenal plane. And this is very far from Nietzschean thought.

It is true that at certain periods of his life Nietzsche denied the existence of a substratum hidden under appearances and admitted only the existence of the latter. The task of the artist became to free himself from appearances and to create in their place a world of moving, varied images that developed in an autonomous fashion; likewise thought, once it had broken out of its logical framework, would be able to develop freely.

Pragmatism, however, rejects this second interpretation along with the first. It does not pretend either to surpass or to go below the surface of the world of immediate reality, in order to substitute for it a world of mental creations. What dominates pragmatism is a realistic sense and a practical sense. The pragmatist is a man of action who, consequently, attaches importance to things. He does not pursue his action in a dream; he never assumes, like Nietzsche, the tone of a prophet or of one inspired; he knows neither anguish nor uneasiness. For him, truth is something to be accomplished.

II. Romanticism

We must also note certain common traits between pragmatism and romanticism, notably the feeling of the complexity, richness, and diversity of life as it is given to us. Romanticism was in part a revolt against the simplistic element in the rationalism and social philosophy at the end of the eighteenth century.

This feeling for the complexity of things human, for the insufficiency of eighteenth-century philosophy, is also found at the basis of the sociology that was just beginning to appear in the works of Saint-Simon and Auguste Comte, who understood that social life was made up not of abstract relationships but of extremely rich material. Such a feeling does not necessarily result in either mysticism or pragmatism. Comte, in particular, was a rationalist to the highest degree. However, he wanted to found a sociology that would be richer, more complex, and less formalistic than the social philosophy of the eighteenth century.

III. The Anglo-Saxon Milieu: Peirce

In order to understand pragmatism it is not necessary to go to doctrines as old as romanticism or to German philosophy.

One needs only to place it in its original setting: the Anglo-Saxon milieu.

The first thinker who employed the word "pragmatism" was the American scholar Peirce.[10] It was he who first presented the ideas that the pragmatists call their own in a paper published in January, 1878, in an American periodical.[11] It was translated in the *Revue philosophique* of January, 1879, under the title "Comment rendre nos idées claires."[12]

These are the essential points. Peirce asks himself why we think. He answers: because we doubt. If we were in a perpetual state of certainty we should not need to think and to make an effort to resolve our doubts. "The irritation produced by doubt forces us to make efforts to try to attain a state of *belief*." However, belief is revealed only through action: belief that does not act does not exist, and action must take on the character of the belief that engenders it. The state of belief is a state of equilibrium and therefore of repose, and this is why we seek it. Consequently, the essential mark of belief is "the establishment of a habit. . . . Our habit has the same character as our actions; our belief as our habit; and our conception as our belief." Thus *doubt* engenders the *idea;* and idea engenders *action,* and, having become *belief,* is revealed by organized movements, by *habit.* The whole sense of an idea lies in the sense of the habit that this idea determines.

Hence this rule: "Consider the practical effects that we believe can be produced by the object of our conception. The conception of all these effects is the complete conception of the object." If, in two cases that one takes to be different the effects are the same, the fact is that one is in the presence of a false distinction: the two objects are the same. The controversies between the Catholics and the Protestants over transubstantiation offer an example of this: The latter see in the Eucharist only a symbol, the former see a real presence. But the final effect is the same for both: the consecrated wafer is food for the soul. Whether or not it is really the flesh and blood of Christ is henceforth of little importance. The discussion is purely a matter of words.[13]

However, all of this is only a very distant forerunner of pragmatism. Moreover, Peirce does not use the word *pragma-*

tism in the article in question. He uses it only in 1902 in his article in J. M. Baldwin's *Dictionary of Philosophy and Psychology*.[14] But he later[15] said that he had been using it in conversation for a long time.

There is obviously some affinity between the thesis that Peirce advanced in his early article and pragmatism. The two doctrines are in agreement in that both establish a close connection between idea and action, set aside all purely metaphysical questions and purely verbal discussions, and end by posing only problems of a practical interest whose terms are borrowed from the world of the senses.

However, there is an essential difference. In Peirce's article, there is no theory of truth. The problem of truth is not posed: the author asks himself how we can succeed in clarifying our ideas, not what conditions are requisite if the idea of a thing is to give a true representation of its sensory effects. Even more important than this is Peirce's admission that under the classical theory truth imposes itself by a sort of "fatality," before which the mind cannot help but bow. Thus the truth is an opinion that possesses its own rights, and all investigators are obliged to admit it. This is the exact opposite of the pragmatist principle.

Consequently, when William James published his works, Peirce refused to identify himself with James and insisted on pointing out certain differences. Peirce stated that he did not repudiate rationalism. For him, if action has value, it is because it is an instrument for the progress of reason. In 1902, in his article in Baldwin's *Dictionary*, he recognized that he had not sufficiently insisted on this point and explicitly dissociated himself from James's interpretations. In the article in the *Monist* of 1905, "What Pragmatism Is," he even invented a new term, "pragmaticism"—which he called "a name so ugly that no one would ever dream of taking it from [me]"—in order to avoid any confusion between his position and that of James. In another article, "The Issues of Pragmaticism,"[16] he calls his own doctrine a "doctrine of common sense." Under these conditions, it is rather curious that James has continued to refer to him as his authority, has saluted him as the father of pragmatism, and has never pointed out these divergences.

WILLIAM JAMES

William James[17] is the true father of pragmatism. In 1896, he published *The Will to Believe*[18] (republished in a new edition in 1911). In this work, he distinguishes between purely theoretical questions that are the affair of science alone—an area in which, if we do not as yet see with perfect clarity, we can expect clarification, for science will someday be able to furnish us with the elements necessary for our belief—and the practical problems, those in which our life is engaged. When faced with the latter, we cannot wait, but must choose and decide, even if we are not sure of the decision; and we do so by obeying personal factors and extra-logical motivations, such as temperament, environment, and so on. We surrender to our urges: one hypothesis seems more alive to us than others; we put it into practice and convert it into actions. This is the same as Pascal's "wager": although the truth cannot be demonstrated or even seen clearly, it is necessary to make a decision and act on the basis of it. Here we have pragmatism's principal point of departure. Truth, as James sees it, has a personal character: truth and life are inseparable.

James is thinking here particularly of religious belief, of which moral belief is, in his opinion, only an aspect. Such preoccupations with religion are found among all pragmatists, and it is through them that pragmatism first appeared in James. Another great pragmatist, F. S. C. Schiller of Oxford, does not go so far as to say with James that it is necessary to have an attitude toward religious questions, but he also declares that truth must not be "depersonalized" or "dehumanized," and he calls his pragmatism "humanism."

Nevertheless, the term "pragmatism" had not yet been used by James. He did so only in his study "Philosophical Conceptions and Practical Results,"[19] which appeared in the *University Chronicle* at Berkeley, California, on September 9, 1898. The essential themes of pragmatism are developed in this work.

1. *Pragmatisme et sociologie.* Cours inédit prononcé à la Sorbonne en 1913-14 et restitué d'après des notes d'étudiants par Armand Cuvillier (Paris: Librairie philosophique J. Vrin, 1955). Lectures 1-5, pp. 27-81; Lectures 13-14, pp. 139-51. [Used by permission of Librairie philosophique

J. Vrin, and Armand Cuvillier. Some of the footnotes accompanying the text are Durkheim's own; the others were added either by the students whose notes were used in reconstructing the course or by Cuvillier. Wherever possible, references to Durkheim's works contained herein have been replaced by references to English translations.—ED.]

2. Lecture of December 9, 1913.

3. This is probably an allusion to the following passage in James's *Pragmatism* (London: Longmans, Green & Co., Ltd., 1907), p. 54: "Against rationalism as a pretension and a method pragmatism is fully armed and militant."

4. Cf. Ferdinand Canning Scott Schiller, *Humanism* (London: Macmillan Co., 1903), pp. 17-19; "From Plato to Protagoras," Essay II (pp. 28-90 in the French translation), and "Protagoras the Humanist," Essay XIV (pp. 388-416 in the French translation), *Studies in Humanism* (London: Macmillan Co., 1907); "Plato or Protagoras?" *Mind*, XVII (1908), 518-26; and "The Humanism of Protagoras," *ibid.*, XX (1911), 181-96.

5. All titles have been added by the editor.

6. *Le pragmatisme chez Nietzsche et chez Poincaré (Un romantisme utilitaire: Etude sur le mouvement pragmatiste*, Vol. I [Paris: Félix Alcan, 1911]).

7. "The Spirit of Gravity," *Thus Spake Zarathustra*, trans. Thomas Common (New York: Macmillan Co., 1911), Part III, p. 239. Cited by Berthelot, *op. cit.*, pp. 36-37, from the French translation, "De l'esprit de pesanteur," in the *Mercure de France* edition of Nietzsche's work.

8. *The Joyful Wisdom*, trans. Thomas Common (New York: Macmillan Co., 1910), Aphorism 112, p. 158. Cited by Berthelot, *op. cit.*, p. 43.

9. *Ibid.*, Aphorism 111, p. 157. Cited by Berthelot, *op. cit.*, p. 42.

10. Charles Sanders Peirce (1839-1914), mathematician and chemist. His *Complete Works* were published at Harvard University in 1931-35.

11. "How to Make Our Ideas Clear," the second paper in the series "Illustrations of the Logic of Science," *Popular Science Monthly*, XII (1878), 286-302.

12. Pages 39-57. The general title of the series of papers by Peirce is "La logique de la science" ("Illustrations of the Logic of Science"). The first article appeared in December, 1878, pp. 553-69.

13. It seems that Durkheim has deliberately modified the meaning of a passage on page 293 of Peirce's article in *Popular Science Monthly*, for a reason that is easy to understand. The French translation in *Revue philosophique*, page 47, follows the original: " . . . we can . . . mean nothing by wine but what has certain effects, direct or indirect, upon our senses; and to talk of something as having all the sensible characters of

wine, yet being in reality blood, is senseless jargon." In his *Pragmatism,* James uses the same example, but in a directly opposite way, to prove that the notion of substance itself is capable of a "pragmatic application" (Cf. *Pragmatism,* Chap. iii).

14. New York: Macmillan Co., 1901-5, Vol. II, pp. 321-22.

15. In the article "What Pragmatism Is," *Monist,* XV (1905), 161-81.

16. *Monist,* XV (1905), 481-99.

17. 1842-1910.

18. *The Will to Believe and Other Essays in Popular Philosophy* (London: Longmans, Green & Co., Ltd., 1896); French translation, 1916.

19. Reprinted in the *Journal of Philosophy,* IV (1904), 673-87, under the title "The Pragmatic Method."

SECOND LECTURE[1]

THE PRAGMATIST MOVEMENT

Thus it was in America, between 1895 and 1900, that pragmatism made its appearance. Although of recent date, the history of its origin is rather difficult to trace, since it developed almost imperceptibly, like a slow, underground movement that extends only gradually beyond the circle of private conversations. James defines it as one of those changes "that opinion undergoes almost without being aware of it."

As we have already mentioned, Peirce used the word only in private conversations. James, though using a term that had already been adopted by others before him, was the first to apply it to an organized group of ideas. For several years, he limited himself to presenting his ideas in various articles in periodicals, the first of which appeared in 1895. In 1909, he collected the main papers he had written up to 1898 in a volume entitled *The Meaning of Truth*[2] (the French translation, *L'Idée de vérité,* appeared in 1913). In 1906, James gave a series of lectures in which he developed his thought in a more complete fashion. They were published in 1907 under the title *Pragmatism*[3] (the French translation appeared in 1911). In 1909, he was intrepid enough to go to Oxford, the citadel of Hegelianism, to expound his doctrine, presenting it from a point of view that made its opposition to Hegelian philosophy most clearly apparent. He gave this group of lectures the title *A Pluralistic Universe*[4] (in 1910, the work was translated into French under the rather inappropriate title, *Philosophie de l'expérience*). His *Essays in Radical Empiricism*, a collection of articles—the first of which had appeared in 1904 under the title "Does Consciousness Exist?"[5]—were published in 1910. This article, important because it poses the question of whether a specific duality exists in the universe, provides, in the form of a French abridgement,[6] the subject matter of an important communication to the Congress of Philosophy (Rome, 1905).

Parallel to James, John Dewey[7] had begun a campaign in a series of articles in which he gradually moved toward pragmatism. A list of these articles is to be found on page 575 of the *Revue de métaphysique* of 1913.[8] We have no work that gives Dewey's over-all position; there are only partial analyses, such as the *Studies in Logical Theory*, a collective enterprise of which he wrote only the first four chapters,[9] or his little book *How We Think*.[10] It was around Dewey that the Chicago school or instrumentalist school developed. Dewey's principal disciple is A. W. Moore.[11]

These ideas crossed the Atlantic at a very early date. At Oxford a group of young philosophers banded together in 1902 to undertake a campaign directed both against materialistic evolutionism and against the theories of Hegel. Under the title *Personal Idealism*[12] they published a collection of articles, the most important of which was F. C. S. Schiller's[13] "Axioms as Postulates." In the following year, Schiller collected his main papers in his book *Humanism*.[14]

In Italy, the magazine *Leonardo*[15] carried pragmatism to an extreme, if not to the point of being paradoxical.

In France pragmatism appears mainly in the neoreligious movement that is called "modernist." Edouard LeRoy claims to have based his religious apologia on principles taken from pragmatism.[16]

We must point out, however, that the pragmatists annex, a little too easily, some thinkers who are far from accepting all their theses. Thus James claims as partisans Henri Poincaré and Henri Bergson.[17] From the latter he borrows certain arguments, simply because Bergson introduced pragmatism to

France in a preface,[18] a preface in which he speaks of it in rather broad terms so that it is easy to observe the reservations he has regarding this doctrine.

THE ESSENTIAL THESES OF PRAGMATISM

Critical Part

Dewey, Schiller, and James are, therefore, the three chief protagonists of pragmatism. Dewey is a logician, and he always tries to be quite precise. His style, however, is often heavy; his developments are laborious; and his thought is sometimes not very clear. James himself admits that he does not fully understand him; Dewey, he says "recently gave a series of lectures entitled *Pragmatism*: they were dazzling flashes of light amidst Cimmerian darkness."[19]

Schiller and James are, on the contrary, very lucid. But their manner is different. Schiller proceeds in a straight line; he has no fear of paradoxes, and far from trying to attenuate the expression of his thought, he aims at shocking and astonishing the reader. He makes his deductions with a surprising, unexpected logic that is brusque and intransigent. James, too, shows a liking for paradox, even in his psychological theories. He enunciates ideas that one would accept much more easily if it were not for the turn he gives them. He begins by presenting his theses in sharp angles, as it were, but in the course of the discussion he displays his ability to round off the corners without abandoning his fundamental principles—one ends up wondering if one does not agree with him. The title of his book on pragmatism clearly indicates this tendency of his mind, for although he shows pragmatism as working a veritable revolution in the very heart of philosophic thought, he entitles his book: *Pragmatism: A New Name for Some Old Ways of Thinking*.[20] According to the circumstances, he presents his doctrine under one or the other of these two aspects. This diversity[21] detracts in some way from the unity of pragmatism (was there not an American writer who counted up to thirteen different varieties of the doctrine?) and makes a general exposition difficult.

In addition, none of the pragmatist philosophers has given us an over-all exposition.[22] We have only articles which are scattered in periodicals or which have been occasionally collected in volumes, or lectures and "popular" addresses. There are no courses in which the lecturer expounded his fundamental thought before students. What we have are lectures delivered before the general public, in which only the high points of certain matters are presented. Each one forms a whole in itself, and what is of secondary importance in one of them becomes the principal matter in another, and vice versa. The whole physiognomy of the doctrine is changed thereby, and it is not easy to discern the major ideas. This rather phantom-like quality of pragmatism has made it possible for some of its adversaries to reproach it for contradicting itself.

However, it is not impossible to discover its fundamental theses and to find a common ground in them. That is what I shall try to do here, without claiming to give a historical explanation; I shall limit myself to pointing out some of the particular nuances that are characteristic of each author. In *The Meaning of Truth*,[23] James declares that he shares Peirce's ideas. Schiller recognizes James[24] as his master. As for Dewey,[25] although he appears to have some reservations, he differs from James mainly on particular points. In all three, therefore, there is an identical orientation. My intention is to bring to light and to demonstrate the major criticisms that the pragmatists direct against rationalism.

Pragmatism is not presented as a completed system. James is quite definite on this point. He says that pragmatism is not a system but a discussion, a movement, whose form may be more clearly determined at a later date. It is less a definitive organization of ideas than a general impulsion in a certain direction. We can characterize it in three ways:[26] (1) as a method, a general attitude of the mind; (2) as a theory of truth; and (3) as a theory of the universe.

1. As a method, pragmatism is nothing else but the attitude or general turn that the mind must adopt in the presence of problems. This attitude consists of directing our attention toward "results, consequences, facts": "The pragmatic method . . . is to try to interpret each notion by tracing its respective practical consequences."[27] This is Peirce's pragmatism, which tries above all to get rid of verbal discussions and useless prob-

lems, and is characterized by its choice of questions and its manner of dealing with them.

2. There is nothing extraordinarily special about this aspect of pragmatism. It is as a theory of truth that pragmatism is of particular interest, and it is from this point of view that we are going to study it. We shall speak of pragmatism as a theory of the universe only to the degree that it will be necessary to do so in order to understand it as a theory of truth. This procedure is indicated by James himself. The strength of pragmatism, he says in *The Meaning of Truth*,[28] lies in the bankruptcy of previous systems; and it is the insufficiency of rationalism in particular that leads us to seek another conception of truth. Unfortunately, James's discussion of rationalism is most of the time mixed up with the exposition of his own conception of truth. It is important to disentangle it, however, because we must above all understand the reasons that have led the pragmatists to believe that rationalism has to be replaced. It so happens that certain thinkers who feel the strength of the objections made by the pragmatists, immediately turn to an acceptance of their soultion. It is very important, however, to separate the solutions from the objections. In order to do so, we must first of all examine the manner in which the pragmatists have represented this rationalist—or let us say more generally—dogmatic[29] conception of truth.

THE DOGMATIC CONCEPTION OF TRUTH

According to James, this conception is based on a very simple principle: The true idea is the idea that conforms to things. It is an image, a copy, of objects: it is the mental representation of the thing. The idea is true when this mental representation corresponds accurately to the object represented. Moreover, this conception is not exclusive with rationalism; it is shared by empiricism. According to John Stuart Mill, for example, the mind does nothing but copy external reality. Ideas are dependent on facts, for they only express sensations. They always refer to sensory images; consequently, thought can do nothing but translate sensations that come to us from the external world.

In spite of appearances to the contrary, it is no different

with rationalism. For it, too, there exists an outside reality that the mind must translate in order to be in truth. The difference is that this reality is not composed of sensory things, but is rather an organized system of ideas which exist by themselves and which the mind must reproduce. Plato's doctrine is recognizable here, and it is Plato, in fact, that Schiller most often attacks.[30] For others, ideas are the thoughts of God. " 'God geometrizes,' it used to be said; and it was believed that Euclid's elements literally reproduced his geometrizing. There is an eternal and unchangeable 'reason'; and its voice was supposed to reverberate in *Barbara* and *Celarent*."[31] For Hegel, whom James bitterly attacks,[32] the absolute "Idea" is identified with "Reason," which envelops everything and is the "absolute all of alls" in which all contradictions are reconciled. But in all these cases, truth is conceived of as existing outside of us: there exists a Reason that dominates all individual reasons, which the latter can do nothing but copy.

The two forms of dogmatism, therefore, consist in admitting that truth is given, either in the world of sensory perception (empiricism) or in the intelligible world as an absolute thought or as reason (rationalism). An example of a third solution is found in Hamelin's idealism in which things are only concepts. But this really amounts to the same thing since the ideal states exist in the things themselves, and the system of truth and reality (which are here identical) is still given to us entirely from outside ourselves.

Thus in all the dogmatic conceptions, truth can only be the transcription of an external reality. Since it is outside individual minds, this truth is impersonal: it does not express man; it does not depend on him. Therefore, it is also performed: it *"holds or obtains,"* says James,[33] and it imposes itself on us in an absolute fashion. The mind does not have to construct it—to copy is not to engender. The mind has no active role. On the contrary, it must efface itself as much as possible and seek simply, in a manner of speaking, a duplication of reality. For if mind had its own activity, if it made its imprint on truth, it would distort it. It would express itself instead of truth. Every contribution of the mind would be a source of error.

Finally, in addition to being external and impersonal, truth, according to dogmatism, is a *completed* system, a complete whole that escapes time and becoming. " '*I have never doubted,*' " says an Oxford Hegelian whom James cites,[34] " 'that truth is universal and single and timeless, a single content or significance, one and whole and complete.' "

A few words of discussion: One is a little surprised, at first glance, to think that Leibnitz and Kant are included in this definition of rationalism and dogmatism. The pragmatists, it is true, are not very careful about specifications. They manifest a certain negligence with respect to doctrines which, in their opinion, are of no major importance.

The objection will immediately be raised that for Leibnitz mind draws all its thought from itself: the monad is without relation to the universe; it is from itself and not from outside that ideas come to it. However, if we look at the pragmatist criticism closely, we see that it applies as much to Leibnitz as to the other rationalists. The monad actually works on a model which it has not created but which it is given, one which is supplied by God. The world is what God has made it, not what the monad wants it to be. The plan that the monad accomplishes, to the extent that it rises to clear thought, is imposed on it. It is not the creator.

For Kant, it is certainly mind which creates truth—but only as long as it is a matter of *phenomenal* truth. Phenomenal truth, however, is mere appearance. In one sense, when compared to the noumenon, it is even error. At the very least, it is only a repercussion of the noumenon, the intelligible world, on the phenomenal plane. The noumenon is a given: we do not create it. The only means of access to it that we have is the moral law, which opens it up to us and tells us that there is something else besides the phenomenal world. Yet what are the characteristics of moral law? They are fixity and impersonality. In one sense, we do discover the moral law within ourselves; but we do not invent it—we only find it. It is not we who have made it, nor is it our mind that has given birth to it. It is, therefore, a reality that is outside us, one that is imposed on us.

401

CRITICISM OF DOGMATISM

What are the objections that pragmatism makes to this conception?

First of all, if truth, it asks, is a simple transcription of reality, what good does it do? It is a useless redundancy.[35] Why do things need a translation? Why do they not suffice by themselves? Such representation adds nothing to what exists. For, according to James, truth must be "not a redoubling, but an addition." He invites us[36] to imagine an individual who for a moment constitutes by himself the whole reality of the universe, and who then learns that another being who will know this reality perfectly is going to be created. What could he hope to obtain from this knowledge? Of what use would this replica of himself in the mind of the newcomer be to him? In what way would his universe be enriched? Nothing is useful but what our mind adds to things. What is important for man is less the substance of things than their secondary qualities: light, color, heat, and so on. What counts is the use we make of reality; if the spirit limited itself to "seeing" reality, of what use would this be?

Let us suppose the existence of a perfect system of objective truths,[37] like the world of Plato's "Ideas." What interest is there in having the "light of intelligence" reflected in the multitude of individual minds that can only reproduce it in a very imperfect fashion? This constitutes a fall, which is also found in the theological hypothesis. Why did God, the sovereign truth, not remain alone in his perfection? What did he add to himself? For if the world comes from him, the world expresses him, but it does so in a very incomplete and deficient fashion!

But, it is said, we are interested in knowing the truth such as it is, with a view, precisely, to action; therefore, this truth must be as faithful a copy of reality as possible. However, we must still show that our thought must copy reality if we are to be permitted to act. Thus we come to make of truth a good in itself, one which imposes itself on its own, and which the mind would seek for the mere happiness of contemplating it. Truth would be established only in order to be thought. It becomes a god to which one raises altars.

There is no doubt that, when we consider an idealism such

as that of Leibnitz, we may wonder what the function of truth is. Each monad copies the totality of the others, that is to say, the universe, and all copy the same universe. Why is there such a waste of intellectual energy if one does not establish the principle that knowledge is a good by itself?

1. Lecture of December 16, 1913.

2. New York: Longmans, Green & Co., Inc., 1909.

3. London: Longmans, Green & Co., Ltd., 1907.

4. New York: Longmans, Green & Co., Inc., 1909.

5. *Journal of Philosophy,* I (1904), 477-91.

6. "La notion de conscience," reprinted in *Essays in Radical Empiricism* (New York: Longmans, Green & Co., Inc., 1912), pp. 206-33.

7. 1859-1952.

8. In the article by Henri Robet, "L'Ecole de Chicago et l'instrumentalisme," Vol. XXI, pp. 537 ff. More complete bibliographies have since been published, notably in Emmanuel Leroux, *Le pragmatisme américain et anglais* (Paris: Félix Alcan, 1922), pp. 346 ff.

9. By John Dewey, with the co-operation of members and fellows of the Department of Philosophy (Chicago: University of Chicago Press, 1903).

10. Boston: D. C. Heath & Co., 1910; French translation, 1925. Dewey later published many other works on the same subjects, notably *Experience and Nature* (1925), *The Quest for Certainty* (1929), and so on.

11. Addison Webster Moore, whose principal works are "Some Logical Aspects of Purpose," *Journal of Philosophy,* VI (1909); *Pragmatism and Its Critics* (Chicago: University of Chicago Press, 1910); "Bergson and Pragmatism," *Philosophical Review,* XXI (1912); and so on.

12. *Personal Idealism: Philosophical Essays by Eight Members of the University of Oxford,* ed. Henry Cecil Sturt (London: Macmillan Co., 1902).

13. Ferdinand Canning Scott Schiller, 1864-1937.

14. London: Macmillan Co., 1903. Other articles, with some original studies, are collected in his *Studies in Humanism* (London: Macmillan Co., 1907).

15. Published in Florence from 1902 to 1906, under the direction of Giovanni Papini and Giuseppe Prezzolini, with the collaboration of G. Vailati, M. Calderoni, and so on. Cf. G. Vailati, "Sur le pragmatisme en Italie," *Revue du mois* (February 10, 1907).

16. At this time, LeRoy had published "Science et philosophie," *Revue de métaphysique et de morale,* VII and VIII (1899 and 1900); "Le problème de Dieu," *ibid.,* XV (1907); *Dogme et critique* (Paris: Bloud, 1907). On LeRoy, see René Berthelot, *Un romantisme utilitaire: Etude sur le mouvement pragmatiste* (Paris: Félix Alcan, 1911), III, 303-8.

17. We could also add Maurice Blondel, cited in the Preface to the French translation of *Pragmatism,* p. 18. But Blondel, who gives a much broader meaning to "action" than does James, has energetically severed connections with pragmatism. Cf. André Lalande, *Vocabulaire technique et critique de la philosophie* (5th ed.; Paris: Presses Universitaires de France, 1947), p. 784 n.

18. The reference is to Bergson's Introduction to the French translation of *Pragmatism,* pp. 1-16.

19. James, *Pragmatism,* p. 23.

20. The complete title is *Pragmatism: A New Name for Some Old Ways of Thinking, Popular Lectures on Philosophy.*

21. In the beginning of his book *Le pragmatisme chez Nietzsche et chez Poincaré,* Vol. I of *Un romantisme utilitaire,* p. 3, Berthelot says that pragmatism is like the cloud that Hamlet shows to Polonius through the windows of the castle of Elsinore. At some times it resembles a camel; at other times, a weasel; at still others, a whale.

22. The same remark is made in respect to Dewey and the Chicago school by Emmanuel Leroux, *op. cit.,* p. 206. As for Schiller, he excuses himself, at the beginning of his *Studies in Humanism,* for the discontinuity of form in which he has presented his thought (p. vii; French translation, p. i).

23. Pages 51-52; cf. James, *Pragmatism,* pp. 46-47.

24. As does Peirce; cf. Schiller, *Studies in Humanism,* p. 5 n.

25. In *Pragmatism,* p. viii, James says that Dewey's *Studies in Logical Theory* "are the foundation" of pragmatism.

26. Cf. James, *Pragmatism,* Lecture II.

27. *Ibid.,* p. 45.

28. Pages 57-59.

29. In *Pragmatism,* p. 11, James presents a picture of the characteristics of the rationalist and the empiricist. The rationalist is shown as dogmatic; the empiricist, as skeptical.

30. Mainly in "Plato and His Predecessors," *Quarterly Review,* CCIV (1906); reprinted as "From Plato to Protagoras" in *Studies in Humanism,* Essay II, pp. 62-88.

31. James, *The Meaning of Truth,* p. 57.

32. The entire third lecture of *A Pluralistic Universe* is devoted to Hegel.

33. James, *Pragmatism,* p. 226.

34. *A Pluralistic Universe,* p. 101.

35. Dewey, *Studies in Logical Theory:* "work of supererogation," p. 36-37; "futilely reiterative," p. 47.

36. *The Meaning of Truth,* p. 79. Cf. p. 235.

37. Here begins a passage in which, in our two versions, the sequence of ideas did not seem perfectly clear. We have re-established them to the best of our ability.

THIRD LECTURE[1]

CRITICISM OF DOGMATISM *(Continued)*

Truth and Human Knowledge

I repeat that I have no intention of giving a history or even a complete outline of pragmatism. What I am trying to do in particular is to identify the general tendency that is common to its various representatives, as well as to discover the motivations that have led them to this way of thinking. To do this, we must first somehow become pragmatists ourselves, setting aside the objections that come to mind. When we have, in this way, grasped what constitutes the strength of pragmatism, we shall be able to become ourselves again and pass on to discussion.

The fundamental element in pragmatism is its criticism of traditional rationalism, or rather dogmatism. In order to understand this criticism, we have tried to see what the pragmatists' idea of dogmatism is. According to them, dogmatism regards the true idea as the copy of external reality, whether this reality consists of material ideas or of thought that originates in the absolute spirit. Thus truth is objective, transcendent, and impersonal. We have already encountered one of the objections that pragmatism makes to this conception: If truth is nothing but a duplication of reality, of what use is it? It seems useless.

Now, however, another difficulty arises. If the reality of which the idea is a copy is external and transcendent, how can we come to know it? If it is outside of us, immanent to the world or transcending it, a part of the world or a totality in itself, how can we attain it? Let us recall the Platonic hypothesis. Ideas, by definition, are beyond the world of experience. How can we raise ourselves to this ideal world that is the only reality? There is an abyss between it and us: how is it possible to bridge it? Or how, on the other hand, can these ideal realities descend into our world? "It is impossible to explain," says Schiller,[2] "how man can rise to the contemplation of eternal truth, or why the idea should descend and distort itself in human thoughts." In vain does Plato attribute special powers to the mind: this does not eliminate the difficulty.

According to Aristotle, too, the divine cannot know the human without degenerating. Inversely, however, one cannot see how man would be able to think of the divine. How could something as finite as the human mind succeed in thinking of the absolute spirit? We should have to admit that there is no separation, that the two worlds are only one.

More generally stated: If thought is a copy of things, we do not see how it can attain things, for there is an abyss between the mind and the object. James says in *The Meaning of Truth*, that thought would have to accomplish a *"salto mortale* across an 'epistemological chasm.' "[3] We can attain the object only by thinking of it. If it is thought of, it is interior to us. Thus it is impossible to control the truth of the idea, that is, to control its conformity with the object, as is required by the hypothesis: thought cannot transcend itself. "In whatever form this 'copy' theory be stated, the question inevitably arises how we can compare our ideas with reality and thus know their truth. On this theory, what we possess is ever the copy; the reality is beyond. In other words, such a theory logically carried out leads to the breakdown of knowledge."[4]

Such is the conception that Schiller, James, and Dewey have of rationalism. Traditional rationalism separates thought from existence. Thought is in the mind; existence is outside it. Hence the two forms of reality can no longer meet. If by a hypothesis one places thought outside existence, the abyss that separates them can no longer be crossed. The only way to solve the difficulty would be to refuse to admit the existence of this gap between existence and thought. If thought is an element of reality, if it is a part of existence and of life, there is no longer any "epistemological abyss" or "perilous leap." We need only to see how these two realities can participate in each other. To connect thought with existence, to connect thought with life—this is the fundamental idea of pragmatism.[5]

Extra-Human Truth and Pure Intellect

There is another difficulty in the dogmatic conception. If truth is impersonal, it is foreign to man, it is extra-human. How, then, can it act on the human mind, attracting and fascinating it? It corresponds to nothing in our nature. It is often said that truth obliges us, that to obey true ideas is a duty, that to seek the truth and to flee from error is a "categorical imperative." But how can we understand this if truth is not something human? What force would ever be able to make us go spontaneously to something that is foreign to us and make us obey it? This is the objection that is often made to the "moral law" as Kant presents it. In reality, however, the pragmatists say, this is not the question. The exigencies of truth, like all others, are always exigencies that are subordinated to certain conditions. In actual life, when a question concerning truth arises, we ask ourselves: When must I adhere to one such truth and when to another? Should my adherence be expressed or remain tacit? And supposing that at some times it should be tacit and at other times expressed, in which of these two cases do I find myself *at this very moment?* Of course, we have the obligation to accept the truth. However, this obligation is relative to the circumstances, for it is never a question of Truth with a capital *T*, of single Truth, of abstract Truth; it is always a matter of "concrete truths" that are more or less expedient depending on the case.[6] If we suppose, on the contrary, that truth is purely objective, it will leave man completely indifferent. To attribute to truth an "independence" with respect to human ends, to assign it an "absolute character" that separates it from life, is to "dehumanize" knowledge.[7]

If one conceives of this idea of a purely objective and impersonal truth, one admits the presence of a very special faculty in man—that is, pure intellect, which has as its function, precisely, to go to truth in a spontaneous and almost mechanical movement, to think truth solely for the sake of thinking and contemplating it. In order to explain how truth, itself extra-human, can be related to man, we assume in him an extra-human faculty for conceiving it, a faculty foreign to all the other factors of life. The pragmatists say, however: "We deny that properly speaking such a thing as pure or mere intellection can occur. What is loosely so called is really also purposive thought pursuing what seems to it a desirable end."[8] According to them, there is no impersonal reason in us, there is an intellect that is a living function and is in close relation to all the other living functions that make up our thought. Far from being impersonal, it shares in all the particularity of consciousness. When we seek the truth, it is always with a goal in mind. Truth can be determined only by means of selection and choice; and it is human interest that determines this choice. According to Schiller, "the development of a mind is a thoroughly *personal* affair. Potential knowledge becomes actual, because of the purposive activity of a Knower who brings it to bear on his interests, and uses it to realize his ends."[9]

One can also say, however, that the pure intellect is in itself a source of pleasure. Just as there is, as Kant admits, a sort of rational sensitivity, a joy that we feel in submitting ourselves to law, so is there a particular pleasure in seeking, discovering, and contemplating truth. This contemplative conception of truth is characteristic of all dogmatism. The pragmatists claim[10] that the idea that the intellect serves only to procure this pleasure is an absurd conception, unless one sees in it a simple game for the amusement of those who are capable of such pleasure. Our intellectual activity cannot, of course, always be in a state of tension. It must relax; there must be moments when the intellect amuses itself in order to rest from the fatigue caused by the assiduous search for truth. This is the pleasure of dreams, of imagination, of disinterested meditation. This play must have only a limited place in our life, however, for it is as susceptible to excess as any other game. It cannot be the principle and constant goal of the intellect, "which is intended for serious work." Its role is best seen in its practical function (in the broadest sense of the term), in its relations with reality. All pragmatists are in agreement on this point: Truth is human; the intellect cannot be isolated from life, nor logic from psychology. James, as well as Schiller, and even Dewey (although Dewey admits the necessity of a certain control of the personal element) refuse to separate these two sciences.[11] According to them, all fundamental logical notions start from psychological processes. Thus truth must be attached to our "interests" as men: truth is made for the life of man.

Ideal Truth and Concrete Truths

There is a new difficulty. If truth is impersonal, if it consists of a system of ideals such as Plato's "Ideas," it must be the same for all men; it must be immutable and unique. One cannot perceive it; but once one attains it, one can see it only as it is: one, identical, and invariable. Concerning such a truth, the pragmatists observe that it contrasts singularly with the truths which men actually attain. Human truths are fugitive, temporary, and perpetually in the process of transformation. Today's truth is tomorrow's error. Can one say that in the course of time truths tend to become fixed? The opposite is more nearly true. Before the sciences were established, the acknowledged truths were almost unchangeable for centuries. Certainly, religious truths did not change, at least for the faithful. It is with the growth of science that we see the emergence of diversity and change. Not so long ago, of course, it was still believed that there existed, at least in science, only one truth; it was even believed that science brings us the truth, whole and definitive. But today we know that this is not so.

> . . . The enormously rapid multiplication of theories in these latter days has well-nigh upset the notion of any one of them being a more literally objective kind of thing than another. There are so many geometries, so many logics, so many physical and chemical hypotheses, so many classifications, each one of them good for so much and yet not good for everything, that the notion that even the truest formula may be a human device and not a literal transcript has dawned upon us.[12]

Truth is thus a living thing that changes ceaselessly; and the more we advance, the clearer this life of truth becomes. A truth that ceased to be flexible and malleable would be no more than "the dead heart of the living tree."[13]

What a change is involved in the shift from the ideal,

immutable truth of dogmatism to the real, concrete truths that we live! Their characters are diametrically opposed. The former can only discredit the latter, since the ideal truth is sufficient in itself. But ideal truth is inaccessible to us. Thus we tend to lose interest in the real truths since they seem to be of little consequence when compared to ideal truth. Intransigent rationalism risks ending up in skepticism,[14] since it places its ideal too high, at a level where we cannot attain it.

Let us see, for that matter, whether the very nature of reality permits us to attribute this unity and fixity to truth. Reality includes both mind and things. And by what are minds[15] characterized if not by their extreme diversity? A single understanding, common to all, does not exist; what exists are understandings that differ greatly from each other. Hence if truth is one, the diversity of minds can only prevent men from discovering this truth that is always one and identical with itself. On the other hand, why are minds so diverse? We have just seen that this diversity is an obstacle to the perfect communion of all men in one truth. Why does it exist if the ideal is an essentially impersonal truth? This dilemma is the source of "logical sin," as well as of moral sin, and it remains totally inexplicable (in Leibnitz' doctrine, in particular, where the plurality of monads raises an insoluble problem).

Is it not simpler and more logical to say that the diversity of minds corresponds to a diversity in truth and in reality itself? "What right have we," asks Schiller, "to assume that even ultimate 'truth' must be one and the same for all? . . . why should not the 'truth,' too . . . adjust itself to the differences of individual experience . . . ?"[16] Why not admit that what is true for one is not necessarily so for another, and, thus, that truth is something much more complex than current rationalism admits? Here, the pragmatists gives us some examples that do not always prove their point, to be sure. Such is the example that Schiller offers us:[17] The judgment, "this is an armchair," can be true for me and not for another; if I am looking for something in which to sit, the armchair is true for me in its function as a seat; but this may not be true, or may be true in a different way, for somebody else—an antique dealer or collector for instance—who sees in it "a piece of antique, ornamental furniture."

According to the pragmatists, the final difficulty presented by the dogmatic conception is that when one admits that there is a single truth, when one does not understand that there is a reason for the diversity of judgment and opinions, one runs the risk of ending up in intolerance. That man has true tolerance who not only admits that among thoughts there are differences that must be respected and that one does not have the right to do violence to the consciences of people, but who also understands that the diversity of opinions and beliefs corresponds to a necessity, to the requirements of affective, intellectual life. In short, the truly tolerant man recognizes that if these divergencies exist, it is good that they do.

Thus pragmatism is very much alive to the diversity of minds and the living character of truth. But it fails to explain them. It runs headlong into a problem of general philosophy which goes far beyond it: Why are there individuals? What is the reason for the existence of the diversity of minds?

1. Lecture of December 23, 1913.

2. F. C. S. Schiller, *Studies in Humanism* (London: Macmillan & Co., Ltd., 1907), Essay II, p. 58.

3. London: Longmans, Green & Co., Ltd., 1909, p. 114.

4. John Dewey, *Studies in Logical Theory* (Chicago: University of Chicago Press, 1903), Essay VI, p. 141. Chapter vi, from which the quotation is taken, is not by Dewey himself, but by one of his collaborators, Simon Fraser McLennan. For a statement by Dewey himself, see Chap. iv, particularly pp. 71-72.

5. Here we have reproduced almost exactly the text of one of our two versions. The other, which has more serious gaps, resembles it very closely. The last sentence is common to the two versions.

6. Cf. James, *op. cit.,* Chap. viii.

7. Cf. Schiller, *op. cit.,* Essay II, p. 69.

8. *Ibid.,* Essay IV, p. 128.

9. *Ibid.,* Essay VII, p. 186.

10. *Ibid.,* Essay I, p. 7.

11. Cf. particularly James, *op. cit.,* p. 153; Schiller, *op. cit.,* Essay III; Schiller, "Psychology and Knowledge," *Mind,* XVI (1907), 244-48; and Dewey, *op. cit.,* pp. 14-15, 185 ff.

12. James, *op. cit.,* p. 58.

13. James, *Pragmatism* (London: Longmans, Green & Co., Ltd., 1907), p. 65.

14. Cf. *ibid.*, pp. 182, 198-99; and Schiller, *Studies in Humanism,* Essay III, p. 73, Essay VIII, etc.

15. With respect to "things," cf. the fourth lecture.

16. *Studies in Humanism,* Essay XVI, p. 360.

17. *Ibid.,* Essay VII, pp. 191-92.

FOURTH LECTURE[1]

CRITICISM OF DOGMATISM *(Continued)*

The Static Conception of Reality

Let us sum up what we have said thus far. (1) If truth is impersonal, it is foreign to man; it is dehumanized and located outside of our lives. (2) If truth is the same for all men, it is impossible to understand the reason for the existence of the diversity of minds, which, nevertheless, must have a function in general life. (3) If truth is identical for all, conformity becomes the rule and dissidence is an evil—and "logical evil" can be explained no better than moral evil.

Let us add that if one represents truth as the rationalists do—as something that is static, immutable in time and space, and the expression of reality—then reality, too, must be conceived of as eternally remaining in a stationary state. If, on the contrary, reality is something alive that continuously changes and engenders something new, truth must follow it in its transformations, and must also change and live.

But it can be asked, Why does reality change? Where does this change come from? If the universe is tending toward something, it is because it lacks something: it is not yet completely reality. Perhaps this change is only illusory, and novelty only appears to be new. It is easy to reply that what is referred to as "illusory" is precisely everything that gives life its interest. To deny or to diminish the reality of change is to eliminate everything that attaches us to things, and to depreciate both their value and the way they affect us. Yet this static conception of reality is so current that we find it even in the writings of those who, it seems to us, should be following a different orientation—an evolutionist like Herbert Spencer, for example. Although Spencer starts from a principle that should have led him to recognize universal change, he depends on such notions as the indestructibility of matter and the conservation of energy, notions which are fundamentally incapable of justifying the conception of real progress or real change in the true meaning of the word.[2] As a result, the change in his system is only apparent; the basis of things always remains the same; and the homogeneity of the universe is restored, "neither richer nor poorer, neither better nor worse."

It is very difficult to rely on a conception which, if pushed to its logical consequences, leads us back to the notion of a reality that is always the same, a notion that can only end in an attitude of detachment from existence. It has been said that the conclusion that one might draw from this notion is that we ourselves are only illusions and transitory appearances and that this is the reason why we attach so much value to something which is merely illusory and passing. But does this not amount to recognizing, in a sense, the reality of what is called illusory? Does it not give a meaning to these so-called appearances?[3]

Our inclination to represent everything under the aspect of immutability is actually only an expediency. It is a means of giving the mind a sort of intellectual security. There are intellects that feel the need to base themselves on something fixed, to have a clearly drawn line of conduct that admits neither hesitation nor doubt, to tell themselves that there are no two ways of acting and thus no necessity to find out which of them is better. Such intellects need a ready-made discipline, a pre-established truth and code of laws. Otherwise they feel disoriented. All change, risk, and attempts at exploration cause them disquiet and uneasiness. Hence the tendency to believe in immutable truth and immutable realities is wholly natural. According to the pragmatists, this is the attitude that is characteristic of the rationalist mind: it represents a need for stability and assurance—in short, for repose.

But at what price, say the pragmatists, is this assurance bought! It quiets us, but it removes the reality of life, it impoverishes life by simplifying it, and the means by which it is obtained is purely illusory. For that matter, what difference does it make whether there is a code of laws written in advance, a predetermined truth? We should still have to discover these laws, and in this sense they would still be of our making. We must discover them with our human faculties, and we must use them with our human forces. For this we can count on no one but ourselves. We are abandoned to ourselves on the "raft of our experience," and even if there were "absolute sailing-directions," the only assurance we have of our being able to follow them lies "in our human equipment." Human caprice and, along with it, human error are always possible. "All the sanctions of a law of truth lie in the very texture of experience. Absolute or no absolute, the concrete truth *for us* will always be that way of thinking in which our various experiences most profitably combine."[4]

The feeling that dominates pragmatism is thus the very opposite of that which inspires dogmatism. It is the feeling for everything that is variable and plastic in things. For it, the universe is something unfinished, something never completely realized; there is a gap between what is and what will be, just as between what is and what was. The world is rich with limitless possibilities, which will appear as circumstances permit. *"For rationalism,"* James says, *"reality is ready-made and completed from all eternity, while for pragmatism it is still in the making, and waits part of its completion from the future.* On the one side, the universe is absolutely secure, on the other it is still pursuing its adventures."[5] And the novelties that can be produced in this way not only concern superficial details, but may also affect the essential.

The principal factor of novelty in the world is consciousness. As soon as consciousnes appears, it introduces something new. Take, for instance, the constellation of the Big Bear.[6] Who made out seven stars in it and counted them? Who noticed its very vague resemblance to the form of an animal? Doubtless, it was man. Of course, we can say that before he did these things, there were the seven stars arranged in this way. But their number and their arrangement were only implicit or virtual. One condition was missing, and this condition was "the act of the mind that counts and compares." Man seems to be limited to translating, to discovering. But in a sense, he also adds and creates: he creates the number seven; he creates the resemblance.

His thought is not a *copy* of the real: it is a true *creation*.

This novelty that the mind contributes is still more apparent where the future is concerned. In this case, our judgments become generators of acts that change the character of future reality. This is particularly true of the representations that precede important acts, that is, beliefs.[7] Belief creates reality itself: belief in success is the best condition for succeeding; belief that one is in good health is a condition for feeling well. Here, thought is not an expression of what is; it is a factor in the reality that is to come. Consequently, reality itself is not something congealed and arrested, something enclosed within unsurmountable barriers. Reality advances ceaselessly with human experience. To the degree that experience extends, it encroaches on the void and is itself enriched. From this arises an essential idea on which all pragmatism rests: thought, tied to action, in a sense, creates reality itself.

This idea is important. The physical world doubtless seems to have reached a sort of equilibrium. We no longer witness the genesis of new species of living beings. Such creations are always taking place in the moral realm, however.[8] All human societies, far from remaining always identical with themselves, are forces that develop. More complex societies in which new forces arise are appearing. We see these forces at work in the present, although we can no longer visualize them in the past except as static. Be this as it may, there is a whole domain of reality that has manifestly been created by thought: social reality. And this example is certainly the most significant that can be cited.

Thus it is understandable that, since reality is not something completed, truth is not something immutable. Truth is not a ready-made system: it is formed, deformed, and re-formed in a thousand ways; it varies and evolves like all things human. In order to make this idea understood, James compares truth to law or justice, to language or grammar. Magistrates and professors sometimes seem to believe that there is only one justice, one code of laws, one truth: the Truth. In reality, according to James, "Truth, law, language fairly boil away from them at the least touch of novel fact. Our rights, wrongs, prohibitions, penalties, words, forms, idioms, beliefs, are so many new creations that add themselves as fast as history proceeds."[9] They are things becoming, not things ready-made; and it is the same with truth as with the rest: truth is an uninterrupted process of changes.

Some remarks are necessary here. The pragmatists are good at showing us how truth is enriched and becomes more complex. But does it necessarily follow that truth changes, properly speaking? If, for example, new species develop, are the laws of life changed thereby? In the same way, it is certain that new social species have appeared; but does this give us the right to conclude from this that the laws of life in society are no longer the same? Let us not confuse the enrichment of truth (or of reality) with the futility of truth. Pragmatism is alive to the fact that what is true for one time may not be true for another. But how inconclusive are its proofs! We said before that its representatives have never forced themselves to give a systematic exposition. Very similar arguments that seem to come to the same conclusion are expounded separately, and the same example is couched sometimes in one form, sometimes in another. Nevertheless, it is the feeling that animates pragmatism, more than its modes of argument, that we are particularly interested in. Pragmatism has always had an intense feeling for the diversity of minds and the variability of thought in time. Hence the diversity of names by which it has designated itself: pragmatism, humanism, pluralism, and so on.

The Pluralist Conception of Reality

The implication of this last point is quite clear. What has preceded shows us that the debate between pragmatism and rationalism involves, according to James,[10] not only the theory of knowledge but also the manner in which "the structure of the universe itself" is conceived. The same antithesis that exists between the static truth of the rationalists and the fugitive truth that is dear to the pragmatists, also exists between the monist and pluralist conceptions of the universe. If the universe is actually *one* in the sense that it forms a closely linked system, all the elements of which imply each other, a system where the whole commands the existence of the parts and where individuals are only appearances that in sum constitute one being, then change is impossible. For the place of each element is determined by the whole, and the whole, in turn, is determined by the elements. This is the monist point of view.

Why, James asks, is there this superstition, this religion of the number "one"?[11] In what way is "one" superior to "forty-three," for example? Moreover, there are many ways of conceiving of this unity. There is no doubt that in one sense, the world is one. But why would it not be one, as it is from the pluralist point of view, in the sense that it is made up of parts which are linked to each other by certain relationships, but which, nevertheless, remain distinct and retain a certain independence, a certain autonomy, so that there is room for change, diversity, and contingency?

Let us place ourselves in the pragmatist position and consult facts and experience.[12] To begin with, we see that the world is one in the sense that it is the object of a representation: it is one for thought and discourse. But this in no way leads us to monism; for, in this sense, chaos, once it is named, has as much unity as cosmos. The world is also one in the sense that all of its parts are continuous[13] in space and time, but this unity is completely external: for pragmatism, space and time are only "instruments of continuity." A more profound unity results from the internal actions and reactions, from the influences that each part of the world exercises on the other parts. The propagation of heat, electricity, and light are examples of these influences that unite everything in the physical world. Thus there is an infinity of networks that are made up of various "lines of influence," networks that are little worlds that serve as a basis for our action. Many things, however, fall outside these lines of influence. In addition, we must choose suitable intermediaries. If, for example, we insert a substance that is a poor conductor into an electrical circuit, the current either does not pass or must make a detour, leaving the substance outside its path. James says that such networks also exist in the moral world. Men are enmeshed in vast networks of social relations. Suppose that A knows B, B knows C, and C knows D: it is then possible to get a message from A to D. But here, too, we are stopped short when we make a bad choice in one of our intermediaries. If by chance B does not know C, the message does not arrive at its destination. There are also lines of sympathy that spread and develop and are organized in different groups. The more a society evolves, the more these lines of sympathy organize themselves and the more they multiply. Thus in every society, there are systems that link individuals to each other—religious systems, professional groups, and so on—and these links cause moral forces to communicate themselves to all members of the group.[14] Sometimes, as in economic relations, this communication is more capricious than at other times. But each group is foreign to the others, so that a society that is one in appearance, is, in reality, composed of a multitude of small groups or small social worlds that, although they sometimes cross each other, live their own lives and remain basically external to one another.

From this we see in what unity and plurality consist for the pragmatists. There is a unity for them, but it is not that of the monists. The world is made up of an incalculable number of networks that unite things and beings with each other. These networks are formed of complicated and relatively independent links. The elements that they connect are not fixed, and the very form of the network is subject to change. Made up of a plurality of small systems, each of which is endowed with an autonomous life, it is ceaselessly formed, deformed, and transformed.

The pluralism of the pragmatists is thus opposed to the monism of the rationalists. For the former, multiplicity is as real as unity: there is both union and disjunction. The "all-form" exists, according to James,[15] but "the each-form," the particular form of each element, "is logically as acceptable and empirically as probable." Indeed, there is an "all," but in this "all" there is a certain free play. The world is a federal republic that leaves a large degree of autonomy to each of its parts; it is not a monarchial society. For example, we can visualize the physical universe as a world in which all things are inert; then, above it, we can envisage a world in which there is only mechanical action, a world of forces, and so on. In the same way, we can conceive of conscious beings doing completely without each other, or of men loving or hating reciprocally; finally, we can imagine all minds entering into communication, intermixing completely. The unity becomes more complete, and yet it always remains partial, relative, and progressive. The world is not, James indicates,[16] anything rigid, limited, and bureaucratic; it does not have the beautiful order that the rationalists perceive in it—the rationalist for whom the pragmatists' world is "a tramp and vagrant world, adrift in space."

In spite of the interest of this argument, one may wonder if it meets what is essential in rationalism. Rationalism admits that the function of truth is to translate reality. Pragmatism tries to show that reality is neither immutable nor the same for all persons, and it concludes that truth cannot be a copy of reality. But why would the copy not evolve like the model? In order to prove that it does not, it would have to be demonstrated that thought cannot be a copy, not only of an immutable reality, but of any reality whatever. It would have to be proved, in other words, that there is a fundamental heterogeneity between reality and thought. The pragmatists have not demonstrated this.[17]

In the last years of his life, however, James gleaned such a demonstration from the works of Bergson. In Bergson, whom he considered the destroyer of intellectualism, James believed that he found his best arguments.

1. Lecture of January 6, 1914.

2. Schiller, *Studies in Humanism* (London: Macmillan Co., 1907), Essay IX, pp. 225-27.

3. Durkheim is alluding to Schiller's criticism of the "appearance-reality" antithesis as it is found in the writings of F. H. Bradley and his disciple A. E. Taylor; cf. *Studies in Humanism*, pp. 239 ff.

4. James, *The Meaning of Truth* (London: Longmans, Green & Co., Ltd., 1909), pp. 71, 72, 73.

5. *Pragmatism* (London: Longmans, Green & Co., Ltd., 1907), p. 257.

6. *The Meaning of Truth*, pp. 92 f.; cf. *Pragmatism*, p. 252.

7. Cf. James, *The Will to Believe* (London: Longmans, Green & Co., Ltd., 1896).

8. Obviously, this commentary expresses not only the pragmatists' thought but also Durkheim's own. Cf. the fourteenth lecture.

9. *Pragmatism,* pp. 241-42.

10. *Ibid.,* p. 259.

11. *Ibid.,* p. 128.

12. Here Durkheim is summarizing Lecture IV of *Pragmatism.*

13. In our two versions, the word is *contiguous.* We have re-established the text of James's lesson.

14. Here Durkheim is giving a loose interpretation of *Pragmatism,* pp. 140 ff.

15. *A Pluralistic Universe* (London: Longmans, Green & Co., Ltd., 1909), p. 34. Cf. *ibid.,* Lecture V and pp. 324-25.

16. *Pragmatism,* p. 260.

17. Cf. the twentieth lecture.

FIFTH LECTURE[1]

PRAGMATISM AND THE CRITICISM OF CONCEPTUAL THOUGHT

Pragmatist criticism, as I said, does not seem to have pushed through to the central principle of rationalism. This criticism mainly attacks the notion of the copy theory of truth. But why, we have asked, should true thought not be the variable copy of a variable model? And, in addition, is it quite so evident that a copy, as a duplicate of reality, is useless? It is not a question, actually, of knowing whether it is useful, but of knowing whether it is true. At the end of the last lecture, I said that in order to establish the pragmatist thesis, it would be necessary to prove that thought and reality are essentially heterogeneous. James attempted this demonstration in Chapter vi of *A Pluralistic Universe,* basing it on Bergson's arguments. This chapter is entitled "Bergson and His Critique of Intellectualism."

Let us examine these arguments as he presents them. According to James, truth presupposes judgments, and judgments presuppose concepts. Thus it is apparently conceptual thought, and it alone, that can be the generator of truth. But in order for this to be the case, there must be a natural affinity between the concept and the things. For James, on the contrary, as for Bergson, the real and the concept have opposite characteristics.

1. The concept[2] is something definite and distinct; it is the

420

very opposite of such vague, shifting, and confused representations as images. Cut out from the stream of our experience, the concept is circumscribed within very narrow limits. Whereas impressions mutually interpenetrate each other in the sensory flux of images, concepts are isolated from each other. There is no contact or confusion among them, such as that which takes place among images.

2. Each concept expresses one aspect of things and only that aspect. Doubtless there are concepts that express things or groups of things, but these are compound concepts. The true and pure concept is simple. It is analagous to what Descartes calls the object of intuition; one moves toward it but never reaches it. In everyday life, of course, we use complex, vaguely contoured concepts, which have not been systematically defined. But the concept, properly speaking, requires definition and limitation, so that when we use it we think it alone and nothing else. The characteristic feature of the concept is to be an isolated representation, because it must express only one thing or one aspect of the thing, one condition, one element.

3. Because concepts have this character, the principle of identity or non-contradiction dominates all of conceptual life: "For conceptual logic, the same is nothing but the same, and all sames with a third thing are the same with each other."[3] The concept is what it is and cannot be anything else. Consequently, in order for conceptual thought to be a copy of reality, reality must be constituted according to the same model, that is to say, it must be made up of stable elements that are entirely distinct from each other and have no reciprocal communication; and things themselves must have the same discontinuous, finite, and separate character. But, says James, nature presents diametrically opposed characteristics: reality is continuous and ceaselessly in formation. "What really *exists,* I repeat, is not things made but things in the making. Once made, they are dead; an infinite number of alternative conceptual decompositions can be used in defining them."[4] If we admit even for an instant that reality consists of stable and distinct elements, how can we tell the number of these elements? In order to be consistent, the rationalists must recognize that this number is infinite, and consequently, that the number of concepts necessary to trans-

late these elements, too, is infinite. But since an infinite number cannot be an actual, real thing, no movement can ever be completed. If a moving object must traverse an infinite number of points, it will never reach the end, since the end always remains outside the series. (This is the old argument of Achilles and the tortoise which was developed by Zeno.) Thus the universe is condemned to immobility.

Yet movement and change do take place. This paradox is bothersome, says James, only if the succession of degrees of change is really divisible by the infinite. But change does not take place in this fashion, by an infinity of infinitesimal modifications; it is rather accomplished by units of a certain size, of a certain extent, that is, by finite quantities. If, when we empty a bottle, it were necessary for its contents to undergo an infinite number of successive diminutions, the operation would never end. The bottle is emptied by a finite number of diminutions, each of a finite quantity. "Either a whole drop emerges or nothing emerges from the spout." It is thus, "by a growing series of distinct pulsations," that change takes place in the world; and every time one of these "pulsations" takes place, we say, "here is something more" or "here is something less." The discontinuity is still more evident when something new appears or something old disappears. "Fechner's term of the 'threshold,' which has played such a part in the psychology of perception, is only one way of naming the quantitative discreteness in the change of all our sensible experiences."[5]

Does James's argument really meet intellectualism? We may well doubt it. The greatest contemporary rationalist, Charles Renouvier, who has demonstrated the impossibility of an actual infinity of parts, takes up Zeno's arguments.[6] Thus to insist on this impossibility is not necessarily to ruin intellectualism. Moreover, the question is secondary. It is much less important to know whether the number of parts making up the world is finite or infinite than it is to know whether these parts are, or are not, distinct.

What are James's arguments on this point? According to him, concepts are something stable. In order to express movement and change, each concept would have to express one of the states through which the movement passes. But to resolve the movement into states is to make of it something fixed. The concept can therefore express movement only by stopping it at a given instant, by immobilizing it.[7] The only way of making concepts coincide with change is to stipulate arbitrarily the points at which the change stops, since it is only these stopping points that our concepts can express. But all we obtain in this way is a discontinuous series of positions and dates, with which it is impossible to reconstitute movement and change. In the first place, a series of concepts that expresses pauses or stops cannot translate what moves. This is the old argument of the Eleatic school: the arrow in flight is motionless because if we consider a position of the arrow at any given moment in its course, this position is necessarily a state of rest. In the second place, if concepts are to be capable of expressing change, change will have to be divided up and fragmented into discontinuous elements. But how can we make the discontinuous over into the continuous? How can we reconstitute the unity of change once this unity is broken? A void, however small it may be, separates concepts that express a position or state of something changing; and this void is impossible to fill. In this way we obtain only "a retrospective patchwork, a post-mortem dissection."[8]

This is all the more serious because what changes is the very soul of things, the essential. Concepts can give us a "synoptic picture" of phenomena; but the metaphysician who is trying to grasp reality in depth, whose curiosity bears on the intimate nature of things and on that which moves them, will have to turn his back on concepts. Thus conceptual thought operates only on the surface of things; it is incapable of penetrating reality.[9]

Here is another way of representing the same idea: What makes up the reality of things is the web of influences they exercise on each other. My thought acts on my body; it animates it. A gesture of my body exteriorizes this thought, and by means of this intermediary my thought communicates with that of others. James writes that things must be able to combine, to "compenetrate and telescope."[10] But, he says, "Intellectualism denies . . . that finite things can act on one another, for all things, once translated into concepts, remain shut up to themselves."[11] Concepts "make the whole notion of a casual influence between finite things incomprehensible."[12] From the point of view of conceptual logic, all distinctions are "isolators." Contagion of concepts would be confusion, and confusion is the logical sin par excellence.

There is an even better reason why life cannot be converted into concepts: "The essence of life is its continuously changing character."[13] A living being is a being who not only is, at a given moment, different from what he was before, but also one who is, at the same instant, himself and different from himself. The Achilles who is pursuing the tortoise is not only the being who, at a given moment, coincides with a certain determined space; he is also the being who is dashing, and this dash is a concrete fact in which the moments of time and the divisions of space are individually involved: "End and beginning come for him in the one onrush."[14]

But it is not life alone that is made up of a web of actions and relationships. Let us consider any being whatever: It is constituted of a group of traits, among all of which and in the whole of which there is solidarity; any one of them can be isolated only artificially. Furthermore, its present can be isolated from its past and future only to a very small degree. The same is true for things. There is no one unique concept of a thing. Each thing includes a plurality of elements; and each element, a plurality of elements.

What is the result of all this? Conceptual thought lives by distinctions, while the world is continuous; and the continuous is vague and confused. This antithesis explains the great prestige that has been given to concepts. Conceptual thought is in love with fixity and hence with precision and clarity; it is very aloof to all that is fleeting. "The ruling tradition in philosophy has always been the platonic and aristotelean belief that fixity is a nobler and worthier thing than change. Reality must be one and unalterable. Concepts, being themselves fixities, agree best with this fixed nature of truth. . . ."[15] When it had succeeded in establishing a system of these immobile concepts, philosophic thought experienced great self-admiration and believed that it had created truth itself. It was Plato's illusion to believe that above this changing and fleeting world there exists a world of fixed and immutable essences. He was taking fiction for reality. Inevitably, James says, "Logic being the lesser thing . . . must succumb to reality."[16] We must bow before the facts; reality must win out over reason. And the result of this chain of reasoning, too, is that the principle of identity and the law of non-contradiction do not apply to reality.[17]

DEFICIENCIES OF THIS CRITICISM

The gravity of this consequence helps us to perceive a deficiency no less grave in James's thought. He does not explain to us how it happens that logical thought, based on the principle of identity, can serve to guide us in the midst of things to which, according to him, the principle of identity does not apply. Actually, none of the pragmatists really thinks that conceptual thought is useless, even though it is not a copy reality. James says that it is largely inspired by "the interests of practice."[18] But how can conceptual thought play this role if it is incommensurate with reality? Moreover, James himself recognizes that these concepts, "cut out from the sensible flux of the past . . . give us knowledge" and have "some theoretic value."[19] It is, in fact, very difficult to escape concepts and logical principles. When James tells us that one cannot make something continuous from something discontinuous, is he not using a logical principle? Is he not affirming with the aid of conceptual thought something that touches on reality itself?[20]

To a very great extent, James bases this whole argument on developments in Bergson. The positive conclusions at which the two men arrive are not identical, but their attitude toward classic rationalism is the same. Both have the same hypersensitivity to everything that is mobile in things, the same tendency to present reality in its obscure and fleeting perspective, the same inclination to subordinate clear and distinct thought to the troubled aspect of things. But the main thing that James has borrowed from Bergson is the form of argumentation that directly challenges conceptual thought. His fundamental ideas had already been in his thought for a long time, as is shown by his earlier *Principles of Psychology,* where he insisted, for example, on the perfect continuity of the "stream" of consciousness.[21]

1. Lecture of January 13, 1914.

2. Cf. James, the three studies, "Percept and Concept," *Some Problems of Philosophy* ([published posthumously] London: Longmans, Green & Co., Ltd., 1911), Chaps. iv, v, and vi, pp. 47-112.

3. James, *A Pluralistic Universe* (London: Longmans, Green & Co., Ltd., 1909), p. 257.

4. *Ibid.*, p. 263.

5. *Ibid.*, pp. 231-32.

6. Cf. Renouvier, *Essais de critique générale* (Paris: Armand Colin, 1912), XI, 42-49. James himself eulogizes Renouvier in *Some Problems of Philosophy*, p. 165 n.

7. *Some Problems of Philosophy*, Chap. v, pp. 81-83, 87-88, etc.

8. *A Pluralistic Universe*, p. 262.

9. Cf. *ibid.*, pp. 251-52. The argument is very much like Bergson's. Cf. *ibid.*, pp. 237-43, where James declares that before Bergson, "rationalism had never been seriously questioned" (p. 237). "Bergson alone has been radical" (p. 238); he alone "challenges the theoretical authority in principle" of conceptual or intellectualist logic (p. 243).

10. *Ibid.*, p. 257.

11. *Ibid.*, pp. 258-59.

12. *Ibid.*, p. 246.

13. *Ibid.*, p. 253.

14. *Ibid.*, pp. 255-56.

15. *Ibid.*, p. 237; cf. James, *The Meaning of Truth* (London: Longmans, Green & Co., Ltd., 1909), p. 247.

16. *A Pluralistic Universe*, p. 207.

17. Cf. the twentieth lecture.

18. *A Pluralistic Universe*, p. 244; cf. pp. 247-48.

19. *Ibid.*, p. 246.

20. In the note that completes the sixth lecture at the end of *A Pluralistic Universe*, James tries to defend Bergson for having himself used "a system of concepts" in order to give us a profounder view of reality than that of the rationalists.

21. In "The Stream of Thought" (Chap. ix), *Principles of Psychology* (New York: Henry Holt & Co., Inc., 1890), Vol. I.

THIRTEENTH LECTURE

GENERAL CRITICISM OF PRAGMATISM

We can now move on to the general discussion of pragmatist doctrines.

They can, first of all, be reproached for certain gaps. As I have already pointed out,[1] the pragmatists too often take liberties with historical doctrines. They interpret them as they wish, and often very inexactly.

Above all, however, we must indicate the abstract character of their argument since it clashes with the general orientation of their doctrine, which they claim is empirical. Most of the time, their proofs have a dialectical character; everything is reduced to a purely logical construction. This constitutes one contradiction.

But their thought presents other flagrant contradictions. Here is an example: On the one hand, we are told that consciousness as such does not exist, that it is nothing original, that it is neither a factor *sui generis* nor a true reality, but is only a simple echo, a "vain noise" left behind by the "soul" that has vanished from the heaven of philosophy.[2] This, as we know, is the theme of the famous paper, "Does Consciousness Exist?" a theme which James took up again in the form of a communication in French to the congress of 1905.[3] On the other hand, however, the pragmatists maintain that reality is a construction of thought, that apperception itself is reality.[4] In so doing they attribute to thought the same power and the same qualities that the idealists ascribe to it. Consequently, they argue both epiphenomenalism and idealism—two theses that are incompatible. Therefore, pragmatism lacks the fundamental characteristics that one has the right to demand of a philosophic doctrine.

Here we must ask ourselves a question: How does it happen that, with such defects, pragmatism has imposed itself on so many minds? It must be based on something in the human consciousness; it must have a strength that we have yet to discover.

THE FUNDAMENTAL MOTIVATION OF THE PRAGMATIST ATTITUDE

Let us ask ourselves, then, what feeling animates the doctrine, what motivation is its essential factor. I have said already that

427

it is not a practical need, a need to extend the field of human action. There is, to be sure, particularly in James, a taste for risk, a need for adventure; he prefers an uncertain, "malleable" world to a fixed world, because it is a world in which there is something to do; this is certainly the ideal of the strong man who wishes to expand the field of his activity. But how, then, can the same philosopher show us as an ideal the ascetic who renounces the world and turns away from it?

Actually, pragmatism is not concerned with designing a particular ideal for us. Its dominant factor is the need to soften the truth, to make it less rigid, as James says—to free it, in short, from the discipline of logical thought. This appears very clearly in James's *The Will to Believe*. With this in mind, everything becomes clear. If thought had as its object simply to "reproduce" reality, it would be the slave of things; it would be chained to reality. It would have nothing to do but to copy servilely the reality that it has before it. If thought is to be freed, it must become the creator of its own object; and the only way to attain this goal is to give it a reality that it has to make or construct itself. Therefore, thought has as its aim not the reproduction of a given reality but the construction of a future reality. It follows that the value of ideas can no longer be assessed by reference to objects but must be determined by the degree of their utility, their more or less "advantageous" character.

In this we perceive the scope of the pragmatist theses. If, in classical rationalism, thought has this character of "rigidity," for which pragmatism reproaches it, it is because in rationalism truth is conceived of as a simple thing, a thing almost divine, that draws its whole value from itself. Since it is sufficient unto itself, it is necessarily placed above human life. It cannot bow to the demands of circumstances and differing temperaments. It is valid by itself and is good with an absolute goodness. It does not exist for us, but for itself. Its role is to let itself be contemplated. It is almost deified; it becomes the object of a true cult. This is Plato's conception. It extends to the faculty by means of which we attain truth, that is, reason. Reason serves to explain things to us, but, in this conception, itself remains unexplained; it is placed outside scientific analysis.

"To soften" the truth is to take from it this absolute and almost sacrosanct character. It is to tear it away from this state of immobility that removes it from all evolution, from all change, and, consequently, from all explanation. We are asked to imagine that instead of being thus confined in a separate world, it is itself part of reality and life—not by a kind of fall or degradation that would disfigure and corrupt it, but because it is naturally part of reality and life.[5] It is placed in the series of facts, at the very core of things having antecedents and consequences. It poses problems: we are authorized to ask ourselves where it comes from, what good it does, and so on. It itself becomes an object of science. Here lies the interest of the pragmatist enterprise: it is an effort to understand truth and reason themselves, to restore to them their human interest, to make of them human things that derive from temporal causes and engender temporal consequences. To "soften" truth is to make it into something that can be analyzed and explained.

It is here that we can establish a parallel between pragmatism and sociology. By applying the historical point of view to the order of things human, sociology is led to pose the same problem. Man is a product of history and hence of a "becoming"; there is nothing in him that is either given or defined in advance. History begins nowhere and it ends nowhere. Everything in man has been made by mankind in the course of time. Consequently, if truth is human, it is also a human product. Sociology applies the same conception to reason. All that constitutes reason, its principles and categories, is made in the course of history.

Everything is a product of certain causes. Phenomena must not be represented in closed series: things have a "circular" character, and analysis can be prolonged to infinity. This is why I cannot accept the statement of the idealists that in the beginning there is thought, nor that of the pragmatists that in the beginning there is action.

But if sociology poses the problem in the same sense as pragmatism, it is in a better position to solve it. Pragmatism, in fact, claims to explain truth psychologically and subjectively. However, the nature of the individual is too limited to explain by itself alone all things human. Therefore, if we envisage individual elements alone, we are led to underestimate the amplitude of the effects that we have to account for. How could reason, in particular, have developed in the course of the experiences undergone by a single individual? Sociology permits us broader explanations. For it, truth, reason, and morality are the results of a becoming that covers the entire unfolding of human history.

Thus we see the advantage of the sociological over the pragmatist point of view. For the pragmatist philosophers, as we have said several times before, experience can take place on one level only. Reason is placed on the same plane as sensitivity; truth, on the same plane as sensations and instincts. But men have always recognized in truth something that in certain respects imposes itself on us, something that is independent of the facts of sensitivity and individual impulse. Such a universally held conception of truth must correspond to something real. It is one thing to call in question the correspondence between symbols and reality, but it is quite another to reject the thing symbolized along with the symbol.[6] However, this pressure that truth admittedly exercises on minds is itself a symbol that must be interpreted, even if we refuse to make of truth something absolute and extra-human.

Pragmatism, which levels everything, deprives itself of the means of making this interpretation by failing to recognize the duality that exists between the mentality which results from individual experiences and that which results from collective experiences. By contrast, sociology reminds us that what is social always possesses a higher dignity than what is individual. We may well assume that truth, like reason and morality, will always retain this character of having a higher value. This in no way prevents us from trying to explain it. The sociological point of view has the advantage of permitting us to analyze even the august thing that is truth.

Up to now there has been no particular pressure to choose between the points of view of sociology and pragmatism. In contrast to rationalism, pragmatism sees clearly that there is not error on one side and truth on the other, but that in reality truths and errors have often been moments in the evolution of truth. In the history of creations, there are unforseeable novelties. How, then, could truth be conceived of as something arrested and definitive?

But the reasons that pragmatism alleges in support of this idea fall under the blow of a great many objections. For the rest, the fact that things change does not necessarily mean that truth changes at the same time. Truth, one could say, is enriched; but it does not actually change. It has certainly been enlarged and increased in the course of the development of history; but it is one thing to say that truth grows, and quite another to say that it varies in its very nature.

1. Cf. pp. 396-97 in this volume. James himself seems to recognize this—for example, when he writes in the Preface to *The Will to Believe* (London: Longmans, Green & Co., Ltd., 1896), p. xiii: "The essay 'On some Hegelisms' doubtless needs an apology for the superficiality with which it treats a serious subject."

2. *Some Problems of Philosophy* (London: Longmans, Green & Co., Inc., 1911), I, 2.

3. Cf. p. 392, in this volume.

4. [Cuvillier makes reference here to p. 96 of the seventh lecture, which has not been included in the present volume.—ED.]

5. Cf. Durkheim, *The Elementary Forms of the Religious Life*, trans. Joseph Ward Swain (Glencoe, Ill.: Free Press of Glencoe, Illinois, 1947), p. 444: "Attributing social origins to logical thought is not debasing it or diminishing its value . . . on the contrary it is relating it to a cause which implies it naturally."

6. Cf. *ibid.*, p. 438: " . . . a collective representation . . . may express this [its subject] by means of imperfect symbols; but scientific symbols themselves are never more than approximative." Cf. also p. 18, where "ideals . . . elaborated on the model of social things" are called "well-founded symbols."

FOURTEENTH LECTURE[1]

THE VARIATIONS OF TRUTH

Let us re-examine the reasons that pragmatism gives in attempting to prove that truth is subject to change. They can be reduced to two: (1) Truth cannot be immutable because reality itself is not; hence truth changes in time. (2) Truth cannot be unique because this oneness would be incompatible with the diversity of minds; hence truth changes in space.

1. In order to be able to say that truth varies in time, one would have to show that a proposition can legitimately be considered true at a given moment and under particular circumstances, and that this same proposition at another moment and in other circumstances cannot be held to be true, even though it relates to the same object. This demonstration has not been made. Pragmatism alleges that reality has changed, but does this mean that old truths become false? Reality can evolve without truth's thereby ceasing to be truth. The laws of the physical world, for example, have remained what they were when life first appeared, and in proportion to the evolution of the biological world.

2. The pragmatists base their argument that truth changes in space on the diversity of individual minds. But does progress not consist precisely in the obliteration of individual differences? Confronted by this argument, will the pragmatists maintain that truth belongs only to the individual? This is a paradox that not even they have dared to attempt to resolve. Nor do they explain what relation exists between the diversity of minds and the diversity of truth. From the fact that in penetrating individual minds, truth takes on diverse forms, it does not follow that truth itself is multiple. In short, pragmatism offers no proof of the thesis that it advances, the thesis that truth is amorphous.

Yet this thesis is not without foundation; it rests on certain facts. However, these facts, which the pragmatists sense only vaguely, must be restored to their true meaning. Let us see what explanation of them is offered by sociology.

Sociology introduces a relativism that rests on the relation between the physical environment, on the one hand, and man, on the other. The physical environment presents a relative fixity. It undergoes evolution, of course; but reality never ceases to be what it is in order to give way to a reality of a new type, or to one consisting of new elements. The original world survives under successive additions that enrich it. New realities are, in a sense, already present in the old ones.[2] The organic world does not abolish the physical world, and the social world does not develop separately from the organic world.

The laws that ruled the movements of the primitive nebulas are conserved in the stabilized universe of today. It seems that the era of great transformation in the organic world ended with the appearance of the human species. Can this be said of man and the social milieus in which he lives? These milieus are the products of different elements, combined and fused together. Our present-day French society is made up of Gallic, Germanic, Roman, and other elements; but these elements can no longer be discerned in an isolated state in our present civilization, which is something new and original, the product of a true creation.[3] Social environments are different from each other since each of them presents something new. Therefore, the institutions of which they are composed must also be different. Nevertheless, these institutions fulfill the same functions as those that preceded them. The family, for instance, has evolved in the course of history, but it has always remained the family and has continued to fulfill the same functions; each of its various forms has been adapted to them. In similar fashion, we see that the same ideal political regime cannot be suitable for all types of societies; the city regime was proper for the ancient cities, and our present political regime is suitable for us. In the same way, there is no one unique morality, and we dare not condemn as immoral the moral systems that preceded ours, for the ideal that they represent was valid for the society in which they were established. The same can be said for religion. In sum, there is not *one* religion, *one* morality, and *one* political regime, but different *types* of religion, *types* of morality, and *types* of political organization. In the practical order, diversity may be considered as established.

Is there any reason why the same condition should not prevail in the theoretical order, in thought itself? If the value of a particular act has changed, speculative thought has changed; and if speculative thought has changed, hasn't the content of truth changed too?

Action cannot be separated from thought. It is impossible for us to claim that the generations which preceded us were capable of living in total error, in complete aberration. For false thoughts lead to erroneous acts. Thus if men had been completely mistaken about the nature of things, their actions would not have produced what was expected of them; and

433

their failures would have engendered suffering which would have led them to seek something else. Nothing authorizes us to think that the affective capacities of men of former times were fundamentally different from our own.

Speculative and theoretical thought varies as practice varies. Aesthetic speculation also shows variations; each people has its own aesthetic. All this leads us to believe that speculation and its value are variable and that, consequently, truth, too, is variable.

These variations take place not only in time but also in space; that is to say, not only between one type of historical society and another but also among the individuals of the same society. In fact, an excess of homogeneity within a society would be its death. No social group can live or—more particularly—progress in absolute homogeneity.[4] Intellectual life as well as practical life, and thought as well as action, need diversity, which is, consequently, a condition of truth. We have renounced the intellectual excommunication of all those who do not think as we do. We respect the truths of others. We "tolerate" them; and this tolerance is no longer the sort that preceded the development of our modern civilization. It is not the kind of tolerance that has its source in fatigue (such as that which appears at the end of wars of religion), nor is it the kind that is born of a feeling of charity. Rather it is the tolerance of the intellectual, of the scientist, who knows that truth is a complex thing and understands that there is an excellent chance that no one of us will see the whole of all its aspects. Such tolerance defies all orthodoxy, but it does not prevent the investigator from expressing the truth as he feels it.

It is in this way that the thesis enunciated by pragmatism is justified from the sociological point of view. Considerations of an abstract or metaphysical order do not furnish us with a satisfactory explanation. It is provided instead by the keenest feeling for what human reality is, the sense of the extreme variability of everything human. We can no longer accept a unique and invariable system of categories or intellectual frameworks. The frameworks that had a reason to exist in former civilizations do not have it today. It goes without saying that this removes none of the value that they had for their own epochs. Variability in time and variability in space are, for that matter, closely connected. If the conditions of life in society are complex, it is naturally to be expected that this complexity and multiple variations of it are to be found in the individuals who make up the social groups.

HOW THESE VARIATIONS CAN BE EXPLAINED

Given this variability of truth in time and space, let us look at the explanation of it that pragmatism offers (up until now, we have seen this dual variability stated, but not explained).

Pragmatism gives us the "why" of these variations in one word: it is the useful that is true. However, it finds the attempt to demonstrate this proposition a rather embarrassing undertaking. In our opinion, the proper way to accomplish it would be to take all of the propositions recognized as true and determine whether or not they are useful, and if so, in what way. But such a procedure would be contrary to the method of pragmatism. If, as pragmatism maintains, there is no true idea but that which is constructed, there can be no given or established idea of truth that can be controlled.

Pragmatism attempts to show that its own theory of truth is useful. For it, the important thing is not so much what truth really is but what it ought to be, even if it is recognized by no one. What the pragmatists are trying to determine is the *ideal* notion of truth. But how can we know that their notion is really the ideal one? Pragmatism can call everything it pleases "ideal truth." Therefore, its method is arbitrary and leads to a purely verbal definition that lacks objective validity. It is analagous to the method used by the classical moralists when they try to determine the ideal notion of morality,[5] a notion which may well be unrelated to morality as it is actually practiced. But just as it is better in seeking a notion of ideal morality to begin by studying moral facts, so does the proper method for determining an ideal notion of truth consist in observing the characteristics of recognized truths.

This is only a question of method, however. Much more important is the pragmatist thesis itself. We shall see that the proposition that the useful is the true is a formula that brings us back to utilitarianism. The pragmatist theory of truth is a logical utilitarianism.

Translated by Charles Blend

1. Lecture of March 17, 1914.

2. This is the version in the only edition available to us. We have serious reservations concerning the authenticity of this formula, however, for it hardly seems to conform with the whole of Durkheim's thought, which is based, as is known, on that of Etienne Emile Marie Boutroux.

3. Cf. *The Elementary Forms of the Religious Life,* trans. Joseph Ward Swain (Glencoe, Ill.: Free Press of Glencoe, Illinois, 1947), p. 446, where society is presented as being endowed with "creative power." Durkheim adds that "all creation . . . is the product of a synthesis," and such syntheses themselves are "productive of novelties."

4. Cf. *The Division of Labor in Society,* trans. and with an Introduction by George Simpson (New York: Macmillan Co., 1933), Chaps. ii and iii, in which Durkheim shows that "mechanical solidarity" which has accomplished maximum homogeneity smothers the personality and therefore progress; and the famous passage in *The Rules of Sociological Method,* trans. Sarah A. Solovay and John H. Mueller (Chicago: University of Chicago Press, 1938), p. 70, in which he calls crime "normal," mainly because a certain elasticity is necessary for social transformations to be possible.

5. Cf. Durkheim's discussion of his exposition of "The Determination of Moral Facts" (1906) in *Sociology and Philosophy,* trans. by D. F. Pocock (Glencoe, Ill.: Free Press of Glencoe, Illinois, 1953), p. 41, where he contrasts the method of the philosophers who "construct" morality, with the sociological method which consists in observing and translating moral "reality."

AN INTRODUCTORY DURKHEIM
BIBLIOGRAPHY

KURT H. WOLFF

The most comprehensive Durkheim bibliography yet to be published appeared in the United States, in Harry Alpert's *Emile Durkheim and His Sociology* (New York: Columbia University Press, 1939), pp. 217-28. An equally extensive one in John M. Foskett's "Emile Durkheim and the Problem of Social Order" (Ph.D. dissertation, Department of Sociology and Social Institutions, University of California, Berkeley, 1939), pp. 224-37, has so far remained unpublished. I have made use of both of these and of a much shorter bibliography, which is also unpublished, by Armand Cuvillier.

In view of the purpose and scope of this volume, I have limited myself to listing Durkheim's books (Section A), his writings which are available in English translation (Section B), and discussions of him and his work (Section C). For the most part, this last section does not list prefaces or introductions to editions of Durkheim's works, either in the original or in translation, although these are often important. Neither does it include books and articles by Durkheim's students, his followers, and others who have been more or less decisively influenced by him, unless these works deal specifically with Durkheim or his ideas. Among the more important and influential of the scholars whose writings fall into this category are Charles Blondel, Francis M. Cornford, Marcel Granet, Maurice Halbwachs, Jane Ellen Harrison, Henri Hubert, Lucien Lévy-Bruhl, Bronislaw Malinowski, Marcel Mauss, Antoine Meillet, Talcott Parsons, Jean Piaget, A. R. Radcliffe-Brown, and many others.

A. Durkheim's Books

1892   *Quid secundatus politicae scientiae instituendae contulerit.* Burdigalae [Bordeaux]: Gounouilhou, 1892. Pp. 75. See 1937 and 1953.

1893   *De la division du travail social: Etude sur l'organisation des sociétés supérieures.* Paris: Félix Alcan, 1893. Pp. ix + 471. (2nd ed., with a new preface entitled, "Quelques remarques sur les groupements professionels," 1902.)

1895   *Les règles de la méthode sociologique.* Paris: Félix Alcan, 1895. Pp. viii + 186. (2nd ed., revised and with a new preface, 1901; new ed., Paris: Presses Universitaires de France, 1947. Pp. xxiv + 150.)

1897   *Le suicide: Etude de sociologie.* Paris: Félix Alcan, 1897. Pp. xii + 462.

1912 *Les formes élémentaires de la vie religieuse: Le système totémique en Australie.* ("Travaux de l'Année sociologique.") Paris: Félix Alcan, 1912. Pp. 647.

1915 a. *Qui a voulu la guerre? Les origines de la guerre d'après les documents diplomatiques.* Written in collaboration with E. DENIS. ("Etudes et documents sur la guerre.") Paris: Armand Colin, 1915. Pp. 67.

b. *L'Allemagne au-dessus de tout: La mentalité allemande et la guerre.* ("Etudes et documents sur la guerre.") Paris: Armand Colin, 1915. Pp. 48.

(Published Posthumously)

1922 *Education et sociologie.* Introduction de PAUL FAUCONNET. Paris: Félix Alcan, 1922. Pp. 160.

1924 *Sociologie et philosophie.* Préface de CÉLESTIN BOUGLÉ. Paris: Félix Alcan, 1924. Pp. xv + 142. (New ed.; Paris: Presses Universitaires de France, 1951. Pp. xvi + 144.)

1925 *L'éducation morale.* Paris: Félix Alcan, 1925. Pp. iv + 326.

1928 *Le socialisme: Sa définition, ses débuts, la doctrine Saint-Simonienne,* edited and with a Preface by MARCEL MAUSS. Paris: Félix Alcan, 1928. Pp. xi + 353.

1937 "Montesquieu: Sa part dans la fondation des sciences politiques et de la science des sociétés," traduction française par F. ALENGRY, *Revue d'histoire politique et constitutionnelle,* I (July-September, 1937), 405-63. A French translation of the 1892 entry.

1938 *L'évolution pédagogique en France.* 2 vols. Paris: Félix Alcan, 1938. Vol. I: *Des origines à la Renaissance,* Pp. 224. Vol. II: *De la Renaissance à nos jours,* Pp. 228.

1950 *Leçons de sociologie: Physique des moeurs et du droit.* Avant-propos de H. NAIL KUBALI; introduction de GEORGES DAVY. ("Publications de l'Université, Faculté de Droit," No. 111.) Istanbul: l'Université d'Istanbul; Paris: Presses Universitaires de France, 1950. Pp. xlii + 264.

1953 *Montesquieu et Rousseau, précurseurs de la sociologie.* Avant-propos d'ARMAND CUVILLIER; note introductive de GEORGES DAVY. ("Petite bibliothèque sociologique internationale.") Paris: Marcel Rivière, 1953. Pp. 200. A new translation by ARMAND CUVILLIER of the 1892 entry, together with a reprint of Durkheim's article, "Le 'Contrat social' de Rousseau," *Revue de métaphysique et de morale,* XXV (1918), 1-23, 129-61.

1955 *Pragmatisme et sociologie.* Cours inédit prononcé à la Sorbonne en 1913-14 et restitué d'après des notes d'étudiants par ARMAND CUVILLIER. Paris: Librairie philosophique J. Vrin, 1955. Pp. 211.

BIBLIOGRAPHY

B. Durkheim's Writings in English Translation

1915   a. *The Elementary Forms of the Religious Life: A Study in Religious Sociology.** Translated by JOSEPH WARD SWAIN. London: Allen & Unwin, Ltd.; New York: Macmillan Co., 1915. Pp. xi + 456. A translation of the 1912 entry.

       b. *Who Wanted War? The Origin of the War according to Diplomatic Documents.* Written in collaboration with E. DENIS; translated by A. M. WILSON-GARINEI. ("Studies and Documents on the War.") Paris: Armand Colin, 1915. Pp. 62. A translation of 1915, a.

       c. *"Germany above All": German Mentality and War.* Translated by J. S. ("Studies and Documents on the War.") Paris: Armand Colin, 1915. Pp. 47. A translation of 1915, b.

1933   *The Division of Labor in Society.** Translated and with an Introduction by GEORGE SIMPSON. New York: Macmillan Co., 1933. Pp. xliv + 439. A translation of the 1893 entry.

1938   *The Rules of Sociological Method.** Translated by SARAH A. SOLOVAY and JOHN H. MUELLER, and edited by GEORGE E. G. CATLIN. Chicago: University of Chicago Press, 1938. Pp. lx + 146. A translation of the 1895 entry.

1947   "On Suicide," translated by W. C. BRADBURY, JR., and with an Introduction by SEBASTIAN DE GRAZIA, *University Observer,* I (Winter, 1947), 51-60. A translation of pp. 272-88 of the 1897 entry.

1951   *Suicide: A Study in Sociology.* Translated by JOHN A. SPAULDING and GEORGE SIMPSON; edited and with an Introduction by GEORGE SIMPSON. Glencoe, Ill.: Free Press of Glencoe, Illinois, 1951. Pp. 405. A translation of the 1897 entry.

1953   *Sociology and Philosophy.* Translated by D. F. POCOCK, and with an Introduction by J. G. PERISTIANY. Glencoe, Ill.: Free Press of Glencoe, Illinois, 1953. Pp. xli plus 97. A translation of the 1924 entry.

1956   *Education and Sociology.* Translated and with an Introduction by SHERWOOD D. FOX; Foreword by TALCOTT PARSONS. Glencoe, Ill.: Free Press of Glencoe, Illinois, 1956. Pp. 163. A translation of the 1922 entry.

1957   *Professional Ethics and Civic Morals.** Translated by CORNELIA BROOKFIELD, and with a Preface by H. NAIL KUBALI and an Introduction by GEORGES DAVY. London: Routledge & Kegan Paul, Ltd., 1957. Pp. xliv + 228. A translation of the 1950 entry.

1958   *Socialism and Saint-Simon.* Translated by CHARLOTTE SATTLER; edited and with an Introduction by ALVIN W. GOULDNER. Yellow Springs, Ohio: Antioch Press, 1958. Pp. xxvii + 240. A translation of the 1928 entry.

1960 a. *Montesquieu and Rousseau: Forerunners of Sociology.* Translated by RALPH MANHEIM, and with a Foreword by HENRI PEYRE. Ann Arbor, Mich.: University of Michigan Press, 1960. Pp. xvi + 155. Contents: "Montesquieu's Contribution to the Rise of Social Science" (1892) and "Rousseau's *Social Contract*" (1918 [posthumous]), by Durkheim; "Durkheim, Montesquieu, and Rousseau," by Georges Davy; and "Note," by A. Cuvillier.

b. The translations in the present volume.

c. A translation of the 1925 entry by Everett K. Wilson, to be issued by the Free Press of Glencoe, Illinois.

(Reprints)

1955 "Division of Labor," in *Small Groups: Studies in Social Interaction,* ed. PAUL A. HARE, EDGAR F. BORGATTA, and ROBERT F. BALES. New York: Alfred A. Knopf, 1955. pp. 5-9. A reprint of pp. 365-66, 396-98, and 406-8 of the 1933 entry.

1956 BORGATTA, EDGAR F., and MEYER, HENRY J. *Sociological Theory: Present-Day Sociology from the Past.* New York: Alfred A. Knopf, 1956. Contains "The Social Shaping of Human Needs," pp. 97-104 (a reprint of pp. 246-54 of the 1951 entry); "The Occupational Group," pp. 287-89 (a reprint of pp. 378-81 of the 1951 entry); "Religious Experience and Religious Organization," pp. 290-97 (a reprint, abridged, of pp. 416-27 of 1915, a.); "The External Reality of Society," pp. 399-403 (a reprint, abridged, of pp. 309-19 of the 1951 entry); "Social Integration and Suicide," pp. 536-42 (a reprint of pp. 208-15 of the 1951 entry); and "Epilogue," p. 547 (a reprint of p. 447 of 1915, a.).

1957 COSER, LEWIS A., and ROSENBERG, BERNARD. *Sociological Theory: A Book of Readings.* New York: Macmillan Co., 1957. Contains "The Internalization of Social Control," pp. 105-10 (a reprint of pp. 35-36 and 40-46 of the 1953 entry); "Suicide and Social Cohesion," pp. 171-80 (a reprint of pp. 156-61, 169-70, and 208-12 of the 1951 entry); "Anomie and Suicide," pp. 480-90 (a reprint of pp. 246-57 of the 1951 entry); and "Causal and Functional Analysis," pp. 513-18 (a reprint of pp. 89-97 of the 1938 entry).

C. SOME DISCUSSIONS OF DURKHEIM

1895 SOREL, GEORGES. "Les théories de M. Durkheim," *Le devenir social,* I (1895), 1-26, 148-80.

1896 TUFTS, JAMES H. "Recent Sociological Tendencies in France," *American Journal of Sociology,* I (1896), 446-56.

1897 BARTH, PAUL. *Die Philosophie der Geschichte als Soziologie.* 4th ed. Leipzig: O. R. Reisland, 1922. Vol. I, pp. 628-42.

1898 a. BELOT, GUSTAVE. "Emile Durkheim: *L'Année sociologique,*" *Revue philosophique,* XLV (1898), 649-57.

BIBLIOGRAPHY

b. Tosti, Gustavo. "Suicide in the Light of Recent Studies," *American Journal of Sociology*, III (1898), 464-78.

c. ————. "The Delusions of Durkheim's Sociological Objectivism," *American Journal of Sociology*, IV (1898), 171-77.

1911 Davy, Georges. "La sociologie de M. Durkheim," *Revue philosophique*, LXXII (1911), 42-71, 160-85.

1913 Leuba, James H. "Sociology and Psychology: A Discussion of the Views of Durkheim and of Hubert and Mauss," *American Journal of Sociology*, XIX (1913), 323-42.

1914 Wallis, Wilson D. "Durkheim's View of Religion," *Journal of Religious Psychology*, VII (1914), 252-67.

1915 Gehlke, Charles Elmer. *Emile Durkheim's Contributions to Sociological Theory.* ("Studies in History, Economics and Public Law," No. 151.) New York: Columbia University Press, 1915. Pp. 188.

1916 Adams, George P. "The Interpretation of Religion in Royce and Durkheim," *Philosophical Review*, XXV (1916), 297-304.

1917 a. Goldenweiser, Alexander A. "Religion and Society: A Critique of Durkheim's Theory of the Origin and Nature of Religion" (1917), *History, Psychology and Culture.* New York: Alfred A. Knopf, 1933. Part IV, Chap. i, pp. 361-73.

b. Worms, René. "Emile Durkheim," *Revue internationale de sociologie*, XXV (1917), 561-68.

1918 a. Branford, Victor. "Durkheim: A Brief Memoir," *Sociological Review*, X (1918), 77-82.

b. Halbwachs, Maurice. "La doctrine d'Emile Durkheim," *Revue philosophique*, LXXXV (1918), 353-411.

c. Lenoir, Raymond. "Emile Durkheim et la conscience moderne," *Mercure de France*, CXXVII (1918), 577-95.

d. Pécaut, Félix. "Emile Durkheim," *Revue pédagogique*, Nouvelle Série, LXXII (1918), 1-20.

1919 Parodi, Dominique. "Emile Durkheim et l'école sociologique" (Chap. v), *La philosophie contemporaine en France: Essai de classification des doctrines.* 2nd rev. ed. Paris: Félix Alcan, 1920. Pp. 113-60.

1919-
1920 Davy, Georges. "Emile Durkheim," *Revue de métaphysique et de morale*, XXVI (1919), 181-98; XXVII (1920), 71-112.

1920 a. Barnes, Harry Elmer. "Durkheim's Contribution to the Reconstruction of Political Theory," *Political Science Quarterly*, XXXV (1920), 236-54.

b. Schaub, Edward. "A Sociological Theory of Knowledge," *Philosophical Review*, XXIX (1920), 319-39.

441

1922 FAUCONNET, PAUL. "The Pedagogical Work of Emile Durkheim," *American Journal of Sociology,* XXVIII (1923), 529-53.

1923 MAUSS, MARCEL. "In memoriam: L'Oeuvre inédite de Durkheim et de ses collaborateurs," *Année sociologique,* Nouvelle Série, I (1923), 7-29.

1924 DENNES, WILLIAM RAY. "Durkheim" (Chap. iii), *The Method and Presuppositions of Group Psychology* ("University of California Publications in Philosophy," No. 6.) Berkeley and Los Angeles: University of California Press, 1924.

1925 LACOMBE, ROGER. "L'interprétation des faits matériels dans la méthode de Durkheim," *Revue philosophique,* XCIX (1925), 369-88.

1926 a. LACOMBE, ROGER. *La méthode sociologique de Durkheim: Etude critique.* Paris: Félix Alcan, 1926. Pp. 168.

   b. PERRY, RALPH BARTON. *General Theory of Value: Its Meaning and Basic Principles Construed in Terms of Interest.* New York: Longmans, Green & Co., Inc., 1926. Chaps. xiv-xvii, pp. 400-519.

1927 a. FAUCONNET, PAUL. "The Durkheim School in France," *Sociological Review,* XIX (1927), 15-20.

   b. OUY, ACHILLE. "La méthode sociologique de Durkheim," *Revue internationale de sociologie,* XXXV (1927), 371-83. A review of 1926, a.

1928 SOROKIN, PITIRIM. *Contemporary Sociological Theories.* New York and London: Harper & Bros., 1928. Chap. viii, Section 4, pp. 463-80.

1930 a. BOUGLÉ, CÉLESTIN; DAVY, GEORGES; GRANET, MARCEL; LENOIR, RAYMOND; and MAUBLANC, RENÉ. "L'oeuvre sociologique d'Emile Durkheim," *Europe,* XXII (1930), 281-304.

   b. RICHARD, GASTON. "La pathologie sociale d'Emile Durkheim," *Revue internationale de sociologie,* XXXVIII (1930) 113-26.

1931 MITCHELL, MARION M. "Emile Durkheim and the Philosophy of Nationalism," *Political Science Quarterly,* XLVI (1931), 87-106.

1932 MARICA, GEORGE M. *Emile Durkheim: Soziologie und Soziologismus.* Jena: Gustav Fischer, 1932. Pp. viii + 174.

1933 a. SIMPSON, GEORGE. "Emile Durkheim's Social Realism," *Sociology and Social Research,* XVIII (1933), 3-11.

   b. ———. "An Estimate of Durkheim's Work," in the 1933 translation of Durkheim's work of 1893, pp. xxv-xliv.

1934 a. MERTON, ROBERT K. "Durkheim's Division of Labor in Society," *American Journal of Sociology,* XL (1934), 319-28.

   b. WILSON, ETHEL M. "Emile Durkheim's Sociological Method," *Sociology and Social Research,* XVIII (1934), 511-18.

1936 APCHIÉ, M. "Quelques remarques critiques sur la sociologie d'Emile Durkheim," *Archives de philosophie du droit et de sociologie juridique,* VI (1936), 182-95.

1937 a. ALPERT, HARRY. "France's First University Course in Sociology," *American Sociological Review,* II (1937), 311-17.

b. GURVITCH, GEORGES. "La science des faits moraux et la morale théorique chez Emile Durkheim," *Archives de philosophie du droit et de sociologie juridique,* VII (1937), 18-44.

c. LOWIE, ROBERT H. *The History of Ethnological Theory.* New York: Farrar & Rinehart, Inc., 1937. Chap. xii, pp. 196-229, esp. 196-212.

d. MARJOLIN, ROBERT. "French Sociology: Comte and Durkheim," translated by ALICE PRICE DUNCAN and HUGH DALZIEL DUNCAN, *American Journal of Sociology,* XLII (1937), 693-704, 901-2.

e. PARSONS, TALCOTT. *The Structure of Social Action: A Study in Social Theory with Special Reference to a Group of Recent European Writers.* New York and London: McGraw-Hill Book Co., 1937. Chaps. viii-xii, pp. 301-470.

1938 a. ALPERT, HARRY. "Durkheim's Functional Theory of Ritual," *Sociology and Social Research,* XXIII (1938), 103-8.

b. BARNES, HARRY ELMER, and BECKER, HOWARD. *Social Thought from Lore to Science.* Washington, D. C.: Harren Press, 1952. Vol. II, Chap. xxii, esp. pp. 829-39.

c. CATLIN, GEORGE E. G. "Introduction to the Translation," in the 1938 translation of the 1895 work, pp. xi-xxxvi.

d. GURVITCH, GEORGES. *La vocation actuelle de la sociologie: Vers une sociologie différentielle.* Paris: Presses Universitaires de France, 1950. Chaps. vi and viii, pp. 351-408, 526-53.

1939 a. ALPERT, HARRY. *Emile Durkheim and His Sociology.* ("Studies in History, Economics and Public Law," No. 445.) New York: Columbia University Press, 1939. Pp. 233.

b. OUY, ACHILLE. "Les sociologies et la sociologie: Deuxième partie, Le sociologisme, Emile Durkheim," *Revue internationale de sociologie,* XLVII (1939), 245-75.

1943 DEGRÉ, GERARD L. *Society and Ideology: An Inquiry into the Sociology of Knowledge.* New York: Columbia University Bookstore, 1943. Chap. iii, pp. 54-84.

1944 PETERSEN, CHRISTIAN. *Emile Durkheim: En historisk kritisk Studie: Medsaerligt Hensyn til hans almindelige Sociologi eller Samfundsfilosofi* ["Emile Durkheim: A Historical-Critical Study with Special Regard to His General Sociology or Social Philosophy"]. Copenhagen: Ejnar Munksgaard, 1944. Pp. 277.

1945 LÉVI-STRAUSS, CLAUDE. "French Sociology" (Chap. xvii), in *Twenti-*

eth Century Sociology, ed. GEORGES GURVITCH and WILBERT E. Moore. New York: Philosophical Library, Inc., 1945. Pp. 503-37.

1947 MASSON-OURSEL, PAUL. "La sociologie de Durkheim et la psychanalyse," *Psyché: Revue internationale de psychanalyse et des sciences de l'homme,* II (1947), 1439-42.

1948 BENOIT-SMULLYAN, EMILE. "The Sociologism of Emile Durkheim and His School" (Chap. xxvii), in *An Introduction to the History of Sociology,* ed. HARRY ELMER BARNES. Chicago: University of Chicago Press, 1948. pp. 499-537.

1950 SIMPSON, GEORGE. "Methodological Problems in Determining the Aetiology of Suicide," *American Sociological Review,* XVI (1950), 658-63.

1951 GINSBERG, MORRIS. "Durkheim's Ethical Theory" (Chap. iv), *On the Diversity of Morals.* New York: Macmillan Co., 1957. Pp. 41-53.

1954 KATTSOFF, LOUIS O. "Comentarios metodológicos sobre sociología," *Revista mexicana de sociología,* XVI (1954), 185-95.

1955 a. FRIEDMANN, GEORGES. "La thèse de Durkheim et les formes contemporaines de la division du travail," *Cahiers internationaux de sociologie,* XIX (1955), 45-58.

b. GINSBERG, MORRIS. "Durkheim's Theory of Religion" (Chap. xiv), *On the Diversity of Morals.* New York: Macmillan Co., 1957. pp. 230-42.

c. KOSEKI, TOICHIRO. "Social Factors in E. Durkheim's Theory," *Japanese Sociological Review,* VI (1955), 51-67.

d. OTTAWAY, A. K. C. "The Educational Sociology of Emile Durkheim," *British Journal of Sociology,* VI (1955), 213-27.

1956 a. KÖNIG, RENÉ. "Drei unbekannte Werke von E. Durkheim," *Kölner Zeitschrift für Soziologie,* VIII (1956), 642-47.

b. WORSLEY, P. M. "Emile Durkheim's Theory of Knowledge," *Sociological Review,* IV, New Series (1956), 47-62.

1958 a. *American Journal of Sociology,* LXII (May, 1958). "Durkheim-Simmel Commemorative Issue."

Relevant articles:

ROSSI, PETER H. "Emile Durkheim and Georg Simmel," p. 579.

NAEGELE, KASPAR D. "Attachment and Alienation: Complementary Aspects of the Work of Durkheim and Simmel," pp. 580-89.

WOLFF, KURT H. "The Challenge of Durkheim and Simmel," pp. 590-96.

SELVIN, HANAN C. "Durkheim's *Suicide* and Problems of Empirical Research," pp. 607-19.

BIBLIOGRAPHY

SCHNORE, LEO F. "Social Morphology and Human Ecology," pp. 620-34.

GOLD, MARTIN. "Suicide, Homicide, and the Socialization of Aggression," pp. 651-61.

ALPERT, HARRY. "Emile Durkheim: Enemy of Fixed Psychological Elements," pp. 662-64.

b. SPENCER, ROBERT F. "Culture Process and Intellectual Current: Durkheim and Atatürk," *American Anthropologist,* LX (1958), 640-57.

1959 a. ALPERT, HARRY. "Emile Durkheim: A Perspective and Appreciation," *American Sociological Review,* XXIV (1959), 462-65.

b. BELLAH, ROBERT N. "Durkheim and History," *American Sociological Review,* XXIV (1959), 447-61.

c. DOHRENWEND, BRUCE P. "Egoism, Altruism, Anomie: A Conceptual Analysis of Durkheim's Types," *American Sociological Review,* XXIV (1959), 466-72.

1960 a. DAVY, GEORGES. "Emile Durkheim," *Revue française de sociologie,* I (1960), 3-24.

b. The contributions in the present volume.

* Reissued after 1947 by the Free Press of Glencoe, Illinois.

445

NOTES ON THE CONTRIBUTORS

CHARLES BLEND teaches French at Ohio State University.

PAUL BOHANNAN was trained at Oxford and has done extensive field research in Africa. He teaches social anthropology at Northwestern. His most recent book is *Justice and Judgment among the Tiv*.

LEWIS A. COSER teaches sociology at Brandeis. He studied with Paul Fauconnet and Célestin Bouglé at the Sorbonne, and at Columbia. He is the author of *The Functions of Social Conflict* (1956), a co-author and co-editor of other books, and an editor of *Dissent*.

HUGH DALZIEL DUNCAN, born in Scotland and trained in philosophy, literature, and sociology at Drake and Chicago, has written *Language and Literature in Society* (1953) and *Social Hierarchy: Communication of Hierarchy in Art and Society* (forthcoming).

JEROME D. FOLKMAN, who holds a Ph.D. degree in sociology from Ohio State, is Rabbi of Temple Israel in Columbus, Ohio.

ROSCOE C. HINKLE, JR., trained at Minnesota and Wisconsin, teaches sociology at Ohio State. His major interest is the sociological analysis of American sociology. He is co-author, with Gisela J. Hinkle, of *The Development of Modern Sociology: Its Nature and Growth in the United States* (1954), and of papers in learned journals and symposiums.

PAUL HONIGSHEIM studied at the universities of Bonn, Berlin, and Heidelberg, and taught at Cologne (where he was also the director of the People's University), Panama, and Michigan State. He has published widely in many fields, including the history of sociology and anthropology, the sociology of religion, art, and knowledge, and adult education.

446

KAZUTA KURAUCHI, professor of sociology at Osaka University, Japan, is the author (in Japanese) of *Sociology of Knowledge* (1932), *Cultural Sociology* (1943), *Culture and Education* (1948), and *An Introduction to Sociology* (1953).

JOSEPH NEYER was trained at Harvard and studied with Marcel Mauss, Paul Fauconnet, Maurice Halbwachs, and other students of Durkheim's. He teaches philosophy at Rutgers and has written for *Ethics, Social Research*, the *Saturday Review*, and other periodicals.

TALCOTT PARSONS, professor of sociology at Harvard, studied at Amherst, the London School of Economics, and Heidelberg. His principal contribution to the study of Durkheim is contained in his book, *The Structure of Social Action* (1937). He is also an author and co-author of several works in sociological theory, including *The Social System* (1951).

J. G. PERISTIANY, senior lecturer in social anthropology at Oxford, wrote an introduction to the English translation of Durkheim's *Sociology and Philosophy* (1953).

HENRI PEYRE, Sterling Professor of French at Yale, was born and educated in France. He has taught in France, England, Egypt, and Argentina, and is the author of numerous books and articles on European and particularly French literature. Among his most recent books is *The Contemporary French Novel* (1955).

ALBERT PIERCE studied sociology at Iowa and Harvard, and has taught at California (Berkeley) and Bucknell; he now teaches at San Fernando Valley State College. His papers have appeared in the *American Sociological Review* and elsewhere.

MELVIN RICHTER, trained at Harvard, teaches political science at Hunter College. He has written on the history of political and social thought in the *Review of Politics, Commentary*, and the *American Sociological Review*.

ALBERT SALOMON teaches sociology at the New School for Social Research. He studied at Heidelberg, taught in Berlin and Cologne, and was editor of *Die Gesellschaft*. He is the author of *The Tyranny of Progress* (1955) and of numerous papers on sociological and political theory and modern intellectual history.

KURT H. WOLFF, who was educated in Germany and Italy, teaches sociology at Brandeis. His main interests are history and philosophy of sociology, and sociology of knowledge. He has written for scientific and literary journals and learned symposiums.

INDEX*

Page numbers in italics indicate passages in the translations.

* Prepared by Herr's Indexing Service, 410 Accomac Road, Wyncote, Pennsylvania.

449

461

Set in Baskerville

Manufactured by The Haddon Craftsmen, Inc.

Published by the Ohio State University Press